POPE PIUS XII LIBRARY, ST. JOSEPH COL.
3 2528 11054 3487

D1519648

ACCULTURATION AND PARENT–CHILD RELATIONSHIPS

Measurement and Development

MONOGRAPHS IN PARENTING SERIES

Marc H. Bornstein, Series Editor

Borkowski, Ramey, and Bristol-Powers Parenting and the Child's World: Influences on Academic, Intellectual, and Social-Emotional Development

Bornstein and Bradley Socioeconomic Status, Parenting, and Child Development

Kalil and DeLeire Family Investments in Children's Potential: Resources and Behaviors That Promote Children's Success

Cowan, Cowan, Ablow, Johnson, and Measelle The Family Context of Parenting in Children's Adaptation to Elementary School

Luster and Okagaki Parenting: An Ecological Perspective (Second Edition)

Bornstein and Cote Acculturation and Parent–Child Relationships: Measurement and Development

Goldberg Father Time: The Timing of Fatherhood in Men's Lives (in preparation)

Bornstein The Parent: Essential Readings (in preparation)

ACCULTURATION AND PARENT–CHILD RELATIONSHIPS

Measurement and Development

Edited by

Marc H. Bornstein
Linda R. Cote
National Institute of Child Health and Human Development

LEA LAWRENCE ERLBAUM ASSOCIATES, PUBLISHERS
2006 Mahwah, New Jersey London

Lawrence Erlbaum Associates, Inc., Publishers
10 Industrial Avenue
Mahwah, New Jersey 07430
www.erlbaum.com

Cover design by Kathryn Houghtaling Lacey

Library of Congress Cataloging-in-Publication Data

Acculturation and parent–child relationships : measurement and development / edited by Marc H. Bornstein and Linda R. Cote

ISBN: 0-8058-5872-5 (alk. paper)

Includes bibliographical references and index.

CIP information for this volume can be obtained by contacting the Library of Congress.

Books published by Lawrence Erlbaum Associates are printed on acid-free paper, and their bindings are chosen for strength and durability.

Printed in the United States of America
10 9 8 7 6 5 4 3 2 1

In memory of
our immigrant grandparents

Contents

Series Foreword
Monographs in Parenting **xi**

PART I. PREVIEW OF ACCULTURATION AND PARENT–CHILD RELATIONSHIPS

1 Introduction to Acculturation and Parent–Child Relationships **3**
Marc H. Bornstein and Linda R. Cote

2 Acculturation: A Conceptual Overview **13**
J. W. Berry

PART II. MEASUREMENT AND ACCULTURATION

3 Issues in the Conceptualization and Assessment of Acculturation **33**
Judit Arends-Tóth and Fons J. R. van de Vijver

4 Conceptual and Measurement Issues in Family Acculturation Research **63**
Kevin M. Chun

5 Acculturation Is Not an Independent Variable: Approaches to Studying Acculturation as a Complex Process **79**
Jean S. Phinney

6 Adaptation of Children and Adolescents With Immigrant Background: Acculturation or Development? **97**
David L. Sam

7 Measurement of the "Acculturation Gap" in Immigrant Families and Implications for Parent–Child Relationships **113**
Dina Birman

8 A Model of Cultural Attachment: A New Approach for Studying Bicultural Experience **135**
Ying-yi Hong, Glenn I. Roisman, and Jing Chen

PART III. DEVELOPMENT AND ACCULTURATION

9 Parenting Cognitions and Practices in the Acculturative Process **173**
Marc H. Bornstein and Linda R. Cote

10 Studying Acculturation Among Latinos in the United States **197**
Robin L. Harwood and Xin Feng

11 Acculturation and Family Characteristics That Facilitate Literacy Development Among Latino Children **223**
JoAnn M. Farver, Stefanie Eppe, and Daniel Ballon

12 The Relation of Language Brokering to Depression and Parent–Child Bonding Among Latino Adolescents **249**
Raymond Buriel, Julia A. Love, and Terri L. De Ment

13 The Prevalence and Consequences of Adolescents' Language Brokering for Their Immigrant Parents **271**
Ruth K. Chao

14 Similarities and Differences Between First- and Second-Generation Turkish Migrant Mothers in Germany: The Acculturation Gap **297**
Birgit Leyendecker, Axel Schölmerich, and Banu Citlak

PART IV. OVERVIEW OF MEASUREMENT AND DEVELOPMENT IN ACCULTURATION

15 An Overview of Acculturation and Parent–Child Relationships **319**
Cigdem Kagitcibasi

About the Authors **333**

Author Index **341**

Subject Index **353**

Series Foreword
Monographs in Parenting

Parenting is fundamental to the survival and success of the human race. Everyone who has ever lived has had parents, and most adults in the world become parents. Opinions about parenting abound, but surprisingly little solid scientific information or considered reflection exists about parenting. *Monographs in Parenting* intends to redress this imbalance: The chief aim of this series of volumes is to provide a forum for extended and integrated treatments of fundamental and challenging contemporary topics in parenting. Each volume treats a different perspective on parenting and is self-contained, yet the series as a whole endeavors to enhance and interrelate studies in parenting by bringing shared perspectives to bear on a variety of concerns prominent in parenting theory, research, and application. As a consequence of its structure and scope, *Monographs in Parenting* will appeal, individually or as a group, to scientists, professionals, and parents alike. Reflecting the nature and intent of this series, contributing authors are drawn from a broad spectrum of the humanities and sciences—anthropology to zoology—with representational emphasis placed on active contributing authorities to the contemporary literature in parenting.

Parenting is a job whose primary object of attention and action is the child—children do not and cannot grow up as solitary individuals—but parenting is also a status in the life course with consequences for parents themselves. In this forum, parenting is defined by all of children's principal caregivers and their many modes of caregiving. *Monographs in Parenting* encompass central themes in parenting . . .

Who Parents?

Biological and adoptive mothers, fathers, single parents, divorced, and remarried parents can be children's principal caregivers, but when siblings, grandparents, and nonfamilial caregivers mind children, their "parenting" is pertinent as well.

Whom Do Parents Parent?

Parents parent infants, toddlers, children in middle childhood, and adolescents, but special populations of children include multiple births, preterm, ill, developmentally delayed or talented, and aggressive or withdrawn children.

The Scope of Parenting

Parenting includes genetic endowment and direct effects of experience that manifest themselves through parents' beliefs and behaviors; parenting's indirect influences take place through parents' relationships with each other and their connections to community networks; the positive and negative effects of parenting are both topics of concern.

Factors That Affect Parenting

Evolution and history; biology and ethology; family configuration; formal and informal support systems, community ties, and work; social, educational, legal, medical, and governmental institutions; economic class, designed and natural ecology, and culture, as well as children themselves—each helps to define parenting.

The Nature, Structure, and Meaning of Parenting

Parenting is pleasures, privileges, and profits as well as frustrations, fears, and failures. Contemporary parenting studies are diversified, pluralistic, and specialized. This fragmented state needs counterforce in an arena that allows the extended, in-depth exploration of cardinal topics in parenting. *Monographs in Parenting* vigorously pursues that goal.

Marc H. Bornstein
Series Editor

I

Preview of Acculturation and Parent–Child Relationships

1

Introduction to Acculturation and Parent–Child Relationships

Marc H. Bornstein
Linda R. Cote
National Institute of Child Health and Human Development, U.S.A.

with

Judit Arends-Tóth, Daniel Ballon, J. W. Berry, Dina Birman, Raymond Buriel, Ruth K. Chao, Jing Chen, Kevin M. Chun, Banu Citlak, Terri L. De Ment, Stefanie Eppe, JoAnn M. Farver, Xin Feng, Robin L. Harwood, Ying-yi Hong, Cigdem Kagitcibasi, Birgit Leyendecker, Julia A. Love, Jean S. Phinney, Glenn I. Roisman, David L. Sam, Axel Schoelmerich, and Fons J. R. van de Vijver

ACCULTURATION AND PARENT–CHILD RELATIONSHIPS

The United States is a nation of immigrants. Even the "Native Americans" immigrated to North America, perhaps across the Bering straits. In the 18th century, when the colonies proclaimed their independence from Great Britain, the colonists were *all* immigrants clinging to a narrow strip of land on the continent's eastern seaboard. Assembled in Philadelphia, the colonists' representatives charged Thomas Jefferson to write out their *Declaration of Independence*. The *Declaration* contains a brief theory of democratic government and a list of 18 grievances the colonists held against the King of England. In Number 7 of the 18, the colonists, being immigrants and wanting to promote immigration, remonstrated that King George "has endeavored to prevent the population of these States; for that purpose obstructing the Laws of Naturalization of Foreigners; refusing to pass others to encourage their migrations hither, and raising the conditions of new Appropriations of Lands." The second President of the United States, John Adams, wrote at that time, "It is our business to render our country an asylum to receive all who may fly to it." America, as one example, is and has always been a country composed of acculturating and acculturated peoples, even if the countries of origin of its naturalizing citizens are constantly shifting.

Going beyond America's borders, immigration and acculturation are contemporaneous international concerns. The International Organization of Migration estimates that in the year 2000 at least 160,000,000 people were living outside the country of their birth or citizenship. In turn, acculturation is a major transforming force on family life, parenting, and child health and human development. Immigrants face multiple challenges in acculturating within the dominant or existing society, including deciding which cultural behaviors or beliefs to adopt from their culture of destination and which to retain from their culture of origin. Yet acculturation as a scientific phenomenon is not at all well understood.

Since the early 1900s, researchers and travelers alike have recognized the thoroughgoing influence of culture on childrearing and child development. Anthropologists were among the first to systematically investigate cultural contributions to family life. Despite the increasing numbers of migrating peoples in the 20th and 21st centuries, research on relations between culture and parent–child relationships has been relatively scarce. The reason for this appears to be the prevalent belief that, once immigrants have lived in their new culture for a time, their beliefs and behaviors come to resemble those of the extant majority and forever relinquish those of their countries of origin (i.e., the assimilationist model). Indeed, in the past some governments forced families to adopt mainstream cultural practices (e.g., by requiring children to speak only the country's official language at school).

However, contemporary investigators who study immigrant families have demonstrated that assimilation is not uniform and that some family cognitions and practices may resist change. Furthermore, previous research on parent–child relationships and the developmental correlates of immigration is not applicable to new generations of immigrant children and families. Moreover, little is known about the cognitions and practices of acculturating groups, and what is known suggests that differences from the majority group (e.g., in parent–child interaction) are likely to have meaningful consequences (e.g., for children's health and development). Patterns of parent–child interactions that lead to cognitive and social competence for ethnic minority children may not necessarily be the same as those that lead to competence for ethnic majority children. Last, immigrant children may perform equally as well as or superior to majority children on measures of health, well-being, and educational achievement, but over time and across generations those advantages tend to disappear. A better understanding of acculturation processes will help to explain and prevent this attenuation.

Culture is composed of the ways in which people process and make sense of their experiences, and culture influences a wide array of family processes including family roles, decision-making patterns, and cognitions and practices about childrearing and child development. Although researchers have studied the effects of culture on parenting and human development for more than a century, for many years acculturation was primarily conceptualized in one of two ways. First, acculturation level was often equated to generation level. Although many acculturation measures in use today incorporate generation level, we now understand that even siblings within the same family—who are the same generation level—may not be equally acculturated (i.e., identify with a new culture to the same degree). Thus, modern acculturation measures attempt to capture a psychological feeling of belonging to a particular culture and are not simply demographic descriptors such as generation level. Second, many acculturation scales measure acculturation as a single point along a single continuum whose endpoints are the cultures of origin and destination, which was consistent with an assimilationist model of acculturation. Since the 1980s, however, researchers have redefined acculturation, which is now viewed as a multidimensional and bidirectional process in which an individual or group retains cognitions and practices of its heritage and simultaneously adopts those of another group with which there is repeated or prolonged contact, regardless of the reason for this contact (e.g., migration, trade). Parenting and child development are shaped in part by current socioeconomic conditions of the environment in which a family lives and in part by cultural heritage. The socialization strategies parents adopt emphasize the development of whatever instrumental competencies are needed for being successful in the environment in which their children are being reared as well as those they inherited; and these two views are not mutually exclusive. A model of parenting and child development that integrates cultural traditions and legacies with current conditions is necessary to acculturation. The degree to which individuals or groups retain their native cultural values will vary, as will the extent to which individuals or groups adopt cognitions and practices of their new culture. A group's adaptive culture is seen as a product not only of its collective history but also of current contextual demands, and this adaptive culture, in turn, has substantial influence on family priorities and parenting practices. Although many researchers generally agree on this (or a similar) basic definition of acculturation, the conceptualization and measurement of acculturation remain controversial.

On this account, the National Institute of Child Health and Human Development sponsored a conference—*Acculturation and Parent–Child Relationships: Measurement and Development*—that brought together scholars who work to define and develop assessments of acculturation and who study the impact of acculturation on families. The goals of the conference were to evaluate both the status of acculturation as a scientific construct and the roles of acculturation in parenting and human development. This volume contains chapters that emanated from that conference. The participant populations range from infants to parents, and the contributors represent many different nations. We felt an international perspective would best shed light on commonalities and differences in the acculturation process and its measurement, which has tended to be dominated by American and Canadian researchers studying immigrants from Latin America and Asia, respectively. The subject matter focuses on the nature of acculturation and its assessment and explores similarities and differences in experiences and the influences of acculturation on parenting and child development both across childhood and in different countries. Although many agree that acculturation is a psychologically salient phenomenon to consider when studying immigrants, as yet no consensus on its measurement has emerged and, relative to its prominence in contemporary life, its manifestations and many impacts are still understudied and ill understood. The goal of this volume is to advance the state of the art.

Part I of this volume previews issues in acculturation and parent–child relationships. *Acculturation* refers to the changes that follow contact between peoples of different cultural backgrounds. In *Acculturation: A Conceptual Overview*, J. W. Berry notes that in cross-cultural psychology, the main interest is on how cultural factors influence the development and display of human behavior; this requires the examination of both cultural-level and psychological-level phenomena. So, too, in the component field of acculturation, both levels are of interest; but, he continues, the task has been doubled because the concern is now with two cultures and two sets of individuals in contact and interaction. Acculturation phenomena include both the processes that take place over time and their longer term outcomes. Earlier views that acculturation inevitably leads to cultural and behavioral loss among nondominant peoples have yielded to a view of acculturation as a highly variable process with diverse outcomes. Many factors that seem to influence the course of these changes have now been identified. Berry's chapter presents a framework that portrays these levels, distinctions, and variations and suggests how these phenomena may affect family life during acculturation.

Part II of this volume turns the reader's attention to central issues of measurement in acculturation. Judit Arends-Tóth and Fons J. R. van de Vijver discuss *Issues in the Conceptualization and Assessment of Acculturation* in an attempt to integrate the growing literature in this field. They start with an overview of its historical roots and present a framework of acculturation variables, distinguishing acculturation conditions, orientations, and outcomes. Frequently observed sources of problems in the assessment of acculturation are outlined, such as mixing different variables into an overall score and using proxy and single-index measures. They contend that the main unresolved issues in the conceptualization and assessment of acculturation are domain specificity, identifying common and group-specific aspects, further delineation of the meaning of integration, and testing attitude–behavior relations. They then discuss an application domain of acculturation assessment, the immigrant family. Examining acculturation in the family domain gives more insight into the dynamic and multifaceted nature of acculturation. They conclude that an essential step in advancing acculturation research is to develop a standardized acculturation instrument or at least a widely endorsed view on what should be included in such a measure. The use of the independent measurement of acculturation orientations (two-statement method) in a range of different domains and situations provides a useful tool to achieve this goal.

In *Conceptual and Measurement Issues in Family Acculturation Research*, Kevin M. Chun gives special attention to the dynamic and multidimensional properties of family acculturation processes and discusses heterogeneous acculturation patterns related to family structures and subsystems, family dynamics, family members' developmental abilities and tasks, and family ecologies. Chun recommends conceptual guidelines and combined qualitative–quantitative measures and strategies for family acculturation research that can improve the construct validity and ecological validity of acculturation findings.

As interest in the study of acculturation increases, methods are needed that take into account the complex, dynamic nature of the process. In *Acculturation Is Not an Independent Variable: Approaches to Studying Acculturation as a Complex Process*, Jean S. Phinney contends that research that treats acculturation as a single psychological construct or independent variable is limited in its contribution to our understanding of the concept. Her chapter explores five research approaches that can help advance the empirical study of acculturation. First, it is useful to distinguish between two types of variables widely used in acculturation research: markers of time in a new culture, such as generation of immigration or length of time following immigration, and within-person variables that change over time, such as language, identity, and values. Second, studying separately the variables associated with acculturation, rather than combining them into a single scale, allows researchers to identify the differing roles of various aspects of acculturative change. Third, both longitudinal and cross-sectional methods provide the opportunity to study differing rates of change among acculturation variables. Fourth, mechanisms or underlying variables that account for acculturation processes need to be identified. Fifth, person-oriented approaches can provide valuable insights that are not evident from variable-oriented approaches. In summary, Phinney maintains that research can be advanced by acknowledging that acculturation is a complex process, not a simple variable.

David L. Sam's chapter, *Adaptation of Children and Adolescents With Immigrant Background: Acculturation or Development?*, focuses on the psychological adaptation of young immigrants from a developmental perspective and argues that immigrant children's adaptation should focus on how they develop competencies to function in a plural society. The chapter critiques current research endeavors on the grounds that they place too much attention on cultural factors (i.e., acculturation) and neglect the fact that immigrant children, just like all other youth, undergo important developmental changes. The chapter argues for an interactive position where acculturation is seen as either embedded in development or where the two are in active interaction with each other. Before taking this interactive position, Sam points to some commonalities between acculturation and development and how acculturation and development confound each other. Working from an interactive position and within a life-span perspective, the chapter presents a model that indicates the difficulties in predicting an individual's adaptive outcome. Development of competencies can go in any direction, depending on the interactions among various factors.

Dina Birman turns our attention to *Measurement of the "Acculturation Gap" in Immigrant Families and Implications for Parent–Child Relationships.* Little empirical research has been conducted on this important topic. Her chapter reviews published studies on the acculturation gap and considers varied conceptual and measurement approaches to examine it. In particular, she argues that findings related to the acculturation gap rest on how acculturation is measured and how acculturation gaps between parents and children are conceptualized and computed. She then offers an example from a study of Soviet Jewish refugee families to illustrate some of the advantages and limitations of varied approaches.

Ying-yi Hong, Glenn I. Roisman, and Jing Chen propose *A Model of Cultural Attachment: A New Approach for Studying Bicultural Experience.* Borrowing from Bowlby's attachment theory, they extend attachment from an interpersonal to a cultural level and argue that people with bicultural experience can develop independent cultural attachments with their native versus new culture. They speculate how different generation cohorts (first-generation immigrants and later generations) face different issues in establishing a secure attachment with their native and new cultures and thus have different developmental trajectories of bicultural identity. They also speculate that the quality of attachment to the two cultures is consequential for individuals' mental health and well-being. To build a foundation for their theory, they tested whether security of cultural attachment can be applied to understand bicultural experience. To that end, they constructed the Cultural Attachment Interview and administered it to a group of Chinese Americans. Based on the coherence of the participants' narratives, they then evaluated the extent to which participants were securely versus insecurely attached to Chinese and American cultures. Their preliminary results show that an insecure attachment to American culture is associated with poorer subjective well-being. Finally, they discuss how their new approach sheds light on some central issues in acculturation.

Part III of this volume takes up the issues of development and acculturation more concretely. Marc H. Bornstein and Linda R. Cote summarize a part of their prospective longitudinal comparative study of Japanese Americans and South Americans in *Parenting Cognitions and Practices in the Acculturative Process,* in relation to children's development. Their chapter reviews research on the acculturation of several parenting cognitions (attributions, self-perceptions, knowledge, and style) and practices (play interactions) among Japanese American and South American mothers of children living in the United States. Their methodological approach examines the acculturation of mothers' parenting cognitions and practices at the individual level by looking at whether immigrant mothers' acculturation level predicts their parenting cognitions and practices. They then explore acculturation at the group level by comparing immigrant mothers' parenting cognitions and practices to those of mothers in the cultures of origin and destination. The body of their research leads to two main conclusions: First, acculturation at the group level appears to be more robust than acculturation at the individual level. Second, their results suggest that parenting practices may acculturate more readily than parenting cognitions.

In the 2000 U.S. Census, Latinos emerged as the largest minority group in the United States. *Studying Acculturation Among Latinos in the United States*, by Robin Harwood and Xin Feng, presents some relevant demographics and examines issues involved in acculturation in this population. The authors give particular attention to internal diversity among Latinos, including country of origin, circumstances of arrival in the United States, socioeconomic status, and generational status. In the past, studies of acculturation among Latinos have tended to ignore sources of internal diversity and focused more narrowly on linguistic adaptation and mental health stressors. The authors correct these past limitations in a study of first- and second-generation Puerto Rican mothers who have migrated to Connecticut.

In their chapter, JoAnn M. Farver, Stefanie Eppe, and Daniel Ballon examine *Acculturation and Family Characteristics That Facilitate Literacy Development Among Latino Children*. Mothers of preschoolers completed questionnaires about their family demography, home environment, perceived parenting stress, and acculturation; they also assessed their children's emergent literacy skills in Spanish and English. In homes where mothers had an integrated style of acculturation, parents read for pleasure and were involved in more frequent home literacy activities, and their children had higher English and Spanish emergent literacy skills than in families where mothers had an assimilated, separated, or marginalized acculturation style. Farver and colleagues' findings highlight within-group variations in the home literacy environments of Latino families as they adjust to life in the United States.

In turn, Raymond Buriel, Julia A. Love, and Terri L. De Ment examine *The Relation of Language Brokering to Depression and Parent–Child Bonding Among Latino Adolescents*. Girls language broker more than boys, they find, and girls also report more depression. There is no gender difference in parent–child bonding or in any education variables. Feelings about language brokering are positively related to parent–child bonding for both girls and boys, as are educational expectations for girls. For both girls and boys, parent–child bonding is negatively related to depression, as well as English proficiency in girls. Language brokering in different places is positively related to depression for boys, but language brokering is unrelated to depression for girls. The authors discuss these results in the context of immigrant Latino family socialization.

Youth from immigrant families provide a striking example of the importance of their contributions to the family through the language translation or brokering they provide their parents. Based on samples of Mexican, Chinese, and Korean immigrants, Ruth K. Chao sought to examine *The Prevalence and Consequences of Adolescents' Language Brokering for Their Immigrant Parents*. Over 70% of youth report they broker for their parents. Among the Mexican and Chinese American youth, Chao found that brokering was positively related to respect for mothers and fathers, but was only related to respect for fathers among the Korean Americans. However, brokering was also related to increases in internalizing and externalizing symptoms among Korean Americans and to increases in internalizing among Chinese Americans. These findings indicate that, although immigrant youth may have increased respect for parents as they broker more, such increases in respect may come at the expense of their own psychological well-being.

About one-half of all marriages in the Turkish community in Germany are between a partner who has spent all or most of his or her life in Germany and a partner who grew up in Turkey. This circumstance is enhanced by the following constraints: Marriage is the only legal way of entry for new migrants from Turkey; migrant families often prefer their children to marry someone "untainted" by a destination culture they perceive as negative; and, as Turkey is easily accessible, migrants stay in close contact with friends and family left behind and they can easily find a partner for themselves or for their children in Turkey. This "marriage migration" has the potential to impact the relationship between the partners, their parenting cognitions and practices, and the acculturation experiences of their children. First, partners have an acculturation gap because only one partner grew up in Germany and has knowledge of German culture and language. In addition, their socialization experiences are likely to differ due to growing up in different countries and in a migrant versus a nonmigrant Turkish culture. Second, partners differ in their positions of power inasmuch as usually only the partner who grew up in Germany has direct family support and knowledge of German culture and language. Third, migrants are more and more likely to live in segregated neighborhoods and to live in a "virtual" Turkey due to access to Turkish television, newspapers, radios, stores, tea houses, and political and religious organizations. For the partner who moved to Germany as an adult, life in a segregated community can decelerate acculturation considerably. Their children, especially if they grow up in a segregated neighborhood, often have little exposure to German culture and language before they enter preschool or school. The impact of partners' joint or "mixed" generational status is likely to be a key for our understanding of acculturation processes within the Turkish migrant community in Germany. Birgit Leyendecker, Axel Schölmerich, and Banu Citlak explore these issues in *Similarities and Differences Between First- and Second-Generation Turkish Migrant Mothers in Germany: The Acculturation Gap*.

In the single chapter in Part IV of this volume, Cigdem Kagitcibasi provides *An Overview of Acculturation and Parent–Child Relationships*. This is a challenging task given the complexity of the issues involved and the diversity of perspectives and research traditions existing in this growing body of scholarship. The different histories of immigration and ethnic relations on the two sides of the Atlantic, from which the present research emerges, are first noted. She then searches for commonalities within diversity. What is shared by the present reports are a micropsychological perspective and a developmental focus, both of which are imperative to better understand the processes underlying family dynamics and parent–child relationships in the context of culture contact. Kagitcibasi notes that studies in this volume attest to the value of developmental science perspectives for enhancing the scope and depth of research questions regarding acculturation. She also identifies some potentially significant issues and topics such as the content of acculturation, context of acculturation, and policy and applications. Going beyond the current work, she notes that greater research attention to these topics would shed further light on the human phenomenon of acculturation and would eventually help serve the groups and societies involved.

The theory and research on acculturation and its relation to parent–child relationships and children's well-being contained in these chapters point to several significant conclusions. For example, individuals within a group or within a family may differ with respect to acculturation, which may create tension and conflict within the family. Typically, individuals with the most contact with the dominant culture, by virtue of participation in the larger community through work, schooling, or other activities, acculturate more rapidly and in more domains than individuals with less contact. Given that schooling, for example, exerts a major socializing influence, it is often the case that children become more acculturated than their parents, which may be a source of tension at home. Because immigrant families straddle two cultures, there may be tension in the family between parents who wish to inculcate the traditional beliefs of their home culture in their children and children who wish to conform to and be accepted by their peers in the new culture. Additionally, school-age children who are fluent in the language of the new culture may be required to act as "culture-brokers" on behalf of their parents who are not fluent in the language, for example, by acting as translators at parent–teacher conferences.

Individuals do not immigrate for the same reasons, and they do not acculturate all facets of their lives in a uniform fashion. For example, an individual may acculturate quickly in one aspect of his or her life (e.g., becoming proficient in and only using the new language) but not in others (e.g., using traditional parenting practices such as sleeping in the same bed as their infants rather than putting the infant to sleep in a crib). Research suggests that parents' practices acculturate more quickly and rapidly than parents' cognitions, even when the same domain of parenting is assessed. Because research on acculturation among those who study families and children's development is still in its infancy and is complex, the effects of these several discordances remain to be understood.

As societies become increasingly diverse and pluralistic, it is imperative that researchers recognize that immigrants do not immediately and forever relinquish the beliefs and behaviors of their cultures of origin and adopt those of the culture of destination. Rather, it is more fruitful to study how families reconcile and implement goals, values, and strategies from both groups and examine the effects of this reconciliation on parent, child, and family development. As the way of the world continues, one can foresee that theoretical and empirical perspectives on acculturation will exert major influences on the research community and inevitably insinuate themselves with social policy as well.

Acculturation and Parent–Child Relationships derives from original presentations delivered at a workshop of the same name held in Ghent, Belgium. The workshop was sponsored by the National Institute of Child Health and Human Development. We are especially grateful to Dr. Owen M. Rennert and Dr. Duane F. Alexander of the National Institute of Child Health and Human Development for sponsoring the workshop and for their continuing support of research into all facets of human growth and children's health. Sincere thanks, too, to the production staff at Lawrence Erlbaum Associates for continuing professionalism and excellence.

2

Acculturation: A Conceptual Overview

J. W. Berry
Queen's University, Kingston, Ontario, Canada

INTRODUCTION

Acculturation is the dual process of cultural and psychological change that takes place as a result of contact between two or more cultural groups and their individual members. At the group level, it involves changes in social structures and institutions and in cultural practices. At the individual level, it involves changes in a person's behavioral repertoire. These cultural and psychological changes come about through a long-term process, sometimes taking years, sometimes generations, and sometimes centuries. Acculturation is a process of cultural and psychological changes that involve various forms of mutual accommodation, leading to some longer term psychological and sociocultural adaptations among both groups. Contact and change occur for a number of reasons, including colonization, military invasion, migration, and sojourning (such as tourism, international study, and overseas posting); it continues long after initial contact in culturally plural societies, where ethnocultural communities maintain features of their heritage cultures. Although acculturation is a process that continues for as long as there are culturally different groups in contact, some longer term adaptation to living in culture-contact settings takes various forms, usually resulting in some form of longer term accommodation among the groups in contact. This often entails, for example, learning each other's languages, sharing each other's food preferences, and adopting forms of dress and social interactions that are characteristic of each group. Sometimes these mutual adaptations take place rather easily (through processes of *culture shedding* and *culture learning*; see Berry, 1992), but they can also create *culture conflict* and *acculturative stress* during intercultural interactions. One key feature of all acculturation phenomena is the variability with which they take place: There are large group and individual differences in the ways in which people seek to go about their acculturation (termed *acculturation strategies*), and in the degree to which they achieve satisfactory adaptations. In addition to cultural group and individual variation, there are variations within families: Among family members, acculturation often proceeds at different rates, and with different goals, sometimes leading to an increase in conflict and stress and to more difficult adaptations.

This chapter outlines the meaning and uses of the concept of acculturation as it is currently used in the fields of cross-cultural and intercultural psychology. Following this discussion of acculturation as a general concept, many of the concepts that have been italicized in this introduction are elaborated in later sections. In my view, acculturation and adaptation are now reasonably well understood; I believe that we are in a position to pursue the development of policies and programs to promote successful outcomes for all parties involved in the contact situation.

THE CONCEPT OF ACCULTURATION

Acculturation has been taking place for millennia, but contemporary interest in research on acculturation grew out of a concern for the effects of European domination of indigenous peoples. Later, it focused on how immigrants changed following their entry and settlement into receiving societies. More recently, much of the work has been involved with how ethnocultural groups relate to each other and change as a result of their attempts to live together in culturally plural societies. Nowadays, all three foci are important, as globalization results in ever-larger trading and political relations: Indigenous national populations experience neocolonization and demonstrate resistance, while new waves of immigrants, sojourners, and refugees flow from these economic and political changes, and large ethnocultural populations become established in most countries. Of increasing concern is the acculturation that is taking place among the long-settled populations as they strive to maintain their societies in the face of increasing cultural diversity in their midst. These two foci of interest (on the established as well as on the newer populations) represent the mutual or reciprocal nature of acculturation: Everyone is involved, and everyone is doing it.

Although much of this initial concern and research was carried out in traditional immigrant-receiving countries (Australia, Canada, New Zealand, United States; see Chun, Balls-Organista, & Marin, 2003), these issues have become more and more important in the rest of the world, where massive population contacts and transfers are taking place (see Sam & Berry, 2006, for an international perspective). Particularly in Asia, where half of the world's population lives in culturally diverse societies, people experience daily intercultural encounters and have to meet the demands for cultural and psychological change. Cross-cultural psychologists take seriously the view that findings from research in one culture area of the world (or even in a few societies) cannot be generalized to others. Thus, as our knowledge of international acculturation experiences, ideologies, and sensitivities increases, we must alter the conceptions and extend the empirical findings that are portrayed in this chapter. Nevertheless, some evidence exists to show that the very concept of acculturation, the various strategies adopted by immigrants and members of the national society, and the nature of the problems that may occur are rather similar to those identified in the research in other countries. It is, of course, up to all societies and their diverse residents to assess the relevance and validity of this existing work for their societies.

Although there are now many competing views about the meaning of acculturation, early views about its nature are a useful foundation for contemporary discussion. Two formulations in particular, have been widely quoted. The first is:

> Acculturation comprehends those phenomena which result when groups of individuals having different cultures come into continuous first-hand contact, with subsequent changes in the original culture patterns of either or both groups . . . under this definition, acculturation is to be distinguished from culture change, of which it is but one aspect, and assimilation, which is at times a phase of acculturation. (Redfield, Linton, & Herskovits, 1936, pp. 149–152)

In another formulation, acculturation was defined as:

> Culture change that is initiated by the conjunction of two or more autonomous cultural systems. Acculturative change may be the consequence of direct cultural transmission; it may be derived from non-cultural causes, such as ecological or demographic modification induced by an impinging culture; it may be delayed, as with internal adjustments following upon the acceptance of alien traits or patterns; or it may be a reactive adaptation of traditional modes of life. (Social Science Research Council, 1954, p. 974)

In the first formulation, acculturation is seen as one aspect of the broader concept of culture change (that which results from intercultural contact) and is considered to generate change in "either or both groups"; that is, acculturation takes place in the settled or dominant group as well as in the nondominant group. Acculturation is distinguished from assimilation (which may be "at times a phase"); that is, there are a number of alternative courses and goals to the process of acculturation. These are important distinctions for psychological work, pursued later in this chapter. In the second definition, a few extra features are added, including change that is indirect (not cultural but "ecological") and delayed (internal adjustments, presumably of both a cultural and psychological character, take time). Importantly, acculturation can be "reactive"; that is, by rejecting the cultural influence from the dominant group and changing back toward a more "traditional" way of life, rather than inevitably toward greater similarity with the dominant culture.

Graves (1967) introduced the concept of *psychological acculturation*, which refers to changes in an individual who is a participant in a culture contact situation, being influenced both directly by the external culture, and by the changing culture of which the individual is a member. There are two reasons for keeping the cultural and psychological levels distinct. The first is that cross-cultural psychology views individual human behavior as interacting with the cultural context within which it occurs. Given these two distinct levels of phenomena, separate conceptions and measurements are required. The second reason is that not every individual enters into, participates in, or changes in the same way; there are vast individual differences in psychological acculturation, even among individuals who live in the same acculturative arena. That is, while general acculturation is taking place at the group level, individuals have variable degrees of participation in them, and variable goals to achieve from the contact situation.

A framework that outlines and links cultural and psychological acculturation and identifies the two (or more) groups in contact is presented in Figure 2.1. This framework serves as a map of those phenomena that need to be conceptualized and measured during acculturation research. At the cultural level (on the left), we need to understand key features of the two original cultural groups (A & B) prior to their major contact, the nature of their contact relationships, and the resulting dynamic cultural changes in both groups and in the emergent ethnocultural groups during the process of acculturation. The gathering of this information requires extensive ethnographic, community-level work. These changes can be minor or substantial, and range from being easily accomplished through to being a source of major cultural disruption. At the individual level (on the right), we need to consider the psychological changes that individuals in all groups undergo, and their eventual adaptation to their new situations. Identifying these changes requires sampling a population and studying individuals who are variably involved in the process of acculturation. These changes can be a set of rather easily accomplished behavioral shifts (e.g., in ways of speaking, dressing, eating, and in one's cultural identity) or they can be more problematic, producing acculturative stress as manifested by uncertainty, anxiety, and depression (Berry, 1976). Adaptations can be primarily psychological (e.g., sense of well-being or self-esteem) or sociocultural, linking the individual to others in the new society as manifested, for example, in competence in the activities of daily intercultural living.

ACCULTURATION CONTEXTS

As for all cross-cultural psychology (Berry, Poortinga, Segall, & Dasen, 2002), it is imperative that work on acculturation be based in examining its cultural contexts. We need to understand, in ethnographic terms, both cultures that are in contact if we are to understand the individuals who are in contact.

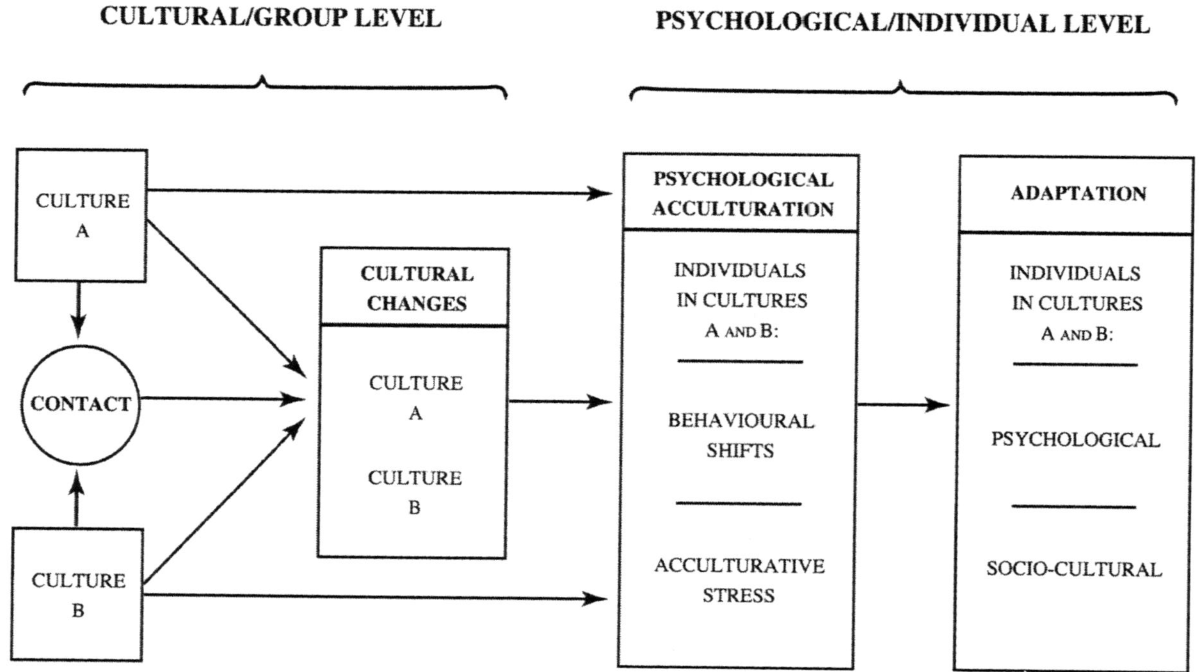

FIGURE 2.1. A general framework for understanding acculturation.

Figure 2.1 shows that there are five aspects of cultural contexts: the two original cultures (A & B), the two changing ethnocultural groups (A & B), and the nature of their contact and interactions. These five sets of phenomena define the nature of the acculturation process at the cultural level, and establish the starting point for the process of acculturation at the psychological level.

Beginning with these culture-level phenomena, and taking the immigration process as an example, we may refer to the society of origin (A) and society of settlement (B), and their respective changing cultural features following contact (changed cultures A and B). A complete understanding of acculturation would need to start with a fairly comprehensive examination of the societal contexts: In the society of origin, the cultural characteristics that accompany individuals into the acculturation process need description, in part to understand (literally) where the person is coming from and in part to establish cultural features for comparison with the society of settlement. The combination of political, economic, and demographic conditions being faced by individuals in their society of origin also needs to be studied as a basis for understanding the degree of voluntariness in the migration motivation of acculturating individuals. Arguments by Richmond (1993) suggest that migrants can be arrayed on a continuum between reactive and proactive, with the former being motivated by factors that are constraining or exclusionary and generally negative in character, and the latter motivated by factors that are facilitating or enabling and generally positive in character; these contrasting factors have also been referred to as push–pull factors in the earlier literature on migration motivation.

In the society of settlement, a number of factors have importance. First, there are the general orientations that a society and its citizens have toward immigration and pluralism. Some societies have been built by immigration over the centuries, and this process may be a continuing one, guided by a deliberate immigration policy. The important issue to understand for the process of acculturation is both the historical and attitudinal situation faced by immigrants in the society of settlement. Some societies are accepting of cultural pluralism resulting from immigration, taking steps to support the continuation of cultural diversity as a shared communal resource; this position represents a positive *multicultural ideology* (Berry & Kalin, 1995) and corresponds to an expectation that the *integration* strategy will be the appropriate way for cultural communities to engage each other. Other societies seek to eliminate diversity through policies and programs of *assimilation*, and still other societies attempt to achieve the *segregation* or *marginalization* of their diverse populations. Murphy (1965) argued that societies that are supportive of cultural pluralism (that is, with a positive multicultural ideology) provide a more positive settlement context for two reasons: They are less likely to enforce cultural change (assimilation) or exclusion (segregation and marginalization) on immigrants, and they are more likely to provide social support both from the institutions of the larger society (e.g., culturally sensitive health care and multicultural curricula in schools), and from the continuing and evolving ethnocultural communities that usually make up pluralistic societies. However, even where pluralism is accepted, there are well-known variations in the relative acceptance of specific cultural, "racial," and religious groups (e.g., Berry & Kalin, 1995; Lebedeva & Tatarko, 2004). Those groups that are less well accepted often experience hostility, rejection, and discrimination, one factor that is predictive of poor long-term adaptation.

ACCULTURATION STRATEGIES

Not all groups and individuals undergo acculturation in the same way; there are large variations in how people seek to engage the process. These variations have been termed *acculturation strategies* (Berry, 1980). These strategies consist of two (usually related) components: attitudes (an individual's preference about how to acculturate), and behaviors (a person's actual activities) that are exhibited in day-to-day intercultural encounters. These two components are kept distinct, both conceptually and empirically, as there is not usually a complete correspondence between them; constraints are often imposed by the dominant group so that individuals are not entirely free to act according to their preferences. Nevertheless, when measures of preferences and behaviors are both included in a composite assessment of how peoples are acculturating, there is usually a pattern that exhibits a consistent strategy (Berry, Kim, Power, Young, & Bujaki, 1989). Which strategies are used depends on a variety of antecedent factors (both cultural and psychological); and there are variable adaptive consequences (again both cultural and psychological) of these different strategies.

The centrality of the concept of acculturation strategies can be illustrated by reference to each of the components included in Figure 2.1. At the cultural level, the two groups (cultures A and B) that are in contact usually have some initial notions about what they are attempting to do (e.g., colonial policies, or motivations for migration), or what is being done to them, during the contact. These notions involve preferences or goals they seek to achieve while in the acculturation arena as well as actual steps taken to achieve them. Similarly, the kinds of changes that are likely to occur in the two cultures following contact will be influenced by their respective acculturation strategies. Both groups exhibit attitudes toward these changes (they may desire them or reject them), and in many cases they are able to act accordingly.

At the individual level (psychological acculturation), both behavior changes and acculturative stress phenomena are now known to be a function, at least to some extent, of what people try to do during their acculturation, and the longer term outcomes (both psychological and sociocultural adaptations) often correspond to the strategic goals set by the groups of which they are members (Berry, 1997).

Four acculturation strategies have been derived from two basic issues facing all acculturating peoples. These two issues are based on the distinction between orientations toward one's own group and those toward other groups (Berry, 1980). These issues involve the distinction between (1) a relative preference for maintaining one's heritage culture and identity, and (2) a relative preference for having contact with and participating in the larger society along with other ethnocultural groups. These issues are presented in Figure 2.2.

Attitudes and behaviors regarding these two issues can range along these two dimensions, represented by bipolar arrows. For purposes of presentation, generally positive or negative orientations to these issues intersect to define four acculturation strategies. These strategies carry different names, depending on which group (the dominant or nondominant) is being considered. From the point of view of nondominant groups (on the left of Figure 2.2), when individuals do not wish to maintain their cultural identity and seek daily interaction with other cultures, the *assimilation* strategy is defined. Here, individuals prefer to shed their heritage culture and become absorbed into the dominant society. In contrast, when individuals place a value on holding on to their original culture, and at the same time wish to avoid interaction with others, then the *separation* alternative is defined. Here, individuals turn their back on involvement with other cultural groups, and turn inward toward their heritage culture. When there is an interest in both maintaining one's heritage culture while in daily interactions with other groups, *integration* is the option. In this case, there is some degree of cultural integrity maintained, while at the same time seeking, as a member of an ethnocultural group, to participate as an integral part of the larger social network. Finally, when there is little possibility or interest in heritage cultural maintenance (often for reasons of enforced cultural loss), and little interest in having relations with others (often for reasons of exclusion or discrimination) then *marginalization* is defined. It is important to note here that assimilation and integration are distinct concepts, involving differing attitudes and behaviors. In some societies, and among some researchers, this distinction is not maintained, leading to confusion in the conception and assessment of acculturation strategies.

This formulation is from the perspective of nondominant peoples, and is based on the assumption that such groups and their individual members have the freedom to choose how they want to acculturate. However, as noted earlier, this option is not always the case. When the dominant group enforces certain forms of acculturation, or constrains the choices of nondominant groups or individuals, then other terms need to be used. In particular, integration can only be "freely" chosen and successfully pursued by nondominant groups when the dominant society is open and inclusive in its orientation toward cultural diversity. Thus a mutual accommodation is required to attain integration, involving the acceptance by both groups of the right of all groups to live as culturally different peoples. This strategy requires nondominant groups to adopt the basic values of the larger society, while at the same time the dominant group must be prepared to adapt national institutions (e.g., education, health, labor) to better meet the needs of all groups now living together in the plural society.

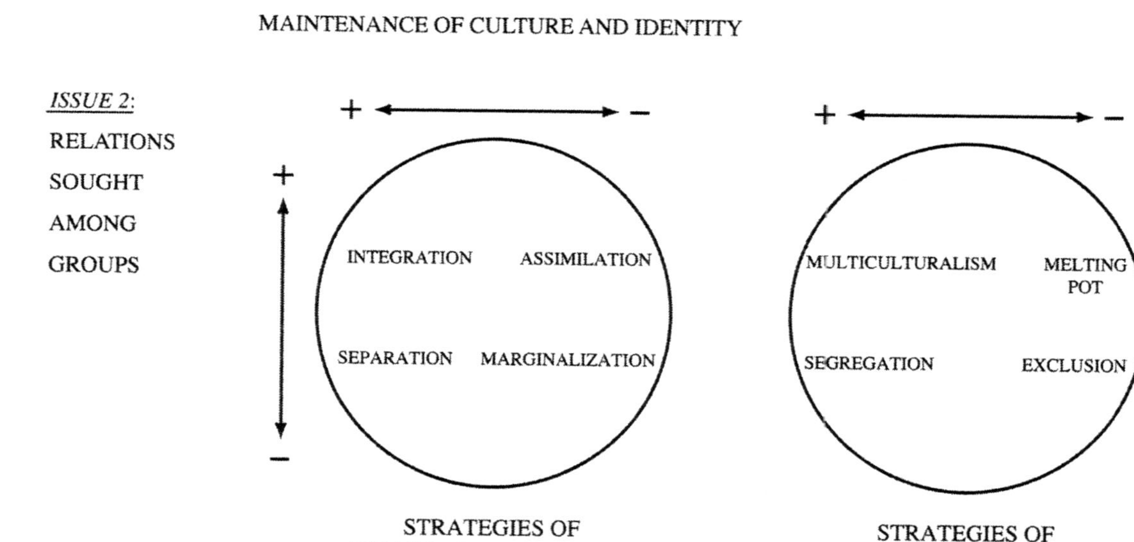

FIGURE 2.2. Four acculturation strategies based on two issues, in ethnocultural groups and the larger society.

Until now, these two basic issues have been approached from the point of view of nondominant ethnocultural groups. However, the original anthropological definition clearly established that *both* groups in contact would engage in the process of mutual or reciprocal acculturation. Hence, a third dimension was added: that of the powerful role played by the dominant group in influencing the way in which acculturation would take place. The addition of this third dimension (Berry, 1980) produces the right side of Figure 2.2. Assimilation, when sought by the dominant acculturating group, is termed the *melting pot*. When separation is forced by the dominant group, it is called *segregation*. Marginalization, when imposed by the dominant group, is called *exclusion*. Finally, integration, when diversity is an accepted feature of the society as a whole, including by all the various ethnocultural groups, is called *multiculturalism*. With the use of this framework, comparisons can be made between individuals and their groups, and between nondominant peoples and the larger society. The ideologies and policies of the dominant group constitute an important element of ethnic relations research (see Berry, Kalin, & Taylor, 1977; Bourhis, Moise, Perreault, & Senecal, 1997), and the preferences of nondominant peoples are a core feature in acculturation research (Berry et al., 1989). Inconsistencies and conflicts between these various acculturation preferences are sources of difficulty for acculturating individuals. Generally, when acculturation experiences cause problems for acculturating individuals, we observe the phenomenon of *acculturative stress*.

One issue of current interest is the appropriate conceptualization of acculturation strategies. The conceptual approach presented here is based on the presence of three underlying dimensions: cultural maintenance, contact and participation, and the power to decide on how acculturation will take place. For a long time, only one dimension was considered: It was assumed that nondominant groups and individuals would move from some "traditional" way of living to a way resembling that of the dominant society. This assimilationist or melting pot conception of the goal of acculturation, the process that leads to it, and its outcome have now been replaced by the multidimensional view presented here. This change occurred for a number of reasons. First, at the ethnographic level of observation (and consistent with early definitions of acculturation), assimilation is not the only form of acculturation; it has not always taken place and it is rarely the goal that is espoused by acculturating groups. Although cultural change is ubiquitous, cultural groups throughout the world have not disappeared, and cultural homogeneity has not resulted from intercultural contact. Resistance to assimilation (separation), and the formation of new cultures following contact are common phenomena. Second, at the psychological level, the central portion of this single dimension is ambiguous: Does it represent preferences and behaviors that represent half-and-half of each culture, or composed of neither culture? In the terms used in this chapter, such a unidimensional conceptualization cannot distinguish between "integration" and "marginalization." In my view, there is no unidimensional acculturation scale that has been able to deal with this problem in a satisfactory way.

However, as we see later, this is a critical problem because stress and adaptation outcomes are vastly different for these two ways of acculturating.

A second current issue is whether these two dimensions and the four acculturation strategies have any empirical basis (see Rudmin & Ahmadzadeh, 2001, for a critique; and Berry & Sam, 2003, for a response to it). One of their claims is that evidence is lacking for the existence of these four ways of acculturating, and that there is no evidence that integration is usually the preferred way to acculturate. Support for the existence of these two basic dimensions has been provided by a number of recent studies (e.g., Ryder, Alden, & Paulhus, 2000). They are found to be empirically distinct dimensions, with distinct correlates in behaviors. Moreover, Berry, Phinney, Sam, and Vedder (2006) studied over 5,000 immigrant youth who settled in 13 countries, and assessed a number of concepts (including attitudes toward the four ways of acculturating, ethnic and national identities, ethnic and national language knowledge and use, and ethnic and national friends). Four distinct acculturation profiles emerged from a cluster analysis of all these attitudinal and behavioral data. The largest number of youth fell into the *integrated* cluster (defined by a preference for integration, positive ethnic and national identities, use of both languages, and a friendship network that included youth from both cultures). The second largest cluster was an *ethnic* one (defined by a preference for separation and a rejection of assimilation, a high ethnic and low national identity, predominant use of the ethnic language, and friends mainly from their own ethnic group). The fourth largest cluster was a *national* one (defined by a pattern of attitudes and behaviors that are the opposite to the ethnic one). Surprisingly, the third largest cluster was a *diffuse* one that resembled marginalization. This was defined by their acceptance of assimilation, separation, and marginalization, and a rejection of integration (suggesting an unformed or diffuse set of acculturation attitudes), low ethnic and national identities (suggesting a feeling of nonengagement or attachment to either group), high proficiency in their ethnic language and low proficiency and use of the national language, and high contact with their own ethnic peers, but low contact with national peers. This finding of four distinct ways in which youth are acculturating provides substantial evidence for the existence of four general acculturation strategies. Because these include a complex set of attitudes and behaviors, they are considered to collectively correspond to the notion of acculturation *strategies*. Contrary to the criticisms already noted, there does appear to be a differential set of ways in which people seek to, and actually do, acculturate. Moreover, the integrative course appears to be the most preferred way to do it.

ACCULTURATIVE STRESS

Three ways to conceptualize outcomes of acculturation have been proposed (Berry, 1992, 1997). In the first (*behavioral shifts*), we observe those changes in an individual's behavioral repertoire that take place rather easily and are usually nonproblematic. This process encompasses three subprocesses: *cultural shedding*, *culture learning*, and *culture conflict*. The first two involve the selective, accidental, or deliberate loss of behaviors and their replacement by behaviors that allow the individual a better "fit" with the society of settlement. Most often this process has been termed *adjustment* because virtually all the adaptive changes take place in the acculturating individual, with few changes occurring among members of the larger society (Ward, Bochner, & Furnham, 2001). These adjustments are typically made with minimal difficulty, in keeping with the appraisal of the acculturation experiences as nonproblematic. However, some degree of cultural conflict may occur, which in the case of assimilation is usually resolved by the acculturating person yielding to the behavioral norms of the dominant group. In the case of those pursuing separation, individuals may withdraw from the acculturation arena in order to avoid continuing cultural conflict. For those seeking integration, conflict can be avoided only when the two groups in contact agree that mutual accommodation is the appropriate course to follow. As noted earlier, this is possible only when there is a multicultural orientation (high multicultural ideology) in the dominant society that matches the preference for integration among the nondominant groups. In the case of marginalization, cultural conflict is a variable feature of daily life and is usually resolved by seeking little involvement in either culture.

When greater levels of cultural conflict are experienced, and these experiences are judged to be problematic but controllable and surmountable, then the second approach (acculturative stress) is the appropriate conceptualization (Berry, Kim, Minde, & Mok, 1987). In this case, individuals understand that they are facing problems resulting from intercultural contact that cannot be dealt with easily or quickly by simply adjusting or assimilating to them. Drawing on the broader stress and adaptation paradigms (e.g., Lazarus & Folkman, 1984), this approach advocates the study of the process of how individuals deal with acculturative problems on first encountering them and over time. In this sense, acculturative stress is a stress reaction in response to life events that are rooted in the experience of acculturation.

Instead of using the term *culture shock* (see Ward et al., 2001) to encompass this second approach, I prefer to use the term *acculturative stress* for two reasons. First, the notion of "shock" carries only negative connotations. The notion of "stress" commonly connotes a negative experience, but in the field of health psychology stress can vary from positive (eustress) to negative (dis-stress) in valence. Because acculturation has both positive (e.g., new opportunities) and negative (e.g., discrimination) aspects, the stress conceptualization better matches the range of affect experienced during acculturation. Moreover, shock has no cultural or psychological theory or research context associated with it, whereas stress (as noted earlier) has a place in a well-developed theoretical matrix (i.e., stress–coping–adaptation). Second, the phenomena of interest have their life in the intersection of two cultures; they are intercultural, rather than cultural in their origin. The term *culture* implies that only one culture is involved, whereas the term *acculturation* draws our attention to the fact that two cultures are interacting and producing the stress phenomena. For both reasons, I prefer the notion of acculturative stress to that of culture shock.

Relating these two approaches to acculturation strategies, some consistent empirical findings allow the following generalizations (Berry, 1997). For behavioral shifts, the fewest behavioral changes result from the separation strategy, whereas most result from the assimilation strategy; integration involves the selective adoption of new behaviors from the larger society, and retention of valued features of one's heritage culture; and marginalization is often associated with major heritage culture loss and the appearance of a number of dysfunctional and deviant behaviors (such as delinquency and substance and familial abuse). For acculturative stress, there is a clear picture that the pursuit of integration is least stressful (at least where it is accommodated by the larger society), but marginalization is the most stressful; in between are the assimilation and separation strategies, sometimes one, sometimes the other being the less stressful. This pattern of findings holds for various indicators of mental health (Berry, 1997; Berry & Kim, 1988).

ADAPTATION

As a result of attempts to cope with these acculturation changes, some long-term adaptations may be achieved; as mentioned earlier, adaptation refers to the relatively stable changes that take place in an individual or group in response to external demands. Moreover, adaptation may or may not improve the "fit" between individuals and their environments. It is thus not a term that necessarily implies that individuals or groups change to become more like their environments (i.e., adjustment by way of assimilation), but may involve resistance and attempts to change environments or to move away from them altogether (i.e., by separation). In this usage, adaptation is an outcome that may or may not be positive in valence (i.e., meaning only well-adapted). This bipolar sense of the concept of adaptation is used in the framework in Figure 2.1 where long-term adaptation to acculturation is highly variable, ranging from well to poorly adapted, varying from situations where individuals can manage their new lives very well to ones where they are unable to carry on in the new society.

Adaptation is also multifaceted. The initial distinction between psychological and sociocultural adaptation was proposed and validated by Ward (1996). Psychological adaptation largely involves one's psychological and physical well-being, whereas sociocultural adaptation refers to how well an acculturating individual is able to manage daily life in the new cultural context. Although conceptually distinct, the two are empirically related to some extent (correlations between the two measures are in the .40 to .50 range). However, they are also empirically distinct in the sense that they usually have different time courses and different experiential predictors. Psychological problems often increase soon after contact, followed by a general (but variable) decrease over time; sociocultural adaptation, however, typically has a linear improvement with time. Analyses of the factors affecting adaptation reveal a generally consistent pattern. Good psychological adaptation is predicted by personality variables, life change events, and social support, whereas good sociocultural adaptation is predicted by cultural knowledge, degree of contact, and positive intergroup attitudes.

Research relating adaptation to acculturation strategies allows for some further generalizations (Berry, 1997; Ward, 1996). For both forms of adaptation, those who pursue and accomplish integration appear to be better adapted, and those who are marginalized are least well-adapted. And again, the assimilation and separation strategies are associated with intermediate adaptation outcomes. This generalization has been challenged (see Rudmin & Ahmadzadeh, 2001); however, despite occasional variations in this pattern, it is remarkably consistent and parallels the generalization made earlier regarding acculturative stress. Evidence for the positive benefits of the integration strategy has been reviewed by Berry and colleagues (1997; Berry & Sam, 1997). In a study of Irish immigrants, Curran (2003) has shown clearly that those pursuing the integration strategy have superior health than those pursuing the other ways of acculturating, especially marginalization. The most substantial evidence in support of this pattern comes from the study of immigrant youth (Berry et al., 2006) mentioned earlier. This project found evidence for the existence of the distinction between psychological adaptation (composed of few psychological problems, high self esteem and life satisfaction) and sociocultural adaptation (good school adjustment, few behavioral problems). When these two adaptation measures were related to the four acculturation profiles, a clear and consistent pattern emerged. Those in the integrated cluster were highest on both forms of adaptation, whereas those in the diffuse cluster were lowest on both. Those in the ethnic cluster had moderately good psychological adaptation, but lower sociocultural adaptation, whereas those in the national cluster had poorer scores on both forms of adaptation. These latest findings suggest that those who pursue integrative strategies (in terms of attitudes, identities, and behaviors) will achieve better adaptations than those who acculturate in other ways, especially those who are diffuse or marginal in their way of acculturating.

APPLICATIONS

There is now widespread evidence that most people who have experienced acculturation actually do survive. They are not destroyed or substantially diminished by it; rather, they find opportunities and achieve their goals sometimes beyond their initial imaginings. The tendency to "pathologize" the acculturation process and outcomes may be partly due to the history of its study in psychiatry and in clinical psychology. Researchers often presume to know what acculturating individuals want, and impose their own ideologies or their personal views, rather than informing themselves about culturally rooted individual preferences and differences. One key concept (but certainly not the only one) to understand this variability has been emphasized in this chapter (acculturation strategies).

There are two areas of application currently receiving considerable attention in research and policy development. One is the domain of family life (including relationships among individuals within the family, and between family members and the world outside). The other is in the area of immigration and settlement policies (including issues of changes in the institutions of a society, and the promotion of cultural diversity).

With respect to family acculturation (Berry et al., 2006), evidence shows that parents and children have different views about parent–adolescent relationships during acculturation. For example, parents have higher scores on a measure of family obligations (e.g., responsibility for various chores) than do their adolescent children; in sharp contrast, immigrant youth have higher scores on a scale of adolescent rights (e.g., independence in dating) than their parents. However, the differences between parents and adolescents in their views about family obligations varied according to which acculturation profile the youth were in: Those in the national profile (i.e., preferring assimilation, having a stronger national identity, and having more national friends) had greater discrepancies from the views of their parents. These discrepancies in family obligations scores (but not rights scores) were associated with poorer psychological and sociocultural adaptation of the adolescents.

A second project dealing with family has been carried out in 30 countries (see Georgas, Berry, van de Vijver, Kagitcibasi, & Poortinga, 2006, for details), dealing with similarities and differences in family structure and function, and with some of their the psychological correlates. This study has demonstrated both variation in family functioning that is linked to their ecological contexts (e.g., reliance on agriculture, general affluence) and variation due to their sociopolitical contexts (e.g., education, religion). In general, family arrangements are hierarchical and extended, and they have more conservative values (including interdependence) in high agrarian and low affluence societies, and with Orthodox Christian or Islamic religions. In contrast, families high in affluence and education and with a Protestant religious tradition are more nuclear, less hierarchical, and exhibit more independence. Although not part of this study, it is expected that following immigration, these variations in family life are likely to set the stage for variations in acculturation strategies, acculturative stress, and psychological and sociocultural adaptation. The basic dimensions of variations established in this project will allow for their use in future studies of immigration and acculturation when individuals migrate between the countries included in the sample of 30 societies.

With respect to public policies, the generalizations that have been made in this chapter on the basis of a wide range of empirical findings allow us to propose that public policies and programs that seek to reduce acculturative stress and to improve psychological and sociocultural adaptation should emphasize the integration approach to acculturation (see Berry, 2000, for a discussion of the social and psychological costs and benefits of multiculturalism). The argument and evidence are presented primarily for nondominant acculturating individuals. However, they are equally relevant for national policies, institutional arrangements, the goals of ethnocultural groups, and for individuals in the larger society. The current debate in political science (e.g., Banting & Kymlicka, 2004) attests to the importance of dealing with these issues at both the national policy and individual psychological levels. Further research is essential, for in the absence of conceptual clarity and empirical foundations, policies may create more social and psychological problems than they solve.

In some countries, the integrationist perspective has become legislated as policies of multiculturalism, which encourage and support the maintenance of valued features of all cultures, and at the same time support full participation of all ethnocultural groups in the evolving institutions of the larger society (see Berry, 1984, and Berry & Kalin, 2000, for an analysis of the Canadian policy). What seems certain is that cultural diversity and the resultant acculturation are here to stay in all countries. Finding a way to accommodate each other poses a challenge and an opportunity to social and cross-cultural psychologists everywhere. Diversity is a fact of contemporary life; whether it is the "spice of life" or the main "irritant" is probably the central question that confronts us all, citizens and social scientists alike.

ACKNOWLEDGMENTS

Much of the conceptual and empirical work reported in this chapter was carried out while the author was the recipient of grants from two agencies: The Social Science and Humanities Research Council of Canada, and the Canadian Ethnic Studies Committee of the Ministry of Multiculturalism.

REFERENCES

Banting, K., & Kymlicka, W. (2004). Do multiculturalism policies erode the welfare state? In P. Van Parijs (Ed.), *Cultural diversity versus economic solidarity* (pp. 227–284). Brussels: Editions De Boeck Université.

Berry, J. W. (1976). *Human ecology and cognitive style: Comparative studies in cultural and psychological adaptation*. New York: Sage/Halsted.

Berry, J. W. (1980). Acculturation as varieties of adaptation. In A. Padilla (Ed.), *Acculturation: Theory, models and findings* (pp. 9–25). Boulder, CO: Westview.

Berry, J. W. (1984). Multicultural policy in Canada: A social psychological analysis. *Canadian Journal of Behavioural Science, 16*, 353–370.

Berry, J. W. (1992). Acculturation and adaptation in a new society. *International Migration, 30*, 69–85.

Berry, J. W. (1997). Immigration, acculturation and adaptation. *Applied Psychology, 46*, 5–68.

Berry, J. W. (2000). Socio-psychological costs and benefits of multiculturalism: A view from Canada. In J. W. Dacyl & C. Westin (Eds.), *Governance and cultural diversity* (pp. 297–354). Stockholm: UNESCO & CIEFO, Stockholm University.

Berry, J. W., & Kalin, R. (1995). Multicultural and ethnic attitudes in Canada. *Canadian Journal of Behavioural Science, 27*, 310–320.

Berry, J. W., & Kalin, R. (2000). Multicultural policy and social psychology. In S. Renshon & J. Duckitt (Eds.), *Political psychology in cross-cultural perspective* (pp. 263–284). New York: Macmillan.

Berry, J. W., Kalin, R., & Taylor, D. (1977). *Multiculturalism and ethnic attitudes in Canada*. Ottawa: Supply & Services.

Berry, J. W., & Kim, U. (1988). Acculturation and mental health. In P. Dasen, J. W. Berry, & N. Sartorius (Eds.), *Health and cross-cultural psychology* (pp. 207–236). Newbury Park, CA: Sage.

Berry, J. W., Kim, U., Minde, T., & Mok, D. (1987). Comparative studies of acculturative stress. *International Migration Review, 21*, 491–511.

Berry, J. W., Kim, U., Power, S., Young, M., & Bujaki, M. (1989). Acculturation attitudes in plural societies. *Applied Psychology, 38*, 185–206.

Berry, J. W., Phinney, J. S., Sam, D. L., & Vedder, P. (Eds.). (2006). *Immigrant youth in cultural transition*. Mahwah, NJ: Lawrence Erlbaum Associates.

Berry, J. W., Poortinga, Y. H., Segall, M. H., & Dasen, P. R. (2002). *Cross-cultural psychology: Research and applications* (2nd ed.). New York: Cambridge University Press.

Berry, J. W., & Sam, D. (1997). Acculturation and adaptation. In J. W. Berry, M. H. Segall, & C. Kagitcibasi (Eds.), *Handbook of cross-cultural psychology, Vol. 3, Social behavior and applications* (pp. 291–326). Boston: Allyn & Bacon.

Berry, J. W., & Sam, D. L. (2003). Accuracy in scientific discourse. *Scandinavian Journal of Psychology, 44*, 65–68.

Bourhis, R., Moise, L. C., Perreault, S., & Senecal, S. (1997). Towards an interactive acculturation model: A social psychological approach. *International Journal of Psychology, 32*, 369–386.

Chun, K., Balls-Organista, P., & Marin, G. (Eds.). (2003). *Acculturation: Advances in theory, measurement and applied research*. Washington, DC: American Psychological Association.

Curran, M. J. (2003). *Across the water—The acculturation and health of Irish people in London*. Dublin: Trinity College and Allen Library.

Georgas, J., Berry, J. W., van de Vijver, F., Kagitcibasi, C., & Poortinga, Y. H. (2006). *Families across cultures: A 30-nation psychological study*. Cambridge: Cambridge University Press.

Graves, T. (1967). Psychological acculturation in a tri-ethnic community. *South-Western Journal of Anthropology, 23*, 337–350.

Lazarus, R. S., & Folkman, S. (1984). *Stress, appraisal and coping*. New York: Springer.

Lebedeva, N., & Tatarko, A. (2004). Socio-psychological factors of ethnic intolerance in Russia's multicultural regions. In B. Setiadi, A. Supratiknya, W. Lonner, & Y. Poortinga (Eds.), *Ongoing themes in psychology and culture. Selected papers from the Sixteenth International Congress of the International Association for Cross-Cultural Psychology* (pp. 507–532). Jakarta: Indonesian Universities Press.

Murphy, H. B. M. (1965). *Migration and the major mental disorders*. Springfield: Thomas.

Redfield, R., Linton, R., & Herskovits, M. (1936). Memorandum on the study of acculturation. *American Anthropologist, 38*, 149–152.

Richmond, A. (1993). Reactive migration: Sociological perspectives on refugee movements. *Journal of Refugee Studies, 6*, 7–24.

Rudmin, F. W., & Ahmadzadeh, V. (2001). Psychometric critique of acculturation psychology: The case of Iranian migrants in Norway. *Scandinavian Journal of Psychology, 42*, 41–56.

Ryder, A., Alden, L., & Paulhus, D. (2000). Is acculturation unidimensional or bidimensional? *Journal of Personality and Social Psychology, 79*, 49–65.

Sam, D., & Berry, J. W. (Eds.). (2006). *Cambridge handbook of acculturation psychology*. Cambridge: Cambridge University Press.

Social Science Research Council. (1954). Acculturation: An exploratory formulation. *American Anthropologist, 56*, 973–1002.

Ward, C. (1996). Acculturation. In D. Landis & R. Bhagat (Eds.), *Handbook of intercultural training* (2nd ed., pp. 124–147). Newbury Park, CA: Sage.

Ward, C., Bochner, S., & Furnham, A. (2001). *The psychology of culture shock*. London: Routledge.

II

Measurement and Acculturation

3

Issues in the Conceptualization and Assessment of Acculturation

Judit Arends-Tóth
Tilburg University, the Netherlands

Fons J. R. van de Vijver
Tilburg University, the Netherlands
North-West University, South Africa

INTRODUCTION

The assessment of acculturation has not yet become an integral part of assessment procedures in multicultural groups despite its relevance for plural societies. A possible reason may be the absence of widely accepted conceptualizations and measurement methods. This chapter discusses conceptual and assessment issues in acculturation research in an attempt to integrate the growing literature in this field. The chapter is divided into four parts. The first part focuses on conceptual issues in acculturation research; it starts with the definition and the presentation of historical roots of acculturation and ends with a framework of acculturation variables. The second part addresses frequently observed sources of problems in the assessment of acculturation. The third part focuses on an application domain of acculturation assessment: the immigrant family. Conclusions are drawn in the final part.

CONCEPTUALIZING ACCULTURATION: DEFINITION AND HISTORICAL ROOTS

When culturally disparate people come into continuous contact with each other, the differences between them tend to become salient and can result in changes in the original cultural patterns of both groups. Although immigration has consequences for both immigrants and members of the receiving society, the former group is usually more affected. Because of its increasing importance in the everyday world as well as in theories and measurement in the social sciences, acculturation experiences of immigrants have frequently been researched in the last three decades, although the field's origin is much older.

From a historical perspective, most research on acculturation has been anthropological in nature and has focused on the acculturation of developing nations to industrial, Western societies (Olmedo, 1979). The term *acculturation* was introduced by American anthropologists, as early as the 1880s, to describe the process of culture change occurring when two different cultural groups come into contact with each other. Numerous definitions of acculturation have been presented in the literature, most of them adaptations of the definition proposed by Redfield, Linton, and Herskovits (1936):

> Acculturation comprehends those phenomena which result when groups of individuals having different cultures come into continuous first-hand contact, with subsequent changes in the original culture patterns of either or both groups. (p. 149)

This definition treats acculturation mainly as a group-level phenomenon; in more recent times, interest has grown in the study of individual-level phenomena, referred to as *psychological acculturation* (Graves, 1967). At the individual level, acculturation refers to changes that an individual experiences as a result of contact with one or more other cultures and of the participation in the ensuing process of change that one's cultural or ethnic group is undergoing.

Early theories and research on acculturation were strongly influenced by medicine and psychiatry and examined the pathological symptoms accompanying culture shock. More recent approaches have paid more attention to establishing links of acculturation models with current theories and models in psychology, mainly clinical and social psychology. For example, acculturation has been studied from a social-psychological perspective by examining its cognitive, affective, and behavioral components. Theoretical frameworks of acculturation have been borrowed from mainstream psychology. Major influences have been drawn from work in stress and coping, social learning and skills, social cognition and intergroup perceptions (Ward, 1996, 1999). For example, adapting a *stress-and-coping approach*, researchers have focused on the influence of life changes, coping mechanisms, cognitive appraisal of the change, personality characteristics, and social support on physical and mental health (e.g., Berry, 1997). The *social-learning approach* is derived from social and experimental psychology. This approach emphasizes the role of learning in the acquisition of culturally appropriate new skills. Variables that promote learning new social skills and that facilitate adaptation to the new culture are frequently studied, including general knowledge about the new culture, cultural distance, length of residence in the new country, and amount of contact with host nationals (e.g., Ward, 1996, 1999; Ward & Kennedy, 1994). In the *social-cognition* approach to acculturation, which draws on the work of Kunda (1999), cognitive elements such as expectations, attitudes toward members of the new culture, cultural identity, perception, attributions, and changes in values as part of the acculturation process have been investigated (e.g., Wong-Rieger, 1984).

Although social and behavioral scientists agree on the definition of acculturation, there is confusion about its conceptualization and measurement. Various assessment procedures have been developed and applied, sometimes based on conflicting underlying theoretical models. In order to set the stage for their description, we first present a taxonomy of acculturation variables that have been frequently reported in the literature.

ACCULTURATION VARIABLES

Variables addressed in psychological acculturation research can be broadly divided into three groups: acculturation conditions, acculturation orientations,[1] and acculturation outcomes (see Figure 3.1).

Acculturation Conditions

Acculturation conditions refer to the contextual limits and demands of the acculturation process. The context in which acculturation occurs often has a major impact on the acculturation process. Relevant aspects at the population or group level involve the type of migration (e.g., temporary versus permanent, voluntary versus involuntary), characteristics of the society of origin (e.g., cultural homogeneity), characteristics of the immigrant group (e.g., ethnic vitality and social attachment), characteristics of the host society (e.g., cultural openness, discrimination, and views on immigrants in general), and intergroup relations (e.g., social inequality and social distance). At the individual level, conditions can refer to changes over time (e.g., age, length of settlement, and generational differences), position in the society, personality characteristics (e.g., social norms and coping strategies), and situational or social context (e.g., social support and stressful situations).

[1]Various terms have been used to refer to acculturation responses, such as *acculturation orientations, strategies, attitudes, modes,* and *styles*. Although all of these terms, if properly defined, can be used, we prefer *acculturation orientations* because this term refers to broad personal preferences, which in our view are crucial in the acculturation process. The term *strategy* implies more conscious rational choice and consistency than we find in the acculturation process; they refer both to attitudes and behaviors (which is an argument against using attitudes as the generic term); similarly, the term *style* could be seen more as referring to behaviors than to attitudes (however, when the term would be used as in "cognitive style," our argument would no longer hold). Finally, the term *mode* may convey the impression of a link with assessment methods, which is undesirable.

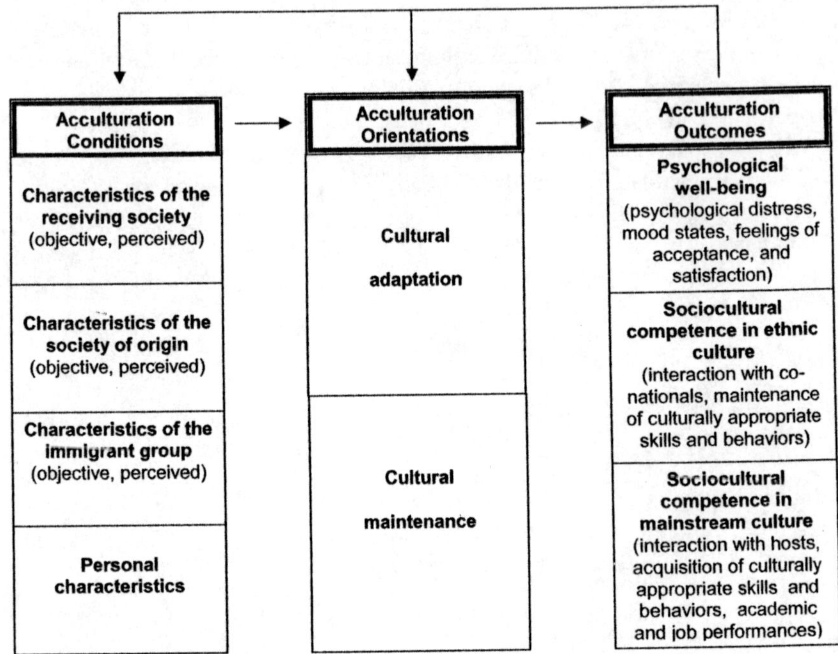

FIGURE 3.1. Framework of acculturation variables.

Understanding acculturation conditions is essential to establishing the context within which the acculturation process takes place. Although there is no generally accepted theoretical model of which background factors affect acculturation in which way, the most elaborated and widely quoted model of acculturation conditions has been proposed by Bourhis, Moïse, Perreault, and Senécal (1997). According to this interactive acculturation model, state immigration and integration policies influence acculturation orientations of both the host majority and immigrant groups. The vitality of immigrant groups was also emphasized in the acculturation process: The more vital the group, the more likely that it would act as a distinctive and collective entity within the larger society, and adopt acculturation orientations reflecting its own priorities rather than those determined by majority group members. The degree to which acculturation orientations of the host community and immigrant group match or mismatch defines their relational outcome. Consensual relational outcomes emerge when the two groups share the same acculturation orientations. Problematic relational outcomes emerge when the majority and the immigrant groups experience only partial agreement in their acculturation orientations. Conflictual relational outcomes occur when there is no overlap in their acculturation orientations. In addition, the integration policy of local, regional, or national authorities may attenuate or accentuate patterns of relational outcomes.

In a study among 155 young Moroccan adults in the Netherlands, Ait-Ouarasse and van de Vijver (2004) found that the acculturation context as perceived by these immigrants was multidimensional. The perceived mainstream context consisted of a tolerance factor (i.e., how tolerant mainstreamers are toward immigrants) and an integration factor (whether mainstreamers want immigrants to integrate). The perceived minority context also consisted of two factors, called permissiveness to adjust (indicating the perceived extent to which the Moroccan community allows its members to adjust to the Dutch culture) and ethnic vitality. The mainstream context factors exerted an influence on work success, whereas the minority context was important for school success and good mental health.

Acculturation Outcomes

Various indices have been examined as outcomes of the acculturation process, such as psychological distress, mood states, feelings of acceptance and satisfaction, the nature and extent of interaction with hosts, the acquisition of culturally appropriate behaviors and skills, academic performance, and job performance. Ward and Kennedy (1994) argued that adaptive outcomes of the acculturative process can be divided into psychological (emotional/affective) well-being and sociocultural (behavioral) competence in the mainstream culture. They found that psychological and sociocultural adjustment were interrelated (their correlation is usually around .30), but that they were predicted by different variables and showed different patterns of fluctuation over time (i.e., sociocultural problems steadily decrease, whereas psychological distress is more variable over time). From a theoretical point of view, it is important to address the level of sociocultural competence in the ethnic culture (e.g., interaction with conationals, maintenance of culturally appropriate skills and behaviors) and changes in this competence as an additional outcome variable. Thus, it is important to study both proficiency in the mainstream culture and maintenance (or loss) of the ethnic culture. Both are relevant outcomes of the acculturation process.

Acculturation Orientations

Many studies of how immigrants cope with intercultural contact focus on acculturation orientations. These orientations are critical to understanding the acculturation process of immigrants and are seen as constituting the most characteristic part of the whole process (e.g., Berry, 1997; Ward, Bochner, & Furnham, 2001) because they link antecedent conditions to outcomes.

Despite the vast number of empirical studies on acculturation orientations, only a few theoretical models have been developed to explain this complex process (Negy & Woods, 1992). Theoretical models of acculturation orientations can be grouped along two lines (see Table 3.1): dimensionality and domain specificity.

TABLE 3.1
A Classification of Acculturation Models
(Domain Specificity and Dimensionality)

	Dimensionality		
Domain Specificity	*Unidimensional Models*	*Bidimensional Models*	*Fusion Models*
Level 1: Trait models (domain-aspecific models)	Migrant adapts to the main culture	Migrant has two attitudes: maintenance of original culture and adaptation to the host culture	A new culture emerges
Domain-specific models - Level 2: Cluster of domains (e.g., public and private domains) - Level 3: Specific life domains (e.g., childrearing, news) - Level 4: Specific situations (e.g., food at home and outside home)	Speed of adaptation varies across domains/situations	Same as above, but now applied for life domains/situations	A new culture emerges in a domain/situation

Dimensionality

Acculturation orientations refer to how an immigrant combines (or does not combine) the culture of origin and the culture of the country of settlement. The former aspect involves the importance attached by the immigrant to maintaining key aspects of the heritage culture. The latter aspect, according to Berry (1997), refers to the extent to which the immigrant wishes to have contacts with and to participate in the society of settlement. Bourhis and his associates (1997) proposed a refinement by changing the nature of the second aspect, making it cultural instead of social. Their dimension of cultural adaptation refers to the perceived importance of adopting key aspects of the majority culture.

The relations between cultural maintenance and cultural adaptation have been described in three ways, resulting in three theoretical models of acculturation. The first, the *unidimensional model*, conceptualizes cultural maintenance and cultural adaptation as opposites (see Figure 3.2). In this model, acculturation is a process of culture change along a single dimension, a shift from maintenance of the immigrant culture to full adaptation to the host culture (Gordon, 1964). Immigrants lose their original culture as they acquire a new culture. For example, the ability to speak the heritage language might be expected to decrease as immigrants become more proficient in the mainstream language.

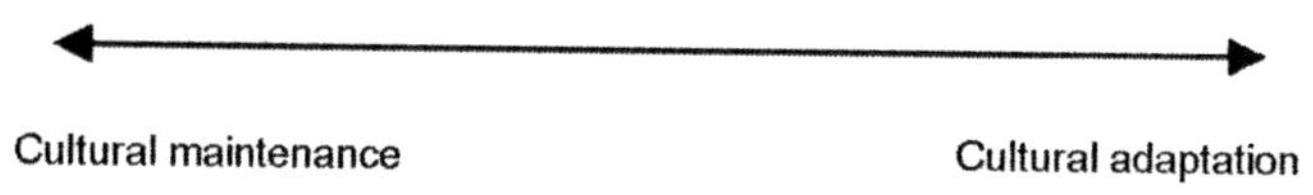

FIGURE 3.2. The unidimensional acculturation model.

The second model is called *bidimensional*. Maintenance and adaptation are treated here as two separate dimensions (Figure 3.3). Various authors view the two dimensions as independent; an increase in adaptation does not require a decrease in cultural maintenance (e.g., Berry, 1997; Hutnik, 1986; Sánchez & Fernández, 1993). For example, the ability to speak the heritage language does not need to influence the ability to speak the language of the mainstream society. The most popular bidimensional model was developed by Berry (chapter 2, this volume). In this model, the two main aspects of acculturation are combined, constituting four acculturation orientations, namely integration, assimilation, separation, and marginalization. Integration reflects an orientation in which key features of the immigrant's culture are maintained, with a simultaneous adoption of elements of the majority culture. Assimilation refers to the loss of the original culture and complete absorption in the majority culture. The separation strategy amounts to the maintenance of the minority culture while rejecting the majority culture. Finally, marginalization amounts to the rejection of both cultures (see Figure 3.3).

In a third kind of dimensionality model, a *fusion model*, an acculturating individual mixes both cultures in a new "integrated culture." This integrated culture contains either a mix of the two cultures (combining "the best of both worlds") or unique and novel aspects that are atypical of either culture (Coleman, 1995; Padilla, 1995). This model sees acculturation as a mixture of cultural characteris-

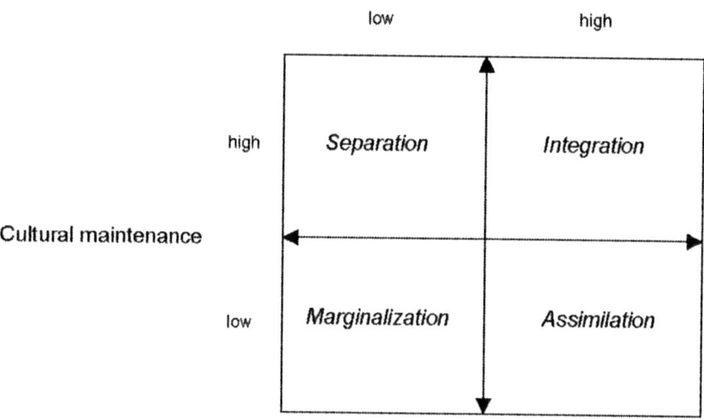

FIGURE 3.3. Berry's bidimensional acculturation model.

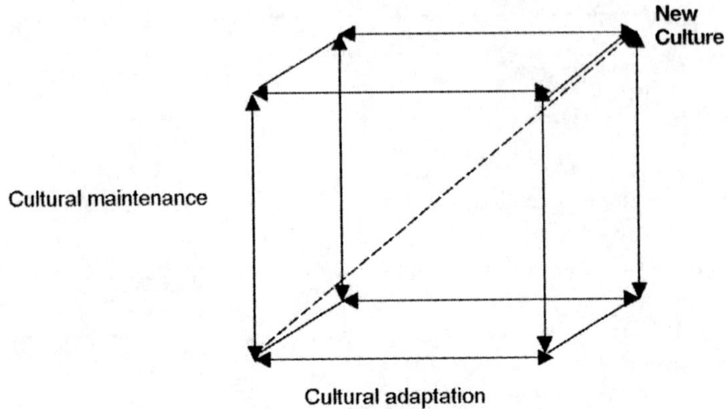

FIGURE 3.4. The fusion model of acculturation.

tics (see Figure 3.4). No studies are available in which the validity of the model has been investigated empirically.

Domain Specificity

Domain-specific models are offshoots of the trait model (which assumes cross-situational consistency). Whereas the contexts in which acculturation occurs were often left out of consideration in the trait model, domain-specific models are based on the assumption that an individual's preference for adaptation and cultural maintenance can (and often will) vary across life domains or situations. For example, one may seek assimilation at work (economic assimilation), speak the languages of the countries of heritage and settlement (linguistic integration), and maintain traditional relationships in family and marriage (separation in private relationships).

The models of domain specificity that have been proposed differ in their levels of abstraction (i.e., the breadth of the domain). We find in our own work that acculturation can be seen as a hierarchical concept, with unidimensionality at the top (a global preference for either adaptation or cultural maintenance). The second level is constituted by two broad, positively related domains: public (functional, utilitarian) domain and private (social–emotional, value-related) domain (Arends-Tóth & van de Vijver, 2003). The public domain involves all activities aimed at participation (broadly defined) in the social life of both majority and minority groups (e.g., education and job). The private domain involves more personal, value-related matters (e.g., childrearing and marriage). Turkish Dutch indicated that they prefer adaptation to the Dutch culture more in the public domain than in the private domain, whereas cultural maintenance was deemed important in both domains; in terms of Berry's (1997) acculturation orientation, this preference amounts to integration in the public domain and separation in the private domain. The third level is formed by specific life domains (e.g., education and language in the public domain, and childrearing and marriage in the private domain). Finally, at the fourth level an individual's preference for adaptation and maintenance may vary across specific situations (e.g., Clement & Noels, 1992; Nagata, 1994; Taylor & Lambert, 1996). Sodowsky and Carey (1988) described certain dual characteristics of first-generation Asian Indians in the United States, who preferred Indian food and dress at home and American food and dress elsewhere. Similarly, Phalet, van Lotringen, and Entzinger (2000) found that Dutch immigrant youth preferred cultural maintenance at home and Dutch culture outside of the home.

ASSESSMENT OF ACCULTURATION

It is still uncommon to take into account an immigrant's acculturation orientation and adjustment in psychological assessment in plural societies (e.g., Cuéllar & Paniagua, 2000; Suzuki, Ponterotto, & Meller, 2001). However, information about an immigrant's acculturation can be highly valuable. For example, it has been found that acculturation orientations are related to mental health, self-esteem, political and social attitudes, social deviancy, alcoholism, recreational drug use, risk of coronary heart disease, suicide, and academic performance (e.g., Berry, 1997; Berry & Kim, 1988; Cuéllar & Paniagua, 2000; Lasry & Sayegh, 1992; Negy & Woods, 1992; Nguyen, Messe, & Stollak, 1999; Padilla, 1995; Pham & Harris, 2001; Ward et al., 2001). In addition, acculturation orientations can be an important moderator affecting the validity of assessment procedures in multicultural groups (e.g., Olmedo & Padilla, 1978). An acculturation measure can serve to establish the extent to which test characteristics obtained among majority group members (e.g., reliability and norms) apply to a specific immigrant, thereby enhancing the quality of the assessment process (e.g., Dana, 2000; van de Vijver & Phalet, 2004).

A vast number of instruments and measurement designs to measure acculturation have been reported in the literature, which preempts a comprehensive presentation within the framework of the current chapter. Therefore, we have adopted another approach. The first part of the section provides guidelines in the assessment of acculturation. The guidelines are not meant to be comprehensive but are based on our view of which problems are commonly met in assessment procedures. The second part focuses on the assessment of acculturation orientations, because these are the most frequently studied aspects of acculturation. Three common ways of assessment are presented. In the final part of this section, two assessment-related acculturation studies are reported; the first compares the three assessment methods, and the second addresses the question of the exchangeability of acculturation attitudes and behaviors.

Some Guidelines for Assessing Acculturation

(1) **Acculturation conditions, orientations, and outcomes usually cannot be combined in a single measure.** An important choice in the assessment of acculturation refers to the question of whether acculturation conditions, orientations, or outcomes are to be measured (Figure 3.1). These three are often mixed in an instrument and aggregated into a single overall score. It is difficult to see how acculturation could "explain" other psychological variables (such as cognitive developmental outcomes) if all aspects of acculturation (background variables, orientations, and outcomes) are used as predictors. For example, length of stay in a country and language proficiency of the country may well be correlated; however, the two variables are conceptually quite distinct, and their causal order is clear. Moreover, if both are used to explain some developmental skill, it could be helpful to use length of stay as predictor, language proficiency as a mediating, moderating, or even outcome variable, and the developmental skill as outcome variable.

Various mixtures of antecedent conditions, orientations, and outcomes can be found in the literature. For example, the attitudinal and (self-reported) behavioral items are often mixed in questionnaires and analyzed in combination, thereby implicitly assuming their interchangeability. However, attitudes and behaviors can refer to quite distinct aspects of the acculturation process. Attitudes belong to acculturation orientations and can be considered as mediating or moderator variables; acculturation behaviors can be viewed as referring either to orientations or to outcomes. An example of an often undesirable mixing of outcomes and orientations could be the use and knowledge of the mainstream language. Language proficiency and use (behaviors) are often used to measure acculturation orientations, but they can also be seen as outcomes of the acculturation process. In the latter case, mixing attitudes and behaviors amounts to combining mediating or moderating variables with outcome variables. A final mixture refers to marginalization. In Berry's (1997) framework, marginalization is an acculturation orientation, but in practice it is often seen as a problematic (undesirable) outcome of the acculturation process.

Unless evidence is reported that all aspects measured constitute a single underlying dimension, we recommend not combining separate indices into a single overall acculturation score.

(2) **A measure of acculturation can only be comprehensive if it contains aspects of both the mainstream and heritage cultures.** Both the heritage and the mainstream cultures are relevant in finding a comprehensive picture of acculturation conditions (i.e., characteristics of the receiving society and characteristics of the society of origin and of the immigrant group) and in acculturation orienta-

tions (i.e., cultural adaptation and cultural maintenance). Attention to both cultures is conspicuously absent in the assessment of acculturation outcomes. Commonly employed indices of sociocultural competence of acculturation outcomes refer to the degree of the success of adaptation to the receiving society (e.g., interaction with hosts, acquisition of culturally appropriate skills and behaviors, academic and job performance) and do not consider the maintenance of the heritage culture at all (e.g., proficiency in the ethnic language). Outcome measures almost never strike a balance between the cultures involved. For example, many studies focus on gains in mainstream language proficiency but few address maintenance of the ethnic language.

An additional problem of not striking a balance between mainstream and heritage culture is that different acculturation aspects (e.g., knowledge, attitudes, behaviors, values, and ethnic identity) are used to assess them. For example, the heritage culture is often assessed by acculturation attitudes only, whereas the mainstream culture is often addressed by self-reported acculturation behaviors. If items are not generated in pairs with regard to aspects, with one item in one aspect referring to heritage culture and the other item in the same aspect referring to the mainstream culture, the obtained differences may be partly due to the differences in measured aspects instead of the two cultures.

(3) **Proxy measures (e.g., generation level, number of years living in the country) can provide valuable complementary information to other measures of acculturation, but are usually poor stand-alone measures of acculturation.** Many acculturation studies use demographic background information to measure acculturation; examples are generation status and number of years of residence in the country of settlement. Although these proxies can provide valuable information about the construct validity of direct measures of acculturation, their value as stand-alone measures is often limited. By operationalizing acculturation as a set of background conditions and leaving out all psychological aspects, a poor rendering of the acculturation process is obtained. For example, Jain and Belsky (1997) found that demographics (e.g., number of years of settlement in the United States) did not predict the father's involvement in children's lives, whereas direct measurements of acculturation orientations (e.g., attitudes) were significant predictors. Measures of acculturation based on demographic variables, such as generational level, age, years living in the receiving society, and socioeconomic status, are good predictors of group trends. They are not, however, sensitive to differences among individuals who have similar demographic characteristics (Mendoza, 1989). McQueen, Getz, and Bray (2003) reported that even when parents and adolescents share the same language and birth country, their views regarding family relationships may differ and these differences may indeed induce conflicts. Therefore, they advise that in order to identify elements of the acculturation process that influence individual and family changes, more direct and diverse measures of acculturation should be used. In general, more direct meas-

ures of acculturation with a firmer psychological basis are preferable (Negy & Woods, 1992).

(4) **The use of single-index measures should be avoided.** Single indices usually are suspect measures of acculturation because of their low content validity (construct coverage); it is difficult to see how the multifaceted complexities of acculturation can be captured in a one-item measure. An additional problem of these measures is their unknown and possibly low reliability. Language preference is an example of such a single-index measure. Some researchers have found language preference to be a very important index of acculturation status (e.g., Padilla, 1980), whereas others have not (e.g., Garcia, 1982; Weinstock, 1964). Weinstock found that the number of friends from the majority group and mass media preference were more adequate indicators of acculturation of Hungarian immigrants than their knowledge of English. It could well be that, as immigrants adapt more to the society of settlement, language preference discriminates less among immigrants and other acculturative aspects may become more important. In general, the literature has not supported any single-item index of acculturation that is reliable, valid across ethnic groups, generations, and countries of settlement, and predicts outcomes.

(5) **Psychometric properties of instruments (validity and reliability) should be reported.** Various measures of acculturation orientations, often based on self-reports, have been developed and used. Reports of studies in which these have been administered often do not describe the psychometric qualities of items and scales. Marín (1992) argued that in many empirical studies acculturation items are summed or averaged, as if they form a single scale, without providing any analysis to support this claim.

Assessment of Acculturation Orientations: One-, Two-, and Four-Statement Methods

There is a need to compare and integrate different acculturation measurement methods that have been proposed in the literature. In this section, we discuss the pros and cons of three widely used measurement methods of acculturation orientations.

One-Statement Acculturation Measurement Method

There tends to be a close link between theoretical models and measurement methods of acculturation orientations. Unidimensional measures following the one-statement measurement method employ a bipolar scale, ranging from cultural maintenance at one pole, with biculturalism at the midpoint of the scale, to adaptation at the other pole. A cumulative scale score is used as an overall index of acculturation status (e.g., Celano & Tyler, 1991; Suinn, Ahuna, & Khoo, 1992). Domain-specific unidimensional measures have been also proposed. In these models and measures, cultural aspects may differ in their level of adjustment (e.g., Triandis, Kashima, Shimada, & Villareal, 1986).

The one-statement method has the advantage of yielding an efficient, short instrument. However, the method cannot distinguish a bicultural individual who strongly identifies with both groups from a marginalized individual who does not identify with either group if individuals score on the midpoint of the scale, referring to equal preference (or equal rejection) of both cultures (e.g., Mavreas, Bebbington, & Der, 1989; Ryder, Alden, & Paulhus, 2000). Adding an answer alternative (no adaptation, no cultural maintenance) to the answer categories solves this problem.

Two-Statement Acculturation Measurement Method

In the two-statement measurement method of the bidimensional model, acculturation is assessed by using two separate scales, one representing attitudes toward the mainstream culture and the other representing attitudes toward the heritage culture (e.g., Donà & Berry, 1994; Padilla, 1995; Sánchez & Fernández, 1993). A study of the association between the heritage and mainstream dimensions of acculturation is theoretically interesting. A strong, negative correlation between the two aspects would support the unidimensional model, whereas a low or zero correlation would support the existence of two orthogonal dimensions, as often assumed in the literature on this model. Empirical studies of the association between cultural maintenance and adaptation have shown considerable disagreement. Correlations have been found to vary from negative (e.g., Birman, 1998; Birman & Trickett, 2001; Laroche, Kim, & Hui, 1997; Nguyen, Messe, & Stollak, 1999; Verkuyten & Thijs, 2002), low and nonsignificant (e.g., Hutnik, 1986; Sánchez & Fernández, 1993; Sayegh & Lasry, 1993), to positive (e.g., Ward & Kennedy, 1994). Too few studies have addressed the issue to warrant a meta-analysis in which results could be synthesized and the effects of possible moderators on the relationship could be studied.

Different procedures have been proposed to transform the two dimension scores into Berry's four acculturation orientations. In the median and mean split procedures, responses are categorized as being lower or higher than a cut-off value (the median or mean of the sample). This procedure employs the characteristics of the sample of the cultural group under study, and categorizes participants into one of the four orientations irrespective of their position on the adaptation and maintenance scale (Ward & Kennedy, 1994). This procedure may give a distorted image in a homogeneous sample, which is the case when many participants have either a high or low score on either or both dimensions (Donà & Berry, 1994). If all immigrants want to combine both cultures (integration is the acculturation orientation that is preferred by most acculturating groups), it is inadequate to artificially split the sample so as to have all four acculturation orientations represented in the sample.

In the midpoint split procedure, scale scores above the midpoint on the Likert scales are taken to indicate agreement to the scale construct and are classified "high" on the scale, and scores below the midpoint refer to disagreement and are classified "low" on the scale. The midpoint split procedure has a firmer theoretical basis than the median and mean split procedures; it avoids the problem of artificially introducing subgroups in a group that has identical acculturation orientations. However, a problem with this procedure is that the midpoint is often an answer option (e.g., a score of 3 on a scale ranging from 1 to 5) and there is no agreement in the literature as to how these midpoint scores should be treated in computing acculturation orientations. In some studies, these scores have been interpreted as disagreement with the item (e.g., Donà & Berry, 1994), in others as agreement (e.g., Lasry & Sayegh, 1992), and in still others as unclassifiable (e.g., Rudmin & Ahmadzadeh, 2001).

According to the proximity procedure, the two dimensions can be seen as defining a two-dimensional space (an adaptation and a maintenance dimension). Each of Berry's (1997) four acculturation orientations can be represented by an "ideal point" in the space. For example, on a 7-point Likert scale (ranging from 1 to 7), the prototypical score of assimilation is 1 on the maintenance scale and 7 on the adaptation scale. The Euclidean distances between the ideal score of each of the four acculturation orientations and the score obtained for an individual can be computed. This procedure has the advantage that it does not classify participants into one of the four categories, but yields a score for all participants on all acculturation orientations. A disadvantage of this scoring method is the lack of independence of the scores on the acculturation orientations (i.e., the same problem that holds for the other scoring procedures based on the two-item measures). Scores for integration and marginalization show a negative correlation, and the same is true for assimilation and separation.

Four-Statement Acculturation Measurement Method

In the four-statement method of the bidimensional model, the attitude toward each of the four acculturation orientations distinguished by Berry (1997) is asked in separate items. The four-statement method is the only one in which the four acculturation orientations are independently assessed. In spite of this advantage, the four-statement method has some limitations. Because acculturation orientations are defined as arising from two attitudes toward two cultures, the Likert items tend to be "double-barreled" (e.g., "Do you like Russian food and do you like American food?"). Participants can interpret such items in different ways or may answer to only a part of the item (the participant may like Russian food and dislike American food; see also Nunnally & Bernstein, 1994). Also, the use of negations (marginalization items tend to have double negations) makes this method cognitively complex (Rudmin & Ahmadzadeh, 2001; Ryder et al., 2000). To overcome the problem of double-barreled items, van Oudenhoven, Willemsma, and Prins (1996) wrote a separate vignette for each of the four orientations and respondents had to indicate the level of agreement with each. The problem with this method is that a vignette should comprehend several domains and situations, which makes a vignette long and complex. It may not be clear then to which features of the vignette the immigrant responded.

Studies on the Assessment of Acculturation in the Netherlands

The Dutch Context

The Netherlands, like all Western European countries, has become culturally diverse. A heterogeneous group of immigrants has taken up permanent residence in the Netherlands, as a result of Dutch colonial history in the Caribbean area (from Surinam and the Dutch Antilles), as a result of the recruitment of cheap labor from the Mediterranean region in the 1960s (from Turkey, Morocco, and Southern Europe), and recently as a result of the influx of refugees mainly from Africa, Eastern Europe, and the Middle East. At present, 18% of the population in the Netherlands is of foreign origin, and by 2010 in the three largest Dutch cities, this figure will rise to 50% (Centraal Bureau voor de Statistiek, 2004). These numbers are unprecedented in Dutch history. Not surprisingly, the acculturation of these groups has become a prominent feature in public discourse.

Turkish Immigrants in the Netherlands

Turkish immigrants form one of the largest groups of immigrants in the Netherlands and are often seen by native Dutch as the prototypical immigrant group (Pettigrew, 1998) with a large cultural distance to the Dutch mainstream culture (in terms of religion, values, gender relationships, and language).

The first Turkish migrants arrived in the Netherlands in the beginning of the 1960s when the Dutch economy had a shortage of unskilled workers. Most of the Turkish immigrants did not intend to stay long in the Netherlands. The aim of their emigration was to earn enough money as "guest workers" (the common term in those days) to build a better life in Turkey. In order to save as much money as possible, they did not invest in their life in the Netherlands and their life circumstances and working conditions in the Netherlands were generally mediocre or poor. Although labor recruitment was brought to an end in 1974, Turkish immigration to the Netherlands continued through family reunification, asylum request, and informal channels. Nowadays, marriages with second-generation Turkish Dutch form the main reason people emigrate from Turkey to the Netherlands.

The orientation and background of Turkish immigrants was not conducive to acquiring a good social position in the Netherlands. The educational level, income, and job position of the first-generation Turkish migrants are, on average, weak in comparison with the Dutch population. The second generation, representing more than a third of the Turkish Dutch population, is better educated and has better jobs than their parents. However, the average educational level of the second generation is still much lower than the national average and unemployment is still much higher among Turkish immigrants than among Dutch mainstreamers (Dagevos, Gijsberts, & van Praag, 2003).

Comparing Acculturation Orientations Across Measurement Methods

Our study examined to what extent the one-, two-, and four-statement methods yield convergent or even identical information about acculturation orientations (Arends-Tóth & van de Vijver, 2005). All three methods of assessing acculturation orientations were studied in seven public (e.g., social contacts, education) and seven private (e.g., childrearing practices, cultural habits) domains in a group of 293 Turkish Dutch youth.[2] Results revealed two-factorial solutions (private items loaded on the first and public items on the second factor) in the two-statement method for both the adaptation and the cultural maintenance scales, in the one-statement method, and in the four-statement method for the integration and the separation scales (subscales of assimilation and marginalization were not included in the model because these acculturation orientations were preferred by very few participants).

To investigate the role of life domains and measurement methods of acculturation simultaneously, a confirmatory factor analysis was performed. A hierarchical model of acculturation with two second-order latent variables showed a good fit (see Figure 3.5). The two second-order latent variables were labeled acculturation attitude, a latent variable with two indicators (public and private life domains) and measurement method, a latent variable with three indicators (one-statement, two-statement, and four-statement method). The two first-order latent variables of the acculturation factor, the public and the private life domains, showed positive loadings, which means that at a global level the immigrants were more inclined either to maintain their Turkish culture (in both public and private domains) or adjust to the Dutch culture. Within both life domains, a similar pattern emerged: Items dealing with Dutch and Turkish culture had opposite signs, indicating that within the domains, individuals tend to prefer either culture. The loadings of the three methods on the method factor showed an interesting pattern. The four-

[2]There were 144 (49.1%) female and 149 (50.9%) male participants, and 15 (5.1%) first- and 278 (94.9%) second-generation immigrants in the sample. The age of the participants varied from 11 to 19 years, with a mean of 14.67 ($SD = 1.69$). Of these students, 18.4% attended vocational training education, 62.1% attended general secondary education, and 19.5% attended professional and academic secondary education.

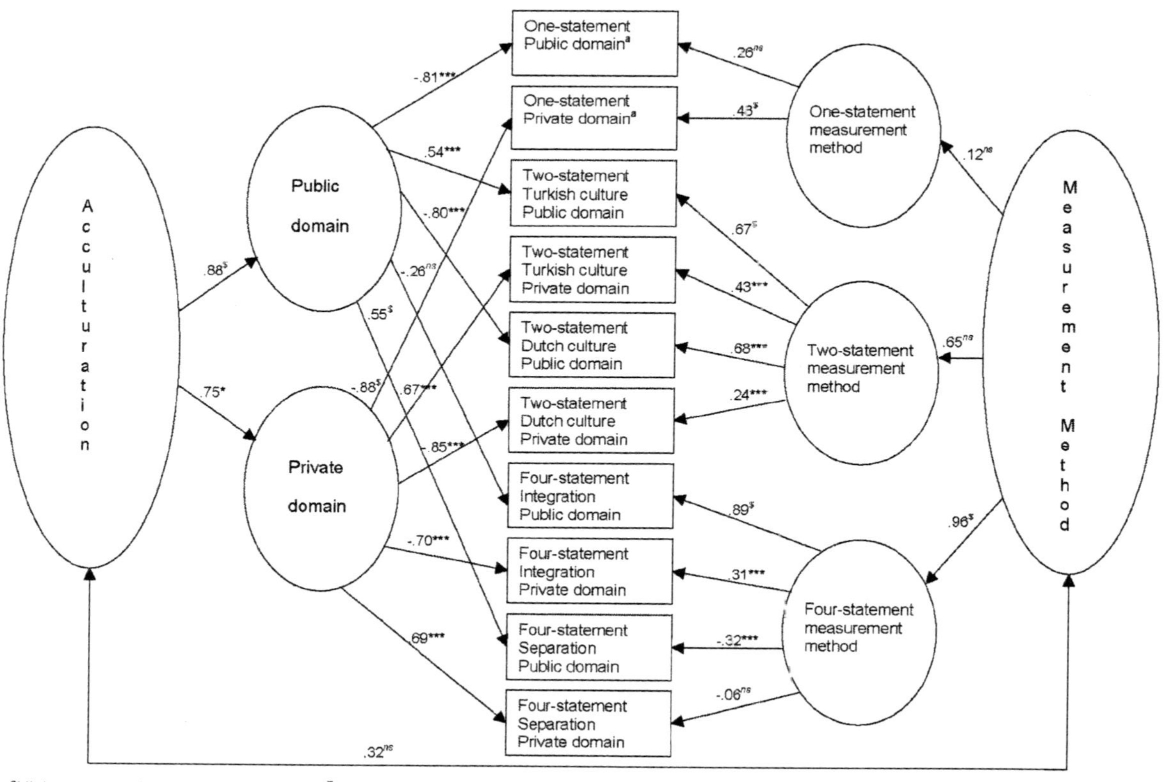

[a]Higher score refers to more adaptation. [$]Fixed at 1 in nonstandardized solution. [ns]Not significant. $^{*}p < .05$. $^{***}p < .001$.

FIGURE 3.5. Hypothesized acculturation model with two second-order latent variables (standardized solution).

statement method was apparently most obtrusive and had more impact on the measurement outcomes than the usage of the one- or two-statement methods. The four-statement method had the highest loading on the second-order method factor, and the loadings of the scales on the first-order factors showed more variability for the four-statement method than for the other factors.

An inspection of mean scores in the two domains in Table 3.2 adds an important element to an analysis of the correlations between domains: The mean score (overall preference) of cultural maintenance was higher in the private than in the public domain (in which both cultures were about equally preferred).

In summary, in order to get a full picture of the acculturation attitudes of the Turkish Dutch, both the correlations of the measures and the patterning of the mean scores in different life domains provide valuable, complementary information.

These results have implications for acculturation theory and assessment. No clear support was found for either the unidimensional or the bidimensional acculturation models if these models conceptualize acculturation as a domain-independent trait. According to our model, acculturation can best be considered as a hierarchical concept with a unidimensional factor at the top (general adaptation vs. cultural maintenance); this general factor constitutes two positively related domain factors, one for the public and one for the private domain. Both domain factors can be seen as made up of a single dimension, ranging from cultural maintenance to cultural adaptation. The four-statement method showed the largest method effect (which, in general, is undesirable as it shows that this method is more obtrusive than the other methods). The two-statement measurement method showed results similar to the one-statement method. In addition, the two-statement method gives more detailed information about preferred acculturation attitudes than the one-statement method. We found that the difference between the public and private domains was larger for adaptation items than for cultural maintenance items, which suggests a stronger distinction between life domains for adaptation than for cultural maintenance (this information cannot be obtained with the one-statement method). Taken together, both the one- and two-statement methods are appropriate measures of acculturation in unidimensional and bidimensional models, respectively. However, unlike the one-statement method, the two-statement method allows for a measure of each of Berry's (1997) acculturation orientations using the same metric (e.g., the distance of the participants to the four orientations). Finally, it is important to include items dealing with both public and private life domains, whichever method is used. Examples of public-domain items would be social contacts, following the news, and language use; examples of private-domain items would be celebrations and childrearing.

Comparing Acculturative Attitudes and Behaviors

It is common in acculturation research to employ questionnaires with items referring to acculturation attitudes and self-reported behaviors, without systematically addressing their relations. It is often tacitly assumed that the two aspects are

TABLE 3.2
Mean Scores and Effect Sizes of the Measurement Methods (One-, Two-, and Four-Statement) in the Two Life Domains

		Two-Statement Method			*Four-Statement Method*				
Domains	*One-Statement Method*	*Dutch Adaptation*	*Turkish Maintenance*	*Effect Size (Dutch Turkish)*	*Integration*	*Separation*	*Effect Size (Int – Sep)*	*Assi*	*Marg*
Mean scores									
Public domain	3.06	3.74	3.78	–.05	3.97	2.29	1.51***	1.95	1.90
Private domain	2.03	2.47	4.36	–1.66***	3.41	3.24	.12*	1.57	1.64
Effect sizes	2.11***	1.86***	–1.12***		.63***	–1.14***		.64***	.45***

Note. Assi = Assimilation. Marg = Marginalization. Int = Integration. Sep = Separation.
$^{*}p < .05$. $^{***}p < .001$.

interchangeable. Our data, however, suggest that attitudes and behaviors in the acculturation process cannot be reduced to each other (Arends-Tóth & van de Vijver, in press). In studies involving Turkish Dutch immigrants, we addressed the relations between acculturation attitudes and self-reported behaviors from an equivalence perspective. Three levels of equivalence were studied: structural equivalence (identity of the internal structure of attitude and behavior), metric equivalence (identity of measurement unit), and scalar equivalence (identity of measurement unit and scale origin). Support for structural equivalence was found, which implies that acculturation attitudes and behaviors can be conceptualized using a single underlying construct. Acculturation can be seen as a higher order construct, with acculturation attitudes and behaviors as lower order indicators. Metric equivalence and scalar equivalence (i.e., direct exchangeability of scores) were higher in the private domain than in the public domain, and higher for identical response formats than for different response formats.

Our study indicated that attitudinal and behavioral aspects refer to the same underlying concept of acculturation; yet, scores of attitudes and behaviors can usually not be interchanged. The mean scores and in some cases even the preferred acculturation strategy may not be the same for attitudes as for behaviors. Our findings suggest that consistency of findings across instruments can only be expected if a clear distinction is made between attitudes and behaviors, if a distinction is made between relevant life domains, and if similarity of stimuli and response categories across attitudes and behaviors is maintained.

UNRESOLVED ISSUES IN THE CONCEPTUALIZATION AND ASSESSMENT OF ACCULTURATION

Although in recent years some excellent studies of immigration and acculturation have been published, many areas of the field remain poorly explored and understood. There is a gap between the huge number of empirical studies on acculturation and the modest developments in acculturation theory and methodology. In the area of conceptualization and measurement, important work remains to be done. There are several directions for future research in this field.

Domain Specificity

Current models of acculturation focus on the dimensionality of acculturation. In our view, acculturation is often more domain and situation specific than implied by current models. A necessary further distinction refers to domain specificity. Among Dutch immigrants, adaptation (integration) is more preferred in the public domain and cultural maintenance (separation) in the private domain. Further research is needed to refine the distinction. For example, social contacts can belong to both the private and the public domain: Informal contacts during leisure time are part of the private domain, whereas formal contacts at the work place or at school belong to the public domain. The validity of the public–private distinction in domains that contain aspects of both still has to be established. Moreover, the applicability of the distinction has to be studied in other countries and ethnic groups. For example, it is not yet clear to what extent ethnic groups differ in how they define both domains. More research dealing with the specification of life domains and situations is required.

On the Delineation of Universal and Group-Specific Aspects of Acculturation

An important question in cross-cultural psychology involves the delineation of widely shared and culture-specific aspects of studied phenomena (Berry, Poortinga, Segall, & Dasen, 2002). The question is also relevant for acculturation. What are the universal and group-specific aspects of acculturation? What processes are common or different across voluntary and involuntary immigrant groups? Some researchers indicate that all individuals, regardless of ethnic group affiliation, undergo similar processes of change with differences in rate in order to adapt to the society of settlement. Immigrants have common experiences of being an immigrant, and there are common cultural demands to adapt to the mainstream society to a certain degree in order to survive economically (e.g., language, social contacts, and education). The process of adaptation is common across many cultural groups, and it is likely that there are common experiences across acculturating individuals. Others suggest that each cultural group is unique and undergoes specific cultural changes. Language loss provides an interesting example (De Bot, 1998). Dutch immigrants in Canada and Australia often show considerable language loss. It is not uncommon to find that the third generation has a poor proficiency in the Dutch language (if any at all). However, Chinese immigrants are often able to maintain knowledge of their first language across several generations.

The Meaning of Integration

Integration, the combination of adaptation and cultural maintenance, is the acculturation orientation most preferred and practiced by immigrants (e.g., Berry & Sam, 1997; van Oudenhoven et al., 1996). However, there may be large variations in what is meant by integration in view of the variety of different possible combinations of cultures. Therefore, the term integration needs to be more precisely defined, and more knowledge is needed about how integration is managed and negotiated in the interactions between immigrants and mainstream society. It could even be argued that, given the massive preference for integration, most variation occurs within integration and not between acculturation orientations.

Integration is an umbrella concept covering a variety of meanings. First, integration can have a connotation of assimilation rather than a preference for both adaptation and cultural maintenance, especially for majority group members. In public discourse in Western European countries, the terms *integration* and *assimilation* were often used interchangeably. Second, integration can refer to any combination of adaptation and cultural maintenance. Does it mean that both cultures contribute to some degree (e.g., 10% ethnic and 90% mainstream) or that both cultures contribute equally? The latter case seems to be the implicit definition in most research. However, even this definition is ambiguous. Does integration refer to "100% adaptation and 100% cultural maintenance" or to "50% adaptation and 50% cultural maintenance"? Does it mean that immigrants combine both cultures in all their behavior or that they switch between cultures? Third, immigrants can have access to both cultural systems and alternate between them depending on the context; for example, "dual monocultural" individuals may switch between cultural maintenance at home and adaptation outside. Finally, integration can refer to merging cultures, creating a "new culture" from the old ones.

It appears, in summary, that integration is an ambiguous term with a high face validity, because almost all immigrants have some aspects of both cultures in their attitudes and behaviors. Research is needed to determine which definition is most valid. Without research and discussion on the topic, the meaning of integration may become too broad to be useful for communication.

Testing Attitude–Behavior Relations in Acculturation

In social psychology, the relation between attitudes and behaviors have received considerable attention, both theoretically and empirically (e.g., Eagly & Chaiken, 1993). The original findings indicating that attitudes and behaviors showed weak relations (if any at all) have not remained unchallenged. The best known model is the theory of planned behavior (Ajzen & Fishbein, 1980), which holds that the relations between attitudes and behaviors is moderated by external factors such as norms about both aspects and the intention to carry out the behavior (e.g., "I know that my smoking is a threat for my health, yet I do not intend to quit smoking."). The theory of planned behavior has been applied successfully in many life domains and may also be useful to account for attitude–behavior relations in acculturation. It is regrettable that the focus in acculturation research on the mediating and moderating role of acculturation orientations and sociocultural and psychological adaptation as outcomes has led to a lack of studies of the relations between attitudes and behaviors. The often incorrectly assumed interchangeability of attitudes and behaviors in assessment questionnaires also suggests that acculturation research should be informed by models about their relation developed in mainstream social psychology.

Assessment

The development of a standardized acculturation instrument or at least a widely accepted procedure to design and evaluate such an instrument is an essential next step in acculturation assessment. Our findings suggest that the two-statement method (involving separate items to measure adaptation and cultural maintenance), with items addressing both public and private life domains, appears to be useful and can significantly contribute to the development of a reliable acculturation instrument. Agreement on how acculturation should be measured will probably help to solve the problem of often conflicting results concerning the relation between acculturation aspects and various psychological processes (e.g., Negy & Woods, 1992; Rogler, Cortes, & Malgady, 1991).

Future research on acculturation should focus more on the questions of how we can incorporate acculturation in assessment in multicultural groups. In this kind of assessment, acculturation is often not the focus of study, but can have an influence on the assessment outcomes. Various ways in which acculturation can be taken into account in assessment have been discussed by van de Vijver and Phalet (2004). An example would be the use of cutoff scores on an instrument that measures adaptation to the mainstream culture. Scores below a minimum value are seen as an indication that the instrument cannot be used in a meaningful way for a particular immigrant. Adaptation then plays the same role as social desirability in personality measurement. In the Eysenck tradition of personality assessment, it is common not to interpret scores on the target dimensions like extraversion if the respondent's level of social desirability is above a minimum value.

AN APPLICATION: FAMILY AND ACCULTURATION

In this section we address the role of acculturation in family relationships. Examining acculturation in the family domain gives more insight into the dynamic and multifaceted nature of acculturation. Again, our focus is on a combination of conceptualization and assessment. We also distinguish between the role of the family in acculturation conditions, orientations, and outcomes.

Family as Condition

The most important function of the family as primary socialization agency has often been stressed in the social and behavioral sciences. For a member of the majority group in the society, the family is an integral part of the whole network of social relationships that constitutes his or her society, and its culture is mainly continuous with that of the main society. For immigrants, the situation is different. The family is usually part of another social system and culture. The immigrant family as socialization agency has a major influence on the acculturation orientations of its members (e.g., Nauck, 2001).

Family as Moderating or Mediating Factor

Among the many factors that can contribute to well-being in acculturating individuals, the family is particularly important. Good family relationships (especially perceived support) can reduce stress experienced during the acculturation process (e.g., Castillo, Conoley, & Brossart, 2004). On the other hand, intergenerational discrepancies between immigrant parents and their children may lead to conflicts within the family, thereby threatening the well-being of its members (e.g., Kaplan & Marks, 1990; Szapocznik & Kurtines, 1993).

An important topic in acculturation research involves intergenerational changes in acculturation orientations between immigrant parents and their children. The overall picture points to acculturation across generations as a development toward the dominant culture, accompanied by either maintenance or loss of the original culture (e.g., Cuéllar, Nyberg, Maldonado, & Roberts, 1997; Mendoza, 1989). However, acculturation does not affect all aspects of the psyche in an identical way. Nagata's (1994) review of acculturation studies pointed to a decrease in ethnic knowledge and behaviors from the first to the second generations, although attitudes did not significantly change.

Acculturation Outcome: Changes in Family Relationships

When immigrants from collectivist cultures come to a more individualist culture (like most of the Western cultures), they are confronted with a culture in which family relationships differ from their culture of origin (Greenfield & Cocking, 1994). The acculturation process can modify the perceived importance of the family. Numerous American studies on the role of acculturation on family relationships do not show convergent results (Chun & Akutsu, 2003). In some studies, more adaptation to the dominant culture was related with less family cohesion, less mutual support, and more family conflict (e.g., Brooks, Stuewig, & Lecroy, 1998). Research with Hispanic families demonstrated that the second-generation and younger immigrants adjust more to the majority culture and display weaker norms of family relationships than first-generation and older immigrants (e.g., Sabogal, Marín, Otero-Sabogal, Marín, & Perez-Stable, 1987). Other studies, however, reported that family relationships were strengthened during the process of acculturation. For example, Mexican Americans who adjusted more to the majority culture indicated that contacts and support among family members increased (e.g., Keefe, 1980). Still other studies showed that acculturation influences only some components of family relationships (Cortes, 1995). For example, in one of these studies, perceived emotional support from the family was not influenced by acculturation; however, giving support to family members became less important (e.g., Sabogal et al., 1987). Finally, some studies do not find significant relations between acculturation and family relationships (e.g., Fuligni, 1998).

There is a need for an overarching framework that permits reconciliation of these findings. The incompatibilities may, at least partly, be due to an insufficient distinction between various components (instrumental, social, and emotional) and variables (attitude and behavior) of family relationships; acculturation may not impact on all these aspects in the same way and at the same pace. Marín (1992) suggested that beliefs and feelings of family solidarity (attitudinal aspects) are less likely to be influenced by acculturation than behavioral aspects (such as visiting patterns). In addition, in previous research insufficient distinction is made between various measures of acculturation, such as proxy measures (generation level and age at immigration) and acculturation attitudes and behaviors, which may also contribute to the conflicting findings with family relationships. In order to have a better insight into the role of acculturation and family relationships, a distinction should be made between the various variables and components of family relationships and of acculturation.

Models of Family Changes

Three models regarding acculturation and family relationships can be envisaged. The first, which is based on modernization theory, holds that acculturation leads to a unidirectional shift in family characteristics toward the Western pattern. Processes of upward educational and occupational mobility expose immigrant family members to the values of the majority group and make immigrants more likely to adopt these values.

The second model holds that some aspects of the family system undergo changes, whereas other aspects remain unaffected. The distinctions among different components of family support (instrumental, social, and emotional) are important because they are differently affected by social change. Emotional dependencies can continue (or even increase) even if material dependencies decrease across generations with increased affluence (Kagitcibasi, 1996).

According to the third model, family relationships are strengthened as a result of acculturative stress. Families provide the "buffer" for immigrants to cope with acculturative stress by social sharing and exchanging information on how to deal with various acculturation-related problems such as discrimination by the majority group. However, a development in which the orientation on the own ethnic group is reinforced is not equally likely to occur in all immigrant groups. The relation between and mutual images of the ethnic group and the majority group in the society could have an influence on the immigrant family. Some cultural groups are evaluated more negatively than others. The evaluation of ethnic groups according to liking and likeness (social distance) is called *ethnic hierarchy* (Schalk-

Soekar & van de Vijver, 2004). In the Netherlands this ethnic hierarchy has been found to be fairly stable across studies. For example, Surinamers and Antilleans are always placed above Turks and Moroccans. Negative images of the majority group influence the rank order of ethnic groups in the hierarchy. Ethnic groups placed lower in the hierarchy are evaluated more negatively than ethnic groups placed higher in the hierarchy. Ethnic groups with a lower position in the hierarchy, that experience more prejudice and discrimination, will depend more on their family and can be expected to show more family solidarity than ethnic groups with a higher position in the hierarchy.

CONCLUSIONS

The main aim of this chapter was to compare and integrate current theoretical models and measurement methods of acculturation. We show that acculturation involves various processes and components; no single measure or method can capture the complexity of acculturation in a comprehensive manner. An essential step in order to advance acculturation research is the development of a standardized acculturation instrument or at least a widely endorsed view on what should be included in such a measure. The use of independent measurement of acculturation orientations (two-statement method) is a useful tool that can contribute to understanding in this area. In order to understand acculturation in context, it is essential to use a range of different contexts and domains.

Contextual features of the acculturation process have received less attention in research. The importance and impact of immigrant cultures depend crucially on acculturation context. Ethnic cultural norms and behaviors are most salient and most easily enforced in private life. Phalet and Swyngedouw (2003) found that Turkish and Moroccan minorities in the Netherlands attributed more importance to cultural maintenance in the home and family context (private domain), whereas the adaptation dimension was more important in school and work situations (public domain).

The family as socialization agent is relevant in all components of the acculturation process; the family provides the cultural background for socializing the child, it influences the acculturation orientation of its members, it moderates relations between background conditions (e.g., acculturative stressors and mental health as an adaptation outcome), and it is influenced by acculturation. In addition, the family plays a role in acculturation outcomes, such as psychological well-being, life satisfaction, and acculturation behavior. The role of the family in acculturation is so vital and involves so many aspects that it is not farfetched to state that if we understand the role of acculturation in the family, we understand the major ins and outs of acculturation. Before we reach that point, however, major advances in the conceptualization and assessment of acculturation are required. We hope that, however modest, the current chapter may help to bring this goal closer within reach.

REFERENCES

Ait-Ouarasse, O., & van de Vijver, F. J. R. (2004). Structure and function of the perceived acculturation context of young Moroccans in the Netherlands. *International Journal of Psychology, 39*, 190–204.

Ajzen, I., & Fishbein, M. (1980). *Understanding attitudes and predicting social behavior*. Englewood Cliffs, NJ: Prentice-Hall.

Arends-Tóth, J., & van de Vijver, F. J. R. (2003). Multiculturalism and acculturation: Views of Dutch and Turkish-Dutch. *European Journal of Social Psychology, 33*, 249–266.

Arends-Tóth, J., & van de Vijver, F. J. R. (2005). *Acculturation attitudes: Conceptual and measurement issues*. Manuscript submitted for publication.

Arends-Tóth, J., & van de Vijver, F. J. R. (in press). The influence of method factors on the relation between attitudes and self-reported behaviors in the assessment of acculturation. *European Journal of Psychological Assessment*.

Berry, J. W. (1997). Immigration, acculturation, and adaptation. *Applied Psychology: An International Review, 46*, 5–34.

Berry, J. W., & Kim, U. (1988). Acculturation and mental health. In P. Dasen, J. W. Berry, & N. Sartorious (Eds.), *Health and cross-cultural psychology: Toward application* (pp. 207–236). London: Sage.

Berry, J. W., Poortinga, Y. H., Segall, M. H., & Dasen, P. R. (2002). *Cross-cultural psychology: Research and applications* (2nd ed.). Cambridge, MA: Cambridge University Press.

Berry, J. W., & Sam, D. L. (1997). Acculturation and adaptation. In J. W. Berry, M. H. Segall, & C. Kagitcibasi (Eds.), *Handbook of cross-cultural psychology: Social behavior and applications* (Vol. 3, 2nd ed., pp. 291–326). Boston: Allyn & Bacon.

Birman, D. (1998). Biculturalism and perceived competence of Latino immigrant adolescents. *American Journal of Community Psychology, 26*, 335–354.

Birman, D., & Trickett, E. J. (2001). Cultural transitions in first-generation immigrants: Acculturation of Soviet Jewish refugee adolescents and parents. *Journal of Cross-Cultural Psychology, 32*, 456–477.

Bourhis, R. Y., Moïse, L. C., Perreault, S., & Senécal, S. (1997). Towards an interactive acculturation model: A social psychological approach. *International Journal of Psychology, 32*, 369–386.

Brooks, A. J., Stuewig, J., & Lecroy, C. W. (1998). A family based model of Hispanic adolescent substance use. *Journal of Drug Education, 28*, 65–86.

Castillo, L. G., Conoley, C. W., & Brossart, D. F. (2004). Acculturation, white marginalization, and family support as predictors of perceived distress in Mexican American female college students. *Journal of Counseling Psychology, 51*, 151–157.

Celano, M. P., & Tyler, F. B. (1991). Behavioral acculturation among Vietnamese refugees in the United States. *Journal of Social Psychology, 131*, 373–385.

Centraal Bureau voor de Statistiek. (2004). *Bevolkingstrends* [Population trends]. Voorburg/Heerlen, the Netherlands: Author.

Chun, K. M., & Akutsu, P. D. (2003). Acculturation among ethnic minority families. In K. M. Chun, P. B. Organista, & G. Marín (Eds.), *Acculturation: Advances in theory, measurement, and applied research* (pp. 95–119). Washington, DC: American Psychological Association.

Clement, R., & Noels, K. A. (1992). Towards a situated approach to ethnolinguistic identity: The effects of status on individuals and groups. *Journal of Language and Social Psychology, 11*, 203–232.

Coleman, H. L. K. (1995). Strategies for coping with cultural diversity. *The Counseling Psychologist, 23*, 722–740.

Cortes, D. E. (1995). Variations in familialism in two generations of Puerto Ricans. *Hispanic Journal of Behavioral Sciences, 17*, 249–255.

Cuéllar, I., Nyberg, B., Maldonado, R. E., & Roberts, R. E. (1997). Ethnic identity and acculturation in a young adult Mexican-origin population. *Journal of Community Psychology, 6*, 535–549.

Cuéllar, I., & Paniagua, F. A. (Eds.). (2000). *Handbook of multicultural mental health: Assessment and treatment of diverse population*. San Diego, CA: Academic Press.

Dagevos, J., Gijsberts, M., & Van Praag, C. (2003). *Rapportage minderheden 2003. Onderwijs, arbeid en sociaal-culturele integratie* [Report on minorities 2003. Education, labor and sociocultural integration]. The Hague: Sociaal en Cultureel Planbureau.

Dana, R. H. (Ed.). (2000). *Handbook of cross-cultural and multicultural personality assessment*. Mahwah, NJ: Lawrence Erlbaum Associates.

De Bot, K. (1998). The psycholinguistics of language loss. In G. Extra & L. Verhoeven (Eds.), *Bilingualism and migration* (pp. 345–361). Berlin: Mouton de Gruyter.

Donà, G., & Berry, J. W. (1994). Acculturation attitudes and acculturative stress of Central American refugees. *International Journal of Psychology, 29*, 57–70.

Eagly, A. H., & Chaiken, S. (1993). *The psychology of attitudes*. Fort Worth, TX: Harcourt Brace Jovanovich.

Fuligni, A. J. (1998). Authority, autonomy, and parent–adolescent conflict and cohesion: A study of adolescents from Mexican, Chinese, Filipino, and European backgrounds. *Developmental Psychology, 34*, 782–792.

Garcia, J. (1982). Ethnicity and Chicanos: Measurement of ethnic identification, identity, and consciousness. *Hispanic Journal of Behavioral Sciences, 4*, 295–314.

Gordon, M. M. (1964). *Assimilation in American life*. New York: Oxford University Press.

Graves, T. (1967). Psychological acculturation in a tri-ethnic community. *South-Western Journal of Anthropology, 23*, 337–350.

Greenfield, P. M., & Cocking, R. R. (Eds.). (1994). *Cross-cultural roots of minority child development*. Hillsdale, NJ: Lawrence Erlbaum Associates.

Hutnik, N. (1986). Patterns of ethnic minority identification and models of social adaptation. *Ethnic and Racial Studies, 9*, 150–167.

Jain, A., & Belsky, J. (1997). Fathering and acculturation: Immigrant Indian families with young children. *Journal of Marriage and the Family, 59*, 873–883.

Kagitcibasi, C. (1996). *Family and human development across cultures: A view from the other side*. Mahwah, NJ: Lawrence Erlbaum Associates.

Kaplan, M. S., & Marks, G. (1990). Adverse effects of acculturation: Psychological distress among Mexican American young adults. *Social Science and Medicine: An International Journal, 31*, 1313–1319.

Keefe, S. E. (1980). Acculturation and the extended family among urban Mexican Americans. In A. M. Padilla (Ed.), *Acculturation: Theory, models, and some new findings* (pp. 85–110). Boulder, CO: Westview.

Kunda, Z. (1999). *Social cognition*. Cambridge, MA: MIT Press.

Laroche, M., Kim, C., & Hui, M. K. (1997). A comparative investigation of dimensional structures of acculturation for Italian Canadians and Greek Canadians. *Journal of Social Psychology, 137*, 317–331.

Lasry, J., & Sayegh, L. (1992). Developing an acculturation scale: A bidimensional model. In N. Grizenko, L. Sayegh, & P. Migneault (Eds.), *Transcultural issues in child psychiatry* (pp. 67–86). Montreal: Editions Douglas.

Marín, G. (1992). Issues in the measurement of acculturation among Hispanics. In K. F. Geisinger (Ed.), *Psychological testing of Hispanics* (pp. 235–251). Washington, DC: American Psychological Association.

Mavreas, V., Bebbington, P., & Der, G. (1989). The structure and validity of acculturation. *Social Psychiatry and Psychiatric Epidemiology, 24*, 233–240.

McQueen, A., Getz, J. G., & Bray, J. H. (2003). Acculturation, substance use, and deviant behavior: Examining separation and family conflict as mediators. *Child Development, 74*, 1737–1750.

Mendoza, R. H. (1989). An empirical scale to measure type and degree of acculturation in Mexican-American adolescents and adults. *Journal of Cross-Cultural Psychology, 20*, 372–385.

Nagata, D. K. (1994). Assessing Asian American acculturation and ethnic identity: The need for a multidimensional framework. *Asian American and Pacific Islander Journal of Health, 2*, 109–121.

Nauck, B. (2001). Intercultural contact and intergenerational transmission in immigrant families. *Journal of Cross-Cultural Psychology, 32*, 159–173.

Negy, C., & Woods, D. J. (1992). The importance of acculturation in understanding research with Hispanic-Americans. *Hispanic Journal of Behavioral Sciences, 14*, 224–247.

Nguyen, H. H., Messe, L. A., & Stollak, G. E. (1999). Toward a more complex understanding of acculturation and adjustment: Cultural involvements and psychosocial functioning in Vietnamese youth. *Journal of Cross-Cultural Psychology, 30*, 5–31.

Nunnally, J. C., & Bernstein, I. H. (1994). *Psychometric theory* (3rd ed.). New York: McGraw-Hill.

Olmedo, E. L. (1979). Acculturation: A psychometric perspective. *American Psychologist, 34*, 1061–1070.

Olmedo, E. L., & Padilla, A. M. (1978). Empirical and construct validation of a measure of acculturation for Mexican Americans. *Journal of Social Psychology, 105*, 179–187.

Padilla, A. M. (Ed.). (1980). *Acculturation: Theory, models and some new findings*. Boulder, CO: Westview.

Padilla, A. M. (Ed.). (1995). *Hispanic psychology: Critical issues in theory and research*. Thousand Oaks, CA: Sage.

Pettigrew, T. F. (1998). Reactions toward the new minorities of Western Europe. *Annual Review of Sociology, 24*, 77–103.

Phalet, K., Lotringen, C., & Entzinger, H. (2000). *Islam in de multiculturele samenleving* [Islam in the multicultural society]. Utrecht: European Research Centre on Migration and Ethnic Relations.

Phalet, K., & Swyngedouw, M. (2003). A cross-cultural analysis of immigrant and host values and acculturation orientations. In H. Vinken & P. Esther (Eds.), *Comparing cultures* (pp. 185–212). Leiden: Brill.

Pham, T. B., & Harris, R. J. (2001). Acculturation strategies among Vietnamese-Americans. *International Journal of Intercultural Relations, 25*, 279–300.

Redfield, R., Linton, R., & Herskovits, M. H. (1936). Memorandum on the study of acculturation. *American Anthropologist, 38*, 149–152.

Rogler, L. H., Cortes, D. E., & Malgady, R. G. (1991). Acculturation and mental health status among Hispanics: Convergence and new directions for research. *American Psychologist, 46*, 585–597.

Rudmin, F. W., & Ahmadzadeh, V. (2001). Psychometric critique of acculturation psychology: The case of Iranian migrants in Norway. *Scandinavian Journal of Psychology, 42*, 41–56.

Ryder, A. G., Alden, L. E., & Paulhus, D. L. (2000). Is acculturation unidimensional or bidimensional? A head-to-head comparison in the prediction of personality, self-identity, and adjustment. *Journal of Personality and Social Psychology, 79*, 49–65.

Sabogal, F., Marín, G., Otero-Sabogal, R., Marín, B. V., & Perez-Stable, E. J. (1987). Hispanic familialism and acculturation: What changes and what doesn't? *Hispanic Journal of Behavioral Sciences, 9*, 397–412.

Sánchez, J. I., & Fernández, D. M. (1993). Acculturative stress among Hispanics: A bidimensional model of ethnic identification. *Journal of Applied Social Psychology, 23*, 654–668.

Sayegh, L., & Lasry, J. (1993). Immigrants' adaptation in Canada: Assimilation, acculturation, and orthogonal cultural identification. *Canadian Psychology, 24*, 98–109.

Schalk-Soekar, R. G. S., & van de Vijver, F. J. R. (2004). Attitudes toward multiculturalism of immigrants and majority members in the Netherlands. *International Journal of Intercultural Relations, 28*, 533–550.

Sodowsky, G. R., & Carey, J. C. (1988). Relationships between acculturation-related demographics and cultural attitudes of an Asian-Indian immigrants group. *Journal of Multicultural Counseling and Development, 16*, 117–136.

Suinn, R. M., Ahuna, C., & Khoo, G. (1992). The Suinn-Lew Asian self-identity acculturation scale: Concurrent and factorial validation. *Educational and Psychological Measurement, 52*, 1041–1046.

Suzuki, L. A., Ponterotto, J. G., & Meller, P. J. (Eds.). (2001). *Handbook of multicultural assessment: Clinical, psychological, and educational applications* (2nd ed.). San Francisco: Jossey-Bass.

Szapocznik, J., & Kurtines, W. M. (1993). Family psychology and cultural diversity. *Hispanic Journal of Behavioral Sciences, 48*, 400–407.

Taylor, D. M., & Lambert, W. E. (1996). The meaning of multiculturalism in a culturally diverse urban American area. *Journal of Social Psychology, 136*, 727–740.

Triandis, H. C., Kashima, Y., Shimada, E., & Villareal, M. (1986). Acculturation indices as a means of confirming cultural differences. *International Journal of Psychology, 21*, 43–70.

van de Vijver, F. J. R., & Phalet, K. (2004). Assessment in multicultural groups: The role of acculturation. *Applied Psychology: An International Review, 53*, 215–236.

van Oudenhoven, J. P., Willemsma, G., & Prins, K. S. (1996). Integratie en assimilatie van Marokkanen, Surinamers en Turken in Nederland [Integration and assimilation of Moroccans, Surinamese, and Turks in the Netherlands]. *De Psycholoog, 31*, 468–471.

Verkuyten, M., & Thijs, J. (2002). Multiculturalism among minority and majority adolescents in the Netherlands. *International Journal of Intercultural Relations, 26*, 91–108.

Ward, C. (1996). Acculturation. In D. Landis & R. Bhagat (Eds.), *Handbook of intercultural training* (pp. 124–147). Thousand Oaks, CA: Sage.

Ward, C. (1999). Models and measurements of acculturation. In W. J. Lonner, D. L. Dinnel, D. K. Forgays, & S. Hayes (Eds.), *Merging past, present and future: Selected papers from the Fourteenth International Congress of the International Association for Cross-Cultural Psychology* (pp. 221–229). Lisse, the Netherlands: Swets & Zeitlinger.

Ward, C., Bochner, S., & Furnham, A. (2001). *The psychology of culture shock*. London: Routledge.

Ward, C., & Kennedy, A. (1994). Acculturation strategies, psychological adjustment, and sociocultural competence during cross-cultural transitions. *International Journal of Intercultural Relations, 18*, 329–343.

Weinstock, S. A. (1964). Some factors that retard or accelerate the rate of acculturation: With specific reference to Hungarian immigrants. *Human Relations, 17*, 321–340.

Wong-Rieger, D. (1984). Testing a model of emotional and coping responses to problems in adaptation: Foreign students at a Canadian university. *International Journal of Intercultural Relations, 8*, 153–184.

4

Conceptual and Measurement Issues in Family Acculturation Research

Kevin M. Chun
University of San Francisco, U.S.A.

INTRODUCTION

Current trends in acculturation research call for analyses of contextual factors and multiple data points to uncover the multidimensional and dynamic properties of acculturation. Such analyses are especially important for understanding how acculturation unfolds in diverse family constellations and environments. Family experiences of acculturation, however, have yet to be fully and systematically explored, largely due to a host of conceptual and methodological challenges. In particular, researchers are often faced with a set of deceptively basic questions at the very outset of investigation: *Whom* and *what* should be studied? *Why* and *how* should it be studied? The inherent difficulty of these questions becomes apparent when considering the somewhat unwieldy nature of acculturation and the complexities of family functioning and organization. Nonetheless, there are compelling reasons to examine acculturation at the family level. First and foremost, acculturation often is a shared family experience. Families play a central role in many immigrants' lives by helping to organize, frame, and make sense of their daily experiences, including new life conditions. This is particularly true for collectivistic persons and immigrant children whose family structures, dynamics, and relationships shape the extent and nature of their acculturation.

Examining families also necessitates a more complex and multilayered conceptualization of acculturation that extends beyond earlier linear and static models. The need for more complex acculturation models is underscored by the different family groupings in which acculturation transpires, the interactive nature of acculturation across family members, and the influence of extrafamilial environments or ecologies on these processes. These considerations frame acculturation as an ongoing and complex process rather than a time-limited or discrete instance of "culture change" as suggested in past research. To this end, acculturation involves different degrees and manifestations of cultural learning and maintenance that are contingent on individual, group, and environmental factors. Acculturation also is dynamic because it is a continuous and fluctuating process. Last, acculturation is multidimensional because it transpires across numerous indices of psychosocial functioning and results in multiple adaptation outcomes.

This chapter explores how these aspects of acculturation are illuminated in a family context. The first section speaks to the broad range of acculturation experiences and issues that arise in families and across different family subsystems. Additionally, the significance of distinct family relationships, developmental tasks and skills, and environments to family acculturation experiences is discussed. The second section offers guidelines and recommendations for resolving conceptual and methodological challenges in studying family acculturation. Special attention is given to a combined qualitative–quantitative research strategy, and specific examples of its possible components are outlined. Finally, promising areas for future family acculturation studies are discussed at the end of the chapter.

SPECIAL CONSIDERATIONS FOR FAMILY ACCULTURATION: FAMILY STRUCTURE AND SUBSYSTEMS, DYNAMICS AND PROCESSES, DEVELOPMENTAL ISSUES, AND ECOLOGIES

The distinct ways in which families organize themselves, function, respond to change, and interact with different contexts contribute to a myriad of acculturation experiences. Family studies must therefore consider the effects of family structure and subsystems, family dynamics and processes, developmental issues, and ecologies on acculturation.

Family Structure and Subsystems

Acculturation can have numerous manifestations in the family and across its various groupings or "subsystems." Families comprise multiple subsystems that arise from characteristic interaction patterns over time (Minuchin & Fishman, 1981). Subsystems have distinct behavioral prescriptions or expectations for the types and range of behaviors that are displayed in families. For example, in the couple subsystem, spouses may have specific gender roles and expectations that inform their daily interactions and communication patterns. However, when the same spouses enter the parent–child subsystem, their behaviors and expectations can radically shift while interacting with their children or elderly parents. Therefore, different acculturation issues can emerge for different subsystems leading to heterogeneous patterns of cultural learning and maintenance in a single family. This is witnessed by the diverse range of acculturation issues that are displayed for the entire family unit, parent–child subsystem, couple subsystem, sibling subsystem, and subsystems defined by other family characteristics.

Family Unit

The entire family unit has received relatively less attention in the acculturation literature as compared to select subsystems or individual family members. However, the family unit deserves added attention because families tend to function as a gestalt or a holistic entity that is greater than the sum of its parts. This is especially true of collectivistic cultures where families are often perceived and experienced as an entity that is greater than any individual member. For instance, Asian Americans who practice filial obligation often focus on the well-being of the family rather than their individual desires and goals (Yee, Huang, & Lew, 1998). Past research has examined the relation of acculturation to various aspects of family functioning, including reported family problems (Boehnlein et al., 1995), family conflict and cohesion (Rosenthal & Feldman, 1989), family satisfaction (Heras & Revilla, 1994), family involvement (Brooks, Stuewig, & Lecroy, 1998), family support (Barrett, Joe, & Simpson, 1991) and familial obligation (Sabogal, Marin, Otero-Sabogal, Marin, & Perez-Stable, 1987). The majority of these studies, however, are based on a few data points, typically self-report data from one or two parents or a child, rendering only a partial snapshot of family acculturation experiences. Thus, the manner in which families collectively understand, experience, and respond to acculturation largely remains a matter of conjecture. It is unclear whether families have collective goals for acculturation, how these goals are formulated, and whether they help to organize or coordinate family interactions. It is plausible that some collective goals (e.g., those with clear and positive outcome expectations) may facilitate overall family adaptation and cohesion whereas others do not (e.g., those with unclear or vague outcome expectations or those with lower consensus across family members).

Parent–Child Subsystem

Of all the subsystems, the parent–child subsystem has received the most attention in family acculturation research. Studies have examined acculturation effects on childrearing techniques, parenting styles and disciplinary methods, parental involvement, socialization, parenting attributions, and parental expectations for their children's behaviors (Chun & Akutsu, 2003). Much attention has been given to parent–child conflict that arises during acculturation. This includes conflict and stress from "role reversals" when children assume adult family roles and responsibilities because they are more proficient in their new culture's language or possess more bicultural competencies than their parents. Children in immigrant households are often expected to serve as translators and to perform various adult tasks. For example, first-generation Chinese American youth are expected to assist their younger siblings with their homework, monitor their academic progress, and attend official school functions on behalf of their parents (Chun, 2004b). Most of their immigrant parents were unable to fulfill these responsibilities because of multiple cultural barriers that included English language difficulties, lack of familiarity with the school system, and extended work hours. The actual effects of role reversals on immigrant children's health have not been extensively studied. The stress that these children face from added and complex family responsibilities may be heightened by parental demands to constantly switch to different, albeit contradictory, family roles at home.

Studies of parent–child conflict also have focused on differences between parents' and children's acculturation levels. This investigative focus rests on the assumption that parents and children experience widening disagreement on cultural beliefs and values as children acculturate more rapidly. Research with Chinese Americans and Latinos indicates that acculturation is positively correlated with disagreements on certain cultural values and negatively correlated with children's obedience to older family members (Chun & Akutsu, 2003). Although this finding captures the experiences of many immigrant parents and their children, it often misleads researchers to believe that parents are more resistant to acculturation than their children. Recent findings, however, show that immigrant parents can acculturate in concert with their children and likewise develop bicultural competencies along their own developmental trajectories (Chun, 2004b).

Finally, most acculturation studies on parent–child relationships are typically limited to the adolescent stage with little, if any, data on other developmental periods. It is therefore difficult to determine if parent–child conflict is due to differential acculturation rates, normative developmental issues in adolescence, or a mixture of both. Also, few studies articulate the meaning of parent–child differences on cultural values and beliefs, resulting in a number of unresolved questions: What scale or magnitude of parent–child differences leads to conflict during acculturation? Are certain issues (e.g., speaking one's native language and dating) more likely to elicit conflict than others during acculturation (e.g., changes to dietary habits and clothing choice)?

Couple Subsystem

The couple subsystem also has a unique set of acculturation issues. Couple interactions are based on implicit rules and explicit agreements that often require modification in a new culture. Studies have focused on acculturation changes to gender role expectations and behaviors, particularly for Latino populations. Study findings generally show more egalitarian or flexible gender roles with higher acculturation (Chun & Akutsu, 2003). However, some studies indicate that educational level is a stronger predictor of gender role expectations than acculturation

(Soto, 1983; Soto & Shaver, 1982). Also, the extent to which acculturation affects couple interactions and dynamics is somewhat unclear. Among new Chinese American immigrants, married couples report lower life satisfaction than their single counterparts, suggesting that marriage may not necessarily be a source of support, but rather a source of stress during acculturation (Ying, 1996). This finding may be related to the adverse effects of traditional gender role attitudes on marital relationships for couples with lower acculturation levels. Preliminary results from a study of Chinese American couples showed that high acculturation was related to egalitarian gender role attitudes, greater emotional expressivity, more sharing in family duties, and greater marital satisfaction (Chun, 2004a).

Last, the couple subsystem provides unique opportunities to explore the interactive nature of family acculturation. Acculturation in couples involves a continual process of cultural exchange, support, and even attenuation of cultural ties depending on the nature of the relationship (Chesla & Chun, 2004). Exclusive attention to individual acculturation experiences overlooks these dynamic aspects of cultural learning and maintenance.

Sibling Subsystem

The sibling subsystem can be children's first peer group where they learn important social and interpersonal skills. Biculturally competent older siblings can transmit and interpret cultural knowledge and assist younger siblings with entry to youth settings (e.g., school settings, peer groups). As "cultural brokers," older siblings instruct their younger siblings in identifying and deciphering cultural trends in popular music, fashion, and recreational pastimes (Chun, 2004b). This cultural information may appear trivial or superficial, but for younger siblings it may be essential to their developmental tasks. From an Eriksonian perspective (Erikson, 1963), the task of establishing friendships with more acculturated peers requires proficiencies in the dialect of youth culture. Knowledge of pop culture thus can be equally as important as formal academic knowledge and skills for immigrant youths' psychosocial adjustment.

Other Subsystems

Acculturation also occurs in other subsystems that are culturally prescribed, task-oriented, and based on functional relations. These include generational subsystems (younger and older family members), gender subsystems (female and male members), task-oriented subsystems (e.g., a grandfather and father or a mother and daughter who operate a family business together), and parenting subsystems that include extended family members or family friends. In short, families organize themselves in ways that are culturally meaningful and oriented toward their shared tasks, goals, and identities. These types of subsystems, unlike the traditionally studied parent–child and couple subsystems, may have greater significance to youth acculturation experiences. For instance, intergenerational households can have a parenting subsystem of grandparents or extended family members who spend considerable time rearing younger family members, teaching bicultural competencies (e.g., bilingual skills, cultural knowledge), and creating opportunities to explore new cultural contexts.

Family members may exhibit varied acculturation patterns when moving in and out of different subsystems. This phenomenon is poignantly illustrated by a first-generation Chinese American mother (Chun, 2004b). In her parent–child subsystem, she showed signs of low acculturation, often insisting that her 12-year-old son follow traditional cultural norms. She also expressed dismay that he was becoming too "Americanized." In contrast, she appeared more acculturated in her couple subsystem, where she resisted traditional gender roles by independently seeking educational and employment opportunities outside of the home. Her varied acculturation behaviors and attitudes point to a fundamental question: How should a family member's acculturation level be characterized given that it can change across different family subsystems and contexts? As I discuss in the section titled "Family Acculturation Research Strategies," certain measurement tools, including ethnographic observation and family narratives, can be used to explore this question.

Family Dynamics and Processes

Family dynamics or underlying processes that drive family relationships and functioning are another special consideration for family acculturation. Some studies treat families simply as an amalgam of isolated or independent individuals or subsystems. However, family systems models posit that family members' actions operate in an interdependent or interconnected fashion (Hoffman, 1981). Family acculturation experiences can thus be "wired" to each other shaping the manner and extent to which cultural learning and maintenance are enacted in the family. For instance, acculturative stress that is experienced in the parental subsystem might adversely affect the parent–child subsystem or vice versa.

Families also have unique tempos and thresholds for change that determine how they move through and respond to a new cultural milieu. Past research indicates that acculturative stress arises when intra- and extrafamilial tempos are incongruent. Immigrant Chinese parents report that "things move too fast in America" and believe that this accelerated tempo compromises their parenting, time spent with their children, and their children's ties to their culture of origin (Chun, 2004b).

According to structural family therapy models, families who resist change experience "homeostasis" when their habitual or old behaviors become ineffective in new life situations (Minuchin & Fishman, 1981). Families can likewise become "stuck" during acculturation when they behave and communicate in ways that were adaptive in a previous cultural setting, but are no longer so in their new one. Among couples, this dynamic can lead to marital conflict or domestic violence when immigrant men resist alterations to traditional gender roles and attitudes (Ho, 1990).

Developmental Issues

Family acculturation experiences are intertwined with individual members' unique developmental abilities and skills. Family members' ability to address acculturation demands are determined by their distinct cognitive, language, and interpersonal skills. To date, most acculturation research focuses on adult and adolescent populations with little reference to younger children. Studies that include children tend to focus on their exchanges with adults (e.g., parent–child relationships), rather than on their interactions with other children. As a result, there is little information regarding the types of cultural information that children exchange with one another and how they accomplish this. Likewise, scant attention is paid to the developmental context of acculturative stress. Acculturation stressors and related coping methods that are unique to children still need to be identified. As previously noted, cultural barriers to fulfilling developmental tasks (e.g., language difficulties, limited access to peer circles) appear to contribute to acculturative stress for first-generation immigrant youth (Chun, 2004b).

Normative family development assumes added complexities when occurring in tandem with acculturation. Life transitions like adjusting to a new marriage, welcoming new members to the family, or dealing with loss and other forms of adversity push families to modify or expand their interactions, organization, and overall functioning. These family life transitions or "chronosystems" (Bronfenbrenner, 1986) become more complex when they transpire in a culturally unfamiliar environment. This was highlighted by a particular Chinese American family (Chun, 2004b). The parents of this middle-class family, both first-generation immigrants in their 40s, appeared to struggle with their two second-generation sons' transition into adolescence. Although the sons did not exhibit behavioral problems, the mother restricted their social activities to their home and their temple and carefully controlled their selection of friends. This situation soon became a source of conflict for the entire family as the sons expressed a growing desire for autonomy. For the parents, living in a new cultural setting complicated matters. The mother was fearful and anxious about living in America, which she perceived as a threatening and dangerous place. The sons, in turn, felt frustrated over being denied opportunities to participate in adolescent rituals and activities that were central to their development. Consequently, the confluence of these developmental and acculturation demands placed considerable strain on their family.

Family Ecologies

Different contexts contribute to different expressions of the self (Minuchin & Fishman, 1981). Acculturation introduces families to multiple, new contexts that can either expand or restrain their behaviors and attitudes. This includes exposure to new "mesosystems" or extrafamilial ecologies that are primarily inhabited by youth (e.g., school settings and peer groups), and new "exosystems" that are inhabited mostly by parents (e.g., work settings, adult social networks; Bronfenbrenner, 1986). Individual members shape family acculturation by bringing new cultural knowledge and behaviors from these different ecologies to the family dinner table. There is some evidence that children use cultural information from their mesosystems to help socialize their parents around new modes of communication and emotional expression. In one study (Chun, 2004b), a first-generation Chinese American mother noted that her two children wanted her to become more openly affectionate after witnessing their more acculturated peers and their parents at school. This bewildered her because her own parents never openly expressed affection to her. After some time, however, she relented and noted that she actually began to appreciate "American" terms of endearment.

Finally, it is important to consider the significance of transnational social fields to family acculturation. Transnational social fields are deterritorialized spaces where familial, economic, religious, and sociopolitical relations and identities are formed and enacted (Mahler, 1998). For example, some Chinese immigrants in San Francisco, California maintain households and active family networks in both San Francisco's Chinatown and Hong Kong (Chun, 2004b). Moreover, their collective family identities and notions of home are not confined to nation-state boundaries, but are instead transnational in character. Transnational social fields are characterized by mobility of persons and materials and the exchange of information and resources. This is pertinent to immigrants who maintain dual citizenship, immigrant youth who seek extended overseas education, and families who maintain close civic, cultural, or economic ties with their countries of origin. The significance of transnational social fields to family acculturation is growing given the omnipresence of globalization. Immigrant families who share the same ethnicity, generational cohort, and country of origin can have altogether different acculturation experiences depending on the demarcations and activities of their transnational social fields. Transnational activities can entail acquiring cultural information about a new country prior to migration and securing capital and other forms of support. Family members may occupy different socioeconomic class positions in their transnational social field—a parent may have relatively low economic standing here in the United States, but have a much higher standing in his or her country of origin. Likewise, ethnic minority immigrants in the United States may belong to the dominant group or have a respected social position in another country. Acculturative stress stemming from "status inconsistency" or the loss of socioeconomic status or social position may thus be offset or diffused by a family's transnational social field. Additionally, a family's transnational social field may support and sustain their cultural practices, belief systems, and identities.

In sum, family acculturation processes illustrate the dynamic and multidimensional properties of cultural learning and maintenance. These properties are closely linked to the varied and complex nature of family organization and relations, family members' unique developmental tasks and skills, and fluctuating and interrelated family ecologies. Researchers thus face the formidable challenge of studying an acculturation process that constantly changes across different contexts and embodies multiple domains of psychological functioning. How does one begin to study this process? Recent advances in acculturation theory and measurement have opened new avenues to address this question more comprehensively and with greater clarity. The following section discusses some of these advancements and offers investigative guidelines that aim to improve the scope and theoretical underpinnings of family acculturation research.

FAMILY ACCULTURATION RESEARCH STRATEGIES

The most tenacious of investigators might be dissuaded from studying family acculturation in light of the many conceptual and methodological problems that can arise. Most problems, however, can be minimized or averted if the rationale for studying acculturation is clearly articulated. It is equally important to critically evaluate the utility and effectiveness of widely used self-report measures that are often adopted without question. A series of fundamental questions that address these and related research issues can serve as helpful starting points for any family acculturation study:

(1) What is the rationale for including acculturation in the study?
(2) What is the hypothesized relation between acculturation and the dependent variable(s)? What are the hypothesized mechanisms underlying this relation?
(3) What is the most appropriate index of acculturation to examine this relation? Should multiple indices be included? Why?
(4) What is the most culturally appropriate method to measure this relation?
(5) Which family grouping is the most relevant unit of analysis for the questions under investigation?

These fundamental questions are sometimes overlooked or given cursory examination because they may appear too rudimentary or intuitive at first glance. However, they are essential investigative starting points because they require: (1) operational definitions of acculturation or consideration of related constructs for investigation, (2) deliberation on the *process* of acculturation, (3) focused selection of acculturation indices that are relevant to the study question(s), (4) attention to equivalence of measures and culturally anchored data, and (5) consideration of nontraditional levels of family analyses. The first three questions are particularly helpful in identifying specific acculturation indices that are proximal to cultural learning and maintenance. Past studies have relied on proxy measures of acculturation (e.g., birthplace, years of U.S. residency, generational status, and language preferences or proficiencies) that often produce inaccurate and isolated snapshots of a highly complex process. The first three questions also promote theoretical frameworks to study family acculturation. A stress-coping model may be a helpful referent for studies that focus on the precursors and psychological sequelae of acculturative stress. However, studies that focus on the mechanisms of cultural learning and maintenance among family members may find social learning theory more useful. Thus, the basic questions outlined here stimulate critical thinking about what actually changes during acculturation, the reasons for these changes, and valid methods to assess them.

Cronbach and Meehl's (1955) construct-validation approach can serve as an overarching framework to study family acculturation. This approach prescribes multiple measures and observations to test the underlying nomological network of assumptions and propositions that define a construct. This is pertinent to acculturation because this construct lacks definitive criterion measures. Additionally, its emphasis on multiple measures and data points pushes for greater flexibility and creativity in acculturation measurement. To date, the preponderance of acculturation studies rely on self-report quantitative measures. Although these measures are beneficial, their exclusive use has been a major methodological limitation because they insufficiently assess the process, nature, and context of acculturation.

The experiences of a 46-year-old first-generation Chinese American mother bring these issues to light (Chun, 2004b). She emigrated from Hong Kong, possessed limited English skills, and had resided in the United States for 17 years. Traditional methods of assessing her acculturation would entail: (1) treating various features of her demographic background (e.g., generational status, years of residency in the United States, place of birth, or English language proficiency) as proxy measures of acculturation or (2) using a global measure of acculturation developed for Asian Americans. This first method assumes that low generational status, fewer years of residency in the United States, foreign birth, and poor English proficiency reflect low acculturation and high acculturative stress. The second method typically involves using the Suinn-Lew Asian Self-Identity Acculturation Scale (SL-ASIA; Suinn, Rickard-Figueroa, Lew, & Vigil, 1987). This 21-item Likert-type scale assesses language preferences and skills, ethnic identity, lifestyle preferences, and choice of friends. Acculturation levels are indicated by low to high individual scores on this measure. Data from both of these traditional assessment methods failed to fully capture this Chinese American mother's acculturation experiences. Ethnographic observations and face-to-face interviews revealed that she was recently in remission from cancer following chemotherapy and a bone marrow transplant. Her husband, a second-generation Chinese American, unexpectedly died 5 months after her transplant, which placed her and her 7-year-old son and 9-year-old daughter in dire economic circumstances. Nonetheless, she was optimistic about her future and reported few acculturation difficulties. She attributed this to her regular attendance at a cancer support group for new Chinese immigrants, her proximity to the culturally familiar environment of San Francisco's Chinatown, and deep Christian convictions that imbued her challenging life situation with meaning. All of these life experiences profoundly affected her adaptation and adjustment to the United States. However, they would have been altogether overlooked by isolated analyses of her demographic background or by exclusive reliance on a self-report measure like the SL-ASIA. There is a pressing need for expanded and creative assessment methods that speak to the complexities of acculturation as depicted. Ultimately, this calls for a paradigm shift in acculturation measurement that incorporates both qualitative and quantitative methods.

Combined Qualitative–Quantitative Methods

Combined qualitative–quantitative assessment methods offer a more comprehensive and accurate portrait of family acculturation. Generally speaking, qualitative methods can provide rich descriptions of the process and context of acculturation. They can illustrate the broad range of acculturation experiences in different family constellations in addition to their underlying conditions or contingencies. Qualitative methods also facilitate hypothesis generation and can inform the selection of quantitative acculturation measures. Quantitative methods are helpful in exploring the significance of specific acculturation indices and isolating causal relationships. Multiple data points from both methods can provide convergent validity for acculturation models. The following discussion outlines qualitative–quantitative measurement tools and strategies that can advance the state of family acculturation research.

Qualitative Assessment

Genograms

These visual illustrations are akin to detailed family trees that outline family structure, household composition, and quality of family relationships (e.g., family coalitions, enmeshed relations, conflicted or detached relationships) and provide overviews of a family's history. Genograms are visual reminders that families can have distinct acculturation experiences based on their unique living conditions, major life events, degree of family support, developmental concerns, and cultural organization. For instance, Asian American families with patrilineal structures and unidirectional parent–child communication may experience and cope with acculturation demands differently from those families who have more egalitarian relationships and bidirectional parent–child communication (Lee, 1997). Genograms provide opportunities to explore such differences by outlining the family context of acculturation.

Ethnographic Observation

This qualitative investigative method is far more encompassing than naturalistic observation and covers a number of techniques (Denzin & Lincoln, 2003). Participant-observation, one of the most widely used ethnographic methods, is particularly useful because it involves acquiring first-hand experience and knowledge of phenomena as they unfold in their natural environments (LeCompte & Schensul, 1999). To study family acculturation, researchers immerse themselves in the ecological niches where immigrant families reside and conduct their daily lives. "Thick descriptions" or detailed observations of family acculturation experiences are then generated. Analyses of these observational data can produce ecologically valid family acculturation models that are grounded in a specific sociocultural context. Participant-observation data can include detailed observations of family interactions, responses to their environments, communication patterns, and individual or collective adaptation goals and motives. Moreover, researchers can witness how these aspects of family functioning fluctuate across different settings, which can provide insights to family acculturation *processes*.

Family Narratives

Families often organize and frame themselves around particular life stories or narratives that speak to their unique characteristics, identities, and histories. Many immigrant and refugee families possess narratives about how and why they journeyed to another country. Overarching themes in these stories (e.g., escaping danger or persecution, survival or resiliency in the face of loss and trauma, hope for better economic and educational opportunities) serve as reference points from which families understand and respond to their new cultural environments. Family interviews can be used to solicit these themes and understand how families construct meaning around their acculturation experiences. Interview questions can include: Why did they leave their country of origin and select their current residence? How did they leave their country of origin? What were their expectations when they came to their new residence? What types of challenges did they face and how did they cope with them? How do they understand their current life situation given their family histories, including their family's strengths and limitations? Unlike most self-report acculturation measures, these types of questions also allow researchers to study family agency or family perceptions of their ability to shape their acculturation.

Mapping Transnational Social Fields

Transnational social fields can significantly affect family acculturation. Researchers can map the various locations where families reside, cultural information and materials that are exchanged, and family activities across these sites. Of particular interest are transnational shifts in family roles and responsibilities and variations in family resources and stressors that affect acculturation. The different types of cultural information that families receive prior to immigration are especially pertinent. In a study of four different Asian American groups in Seattle, it was found that new immigrants who had knowledge of the United States prior to immigration were less likely to show depressive symptoms (Kuo & Tsai, 1986). Mapping transnational social fields allows researchers to detail the types of cultural information that are beneficial to immigrant families and the manner in which this information is transmitted and shared among family members.

Quantitative Assessment

Domain-Specific Versus Global Acculturation Assessment

Focusing on a specific acculturation domain, rather than a global acculturation score comprised of multiple domains, may be more appropriate when the domain has clearer or direct conceptual links to the construct under investigation. To illustrate this point, individual scores on the SL-ASIA comprise multiple acculturation domains, as previously noted (including one that confounds ethnic identity with acculturation). However, the conceptual links between some domains (e.g., food and music preferences, ethnicity of friends) and certain outcome variables (e.g., parent–child conflict) may be unclear or based on tenuous assumptions. Analyzing a specific acculturation domain or a select few that are conceptually related to the outcome variable potentially strengthens a study's theoretical basis. This approach might involve disaggregating domains on a global acculturation measure to examine their differential relations with the dependent variable. Analyzing a global acculturation score, however, is indicated if overall or pervasive life changes are an investigative focus.

Measuring Constructs That Influence Family Functioning and Covary With Acculturation

Acculturation measures are not always indicated when studying acculturation effects on family functioning. Instead, measures of constructs that influence family functioning and are known to covary with acculturation may be more useful. For instance, constructs such as "self-construals" (measured along interdependent–independent dimensions; Markus & Kitayama, 1991), social orientations (involving individualistic–collectivistic dimensions; Triandis, 1989), and "loss of face" for Asian Americans (Zane & Mak, 2003), drive family organization, dynamics, and relations. These constructs also change with acculturation: Greater acculturation in the United States is associated with an independent self-construal, individualistic orientation, and less emphasis on loss of face (Chun, Balls Organista, & Marin, 2003). By directly measuring these constructs, researchers can effectively pinpoint acculturation changes in underlying mechanisms of family functioning. This measurement strategy provides more detailed and cogent information on the nature of family acculturation, unlike a global acculturation measure or an isolated acculturation domain.

CONCLUSIONS

Future family studies should aim to provide more contextualized, developmentally focused, process-oriented, and multidimensional portraits of acculturation. In respect to context, studies can examine shifts in acculturation behaviors and goals as families move through different social, familial, occupational, and educational spheres. This study approach permits exploration of fluctuating environmental demands that bear on family acculturation, interact with family characteristics, and elicit heterogeneous acculturation patterns.

Future studies also can tailor their research questions to specific phases of family development. For instance, in the couple formation phase when spouses meet and begin to form their family, a question might be: How does acculturation affect couple intimacy and marital relations? For families with children, another question might be asked: How do new immigrants access health and educational resources for their children? Studies of families with elderly members might focus on acculturation effects on aging. This can include identifying unique acculturation stressors for older adults and specific changes to family roles and responsibilities.

The process of acculturation also should receive special attention. Investigations can identify specific dynamics and behaviors that cause families to become "stuck" at different points of their acculturation. Findings from these investigations can inform culturally appropriate family interventions that alleviate acculturative stress and help to recalibrate family interactions for their new cultural settings. Similarly, studies can identify specific family behaviors and characteristics that facilitate acculturation. Some immigrant families might exhibit "niche picking" in which they deliberately select environments where they can express certain cultural characteristics and attributes. This adaptive strategy might enhance their efforts to maintain their culture and stabilize their family functioning.

In regards to multidimensionality, future studies should expand assessment of acculturation domains. Religious and spiritual beliefs and practices have been largely overlooked by acculturation research. Many immigrants and refugees, however, turn to religion in the event of tremendous change, upheaval, or loss, including those incurred during acculturation. This is perhaps most poignantly illustrated for Southeast Asian refugee families who endured multiple traumas and stressors (Abueg & Chun, 1996). For these families, religion and religious institutions may serve as primary coping resources, particularly when they are situated in their ethnic communities and provide cultural forms of support.

ACKNOWLEDGMENTS

This chapter was supported in part by a grant from the Pew Charitable Trusts for the University of San Francisco Religion and Immigration Project (TRIP).

REFERENCES

Abueg, F. R., & Chun, K. M. (1996). Traumatization stress among Asians and Asian Americans. In A. Marsella, M. Friedman, E. Gerrity, & R. Scurfield (Eds.), *Ethnocultural approaches to understanding post-traumatic stress disorder: Issues, research, and clinical applications* (pp. 285–299). Washington, DC: American Psychological Association.

Barrett, M. E., Joe, G. W., & Simpson, D. D. (1991). Acculturation influences on inhalant use. *Hispanic Journal of Behavioral Sciences, 13*, 276–296.

Boehnlein, J., Tran, H., Riley, C., Vu, K. C., Tan, S., & Leung, P. (1995). A comparative study of family functioning among Vietnamese and Cambodian refugees. *The Journal of Nervous and Mental Disease, 183*(12), 768–773.

Bronfenbrenner, U. (1986). Ecology of the family as a context for human development: Research perspectives. *Developmental Psychology, 22*, 723–742.

Brooks, A. J., Stuewig, J., & Lecroy, C. W. (1998). A family based model of Hispanic adolescent substance use. *Journal of Drug Education, 28*(1), 65–86.

Chesla, C., & Chun, K. M. (2004). Accommodating type 2 diabetes in the Chinese American family. *Qualitative Health Research.*

Chun, K. M. (2004a). *Relationship of gender role expectations to disease management for Chinese American couples*. Manuscript in preparation.

Chun, K. M. (2004b). Religious organizations in San Francisco Chinatown: Sites of acculturation and adaptation for Chinese immigrants. In L. A. Lorentzen, K. M. Chun, J. Gonzalez, & H. D. Do (Eds.), *On the corner of bliss and nirvana: The intersection of religion, politics, and identity in new migrant communities*. Manuscript submitted for publication.

Chun, K. M., & Akutsu, P. D. (2003). Acculturation processes among ethnic minority families. In K. M. Chun, P. Balls Organista, & G. Marin (Eds.), *Acculturation: Advances in theory, measurement, and applied research* (pp. 95–119). Washington, DC: American Psychological Association.

Chun, K. M., Balls Organista, P., & Marin, G. (Eds.). (2003). *Acculturation: Advances in theory, measurement, and applied research*. Washington, DC: American Psychological Association.

Cronbach, L., & Meehl, P. (1955). Construct validity in psychological tests. *Psychological Bulletin, 52*, 281–302.

Denzin, N., & Lincoln, Y. (Eds.). (2003). *Collecting and interpreting qualitative materials* (2nd ed.). Thousand Oaks, CA: Sage.

Erikson, E. H. (1963). *Childhood and society*. New York: W.W. Norton & Co.

Heras, P., & Revilla, L. (1994). Acculturation, generational status, and family environment of Philipino Americans: A study in cultural adaptation. *Family Therapy, 21*(2), 129–138.

Ho, C. (1990). An analysis of domestic violence in Asian American communities: A multi-cultural approach to counseling. In L. Brown & M. Root (Eds.), *Diversity and complexity in feminist therapy* (pp. 129–150). New York: Haworth Press.

Hoffman, L. (1981). *Foundations of family therapy*. Basic Books.

Kuo, W. H., & Tsai, Y. M. (1986). Social networking, hardiness and immigrants' mental health. *Journal of Health and Social Behavior, 27*, 133–149.

LeCompte, M. D., & Schensul, J. J. (1999). *Designing and conducting ethnographic research*. Walnut Creek, CA: Altamira Press.

Lee, E. (1997). Overview: The assessment and treatment of Asian American families. In E. Lee (Ed.), *Working with Asian Americans: A Guide for Clinicians* (pp. 3–36). New York: Guilford.

Mahler, S. J. (1998). Theoretical and empirical contributions toward a research agenda for transnationalism. In M. P. Smith & L. E. Guarnizo (Eds.), *Comparative urban & community research: Vol. 6. Transnationalism from below* (pp. 64–100). New Brunswick, NJ: Transaction Publishers.

Markus, H. R., & Kitayama, S. (1991). Culture and the self: Implications for cognition, emotion, and motivation. *Psychological Review, 98*(2), 224–253.

Minuchin, S., & Fishman, H. C. (1981). *Family therapy techniques*. Cambridge, MA: Harvard University Press.

Rosenthal, D., & Feldman, S. (1989). The acculturation of Chinese immigrants: Perceived effects on family functioning of length of residence in two cultural contexts. *The Journal of Genetic Psychology, 151*(4), 495–514.

Sabogal, F., Marin, G., Otero-Sabogal, R., Marin, B., & Perez-Stable, E. J. (1987). Hispanic familism and acculturation: What changes and what doesn't? *Hispanic Journal of Behavioral Sciences, 9*, 397–412.

Soto, E. (1983). Sex-role traditionalism and assertiveness in Puerto Rican women living in the United States. *Journal of Community Psychology, 11*(4), 346–354.

Soto, E., & Shaver, P. (1982). Sex role traditionalism, assertiveness, and symptoms of Puerto Rican women living in the United States. *Hispanic Journal of Behavioral Sciences, 4*(1), 1–19.

Suinn, R. M., Rickard-Figueroa, K., Lew, S., & Vigil, P. (1987). The Suinn-Lew Asian Self-Identity Acculturation Scale: An initial report. *Educational and Psychological Measurement, 47*, 401–407.

Triandis, H. C. (1989). The self and social behavior in differing cultural contexts. *Psychological Review, 93*(3), 506–520.

Yee, B. W. K., Huang, L. N., & Lew, A. (1998). Families: life-span socialization in a cultural context. In N. W. S. Zane & L. Lee (Eds.), *Handbook of Asian American Psychology* (pp. 83–136). Thousand Oaks, CA: Sage.

Ying, Y. W. (1996). Immigration satisfaction of Chinese Americans: An empirical examination. *Journal of Community Psychology, 24*, 3–16.

Zane, N. W. S., & Mak, W. (2003). Major approaches to the measurement of acculturation among ethnic minority populations: A content analysis and an alternative empirical strategy. In K. M. Chun, P. Balls Organista, & G. Marin (Eds.), *Acculturation: Advances in theory, measurement, and applied research* (pp. 39–60). Washington, DC: American Psychological Association.

5

Acculturation Is Not an Independent Variable: Approaches to Studying Acculturation as a Complex Process

Jean S. Phinney
California State University, Los Angeles, U.S.A.

INTRODUCTION

Acculturation is a complex process involving multiple changes that take place following contact among individuals and groups from differing cultural backgrounds. It involves changes in many areas, including attitudes, feelings, beliefs, and behaviors. Like acculturation, human development is a multifaceted process involving many changes that take place over time. For both acculturation and development, changes occur at the individual and group levels and are influenced by many individual and contextual factors and their interactions.

Developmental scientists are familiar with the difficulty of studying complex changing phenomena, and they have developed various ways of dealing with dynamic processes. In contrast, although acculturation is becoming increasingly recognized as an important psychological concept, acculturation researchers have been slower to take seriously its multifaceted and dynamic nature. With the increasing interest in the topic, more researchers have become involved in studying populations undergoing acculturation. Many empirical methods have been used, with some being more effective than others. To advance our understanding of the topic, researchers need to recognize the complexity of acculturation. In particular, they need to consider the limitations of treating acculturation as a single psychological construct or an independent variable that can predict outcomes such as academic achievement or substance abuse.

The ways of developing better research strategies are not simple or obvious. This chapter explores a number of research approaches that can help advance the empirical study of acculturation. In the chapter, I present and illustrate five approaches that can be used in acculturation research and can enhance our understanding of this complex topic.

First, because of the complexity of acculturation phenomena, it is important to recognize and distinguish among its component parts. An initial distinction should be made between two types of variables that are central to acculturation research: *markers of time*, such as generation of immigration, that are simply an index of length of time in a new cultural setting, and *variables that change*, such as language proficiency and social networks, that vary within individuals experiencing acculturation. A second, related, issue is the need for examining the components of acculturation separately in terms of their relation to influences and outcomes of interest, rather than combining many variables into a single scale. Third, because various features of acculturation, such as language and customs, change at differing rates, it is important to use methods, both longitudinal and cross-sectional, that can identify and take into account differing rates of change. Fourth, an understanding of the acculturation process requires that we go beyond simply describing acculturative change; rather, we should identify the mechanisms or underlying variables that account for differences across time or individuals. Fifth, because acculturation proceeds along varied trajectories, person-oriented approaches can provide valuable insights that are not evident from variable-oriented approaches.

In the following sections, I discuss each of these approaches in the study of acculturation and provide examples to illustrate them. These examples are based primarily on studies carried out over the last decade among adolescents and adults from immigrant backgrounds in the Los Angeles area.

DISTINGUISHING *MARKERS OF TIME* FROM *VARIABLES THAT CHANGE OVER TIME* IN ACCULTURATION RESEARCH

To begin to unravel the process of acculturation, it is helpful to distinguish between two types of variables that are typically involved in research on acculturation: *markers of time* and *variables that change over time*. Historically, markers of time, such as generation of immigration or length of time in a new cultural context, have been the most widely used variables in acculturation research. Such markers assess the length of time that has passed following cultural contact. These markers are between-person variables; that is, they differ across individuals but are stable within an individual. They are proxy or surrogate variables that are assumed to indicate the extent of change among people experiencing acculturation based simply on time in a particular setting. They are relatively unambiguous and relatively simple to measure, as they are based on factual information.

Generation is perhaps the most widely used marker of time. It is useful in providing a broad picture of differences that are likely to be seen across first, second, and third generations of immigrants. *Length of time* in a new cultural context, such as years since immigration, can be used as an indicator of changes such as the likelihood of having acquired skill in a new language. Markers of time are valuable in acculturation research because the alternatives, such as longitudinal studies that follow migrants over time, are difficult to conduct and far less common. However, they are limited in that they give no insight into processes of change. Furthermore, individual experiences differ widely, with some people changing dramatically in a short period and others remaining virtually unchanged for a long period. Length of time is confounded with the age at which one arrived; for example, language acquisition is typically easier at younger ages. Therefore, such markers should be used together with other variables that can elucidate the underlying processes.

In contrast to markers of time are *variables that change* as part of the acculturation process. These are within-person or within-group variables that show change at the individual and group levels following cultural contact. Although researchers lack agreement on exactly what aspects should be included in the concept of acculturation, the most salient changes that have been identified are those related to language, customs, social networks, identity, and values (Zane & Mak, 2003). Much early research assumed that these variables showed a linear trend, changing from an orientation toward the culture of origin to an orientation toward the new culture. However, current conceptualizations recognize that these aspects of acculturation can be thought of as varying along two independent dimensions of change, one in relation to the ethnic culture and the other in relation to the culture of settlement (e.g., Berry & Sam, 1997).

By making a distinction between *markers of time* and *variables that change*, researchers can more clearly link processes of acculturation to outcomes of interest and can avoid the confusion that results when different types of variables are combined into a single concept.

EXAMINING ACCULTURATIVE CHANGE VARIABLES SEPARATELY

Both human development and the acculturation of immigrants involve changes that, although interrelated, can best be understood initially by being considered separately. In the case of developmental change, particular phenomena are generally examined as distinct processes before researchers consider how they are interrelated; for example, pubertal changes and parent–child relationships must each be understood before their association can be studied. For acculturation, in addition to the distinction between markers of time and changes over time, it is important to distinguish among the changes that take place and consider them separately. As noted, the most commonly studied changes include language proficiency and use, customs, social networks, values, and identity. In each case, there is assumed to be a weakening or decline in those aspects associated with the culture of origin and an increase or strengthening of those associated with the new society.

These types of change are to some extent correlated, so the urge to simplify the construct by combining them into single scales is compelling. However, combining several acculturation variables (for example, language, identity, and values) into a single index and considering it to be a variable that can be used to predict specific outcomes, such as academic achievement, is like combining a number of factors in development, such as social class, family structure, parenting style, and ethnicity into a single index to predict developmental outcomes. Even though the variables may be correlated, they have separate and clearly distinguishable implications.

A study of traditional sex role attitudes in a sample of Latino adults (Phinney & Flores, 2002) illustrates the importance of distinguishing among aspects of acculturation and identifying which aspects are important with reference to a particular outcome. The goal was to determine how sex role attitudes varied as part of the acculturation process and what accounts for such variation. The participants were 170 Latino adults, with equal numbers of males and females, from diverse generational backgrounds, including first generation (born in a Latin American country), second generation (born in the United States, with one or both parents born in a Latin American country), and third generation (self and parents born in the United States). They also varied in educational background from high school completion or less to completion of a bachelor's degree.

Rather than using a scale of acculturation, we assessed separate elements of acculturation to determine their individual contributions to sex role attitudes. These elements were measured along two dimensions, an ethnic dimension based on one's relation to Latino culture and a dimension based on one's relation to the larger society. The ethnic dimension was assessed with two variables, Spanish language proficiency and use and number of Latino friends. The larger society dimension was assessed with English language proficiency and use and number of non-Latino friends. Language and friendship networks are only two of many possible factors that could be included, but they are among the most widely used in acculturation research (Zane & Mak, 2003). The outcome variable was the endorsement of traditional sex role attitudes, measured on a scale with four items such as, "Girls should help out with housework more than boys." Generation of immigration was used as a marker of time, and the demographic variables of gender and education were included in the analyses.

Multiple regression analysis was used to examine the combined effects of the predictor variables on sex role attitudes (see Table 5.1). With demographic vari-

TABLE 5.1
Multiple Regression Analysis Using Generation, Demographic Characteristics, Language, and Friends to Predict Sex Role Attitudes

	Beta	*t*	*Significance*
Generation	−.196	−2.83	.01
Education	−.221	−3.31	.001
Gender	.36	5.83	.001
English	−.096	−1.32	*ns*
Spanish	.027	.36	*ns*
Non-Hispanic friends	−.22	−3.12	.01
Hispanic friends	.058	.88	*ns*

Note. From Phinney & Flores, 2002. Reprinted with permission.
$R^2 = .40$. $F\ (7,162) = 15.25$. $p < .001$.

ables and the marker of time (generation) controlled, only one change variable, number of non-Hispanic friends, remained a significant predictor of attitudes: Specifically, having more non-Hispanic friends was related to less traditional sex-role attitudes. However, Hispanic friendships and Spanish and English language use were unrelated to attitudes.

Generation of immigration was also a significant predictor, with later generations having less traditional attitudes than earlier. However, as Table 5.1 shows, the demographic variables of education and gender were stronger predictors of attitudes than generation. Analysis of variance of sex role attitudes, with generation, gender, and education as factors, revealed a three-way interaction that underscores the complexity of the process (see Figure 5.1). For males without a college education, generation of immigration made little difference in attitudes; all of the less educated males retained traditional attitudes across three generations. For those males with a college education, attitudes became less traditional across generations. In contrast, for females, attitudes became less traditional with both increased education and later generation.

Correlational analyses among the variables showed that generation of immigration, which has been perhaps the most widely used marker of time in acculturation research, was unrelated to the variables that independently predicted sex role attitudes. Specifically, in bivariate correlations, generation was unrelated to having Latino and non-Latino friends, or to English language proficiency and usage, or to educational level. The only significant relation with generation was a negative correlation with Spanish proficiency and usage. However, Spanish language was not a predictor of sex role attitudes. Thus, generation alone was a crude predictor of sex role attitudes; more important was having non-Hispanic friends and being more educated. Although there were generational differences, knowing whether a person was first, second, or third generation revealed little about the factors that account for differences in attitudes resulting from cultural contact.

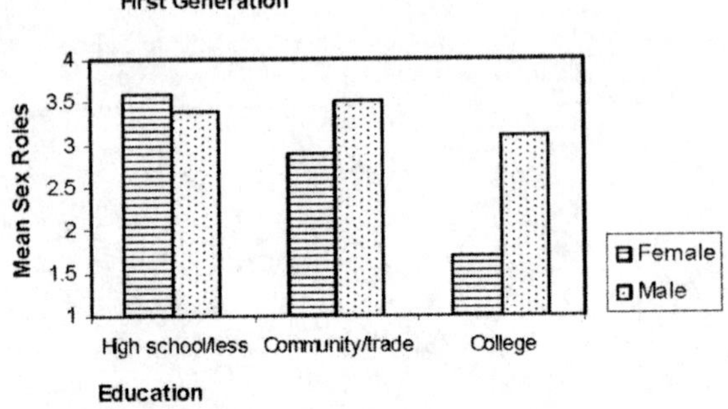

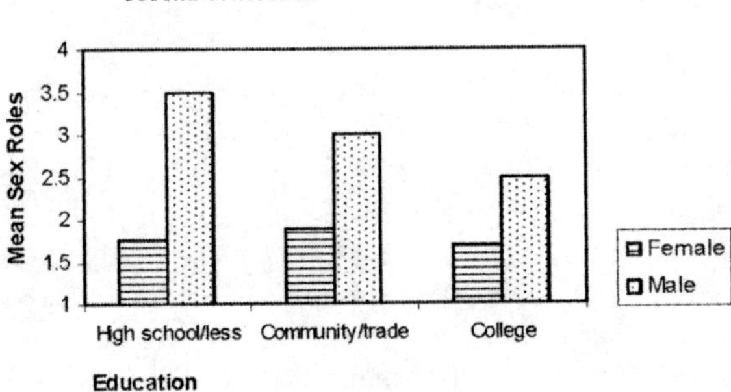

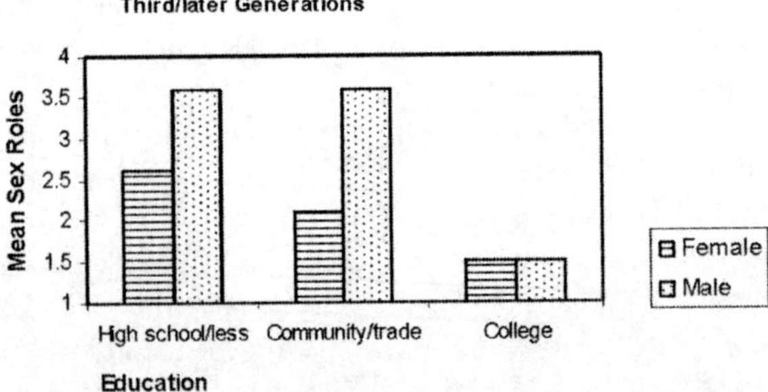

FIGURE 5.1. Mean scores on traditional sex role attitudes among Latino adults, by generation of immigration, education level, and sex. From Phinney and Flores (2002). Reprinted with permission.

In summary, this research illustrates the importance of recognizing the complex, multivariate nature of the acculturation process and examining its components separately. The research shows, furthermore, that factors that change with time are more useful than markers of time in understanding the process of acculturation.

STUDYING CHANGE OVER TIME

Although acculturation is defined as change, very little acculturation research actually examines change. In developmental science, longitudinal studies are recognized as essential to the understanding of processes of change in children. Long-term longitudinal studies provide valuable evidence of developmental pathways and factors that influence them. Fuligni (2001) stated similarly that longitudinal studies of immigrant children are needed to provide a better understanding of acculturation. He suggested that only by following immigrant children over time can researchers learn about the influences on acculturative change. Clearly, longitudinal methods provide the best approach to understanding both development and acculturation.

However, longitudinal studies are difficult, time-consuming, and expensive. Although we should carry out longitudinal research to the extent possible, we cannot depend on research that takes decades in order to gain understanding of current acculturation issues. In the meantime, other approaches are available to understand acculturation over time. Cross-sectional studies are necessary and are useful as long as we clearly distinguish markers of time, which are fixed properties of each immigrant, from those aspects of acculturation that change within individuals over time. Although generation is the most widely used among markers of time since immigration, others can be as useful or more so. The proportion of life and number of years spent in the new society are both continuous measures that provide a more sensitive index of time since immigration. They are particularly useful with first-generation immigrants. However, they can be used in samples that mix first and second generation; in that case, for the second generation the proportion of life is 100% and the number of years in the society equals age.

Cross-sectional studies that use markers of time, such as proportion of life or number of years since immigration, are valuable in showing that aspects of acculturation change at different rates. Some changes occur very quickly, over a few months or years, whereas others occur over decades or longer. Furthermore, the rate varies greatly with age of immigration and with the context. Acquisition of the national language is likely to occur rapidly, especially in young immigrants who attend school in the new society and in workers who need the language for their jobs. An ethnic language is less likely to change, at least among adult immigrants, who rarely forget their ethnic language, but children may lose their ethnic language facility if it is not reinforced at home.

On the other hand, cultural identity, which is often included in measures of acculturation (e.g., Cuellar, Arnold, & Maldonado, 1995), is very slow to change. Adult migrants generally maintain a primary identification with their country of origin and never take on a national identity in their country of settlement, so that there is little measurable change over the life of the individual (Phinney, 2003). In contrast, their children, born in the new society, generally identify with the national culture, even though they retain a clear ethnic identity, so that they are often biculturally identified. There is considerable variation across individuals in cultural identity, with some people feeling more ethnically identified and others more nationally identified (Phinney & Devich-Navarro, 1997). There is also situational variability in ethnic identity within individuals on a day-to-day basis (Yip & Fuligni, 2002). However, there is little evidence of substantial ethnic identity change within generations; most first-generation immigrants identify with their country of origin, and most second-generation residents, at least in the United States, are likely to be bicultural, that is, to identify with both their ethnic and national cultures (Phinney, 2003).

Because of differences in rates of change and in influences on change, the markers of time used in research should be selected depending on the issues being studied. The study of sex role attitudes discussed earlier (Phinney & Flores, 2002) showed that although generation of immigration was correlated with sex role attitudes, it was less useful as a predictor than specific variables that can change with time, such as friendships outside one's ethnic group. Nevertheless, for changes that occur very slowly, such as cultural identity, generation may provide a useful index (Phinney, 2003).

Markers such as proportion of life or time since immigration are an alternative method of studying variation across aspects of acculturation. In a large international study of immigrant adolescents in 13 countries (Berry, Phinney, Sam, & Vedder, 2006), a continuous variable, proportion of life in the new country, was created to provide a more fine-grained marker of time following immigration than generation.

The participants were over 5,000 adolescents from immigrant families, from age 13 to 18, sampled from 13 immigrant-receiving societies, including the United States, Canada, European countries, Australia, and New Zealand. About two thirds were children of immigrants or had immigrated before the age of 7, and one third were immigrants who arrived at age 7 or later. Multiple aspects of acculturation were assessed separately. Variables were assessed along two dimensions (an ethnic orientation and an orientation toward the larger, or national, society) and included strength of ethnic and national identities, ethnic and national language proficiency and use, and ethnic and national peer social contacts. Additional aspects of acculturation were acculturation attitudes (integration, separation, assimilation, and marginalization) and perceived discrimination.

Correlational analyses showed wide variation in the relation of proportion of life in the new country to other aspects of acculturation (Phinney, Berry, Liebkind, & Vedder, 2006). The strongest correlations (r = .30 or larger) were found between language variables and proportion of life in the new society; there was a negative relation of proportion of life with ethnic language proficiency (r = −.32), and positive relations with national language proficiency (r = .44) and use (r = .32). Small correlations (r = .10 or above) were found between proportion of life and perceived discrimination (r = −.16), ethnic identity (r = .15), peer contacts outside one's group (.14), assimilation attitudes (r = −.14), and separation attitudes ($r = -.10$). Negligible relations were found with other acculturation variables, such as national identity, ethnic peer contacts, and cultural values.

The results highlight the fact that some acculturation variables are strongly linked to time following immigration, whereas others show little or no relation. In general, acquisition of the national language was most strongly related; this finding may reflect the fact that participants in this case were all adolescents and all were attending school. Results would probably be very different for older immigrants, who are slower to learn a new language and rarely give up their ethnic language. Nevertheless, many immigrants acquire the new language rapidly out of necessity. The results are also likely to vary depending on the characteristics of the particular ethnic community and its relation to the larger society.

The results raise questions about scales of acculturation that rely primarily on language as an indicator of acculturation. Findings may provide misleading results if other aspects of acculturation that are important but that change more slowly are not taken into consideration, such as identity and cultural values. The variation in the relation between time in the society and acculturation variables again emphasizes the need to study these variables separately, rather than assuming that an inclusive index of acculturation can accurately capture the complexity of the acculturation process.

IDENTIFYING FACTORS THAT UNDERLIE VARIATION IN ACCULTURATION: ETHNIC GROUP DIFFERENCES AND CULTURAL VALUES

In both developmental and acculturation research, it is important to identify the underlying factors that may account for change. In both cases, researchers need to recognize the limitations of trying to understand these processes solely with reference to common markers of time, such as age (in the case of development) or generation of immigration (in the case of acculturation). Age is an obvious indicator of development and has been central from the beginnings of developmental research to describe the process of growing up. Age can be used to group developing humans into stage-like categories that convey a broad picture of development. Yet developmental scientists are well aware that age alone does not explain developmental change. Although developmental changes are linked to age, age is not the only determining factor. The best developmental research identifies and assesses underlying factors, such as the biological substrate, cognitive functioning, contextual influences, and their interactions, that account for observed changes over time. Development is not a variable that causes changes, for example in parent–child relationships. Parent–child relationships change due to specific factors linked to development, such as a child's cognitive abilities and external social pressures.

Similarly, although acculturative changes are linked to markers of time, such as generation of immigration, these markers do not explain such changes, as shown in the study of sex role attitudes discussed earlier (Phinney & Flores, 2002). Generation is what Bronfenbrenner (1988) called a "social address," a label that categorizes people but provides no understanding of characteristics that may be associated with the categories. Rather, specific factors associated with the social address need to be identified.

A study on adolescent–parent relationships in immigrant and nonimmigrant families (Phinney, Kim-Jo, Osorio, & Vilhjalmsdottir, 2005) illustrates the importance of identifying underlying factors that may explain variation in immigrant samples. The goals of the study were to examine differences in the ways in which adolescents and young adults from diverse backgrounds handle disagreements with their parents and, more importantly, to identify factors that predict such differences. Cultural values were examined as an underlying factor that may explain variation in the handling of disagreements, and ethnic group differences were explored. For this chapter, data on number of years in the new society, not analyzed previously, were used to provide a marker of time following immigration.

We focused on adolescents' responses to hypothetical situations in which their own wishes differed from those of their parents. Adolescents reported what they would do; that is, whether they would assert themselves and do what they wanted, or comply and do what their parents wanted them to do. Obedience to parents is a value common in the cultures of many immigrant groups (Fuligni & Tseng, 1999; Phinney, Ong, & Madden, 2000), including those we studied from Korean, Armenian, and Mexican backgrounds. We wanted both to determine the extent to which self-assertion varies over time in the United States among immigrant youth and to identify factors that may account for the variation. Because time does not provide an explanation of change, we assessed the cultural value of family interdependence, which is assumed to underlie and account for behavior toward parents, in this case, self-assertion. Because self-assertion is also assumed to change as young people develop, age was included both for descriptive purposes and as a step toward distinguishing developmental from acculturative change.

The data presented here, a subset of the larger study (Phinney et al., 2005), are based on 180 young people, 60 each from three American immigrant groups (Korean American, Armenian American, and Mexican American), equally represented across three age groups (14–15 years, 16–18 years, and 19–22 years), with equal numbers of males and females (for details, see Phinney et al., 2005). All three ethnic groups included both foreign-born and U.S.-born youth, that is, first and second generation; all participants had foreign-born parents. The study was not longitudinal, so actual change could not be determined. For the current analyses, the variable *years in the United States* was created by subtracting age of arrival in the United States from current age; for those who were United States born, this variable was equal to their age. Years in the United States was used as a marker of time, and age was a marker of developmental change. We could thus examine together the two types of change. The inclusion of three different ethnic groups permitted the examination of cultural differences in both processes.

Participants read six vignettes describing hypothetical situations likely to create disagreement with parents. Some examples of these situations are: a young person wanting to watch television rather than do chores, or wanting to date someone from a different ethnic group when parents want him or her to date within the group. Participants wrote open-ended responses, indicating what they would do in dealing with each disagreement. Responses were then coded into one of three categories: compliance, self-assertion, or negotiation. In cases where the youth agreed with the parents, there was no conflict, and responses were not used.

We focus here on self-assertion, that is, cases where the young person reported doing what he or she wanted to do when the parents wanted him or her to do something else. We expected that self-assertion would occur more often with development, as indicated by age, and with longer residence in the new culture. The cultural value of family interdependence, which included items such as putting family's needs before one's own and consulting with parents before making decisions, was expected to be a negative predictor of self-assertion and also to be less strongly endorsed in older participants and those who had lived longer in the United States. In summary, self-assertion was expected to be related positively to age and to years in the United States and negatively to family interdependence. A key question was whether family interdependence would explain differences based on age and years of residence. We also wanted to distinguish processes associated with development from those related to acculturation and to explore ethnic group variation.

Bivariate correlations showed the expected interrelations (see Table 5.2). The more years spent in the United States, the greater the self-assertion and the weaker the value of family interdependence. Self-assertion was higher among the older participants, but age was also related to years in the United States. Furthermore, stronger endorsement of family interdependence was related to less self-assertion. The strength of the correlations differed across the three ethnic groups.

A series of regression analyses was carried out to examine the possible mediating effect of family interdependence. An initial regression analysis using age and

TABLE 5.2
Correlations Among Years in U.S., Age, Family Interdependence, and Self-Assertion

	Years in United States	*Age in Years*	*Family Interdependence*
Age in years	.20**		
Family interdependence	–.24**	–.11	
Self-assertion	.24**	.19*	–.39**

Note. Based on data from Phinney et al., 2005.
$N = 180$.
$*p < .05$. $**p < .01$.

years in the United States as predictors showed that both of these variables significantly predicted self-assertion. When family interdependence was added to the model, age and years in the United States were no longer significant predictors of self-assertion, showing that family interdependence mediated the effects of age and time on self-assertion. Family interdependence is thus an example of an underlying variable that provides an explanation of acculturative change in family relationships; with age and longer time in the United States, there was weaker endorsement of family interdependence, and this in turn was associated with more self-assertion.

Nevertheless, there were differences among the three ethnic groups in the prediction of self-assertion that highlight variation in the process of acculturation across ethnic groups. The results of regression analyses carried out for each ethnic group separately are shown in Table 5.3. Across all three groups, higher levels of family interdependence were associated with less self-assertion, although the effect was not significant for the Armenian youth. For the Armenian American youth, years in United States was a stronger predictor of self-assertion than family interdependence, suggesting that there are other changes occurring in their lives, not assessed in this study, that may influence adolescents' relationships with their parents. For the Mexican American youth, family interdependence was a strong and highly significant predictor of self-assertion, whereas age did not influence self-assertion.

For Korean American young people, family interdependence was also a significant predictor of self-assertion. However, Korean Americans showed little difference in self-assertion with either age or years in the United States. This unexpected finding was explored in an extension of the study. Kim-Jo (2003) sampled a group of Korean youth of the same ages living in Korea and compared them to the Korean American youth in the United States. Results showed that the Korean American youth reflected stronger Korean cultural values than the young people in Korea. Qualitative observations in Korea and in the Korean American community suggested that in Korea, society is changing rapidly with Westernization and

TABLE 5.3
Separate Regression Analyses by Ethnic Group, Predicting Self-Assertion From Age, Years in the United States, and Family Interdependence

Predictor	*Korean Americans* β	*Armenian Americans* β	*Mexican Americans* β
Age	−.031	.153	.172
Years in U.S.	−.075	.346**	.126
Family interdependence	−.295*	−.226	−.426***
R^2	.08	.27***	.25***
N	60	60	60

*$p < .05$. **$p < .01$. ***$p < .001$.

the weakening of traditional values, whereas in America, Korean parents exert strong pressure on young people to preserve traditional Korean values. The latter may account for the lack of difference in self-assertion with age and years in the U.S. among Korean Americans.

Overall, the cultural value of family interdependence was the best predictor of self-assertion, with age and years in United States included in the analyses. Changes that accompany acculturation in the family, such as increased self-assertion in adolescents, may be explained in part by developmental changes during adolescence that are common across groups. However, as this research shows, immigrant adolescents' attitudes and behaviors are strongly influenced by their cultural values regarding the family. These values are likely to change with exposure to the values of the larger society and, in turn, to influence behavior. In fact, changes in self-assertion over time were associated more strongly with changes in cultural values than with age. Nevertheless, caution must be used in generalizing about the impact of changing cultural values, as the process plays out differently across ethnic groups.

USING A PERSON-ORIENTED APPROACH TO UNDERSTANDING ACCULTURATION

The vast majority of studies of acculturation are variable-oriented. Because variables related to acculturation are typically intercorrelated, methods that combine variables can be useful in gaining a broad view of the acculturation process. However, variable-oriented approaches provide information only on relations among variables and therefore may mask individual differences. This is particularly true in cases where two variables, such as ethnic identity and national (e.g., American) identity, are positively correlated for some individuals (e.g., bicultural people who are high on both) but negatively correlated for others (e.g., assimilated people who are low on ethnic identity but high on national identity).

In contrast to variable-oriented approaches, person-oriented approaches allow for the grouping of individuals based on their similarity on a number of variables of interest (Aldenderfer & Blashfield, 1984). Bergman, Magnusson, and El-Khouri (2003) argue that a person-oriented approach can provide for a better understanding of individuals than do methods based on variables. Cluster analysis, which identifies clusters of individuals who share particular characteristics, is one such method.

In the international study of immigrant adolescents discussed earlier, cluster analysis was used to identify profiles of acculturation that are shared by groups of immigrant youth (Phinney et al., 2006). The cluster analysis was based on a wide range of aspects of acculturation, including acculturation attitudes (toward integration, separation, assimilation, and marginalization), ethnic and national identities, language, peer contacts, and family relationships: Of these, identities, language, and peer contacts were assessed in relation to both the ethnic culture and the wider society. Cluster analysis resulted in the identification of four distinct and reliable profiles of acculturation into which immigrant adolescents could be grouped: an integration profile, an ethnic profile, a national profile, and a diffuse profile. These four statistically derived profiles mirror, to a large extent, Berry, Kim, Power, Young, and Bujaki's (1989) conceptually derived model of four acculturation strategies: integration, separation, assimilation, and marginalization.

The most frequently occurring profile consisted of adolescents whose attitudes and behaviors reflected integration. These young people showed relatively high involvement in both their ethnic and national cultures. They were high on both ethnic and national identities, and they strongly endorsed integration attitudes. They reported high national language proficiency and average ethnic language proficiency; their language usage suggested balanced use of both languages. They had peer contacts with members of both their own ethnic group and the national group. These adolescents appear to be comfortable in both the ethnic and national contexts, and thus exemplify integration as way of dealing with the immigrant experience.

The ethnic profile consisted of adolescents who showed a clear orientation toward their own ethnic group, with high ethnic identity, ethnic language proficiency and usage, and social contacts within their own group. Their support for traditional cultural values regarding the family was well above the average. They scored low on national identity and contacts with the national group, and endorsed separation attitudes. They represent an ethnic solution to the immigrant experience, in that they are largely embedded within their own cultural milieu and show little involvement with the larger society.

The national profile defined immigrant adolescents who showed a strong orientation toward the society in which they had settled. They were high on national identity and on assimilation attitudes and very low on ethnic identity. They were proficient in the national language and used it predominantly. Their social contacts were largely with members of the national group, and they showed low support for family obligations. These adolescents presented a national profile that exemplifies the idea of assimilation, indicating relatively low retention of their ethnic culture.

The diffuse profile shows a pattern that suggests youth who are in transition and unsettled regarding how to deal with their immigrant experience. These youth reported high proficiency in and usage of the ethnic language, but also reported low ethnic identity. They had low proficiency in the national language, and they reported somewhat low national identity and national social contacts. They endorsed two conflicting acculturation attitudes, assimilation and marginalization. These young people seem uncertain about their place in society, perhaps wanting to be part of the larger society but lacking the skills and ability to make contacts, and thus reflect a diffuse identity as described by Marcia (1994). This profile appears similar to people described in the classic acculturation literature as marginalized (Stonequist, 1961).

The profiles, when examined in relation to a marker for length of residence in the new society, suggest that immigrants follow different trajectories in the acculturation process and these trajectories vary over time. Among the most recent arrivals, the diffuse profile dominated, and the national profile was very low. For those with the longest residence in the society of settlement, the integrated profile dominated, and the national profile was second in frequency; the diffuse profile was dramatically less frequent. The ethnic profile was almost equally frequent across length of residence. Overall, these results suggest a trend over time away from a diffuse profile, toward an integrated or national profile. Nevertheless, a substantial group of adolescents shows strong and enduring involvement with their ethnic culture regardless of length of residence.

These distinct profiles of acculturation reinforce the idea that acculturation is a complex experience that individuals and groups handle in different ways. Correlations among aspects of acculturation can vary across different samples. For individuals who show an integrated or bicultural profile, ethnic and national aspects of their lives (identity, language, and social contacts) are positively correlated, that is, one can hold simultaneously both orientations. For those with ethnic or national profiles, the ethnic and national aspects are negatively correlated; individuals exhibit one or the other orientation, but not both.

In summary, acculturation does not proceed along a single trajectory that can be defined with one variable. Rather, individuals take varied paths as they face the challenges of living in a culture that differs from their heritage culture. A person-oriented approach such as cluster analysis provides a useful means of moving beyond the idea of acculturation as a unified construct and can help us to gain understanding of the varied experiences of immigrants.

CONCLUSIONS

With the growing importance of immigration in modern societies, research is needed to address the many issues of acculturation facing immigrant children and families and the societies in which they settle. The material presented in this chapter suggests a number of approaches to address this need.

Foremost is the importance of recognizing that acculturation is a process that is made up of many distinct elements. Researchers need to distinguish between-person markers of time in a new cultural context and within-person variables that change over time in such a context. Because time is a variable that provides no insight into processes of change, it is important to identify underlying factors that may explain change. Furthermore, the many factors that vary over time, such as language, identity, and others, change at differing rates and are associated in different ways with outcome variables of interest. Although most aspects of acculturation are interrelated, the relations vary in strength and even direction in different individuals, groups, and contexts, so that combining them for purposes of study may result in diluting or washing out critical causal associations. The differing ways in which aspects of acculturation may be interrelated can be seen in the use of person-oriented approaches, such as cluster analysis, that suggest different profiles of acculturation.

There is growing awareness of the complexity of the construct of acculturation and of the need for more nuanced approaches. A recommendation for advancing the study of acculturation is to use language more precisely in order to make clear the complex, multivariate nature of the phenomenon. A useful starting point would be to use the word *acculturation* only to refer broadly to the phenomena encompassing the many changes that result from cultural contact; in this broad sense, it is useful in referring to acculturation processes, acculturation research, or acculturative change. However, the use of the term in phrases such as the "effects of acculturation" and "higher levels of acculturation" contributes to the tendency to oversimplify the construct, implying that there is a single entity that can describe and explain the processes of change among immigrants.

Because acculturation is multifaceted and dynamic, it cannot be understood in any depth as long as we think of it as a single variable. Rather, it is important to recognize that multiple aspects of acculturation, themselves changing with time, have varying relations to the experiences of immigrants and the differing outcomes that result. To understand the changes that occur following immigration, researchers need to recognize this complexity and incorporate it into research designs. Acculturation, like human development, is a process, not a variable.

ACKNOWLEDGMENTS

Preparation of this chapter was supported in part by Grant S06 GM-08101 from the NIH MBRS SCORE Program.

REFERENCES

Aldenderfer, M., & Blashfield, R. (1984). *Cluster analysis*. Beverly Hills, CA: Sage.

Bergman, L., Magnusson, D., & El-Khouri, B. (2003). *Studying individual development in an interindividual context*. Mahwah, NJ: Lawrence Erlbaum Associates.

Berry, J., Kim, U., Power, S., Young, M., & Bujaki, M. (1989). Acculturation attitudes in plural societies. *Applied Psychology: An International Review, 38*, 185–206.

Berry, J., Phinney, J., Sam, D., & Vedder, P. (Eds.). (2006). *Immigrant youth in cultural transition: Acculturation, identity, and adaptation across national contexts*. Mahwah, NJ: Lawrence Erlbaum Associates.

Berry, J., & Sam, D. (1997). Acculturation and adaptation. In J. Berry, M. Segall, & C. Kagitcibasi (Eds.), *Handbook of cross-cultural psychology, Vol 3, Social behavior and applications* (pp. 291–326). Boston: Allyn & Bacon.

Bronfenbrenner, U. (1988). Interacting systems in human development: Research paradigms, present and future. In N. Bolger, A. Caspi, G. Downey, & M. Moorehouse (Eds.), *Persons in context: Developmental processes* (pp. 25–49). New York: Cambridge University Press.

Cuellar, I., Arnold, B., & Maldonado, R. (1995). Acculturation rating scale for Mexican Americans–II: A revision of the original ARSMA scale. *Hispanic Journal of Behavioral Sciences, 17*, 275–304.

Fuligni, A. (2001). A comparative longitudinal approach to acculturation among children from immigrant families. *Harvard Educational Review, 71*, 566–578.

Fuligni, A., & Tseng, V. (1999). Family obligation and the academic motivation of adolescents from immigrant and American-born families. In T. Urdan (Ed.), *Advances in motivation and achievement* (pp. 159–183). Stanford, CT: JAI Press.

Kim-Jo, T. (2003). *Cultural values among Korean and Korean American adolescents*. Unpublished master's thesis, California State University, Los Angeles.

Marcia, J. (1994). The empirical study of ego identity. In H. Bosma, T. Graafsma, H. Grotevant, & D. de Levita (Eds.), *Identity and development: An interdisciplinary approach* (pp. 67–80). Thousand Oaks, CA: Sage.

Phinney, J. (2003). Ethnic identity and acculturation. In K. Chun, P. Organista, & G. Marin (Eds.), *Acculturation: Advances in theory, measurement, and applied research* (pp. 63–81). Washington, DC: American Psychological Association.

Phinney, J., Berry, J., Liebkind, K., & Vedder, P. (2006). The acculturation experience: Attitudes, identities, and behaviors of immigrant youth. In J. Berry, J. Phinney, D. Sam, & P. Vedder (Eds.), *Immigrant youth in cultural transition: Acculturation, identity, and adaptation across national contexts*. Mahwah, NJ: Lawrence Erlbaum Associates.

Phinney, J., & Devich-Navarro, M. (1997). Variations in bicultural identification among African American and Mexican American adolescents. *Journal of Research on Adolescence, 7*, 3–32.

Phinney, J., & Flores, J. (2002). "Unpackaging" acculturation: Aspects of acculturation as predictors of traditional sex role attitudes. *Journal of Cross-Cultural Psychology, 33*, 320–331.

Phinney, J., Kim-Jo, T., Osorio, S., & Vilhjalmsdottir, P. (2005). Autonomy and relatedness in adolescent–parent disagreements: Ethnic and developmental factors. *Journal of Adolescent Research, 20*, 8–39.

Phinney, J., Ong, A., & Madden, T. (2000). Cultural values and intergenerational value discrepancies in immigrant and non-immigrant families. *Child Development, 71*, 528–539.

Stonequist, E. (1961). *The marginal man: A study in personality and culture conflict*. New York: Russell & Russell.

Yip, T., & Fuligni, A. (2002). Daily variation in ethnic identity, ethnic behaviors, and psychological well-being among American adolescents of Chinese descent. *Child Development, 73*, 1557–1572.

Zane, N., & Mak, W. (2003). Major approaches to the measurement of acculturation among ethnic minority populations: A content analysis and an alternative empirical strategy. In K. Chun, P. Organista, & G. Marin (Eds.), *Acculturation: Advances in theory, measurement, and applied research* (pp. 39–60). Washington, DC: American Psychological Association.

6

Adaptation of Children and Adolescents With Immigrant Background: Acculturation or Development?

David L. Sam
University of Bergen, Bergen, Norway

INTRODUCTION

This chapter focuses on immigrant children's adaptation from a developmental perspective and argues that immigrant children's adaptation should be seen as a form of development rather than as two separate processes: acculturation and development. The chapter has two main parts. The first part discusses the need for a better understanding of immigrant children's adaptation, the limitations of current research efforts in acculturation, and the need to bring developmental issues into acculturation. In the second part of the chapter, a theoretical model together with a partial support to the model are presented.

In almost every aspect of society, children receive special attention, and immigration is no exception (Mautino, 2001). Nevertheless, research and theories on immigrant children's adaptation is surprisingly lacking considering that immigrant children constitute the fastest growing sector of the population in many Western industrialized countries (Aronowitz, 1984). For instance, it was estimated that during the 7-year period between 1990 and 1997, the number of children with immigrant backgrounds in the United States grew by 47%, compared to the 7% increase in the number of children of nationals (Hernandez, 1999). Similar trends have been found in other countries including the United Kingdom (www.statistics.gov.uk) and Canada (www12.statcan.ca/english/census01).

The ubiquity of immigrant children in several Western industrialized countries has in recent years attracted some research attention aimed at understanding how they adapt to the two often opposing cultures they face at home and within the larger society they live in. Early waves of research among immigrant children were more concerned with how well they are adapting, probably as a response to the recurrent association between immigrant status and psychological disorders (see Evans, 1987; McKay, Macintyre, & Ellaway, 2003; Murphy, 1977), and in the light of theories that asserted that children may be particularly vulnerable to the stresses of migration (Bashir, 1993). As Fuligni (2003) pointed out, results from these studies indicate, at least in the United States, that immigrant children and adolescents show a remarkably good adaptation, ranging from good school adjustment and academic records (Fuligni, 1997, 1998a, 1998b) through few problem behaviors (Harris, 1999) to comparably good psychological adjustment (Harris, 1999). In recent years, similar findings have been reported in other countries (see Berry, Phinney, Sam, & Vedder, in press), including Sweden (Virta & Westin, 1999) and Norway (Virta, Sam, & Westin, 2004).

This paradox (i.e., good adaptation in spite of poor socioeconomic background and the hardships associated with migration) calls for an explanation. Unfortunately, not only is there a lack of research that examines the processes by which immigrant children and their families adapt to new societies, but there is also a dearth of theories that can account for immigrant children's successful adaptation (Garcia Coll & Magnuson, 1997). Several researchers (e.g., Garcia Coll & Magnuson, 1997; Laosa, 1997; Siantz, 1997) have pointed out that to fully understand the acculturation of immigrant children, theoretical models need to draw more heavily on developmental theories. But to date, developmental theories are still very much ignored in acculturation theories about children, and the few existing attempts (Fuligni, 1998b, 2003; Sam, 1995; Siantz, 1997) have merely described experiences such as the family conflicts between immigrant children and their parents and the development of autonomy among immigrant children in different developmental phases, rather than positing an integrated conceptual model or theory.

The fact remains that there is no single overarching theory of human development, and to think of an acculturation theory that adequately incorporates human development is a challenging task. Thus, the goal of this chapter is not to propose an overarching theory of the process of acculturation of immigrant children and their subsequent adaptation, but to highlight and integrate different aspects of immigrant children's acculturation experiences into a model that is cognizant of the fact that immigrant children, just like all other children, traverse developmental changes in addition[1] to their acculturation experiences.

PSYCHOLOGICAL ACCULTURATION AND ONTOGENETIC DEVELOPMENT

Some Commonalities and Erroneous Assumptions

Paradoxically, both psychological acculturation and ontogenetic development are concerned with change, yet these two subject areas have tended to ignore each

[1]The expression "in addition" is used here as a generic term to indicate a combined influence of acculturation and development, and not to suggest an additive contribution. The author is of the opinion that acculturation is embedded in development and the two are in active dynamic interaction.

other. From a developmental perspective, change arises from a dynamic interaction between biological and maturational processes on one hand and environmental learning experiences on the other (Lerner, 2001). Except perhaps for social identity theory, change in acculturation is often attributed to either a coping mechanism in response to a stressful situation that is induced by an encounter with an unfamiliar cultural context, or as a need on the part of an individual to learn specific cultural skills so as to survive and thrive in a given cultural context. The reaction to the stress induced by acculturation is believed to result in the learning of coping skills that are adaptive and functional, otherwise the person is said to be maladapted (Ward, 2001). Whereas acculturation can primarily be conceived of as a learning phenomenon, development entails both learning and maturation. This means that some changes in individuals attributed to acculturation may in reality be developmental changes.

Age and *time* are two factors that both acculturation and development theorists regard as closely related to change. For instance, the younger the child at the time of migration, the easier the adaptation process (Berry, 1997; Berry & Sam, 1997; Zhou, 1997). Similarly, the length of residence is suggested to affect one's social skills such as the acquisition of the national language (Kwak, 1991). Similarly, human development theories are full of such trends as age-related abilities (e.g., Piaget's cognitive development).

Developmental changes are often seen as involving both *continuity* and *discontinuity* (i.e., the debate whether the factors responsible for human development remain the same—*continuity*—or are different—*discontinuity*—during the life span; Lerner, 2001). Acculturation changes often assume continuity even though this assumption has rarely been discussed and has not always been possible to demonstrate. A typical continuity assumption in acculturation is the belief that with the passage of time, immigrant children's ethnic identity will wane as their national identity strengthens (Costigan & Su, 2004; Liebkind, 2001). However, in a 13-country comparative study involving over 30 different ethnic groups, Berry, Phinney, Sam, and Vedder (in press) could not find support for this assumption. It is possible that some of the changes in immigrant children's ethnic identity follow a qualitative discontinuity rather than quantitative continuity as assumed. The point being made here is that, whereas acculturation changes are often seen as continuous, some aspects may be discontinuous. Along this line, it is perhaps more correct to think of acculturation as embedded in development rather than as a separate phenomenon. This reasoning implies that development invariably confounds acculturation.

In addition to the assumed continuity changes, acculturation studies also assume that when an individual finds him- or herself in an acculturation situation, development stops and acculturation takes over. Not only is this an unsubstantiated assumption, but current theories in human development all point to a life-span perspective that development continues throughout one's life. Thus, development continues whether one experiences acculturation or not, further underscoring the potential confounding role ontogenetic factors may have on acculturation. Somehow efforts to eliminate the confounding role of development on acculturation appear not to have yielded the warranted research attention.

Because acculturation involves contact between individuals and groups of different cultural backgrounds, it is often assumed that *cultural factors* are directly implicated when differences are found between host nationals and immigrant groups just as in other areas of cross-cultural psychology (Berry, Poortinga, Segall, & Dasen, 2002). However, not all aspects of an acculturation experience are cultural (e.g., the duration of the contact between the two groups). There is no gainsaying that some problems immigrant children experience (e.g., ethnic identity crisis) may be rooted in the process of acculturation, but some may very well arise from the developmental transition (i.e., identity development), or an interaction between the two processes (i.e., acculturation and development). By simply limiting oneself to "acculturation factors," one may overlook other possible explanations for the observed problem.

It has often been contended that adolescents and children of immigrant background are particularly vulnerable to psychological problems (Bashir, 1993). One explanation given to this vulnerability is intergenerational family conflict between immigrant children and their parents (Szapocznik & Kurtines, 1993). The assumption is that immigrant children acculturate (assimilate) faster to prevailing cultural values and norms of the host society than do their parents (Buriel & de Ment, 1997; Rick & Forward, 1992). Thus, with the passage of time, immigrant children and their parents may differ in cultural values, and these value discrepancies may be the basis for psychological maladaptation.

As intuitive as this hypothesis sounds, a cross-sectional study involving two cohorts (parents and their children) of immigrant and host-nation families in Norway and Sweden could not find support to the hypothesis that intergenerational value discrepancies were particularly larger in immigrant families than in host national families (Sam & Virta, 2003). Neither could the intergenerational differences in values be related to mental health problems. In a similar study, Phinney, Ong, and Madden (2000) did not find larger intergenerational value discrepancies in immigrant families compared to their European American host counterparts. Although in a follow-up study Phinney and Ong (2002) found a negative relation between intergenerational value discrepancies and satisfaction with life, the impact of the discrepancy on life satisfaction was no greater in a Vietnamese sample than in European Americans.

All three studies cited questioned the validity of the assumption that psychological problems among immigrant children might be due to acculturation factors, and pointed out that perhaps the observed findings might reflect normal developmental processes. (See Kwak, 2003, for a recent review.) However, it has been difficult to draw a clear conclusion as to whether the observed findings are developmental or acculturation as the studies themselves were cross-sectional. There is no doubt that more rigorous studies are needed to help isolate the confounding role of development on acculturation, even though we believe that this is an extremely difficult task when acculturation is conceptualized as a phenomenon in active interaction with, or embedded in, development.

Theoretical Problems

A problem with many acculturation theories, and in particular those involving children and adolescents, is their failure to take into consideration the unique situation of young people (Sam & Oppedal, 2002). Immigrant children and adolescents face different adaptation challenges than their parents (Zhou, 1997), but their adaptation experiences have often been attended to using theories developed for adult immigrants (Aronowitz, 1984). For many adult immigrants, the motivating factor for their immigration is either to improve their economic circumstances (in the form of labor immigration), flee political or ethnic persecution (as a refugee), or for the purposes of adventure. With respect to children, other than those with refugee background, many migrated as part of family reunification programs (where they accompany their parents as "baggage"), or were actually born in the host country to an immigrant family. This latter group actually does not have direct experience with the uprooting part of immigration. Thus, using models developed for first-generation adult immigrants may be inappropriate. It should therefore not be surprising that, in contrast to the earlier studies that contended that immigrant children were poorly adapted (see e.g., Bagley, 1972; Minde & Minde, 1976; Rodriguez, 1968; Schaller, 1972, 1974), recent studies on immigrant children suggest that they adapt very well (Berry et al., in press; Fuligni, 1998a, 1998b). One possible explanation for this is that the children are now being studied in their own right and with theories and models developed specifically for their situation, namely that they are undergoing both acculturation and development.

One problem with many human development theories is that they tend to lack specific information about how culture influences developmental processes. When the theory includes a cultural perspective, however, it often does so by assuming that only a single, monoculture is involved. This monoculture perspective is further presented as a background periphery context within which developmental processes have to be understood (see e.g., Bronfenbrenner, 1979). Culture is often portrayed as distal to the behavior and social interactions that take place during development. Because of the underlying monoculture assumption of existing human developmental models, two major problems that developmental models of acculturation have to overcome are, first, to incorporate two or more cultures in contact, and second, to specify how these influence the developmental outcome.

To overcome these problems, Oppedal (in press) and her colleague (Sam & Oppedal, 2002) have suggested that acculturation should be seen as an integral part of, or as embedded within, development, where children and adolescents with immigrant backgrounds' acculturation should be viewed in terms of how they develop competencies to function effectively in one or more cultural contexts. The extent to which these children manage to develop competencies within one or more contexts depends on both personal factors such as age, gender, and motivation, and contextual factors such as cultural diversity, settlement policies of the society, how much time they spend within each of the contexts, and the extent to which different contexts interact with each other. The acquired competences will affect their overall adaptation and well-being.

From a life-span developmental perspective, the interactions between the individual and the context may follow a variety of possible pathways (Valsiner & Lawrence, 1997), and for that reason it may be difficult to predict what an outcome will be. Acculturation—or bicultural development with the ability to function effectively in more than one cultural context—is one possible pathway for immigrant children and other children (including nonimmigrants) growing up in a multicultural context. Another pathway could be competence in only one culture.

ACCULTURATION DEVELOPMENT

The Model

Acculturation has classically been defined as the changes that arise when individuals and groups of different cultural backgrounds come together (see Berry, chapter 2, this volume). However, in conceptualizing acculturation as a form of development, acculturation is seen as a process whereby an individual acquires competence to function in one or more cultural contexts when the cultures in question come into contact with each other. In essence, acculturation development is akin to the cultural learning perspective (see Ward, 2001; Masgoret & Ward, in press; Berry, chapter 2, this volume). However, acculturation development differs from the cultural learning perspective on the grounds that the acquisition of competence is seen as a normal developmental process where the developing child undergoes both formal socialization as well as enculturation. In the cultural learning perspective, acculturation is seen more or less as a form of resocialization. From the acculturation development perspective, failure to acquire competence in a given context does not mean that acculturation has not taken place, but rather that the developmental changes that arose following the meeting between the two cultures followed a different pathway that may be less functional in the cultural context(s) in which the child is developing.

Human development involves a continuous, reciprocal, and dynamic interaction between the organism and the context, and this is the position taken in the acculturation development model (see Figure 6.1). Taking a developmental niche perspective, the child is the focal point of attention, placed in the center (together with his or her family) of not one, but two cultural settings: the ethnic society and the dominant host society. The outermost portion of the model is the context of a plural society. This plural society is influenced by other societies by way of immi-

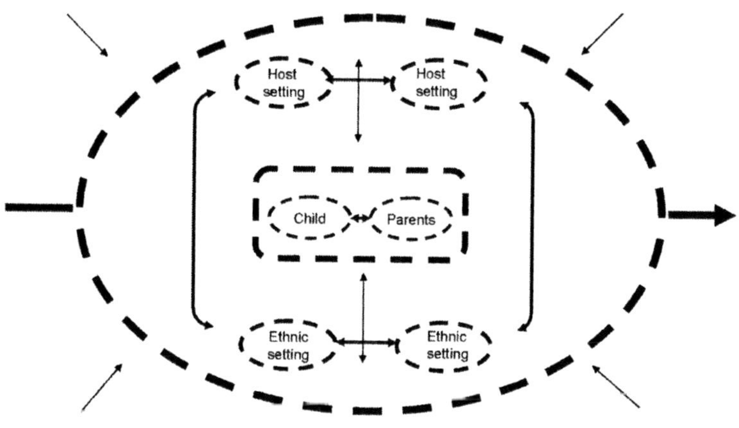

FIGURE 6.1. A general model of acculturation development pathway.

gration, globalization, et cetera (hence the perforated boundary). At the center of the model is the developing child in close interaction with his or her parents, family, and extended family (which collectively and subsequently are referred to as parents). The parent–child dyad is central to a child's development, and this "unit" is partially isolated. The partial isolation is reflected in the perforated boundary of the unit, which indicates that it is not entirely free from other contextual influences. At the two opposite poles of the main plural society are two settings: the host society cultural context, and the ethnic cultural context. These two contexts have their own particular characteristics. The dominant host society context is characterized by such settings as the school, media, health care system, and work. The ethnic context is characterized by such settings as the ethnic community traditions, religious groups and affiliation, ethnic clubs, and so on. Although these various settings are separated from each other, they are in reciprocal and mutual interaction with each other and influence each other. These are illustrated by the reciprocal arrows and perforated boundaries of the various settings. Furthermore, all the settings influence and are influenced by the developing child, either directly or indirectly through, for example, other family members. Finally, the larger plural society is influenced by other global events such as globalization and international politics. These are illustrated in the model using four arrows pointing toward the larger plural society.

Because individuals have the potential to change throughout their lives, an arrow passing through the larger context is used to depict the time-related aspect of development. As previously pointed out, the continuous dynamic interactions between individuals and the various elements of their contexts will lead to developmental changes that run along a variety of pathways. The followed pathways may be indicative of the kinds of interactions that have taken place.

Acculturation Developmental Pathways

Any particular developmental pathway is not fixed or invariant to the extent that it cannot change over the life span. On the contrary, acculturation developmental pathways have the potential to change direction in the course of the life span depending on interactions among a number of factors. These factors may include the nature of the interactions within the parent–child dyad (e.g., parenting styles), interactions between the parent–child dyad and their immediate ethnic and host contexts (e.g., the kinds of acculturative strategies preferred—see Berry, chapter 2, this volume), and interactions between the two respective ethnic and host societies (e.g., ethnic discrimination and policies that are implemented by the larger host society). All these interactions are further dependent on the personal characteristics within the parent–child dyad (e.g., age, personality), the historical point in time that the interactions are taking place, and influences from cultures and societies outside the immediate larger plural society (e.g., worldwide migration and globalization and international politics).

To further elaborate our acculturation developmental pathway, let us assume that all the interacting factors remain constant except the amount and the nature of the interactions between the parent–child dyad and the immediate ethnic and host contexts. In situations when there is equal amount of time and interactions between the two contexts, and perfect harmony within the parent–child dyad, one could expect a bicultural or integrated developmental pathway as illustrated in Figure 6.2. Similarly, it could be that both the child and the parents have closer

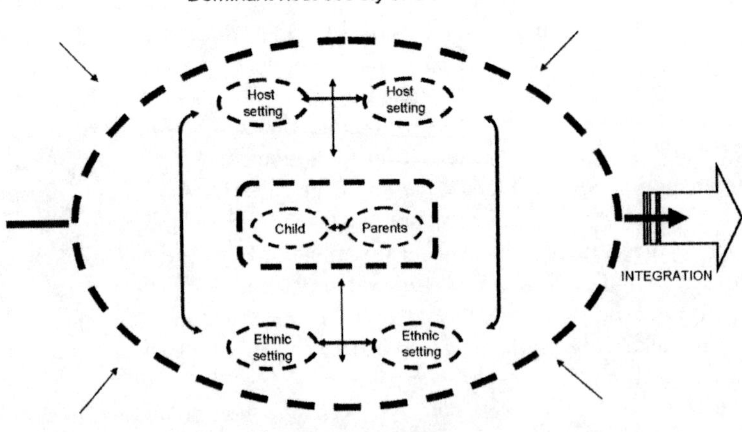

FIGURE 6.2. A model showing a possible integration pathway with balanced interactions among the factors.

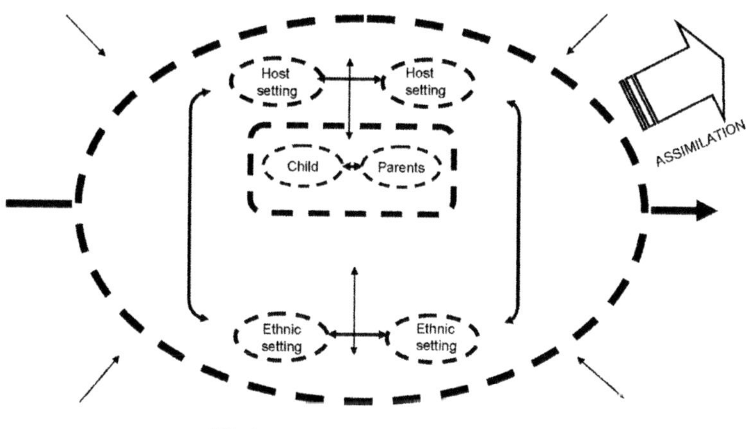

FIGURE 6.3. A model showing a possible assimilation pathway with interactions heavily in favor for host society factors.

and more interaction with the larger host community than the ethnic community. This may also follow a different pathway, such as assimilation or consonant acculturation (see Portes & Rumbaut, 2001), and this is illustrated in Figure 6.3.

In the event that both the child and parent spend more time and interaction with the ethnic context than the host context, yet a different pathway may result. This could be separation or a consonant resistance to acculturation (see Figure 6.4). It is also possible that the child may have closer and more interactions with the host context, but parents have closer interaction with the ethnic context (see Figure 6.5), leading to perhaps dissonant acculturation. Another possible pathway might be the situation where the child has closer and more contact with the ethnic context than the parents have with the ethnic context, but the parents have more contact with the host context (see Figure 6.6). This situation is thought of as unlikely, and therefore no term describing this pathway has been found in the literature. However, from the acculturation development pathway, everything is possible, and finding no term in the literature is possibly because these types of interactions have not been explored in acculturation studies.

Assuming that all other factors are held constant, the different pathways described depend largely on the amount of interaction the child and the parents have with the different cultural contexts. However, in real-life settings, all these other factors are constantly changing and interacting with each other. Within the parent–child dyad, the interactions may not be as simple as portrayed here, in that the interactions between the mother and the child may be different from the one between the father and the child, and these may differ between the child in question and his or her respective siblings (see the developmental niche model of Super

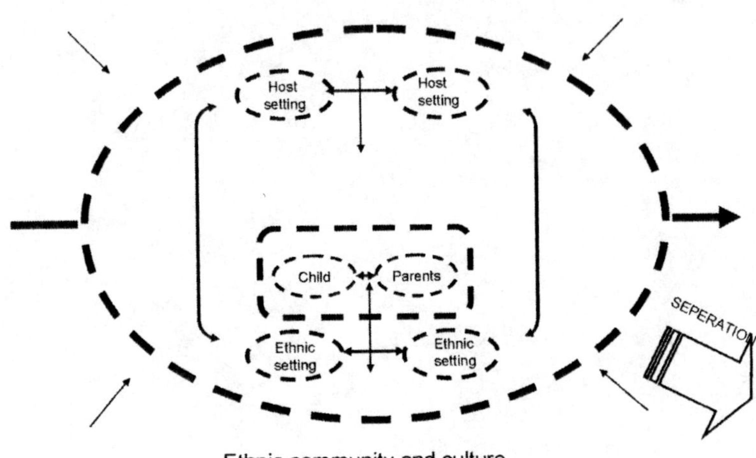

FIGURE 6.4. A model showing a possible separation pathway with interactions heavily in favor for ethnic community factors.

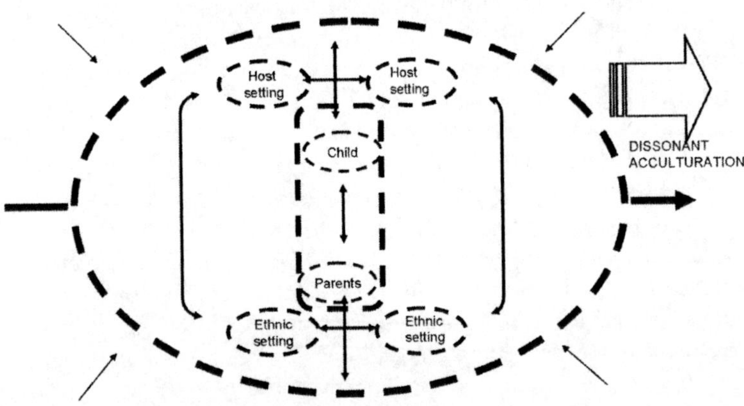

FIGURE 6.5. A model showing a possible dissonant acculturation with different interactions between the child and the parents and the host and ethnic communities.

& Harkness, 1997). Taking all the interactions together, it is impossible to predict the developmental outcome of an individual, except to speak of a "here and now" outcome. Any given developmental pathway will affect the person's psychological and sociocultural adaptation. In our models we have used terms such as *consonant acculturation* and *integration* to describe different pathways and

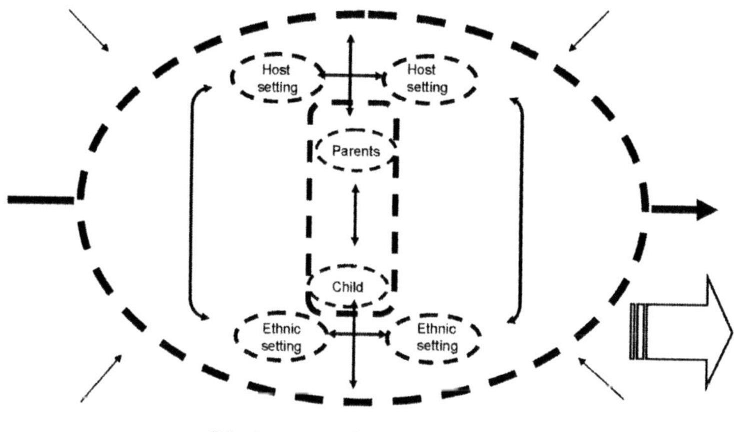

FIGURE 6.6. A model showing a possible pathway with different interactions between the child and the parents and the host and ethnic communities.

outcomes. However, the use of these terms should be seen only as approximations of immigrant children's acculturation development experience at a particular time and in a given cultural context.

Partial Support for the Model

According to the acculturation development model, an immigrant child's adaptation is a reflection of the competencies he or she has developed in his or her interaction with the two contexts: the ethnic community and the dominant host societies. Generally, the amount of time spent within the context will affect the quality of competence one develops. Furthermore, the interactions within the different contexts will influence the amount of social support the child receives from the particular context. How much competence the child develops will, in the long run, affect the child's self-concept and his or her mental health.

From the acculturation development perspective, one should therefore expect two parallel lines of development (i.e., competence), one arising from interactions with the host society resulting in host culture competence, and the other arising from interactions within the ethnic community resulting in ethnic competence. These two lines of development will result in the child's self-concept and then his or her overall mental health. This model was partially tested in a 1-year longitudinal study among 137 immigrant youth living in Oslo (Oppedal, Røysamb, & Sam, 2004). The first data collection for the study took place when the youth were in the 8th grade (average age was 13 years old) and the second data collection took place a year later when they were in the 9th grade.

In testing out the model, interaction between parents and child was examined as family social support and was part of the interactions within the ethnic community. Included in this development path was social support from ethnic friends. Regarding interactions within the host society, the researchers examined different forms of social support at school, support from teachers, and support from classmates. In addition, perceived ethnic discrimination was examined as part of the within-host culture interactions. Ethnic and host competence in the study were assessed using mastery in their own ethnic and the relevant host national language (i.e., Norwegian); number of friends among their own ethnic group versus the dominant host group, and frequency of interactions with these friends and ethnic versus host national identity. Self-esteem and mental health were respectively measured using Rosenberg's (1965) 10-item scale and the 25-item Hopkins Symptom Check List (Derogatis, Lipman, Richels, Uhlenhuth, & Covi, 1974).

Using a structural equation model, the researchers found support (following some modifications of the original model) for the fact that there are indirect paths for the effect of acculturation on mental health change. One path passes through culture domain-specific social support and the other through self-esteem. Significant interaction effects between social support and culture competencies were demonstrated, in addition to buffer effects of social class support on perceived ethnic discrimination.

CONCLUSIONS

In this chapter, we argued for the need to understand young immigrants' acculturation as part of their development rather than as a separate process. Furthermore, we argued that the essence of acculturation development is to acquire competencies so as to function effectively in the two cultures in contact. The acquisition of competence is dependent on how much the child interacts with his or her ethnic community and the dominant host society, as well as the nature of the interactions the child has with his or her family.

Although most acculturation studies are concerned about attitudes and behaviors toward the ethnic culture and the host society, these are not enough in providing full understanding of how the child gains competence. The amount of time the child spends interacting with each of the two settings and how the two settings interact with each other should be incorporated into research designs. Whereas information from the former area (i.e., how much time the child spends interacting with the two settings) can be obtained from the child, the latter source of information requires ethnographic information. Inasmuch as development is an ongoing process, it is important that research is not limited to one-time data collection as is the case in cross-sectional studies. Including longitudinal studies will help tease out what changes are taking place and which factors are responsible for the different changes.

Although this chapter has essentially focused on immigrant children, it is important to mention that nonimmigrant children also experience some form of acculturation and their development is affected by being in contact with other ethnic groups. In essence, studies on the development of nonimmigrant children in plural societies will benefit greatly by examining acculturation issues among these children as well.

ACKNOWLEDGMENTS

Portions of this chapter were adapted from:

Sam, D. L., Kosic, A., & Oppedal, B. (2003). Where is "development" in acculturation theories? *International Society for the Study of Behavioural Development (ISSBD) Newsletter, 44*, 24–27.

REFERENCES

Aronowitz, M. (1984). The social and emotional adjustment of immigrant children. A review of literature. *International Migration Review, 18*, 237–257.

Bagley, C. (1972). Deviant behaviour in English and West Indian school children. *Research in Education, 8*, 47–55.

Bashir, M. R. (1993). Issues of immigration for the health and adjustment of young people. *Journal of Paediatrics and Child Health, 9*(Supplement 1), 42–45.

Berry, J. W. (1997). Immigration, acculturation and adaptation. *Applied Psychology, 46*, 5–68.

Berry, J. W., Phinney, J. S., Sam, D. L., & Vedder, P. H. (in press). *Immigrant youth in cultural transition: Acculturation, identity, and adaptation across national contexts*. Mahwah, NJ: Lawrence Erlbaum Associates.

Berry, J. W., Poortinga, Y. H., Segall, M. H., & Dasen, P. R. (2002). *Cross-cultural psychology: Research and applications* (2nd ed.). Cambridge, UK: Cambridge University Press.

Berry, J. W., & Sam, D. (1997). Acculturation and adaptation. In J. W. Berry, M. H. Segall, & C. Kagitcibasi (Eds.), *Handbook of cross-cultural psychology: Vol. 3. Social behavior and applications* (2nd ed., pp. 291–326). Boston: Allyn & Bacon.

Bronfenbrenner, U. (1979). *The ecology of human development*. Cambridge: Harvard University Press.

Buriel, R., & de Ment, T. L. (1997). Immigration and sociocultural change in Mexican, Chinese and Vietnamese American families. In A. Booth, A. C. Crouter, & N. Landale (Eds.), *Immigration and the family: Research and policy on U.S. immigrants* (pp. 165–200). Mahwah, NJ: Lawrence Erlbaum Associates.

Costigan, C. L., & Su, T. F. (2004). Orthogonal versus lineal models of acculturation among immigrant Chinese Canadians: A comparison of mothers, fathers, and children. *International Journal of Behavioral Development, 28*, 518–527.

Derogatis, L. R., Lipman, R. S., Richels, K., Uhlenhuth, E. H., & Covi, L. (1974). The Hopkins Symptom Check List (HSCL): A self-report symptoms inventory. *Behavioral Science, 19*, 1–15.

Evans, J. (1987). Introduction: Migration and health. *International Migration Review, 21*, v–xiv.

Fuligni, A. J. (1997). The academic achievement of adolescents from immigrant families: The role of family background, attitudes and behavior. *Child Development, 68*, 261–273.

Fuligni, A. J. (1998a). The adjustment of children from immigrant families. *Current Directions in Psychological Science, 7*(4), 99–103.

Fuligni, A. J. (1998b). Adolescents from immigrants families. In V. C. McLoyd & L. Steinberg (Eds.), *Studying minority adolescents: Conceptual, methodological and theoretical issues* (pp. 127–143). Mahwah, NJ: Lawrence Erlbaum Associates.

Fuligni, A. J. (2003). The adaptation of children from immigrant families. *Newsletter of International Society for the Study of Behavioral Development, 44*, 2–11.

Garcia Coll, C., & Magnuson, K. (1997). The psychological experience of immigration: A developmental perspective. In A. Booth, A. C. Crouter, & N. Landale (Eds.), *Immigration and the family: Research and policy on U.S. immigrants* (pp. 91–132). Mahwah, NJ: Lawrence Erlbaum Associates.

Harris, K. M. (1999). The health status and risk behaviors of adolescents in immigrant families. In D. J. Hernandez (Ed.), *Children of immigrants: Health, adjustment and public assistance* (pp. 286–315). Washington, DC: National Academy Press.

Hernandez, D. J. (1999). Children of immigrants: Health, adjustment and public assistance. In D. J. Hernandez (Ed.), *Children of immigrants: Health, adjustment and public assistance* (pp. 1–18). Washington, DC: National Academy Press.

Kwak, K. (1991). *Second language learning in a multicultural society: A comparison between the learning of a dominant language and a heritage*. PhD thesis, Queen's University, Kingston, ON, Canada.

Kwak, K. (2003). Adolescents and their parents: A review of intergenerational family relations for immigrant and non-immigrant families. *Human Development, 46*, 115–136.

Laosa, L. M. (1997). Research perspectives on constructs of change. Intercultural migration and developmental transitions. In A. Booth, A. C. Crouter, & N. Landale (Eds.), *Immigration and the family: Research and policy on U.S. immigrants* (pp. 133–148). Mahwah, NJ: Lawrence Erlbaum Associates.

Lerner, R. M. (2001). *Concepts and theories of human development* (3rd ed.). Mahwah, NJ: Lawrence Erlbaum Associates.

Liebkind, K. (2001). Acculturation. In R. Brown & S. Gaetner (Eds.), *Blackwell handbook of social psychology: Vol. 3. Intergroup processes* (pp. 386–406). Oxford: Blackwell.

Masgoret, A.-M., & Ward, C. (in press). Cultural learning perspective to acculturation. In D. L. Sam & J. W. Berry (Eds.), *Cambridge handbook of acculturation psychology*. Cambridge, UK: Cambridge University Press.

Mautino, K. S. (2001). Health issues among immigrant children. *Journal of Immigrant Health, 3*, 169–171.

McKay, L., Macintyre, S., & Ellaway, A. (2003). Migration and health. A review of the international literature. *Occasional Paper 12*. Glasgow, Scotland: Medical Research Council, Social and Public Health Sciences Unit.

Minde, K., & Minde, R. (1976). Children of immigrants: The adjustment of Ugandan Asian primary school children. *Canadian Psychiatric Association Journal, 21*, 371–381.

Murphy, H. B. M. (1977). Migration, culture and mental health. *Psychological Medicine, 7*, 677–684.

Oppedal, B. (in press). Acculturation development. In D. L. Sam & J. W. Berry (Eds.), *Cambridge handbook of acculturation psychology*. Cambridge, UK: Cambridge University Press.

Oppedal, B., Røysamb, E., & Sam, D. L. (2004). The effect of acculturation and social support on change in mental health among young immigrants. *International Journal of Behavioural Development, 28*, 481–494.

Phinney, J., & Ong, A. (2002). Adolescent–parent disagreements and life satisfaction in families from Vietnamese- and European-American backgrounds. *International Journal of Behavioral Development, 26*, 556–561.

Phinney, J., Ong, A., & Madden, T. (2000). Cultural values and intergenerational value discrepancies in immigrant and non-immigrant families. *Child Development, 71*, 528–539.

Portes, A. R., & Rumbaut, R. G. (2001). *Legacies: The story of immigrant second generation*. Berkeley: University of California Press.

Rick, K., & Forward, J. (1992). Acculturation and perceived intergenerational differences among youth. *Journal of Cross-Cultural Psychology, 23*, 85–94.

Rodriguez, R. (1968). Difficulties of adjustment in immigrant children in Geneva. *Medecine et Hygiene, 845*, 1–6.

Rosenberg, M. (1965). *Society and the adolescent self-image*. Princeton, NJ: Princeton University Press.

Sam, D. L. (1995). Acculturation attitudes among young immigrants as a function of perceived parental attitudes towards cultural change. *Journal of Early Adolescence, 15*, 238–258.

Sam, D. L., & Oppedal, B. (2002). Acculturation as a developmental pathway. In W. J. Lonner, D. L. Dinnel, S. A. Hayes, & D. N. Sattler (Eds.), *Online readings in psychology and culture* (Unit 8, Chapter 6). Available online: http://www.wwu.edu/~culture

Sam, D. L., & Virta, E. (2003). Intergenerational value discrepancies in immigrant and host-national families and their impact on psychological adaptation. *Journal of Adolescence, 26*, 213–231.

Schaller, J. (1972). Residential change and emotional maladjustment in children and adolescents: A review of Research. *Gotenberg Psychological Reports, 2*, 1–11.

Schaller, J. (1974). The relations between geographic mobility and school behaviour. *Gotenberg Psychological Reports, 4*, 1–17.

Siantz, M. L. d. L. (1997). Factors that impact developmental outcomes. In A. Booth, A. C. Crouter, & N. Landale (Eds.), *Immigration and the family: Research and policy on U.S. immigrants* (pp. 149–161). Mahwah, NJ: Lawrence Erlbaum Associates.

Super, C., & Harkness, S. (1997). The structuring of child development. In J. W. Berry, P. R. Dasen, & S. Saraswathi (Eds.), *Handbook of cross-cultural psychology: Vol. 2. Basic processes and human development* (2nd ed., pp. 1–39). Boston: Allyn & Bacon.

Szapocznik, J., & Kurtines, W. (1993). Family psychology and cultural diversity. *American Psychologist, 48*, 400–407.

Valsiner, J., & Lawrence, J. (1997). Human development in culture across the life span. In J. W. Berry, P. R. Dasen, & T. S. Saraswathi (Eds.), *Handbook of cross-cultural psychology: Vol. 2. Basic processes and human development* (2nd ed., pp. 69–106). Boston: Allyn & Bacon.

Virta, E., Sam, D. L., & Westin, C. (2004). Adolescents with Turkish background in Norway and Sweden: A comparative study of their psychological adaptation. *Scandinavian Journal of Psychology, 45*, 15–25.

Virta, E., & Westin, C. (1999). Psychological adjustment of adolescents with immigrant background in Sweden. *Occasional Papers, No 2*. Stockholm: Stockholm University.

Ward, C. (2001). The ABCs of acculturation. In D. Matsumoto (Ed.), *Handbook of psychology and culture* (pp. 411–445). Oxford, UK: Oxford University Press.

Zhou, M. (1997). Segmented assimilation: Issues controversies and recent research on the new second generation. *International Migration Review, 31*, 975–1008.

Internet References

http://www.statistics.gov.uk

http://www12.statcan.ca/english/census01

7

Measurement of the "Acculturation Gap" in Immigrant Families and Implications for Parent–Child Relationships

Dina Birman
University of Illinois at Chicago, U.S.A.

INTRODUCTION

One of the most important challenges that immigrant and refugee families confront involves what researchers have called the *acculturation gap* between parents and children (Kwak, 2003; Merali, 2002). Acculturation is a developmental process, as children and adults acculturate to a new culture and retain affiliation with the culture of origin at different rates (Birman & Trickett, 2001). As a result, acculturation gaps arise between parents and children, and these gaps are thought to be potentially problematic for parent–child relationships.

A great deal has been written about the importance of acculturation gaps in immigrant families, but empirical studies that describe such gaps and document the links between acculturation gaps and family relationships are only beginning to emerge. This chapter reviews this emerging literature and makes recommendations for future research. First, the chapter reviews the varied research designs used in published studies on the acculturation gap. Next, a discussion of the ways that acculturation gaps have been conceptualized and measured in these studies is provided. This is followed by an example from the author's research that illustrates differences in measurement approaches. The chapter concludes with recommendations for research design and measurement on this topic.

THE ACCULTURATION GAP

As discussed in the literature, the acculturation gap is seen as extending across a variety of life domains and aspects of parent–child relationships. For example, children adapt to the norms of their peer group relatively quickly, but their parents, who immigrated as adults, may never acquire sufficient comfort with the new language and culture to become socially integrated into their new country. In addition, immigrant children may have few opportunities to participate in and learn about their native culture, and they lack access to the kinds of formal instruction and informal socialization that they would have received in their country of origin. As a result, over time, immigrant parents and children increasingly live in different cultural worlds, which can make it difficult for them to understand one another and can create difficulties in their relationships.

The implications of this gap for parent–child relationships are potentially broad in impact. Immigrant parents often know little about their children's lives outside the home. Consider the experience of immigrant families in the United States. Not having grown up in American society themselves and gone to its schools, immigrant parents are unfamiliar with how American schools operate and may not have the English language skills to communicate with the teachers and other staff (Delgado-Gaitan, 1985, 1994a, 1994b; Grolnick, Benjet, Kurowski, & Apostoleris, 1997). Immigrant parents may also lack knowledge and connection to programs and resources available to their children outside or after school. As a result, immigrant parents may find it difficult to guide and to monitor their children's activities (Hao & Bonstead-Bruns, 1998; Mau, 1997).

For immigrant children, it can be difficult to live with the expectations and demands of one culture in the home and another at school and elsewhere outside the home. Children may not turn to their parents with problems and concerns, believing that their parents do not know the culture and its institutions well enough to provide them with good advice or assistance. In addition, they may see their parents as already burdened with the multiple stresses of resettlement and as psychologically unavailable more generally. At the same time, immigrant parents often rely on children to help them with the new language and culture in such situations as doctors' appointments, parent–teacher conferences, and with financial and legal documents (Buriel, Love, & De Ment, chapter 12, this volume; Chao, chapter 13, this volume). This "culture broker" role can place great responsibility on children and at the same time undermine their parents' authority in their eyes (Jones & Trickett, 2005; Portes & Rumbaut, 1990).

Alternatively, adolescents may embrace the opportunity to engage in unsupervised activities and may have ambivalent feelings about their parents' inability to fully understand their experience. Szapocznik, Scopetta, Kurtines, and Aranalde (1978) suggested that immigrant adolescents who become overly acculturated to the American culture and disconnected from their native culture are at particularly high risk for substance abuse and other high-risk behaviors. Such "overacculturation" has been a target of interventions designed to reduce adolescent conduct problems and improve family relationships in Hispanic immigrant families (Szapocznik, Rio, Perez-Vidal, Kurtines, & Santisteban, 1986; Szapocznik, Santisteban, Kurtines, Perez-Vidal, & Hervis, 1984).

STUDIES OF ACCULTURATION GAP AND FAMILY RELATIONSHIPS

Empirical studies of the acculturation gap and its implications for family functioning have adopted a range of approaches to conceptualizing and measuring both acculturation and the gap. Each approach involves a distinctive set of assumptions and asks slightly different questions. They include comparative studies of conflict in immigrant and nonimmigrant families, studies of the link between acculturation of adolescents and family relationships, and studies of the link between an acculturation gap between parents and children and family relationships.

Comparative Studies

One approach to establishing the existence and impact of the acculturation gap has been to conduct comparative studies assessing the degree of conflict between immigrant and nonimmigrant parents and children. For example, Dinh, Sarason, and Sarason (1994) compared Vietnamese immigrant and U.S.-born families and found greater levels of conflict and reports of less positive relationships between immigrant parents and children. Nguyen and Williams (1989) also compared Vietnamese immigrant and European American families in the United States and found a greater generation gap with respect to values and beliefs among Vietnamese families. Furthermore, differences in values and beliefs between Vietnamese parents and their children were found to increase with length of time in United States. Similarly, Rosenthal (1984) measured the amount of disagreement between parents and children among Anglo Australians and Greek and Italian immigrants to Australia. Anglo Australian adolescents, mothers, and fathers reported significantly less family conflict than did Greek and Italian immigrants. These studies suggest that there is greater disagreement and conflict among parents and children in immigrant compared to nonimmigrant families in the U.S. and Australian samples studied.

In general, comparative studies *infer* that the level of conflict in immigrant families can be attributed to the acculturation gap between parents and children. However, other explanations for the differences found are also possible. For example, Rosenthal and colleagues (Rosenthal, 1984; Rosenthal, Bell, Demetriou, & Efklides, 1989; Rosenthal & Bornholt, 1988) pointed out that greater conflict in Greek and Italian immigrant families may be due to differences in expressions of emotion across these cultures, with Anglo Australians being less likely to express conflict and disagreement directly than the immigrant groups. On the other hand, Vietnamese immigrant families may display greater conflict with length of residence in the United States because intergenerational conflict may be more acceptable in the American culture to which they are acculturating. Thus, greater conflict, if found in immigrant families and over time, may be due to cultural differences in the ways that family members relate to each other, rather than problems in parent–child relationships.

In addition, Gil and Vega (1996) found that the presence of parent–child conflicts in Cuban and Nicaraguan immigrant families in Miami was related to the level of acculturative *stress* reported by parents. Although this study did not assess the acculturation gap, the study offers an alternative explanation for why parent–child conflict may be more likely to occur in immigrant families. Here, it is the amount of stress and difficulties experienced by parents in resettlement that may contribute to parent–child conflicts, rather than an acculturation gap between parents and children per se. Thus overall, comparative studies are helpful in identifying differences between immigrant and nonimmigrant families, but they do not definitively answer the question of whether the acculturation gap creates parent–child conflicts in immigrant families.

Studies of Acculturation and Family Adjustment

Another approach to understanding the impact of acculturation gaps has been to examine the link between the child's level of acculturation and family adjustment. Here, as in the comparative studies, the acculturation gap is inferred rather than measured directly. For example, several studies have suggested that the greater the child's acculturation to their native culture, the better the family adjustment for immigrant children. In a study of Chinese immigrants, children's Chinese language proficiency was positively related to mother–child cohesion (Luo & Wiseman, 2000). Another study of Chinese American children found that bilingual and Chinese monolingual children experienced less family conflict than children who are English monolingual (Portes & Hao, 2002). Here, the assumption was that retention of native culture and language *implied* less of a parent–child gap with respect to native culture, which in turn positively affected family functioning.

In addition, some studies have demonstrated that higher levels of acculturation to the new culture in immigrant adolescents were related to positive family adjustment, contrary to expectations of acculturation gap theories. In a study of multiethnic Asian American college students, those belonging to the "acculturated" group reported lower intergenerational conflict than those in the low acculturated and bicultural groups (Chung, 2001). Another study found that acculturation to American and not Latino culture was related to perceived competence as a family member on the part of Central American immigrant adolescents (Birman, 1998). Different alternative explanations for these findings were offered. Chung (2001) invoked an acculturation gap explanation, reasoning that the acculturated students reported lower conflict because they were mostly second generation or higher, which increased the likelihood of their parents also being American acculturated. This, in turn, would decrease the acculturation gap and result in lower family conflict. Birman (1998), however, suggested that Americanized adolescents were better able to function as culture brokers for their parents, leading to more positive assessments of themselves as family members. These findings do not support the notion that adolescents who have higher levels of acculturation to the new culture have worse relationships with their parents, and do not support the acculturation gap hypothesis.

Other studies have found that acculturation to *both* the native and the American culture may be beneficial for family adjustment of immigrant adolescents. Nguyen, Messe, and Stollak (1999) found that Vietnamese American adolescents' involvement with Vietnamese culture and their involvement with U.S. culture were both positively associated with their report of family relationship quality. Similarly, in two different studies of immigrants and refugees from the former Soviet Union, we found that both Russian and American acculturation of adolescents predicted perceived support from parents (Birman, Trickett, & Buchanan, 2005; Birman, Trickett, & Vinokurov, 2002). These findings are also inconsistent with the acculturation gap hypothesis, which would predict that adolescents' acculturation to the American culture may widen the acculturation gap with their parents and decrease the quality of parent–child relations.

Overall, the studies reviewed suggest a link between adolescent acculturation and family relationships for new and later generation immigrant families. However, if some of these studies suggest that greater levels of acculturation to the native culture for the child imply a smaller acculturation gap with parents, and thus better family adjustment, other studies do not support this assumption. In addition, none assessed the acculturation gap directly, although some invoked it as a post hoc explanatory concept. To assess the impact of the acculturation gap, research must explicitly assess levels of acculturation of both the parent and the child in the same study, rather than assume it.

Studies of Acculturation Gaps: Perceived Gaps

Increasingly, research is emerging that assesses the acculturation *gap* between parents and children. To date, most of these studies have assessed "perceived" gaps. In other words, they assessed the discrepancy in levels of acculturation between parents and children through either parent or child report only. Rick and Forward (1992) reported on a study of Hmong high school students who were asked to rate their own acculturation and their perception of their parents' acculturation level. Students reported higher American acculturation levels for themselves than for their parents. Greater acculturation levels of adolescents predicted greater perceived acculturation gaps with their parents. However, acculturation gaps did not predict greater family conflict.

Buki, Ma, Strom, and Strom (2003) assessed Chinese immigrant mothers who reported on their own level of acculturation and their perceptions of acculturation of their teenage children. The acculturation gap was computed by subtracting the mother's score from the child's score. Larger acculturation gaps were related to mothers' reports of greater difficulty communicating with children, as well as more uncertainty and less satisfaction with their own parenting behavior.

Lee, Choe, Kim, and Ngo (2000) studied Asian American college students who completed acculturation measures for themselves and a two-item perceived parents' acculturation index. Results suggested that parents' perceived level of acculturation, as well as the interaction between students' and parents' acculturation, were associated with greater family conflict. Post hoc analyses divided the families into four groups based on combinations of parents' and children's acculturation score levels: both high, both low, parents high and children low, or children high and parents low. Family conflict was lowest when both children and parents had high acculturation scores, suggesting greater conflict for families with acculturation dissonance.

Although some of these studies suggest that the acculturation gap is associated with greater degree of conflict and parent–child disagreement in immigrant families, one shared limitation is that acculturation as well as family adjustment were assessed from only one perspective, either the parent (Buki et al., 2003) or the child (Lee et al., 2000; Rick & Forward, 1992). There are at least two potential problems with this approach. One is that children and parents may over- or underestimate each other's level of acculturation. The second is that self-reported perceptions of the gap may inadvertently be confounded with perceptions of family discord.

The over- or underestimation issue was examined by Merali (2002) in a study of Hispanic refugee parent–child dyads. Parents and adolescents reported on their own level of assimilation as well as their perceptions of their parent's or child's level of assimilation. Perceived disparity was computed by subtracting one's own score from the perceived other's score (similar to procedures used by Rick & Forward and Buki et al.), whereas the actual disparity was computed by subtracting actual scores of each family member from scores of the other. An error score was calculated for each dyad using the absolute value of the difference between perceived disparity and the actual disparity. Only one parent and four adolescents out of a sample of 50 families made accurate judgments about the other's assimilation level, ending up with the same score for the perceived and actual acculturation levels. The majority of parents (72%) and adolescents (54%) underestimated the disparity between them. These findings suggest the importance of including both parent and child measures of acculturation and not only the perceived gap reported by one or the other.

The issue of the potential confound of self-report acculturation discrepancies with family discord may occur under a variety of conditions. For example, children may attribute normative parent–adolescent conflict around such issues as autonomy to acculturation discrepancies rather than other reasons. As Merali (2002) pointed out, "An overestimation of the actual degree of inter-generational gaps can be considered to be a negative illusion or health-compromising belief. This type of misappraisal would be most likely to relate to the experience of depression" (p. 65). The only way to disentangle such potential confounds is to assess acculturation of parents and children independently, and assess family adjustment from both perspectives.

Studies of Acculturation Gaps: Actual Gaps

Actual gaps refer to the gaps between child and parent reports of their own levels of acculturation. Several studies have assessed parents and children independently and computed these actual acculturation gaps. Farver, Narang, and Bhadha (2002) assessed Asian Indian adolescents and parents using the ARMSA-II acculturation scale (Cuellar, Arnold, & Maldonado, 1995), adapted for Asian Indians, as well as an Issues Checklist that documented the degree of frequency and intensity of parent–child conflicts. Parents and children were classified into one of four acculturation style groups derived from this acculturation measure: assimilated, marginal, separatist, and bicultural styles. Families were then sorted into two groups based on whether the parents and children were matched or mismatched in acculturation style. Lower frequencies and intensity of conflict were found in the matched groups, suggesting that mismatch on acculturation was related to greater family conflict and disagreement between parents and adolescents. Furthermore, adolescents in mismatched families reported lower self-esteem and higher anxiety. Thus, the study suggests that family acculturation gaps may contribute, not only to increased family conflict, but also to negative psychological outcomes for adolescents.

Pawliuk et al. (1996) studied families from diverse immigrant backgrounds at a Montreal pediatric clinic. The acculturation gap groups were derived in a similar way as in the Farver, Narang, and Bhadha (2002) study, by assigning children and parents to one of four acculturation groups and then grouping them into those who were matched or mismatched on acculturative styles. Children who adopted the same acculturation style as their parents scored significantly higher on the social competence subscale than did children whose acculturation style differed from their parents, suggesting a negative impact of the gap.

Overall, a number of different types of studies have been conducted to answer the question of whether acculturation gaps in immigrant families are related to problems in family relationships. These include comparative studies of immigrants and nonimmigrants, studies of how the acculturation of adolescents links to family relationships, and studies of both parent and adolescent acculturation. Of these, studies that have independently assessed actual acculturation gaps are best able to address the question of whether acculturation gaps contribute to difficulties in parent–child relationships directly. Most studies suggest that acculturation gaps are related to difficulties in family relationships for the few immigrant groups studied.

However, each of these studies has computed or operationalized both acculturation and the acculturation gap in a slightly different way. In order to advance this line of research, a more precise understanding of these different approaches to conceptualizing and operationalizing acculturation gaps is needed to ensure that there is agreement with respect to the meaning of the construct and, hence, the gap. To that end, the next section reviews the differences in measurement of acculturation and computation of acculturation gaps across studies. The focus is on studies that assessed either the perceived or actual acculturation gap.

ISSUES IN CONCEPTUALIZING AND COMPUTING ACCULTURATION GAPS

Each of the studies described that assessed acculturation of both parents and children used a different procedure to compute the acculturation gap. The specific computation used rests in part on the model and measurement of acculturation used in a particular study. Furthermore, the different procedures used are derived from slightly different conceptualizations of the meaning of the gap.

Computation of Acculturation Gaps: Acculturation Models Used

The way in which the gap is computed in a given study rests in part on the measures of acculturation used and the ways in which acculturation scores are derived. Broadly, the main distinction in acculturation research is between studies that conceptualize acculturation as a one-dimensional process and those that view it as two-dimensional. The implications of these two different conceptualizations for measurement of acculturation and computation of acculturation gaps in families are summarized in Table 7.1, and described next.

The one-dimensional approach to acculturation (see Table 7.1) views it as a zero-sum process of assimilation, with acquisition of aspects of the new/host culture displacing acculturation to the native culture over time. Items in such measures generally assume that the greater one's acculturation to the host culture, the less is acculturation to the native culture (e.g., Cuellar, Harris, & Jasso, 1980; Suinn, Knoo, & Ahuna, 1995; Szapocznik et al., 1978). The resulting acculturation score indicates an individual's position on a continuum between the new and the old culture. With respect to the acculturation gap literature, for example, Buki et al. (2003) and Merali (2002) used such measures.

Two-dimensional approaches argue that acculturation involves two independent processes of acculturation, one to the new culture and the other to the native culture. Two different two-dimensional measurement approaches have been used in acculturation research, the four-fold paradigm approach (see Table 7.1) and the "orthogonal" or independent measurement approach. The four-fold

TABLE 7.1
Conceptualization and Measurement of Acculturation, and Computation of Acculturation Gaps in Select Studies

	Conceptualization of Acculturation		
	One-dimensional: Acculturation to the new culture is inversely related to acculturation to the native culture	*Two-dimensional: Acculturation to new and native cultures occur independently*	
1. Types of measures	One-dimensional	Four-fold	Independent ("Orthogonal")
2. Acculturation score(s) obtained	1 score signifying "assimilation"	4 scores representing extent of endorsement of each of the 4 categories (assimilation, marginality, integration and separation), or sample is divided into the 4 groups	2 scores, one for acculturation to the new, and one for acculturation to the native culture
3. Computation of acculturation gap	Differences Score (child's acculturation score minus parent's)	Formed 2 groups of families: parents and children matched on acculturation style, and mismatched	Examined interaction of parent and adolescent acculturation
4. Examples of acculturation gap studies using these measures	Buki et al. (2003) Merali (2002)[a] Rick and Forward (1992)	Farver, Narang, and Bhadha (2002) Pawliuk et al. (1996)	Birman (2005) Lee et al. (2000)

[a]Used absolute value of the difference score.

measurement paradigm, suggested by Berry (chapter 2, this volume; Berry, Trimble, & Olmedo, 1986) locates acculturating individuals in one of four categories of acculturative styles: assimilation, marginality, separation, or integration. Studies using this approach (e.g., Kwak & Berry, 2001) assess the extent to which respondents endorse each of the four acculturation attitudes and obtain four scores for each respondent, indicating the extent to which she or he endorses each of these attitudes.

A different, two-dimensional approach is to use "orthogonal" or independent measures (e.g., Oetting & Beauvais, 1990). These types of measures include two separate scales that assess acculturation, one with respect to the new culture, and one with respect to the native culture. The resulting scores can then be used independently or as in interaction to predict outcomes of interest (Birman, 1998; H. Nguyen et al., 1999).

Each of these ways of measuring acculturation yields somewhat different information. One-dimensional measures have been criticized as providing somewhat misleading information about one's acculturation status by forcing individuals to choose either one culture or another, rather than giving them opportunities to endorse a bicultural acculturative style. In response, some authors have revised their one-dimensional scales to make them two-dimensional (e.g., Cuellar et al., 1995; Szapocznik, Kurtines, & Fernandez, 1980). The two-dimensional measurement approaches are seen as providing more accurate information about an individual's acculturative stance.

In addition, the four-fold paradigm yields different information than the "orthogonal" approach because it classifies respondents into broad acculturation "styles," whereas the "orthogonal" or independent measurement approach provides information about each individual's standing with respect to each culture. Importantly, each of the ways of measuring acculturation has very specific implications for how the acculturation gap between parents and children is conceptualized and computed.

Computation of Acculturation Gaps: Operationalizing Parent–Child Discrepancies

In addition to different ways of conceptualizing and measuring acculturation, different strategies for computing the acculturation gap are also reported. One approach is to compute or establish the degree of discrepancy in acculturation between parents and children regardless of the types of discrepancies that occur. The other approach is to determine whether particular combinations of parent and child acculturative styles are related to parent–child relationships and family adjustment. These approaches are also summarized in Table 7.1.

Acculturation Gap as Difference Scores

Rick and Forward (1992), Merali (2002), and Buki et al. (2003) computed difference scores between parent and child levels of acculturation by subtracting the parent's score from the child's. Because these studies assessed acculturation based on a one-dimensional framework examining the extent of assimilation to the new culture, the difference score summarized the extent of *assimilation* discrepancy between parents and children.

One issue in using difference scores is that they assume that differences between parents and children always occur in the same direction, with children more acculturated to the new/host culture than the parents, and parents more acculturated to the native culture than the children. However, several studies suggest that this may not always be the case. For example, Birman and Trickett (2001) and

Farver, Bhadha, and Narang (2002) found that some immigrant children scored higher on measures of ethnic identity than their parents, an unexpected finding given the assumption in the literature that parents are more attached to native culture than children. When such patterns occur in families, the difference score procedure would create positive gap scores for some families and negative scores for others. To address this issue, Merali (2002) used the absolute value of the difference in parent–child acculturation scores to compute the gap. In this way, the difference score represents the extent of parent–child dissonance, regardless of the direction of the difference.

Matched/Mismatched Groups

A similar approach to operationalizing the acculturation gap has been to use the four-fold classification of acculturative styles (assimilation, integration, marginalization, separation) to derive two groups of families: those families where parents and children were matched on their acculturation style and those families where the acculturation styles were mismatched (e.g., Farver, Narang, & Bhadha, 2002; Pawliuk et al., 1996). Both the difference score and the matched/mismatched group approach allow the researcher to conceptualize and summarize the gap as the presence of acculturation discrepancies between parents and children. Analyses can then be conducted to test the assumption that it is the discrepancies in families that contribute to family conflicts and maladjustment.

However, several limitations of both these strategies affect our understanding of the nature of the acculturation gap and its implications for family functioning. Some limitations have already been mentioned, such as the conceptual concern with one-dimensional measures of acculturation. The literature on acculturation suggests that the acculturation–family discord relationship is more complex than represented by a simple difference or discrepancy between parents and children. Rather, the literature suggests that it is *particular combinations* of parent and child acculturation levels that may lead to family discord. Specifically, families where children have high acculturation to the new culture and low acculturation to the native culture, and families where parents have high acculturation to the native culture and low acculturation to the new culture, are thought to experience greater conflict. To examine this complex set of combinations, researchers need to find ways to summarize information about particular groupings of families based on both *types* and *direction* of differences in parent and child acculturation. One way is to conceptualize the acculturation gap as an interaction between parents' and children's acculturation scores.

The Acculturation Gap as Interaction

An interaction approach to the acculturation gap can explore a number of different possible combinations of parents' and children's acculturation levels or styles. For example, as illustrated in Table 7.2, parents and children may have high or low scores on a measure of American acculturation, resulting in four possible combinations within families:

(1) parents are low and children high on American acculturation;
(2) both parents and children are high;
(3) both parents and children are low;
(4) the parents are high and children low.

Conceptually, acculturation gap theories suggest that it is Group 1, where parents are low and children high on American acculturation, that is at risk for family maladjustment. On the other hand, the situation where children are low and parents high (Group 4) is often assumed not to exist in the current literature, although it is possible, such as in families where parents may have had prior experiences traveling or working in the United States, or had excellent English language skills even prior to migration.

Situations where parents and children are both low on American acculturation (Group 3) may not result in problems in family relationships, but may occur when the family is newly arrived in the country and no acculturation has yet occurred for either parent or child. Neither would acculturation be expected to be problematic for families when both parents and children are high on acculturation (Group 2), as might be the case after a long length of residence in the United States or for second-generation immigrants (Chung, 2001). In these situations, gaps or discrepancies would be expected to be minimal and of little significance with respect to family dynamics. A similar typology can be constructed for acculturation to the native culture, consisting of four possible combinations of parent and child acculturation levels.

Conceptually, the interaction and discrepancy approaches ask somewhat different questions of the data. The "matched/mismatched" and discrepancy approaches do not allow an exploration of all the potential types of parent–child

TABLE 7.2
Interaction Model of Parent and Child American Acculturation and Acculturation Gaps

Children's Acculturation	*Parents' Acculturation*	
	Low	*High*
High	Group #1 Mismatched High risk	Group #2 Matched Both acculturated
Low	Group #3 Matched Both not acculturated	Group #4 Mismatched Unexpected gaps

acculturative gaps as seen in Table 7.2. The "matched versus mismatched" approach used by Farver, Narang, and Bhadha (2002) asks the question of whether a discrepancy or gap between parents and children is related to family adjustment, regardless of the direction of the gap or the specific acculturative styles involved. Essentially, this approach tests differences between Groups 1 and 3 (mismatched) versus Groups 2 and 4 (matched; see Table 7.2). Using the absolute value of the difference score between parents and children amounts to essentially asking the same question of the data, but with continuous rather than discrete variables. The absolute value of the difference score approach essentially splits the sample into families where gaps occur (of any kind) and those where no gaps occur (regardless of whether parents and children both have high or low acculturation levels).

On the other hand, a difference score as used by Buki et al. (2003) potentially separates the sample into three groups: 1, 3, and a combined group made up of 2 and 4 (see Table 7.2). When both parents and children have the same high score, or the same low score, the difference between them would be zero. When children have higher scores than parents, the differences score would be positive. When parents have higher scores than children, the difference score would be negative. Thus, the difference score approach assigns the same score to Groups 2 and 4. However, Buki et al. (2003) did not report whether negative gap scores occurred, and if they did, how they impacted interpretation of their findings. Furthermore, a number of statistical problems with using difference scores are of concern when used in these studies (Cohen & Cohen, 1983; Collins & Horn, 1990; Cronbach & Furby, 1970).

In contrast, the interaction approach has the potential to explore differences among all four groups illustrated in Table 7.2. This approach asks whether particular combinations of parent and child acculturation levels are responsible for difficulties in family adjustment. The interaction approach does not rule out the importance of "main effects" or the notion that it is the child's acculturation level, irrespective of the parent, or the parent's acculturation level, irrespective of the child, that contributes to family adjustment. The presence of a significant interaction allows the researcher to explore whether it is one particular group (such as when parents are low and children high in American acculturation) that is related to family maladjustment, or whether acculturation discrepancies more generally and regardless of direction are problematic.

As a consequence, the interaction model allows researchers to examine a fuller range of kinds of combinations of levels of acculturation for parents and children in immigrant families than do the matching or difference-score approaches. Collecting data on acculturation using bidimensional measures from parents and adolescent children creates opportunities for researchers to explore in greater detail the kinds of gaps that emerge in families, and how they link to family relationships. The next section provides an illustration of the kinds of information that different kinds of computations of acculturation gaps yield.

ACCULTURATION GAP AND FAMILY DISAGREEMENT: A STUDY OF REFUGEE FAMILIES FROM THE FORMER SOVIET UNION

A study of the link between acculturation gaps and family disagreements was conducted in a Soviet Jewish refugee community in Maryland. The sample is described in greater detail elsewhere (Birman, in press; Trickett, Birman, & Persky, 2004). The final sample of 115 families with adolescent children was drawn from a larger random sample of 270 refugee families from the former Soviet Union resettled in Maryland during a 10-year time frame. Parent data were based on responses of mothers in 70% of the families, and fathers in 30%, based on who chose to participate. Parents and their adolescent children completed questionnaires on their own acculturation using the Language, Identity, and Behavior scale (LIB; Birman & Trickett, 2001), a two-dimensional orthogonal measure that assessed acculturation to American and Russian cultures separately. In addition, the scale assessed three distinct domains of acculturation, including language competence, behavioral acculturation, and identity. Thus, the measure yielded six separate acculturation scores (three dimensions × two cultures) for each parent and child. Quality of family relationships was assessed using the Problem Solving Checklist (Rueter & Conger, 1995), completed by the parent and the child. This 27-item measure asks participants to rate, on a 5-point scale, how often they disagree or get upset with their parents/adolescent about a variety of topics including money, school grades/homework, choice of friends, and use of free time. Individual item scores were summed to produce a total score reflecting the extent of disagreement reported.

To illustrate differences between the acculturation gap as discrepancy and the acculturation gap as interaction, analyses were conducted in two different ways (see Table 7.3). The first approach used the absolute value of the difference scores (Model 1) in acculturation, along each of the six dimensions assessed. The second approach conceptualized the gap as the interaction between acculturation levels of parents and children (Model 2).

When conceptualized as difference scores (Model 1, see Table 7.3), multiple regressions were conducted regressing parent and adolescent reports of family disagreements on each of the six types of acculturation gaps (gaps in American identity, language competence, and behavior, and gaps in Russian identity, language competence, and behavior). Two types of acculturation gaps predicted parent report of family disagreements in the expected direction, with the larger gaps predicting greater conflict and disagreements: American identity and Russian language ($\beta = .28$ and $\beta = .24$, respectively, both at $p < .05$ levels). Two types of acculturation gaps predicted adolescent report of family disagreements, also in the expected direction: American identity ($\beta = .15, p < .05$) and American behavior ($\beta = .37, p < .001$).

When conceptualized as main effects and interactions of parent and child acculturation scores (Model 2, see Table 7.3), the results confirmed the findings with the

TABLE 7.3

Significant Findings in Regressions of Family Disagreements on Parent–Adolescent Acculturation Gaps Operationalized as Absolute Value of Parent–Child Difference Scores (Model 1) and as Main Effects and Interactions of Parent and Adolescent Acculturation Variables (Model 2), Controlling for Adolescent Age, Gender, and Length of Residence in the United States

		Model 1 Gap as Difference Score		*Model 2 Gap as Main Effects and Interactions*				
DVs	*IVs*			*Main Effects*			*Interactions*	
Family disagreements:	Acculturation gap domains:	ΔR^2	β		ΔR^2	β	ΔR^2	β
Parent report	American identity	.10*	.21*	n.s.	n.s.	n.s.	.06**	−.26**
	Russian language	"	.28*	Adolescent	.06*	−.32**	n.s.	n.s.
Adolescent report	American identity	.11*	.15*	n.s.	n.s.	n.s.	.06**	−.27**
	American behavior	"	.32***	Parent	.07**	−.26**	n.s.	n.s.

Note. n.s. = not significant.
$^*p < .05$. $^{**}p < .01$. $^{***}p < .001$.

difference scores, but also provided more detail about the underlying processes of acculturation. It was the main effect for adolescent Russian language acculturation that predicted parent report of disagreements, whereas the interaction between parent and child Russian language acculturation was not significant. Thus, difference score analyses suggested that it was the *discrepancy* in Russian language that was linked to disagreements, and the interaction model analyses clarified that it was the *child's* level of Russian language competence that was contributing to family disagreements. In fact, there was almost no variability in Russian language competence of the parents, as all reported excellent competence.

Findings with respect to American behavior gap and adolescent report of disagreements using Model 2 suggested that it was the main effect for *parent* American behavioral acculturation that contributed uniquely to reported disagreements. The interaction of the parent-and-child American behavioral acculturation was not significant. This pattern of findings suggests that it is not the discrepancy in American behavioral acculturation between parents and children that is linked to disagreements, but the low acculturation of parents.

With respect to the findings for American identity, the presence of a significant interaction confirmed the results with difference scores that it was the discrepancy between parents and adolescents that contributed to parent report of disagreements. Plotting the interaction revealed that both "mismatched" groups, where parents were high and children low on acculturation, and those where children were high and parents low on American identity had higher disagreement scores than "matched" groups. In this case, the interaction results confirmed the difference score (Model 1) findings and clarified that they held regardless of the direction of the difference.

Thus, findings obtained with the interaction model clarify that in some cases the acculturation gap involves a discrepancy between acculturation of parents and children, such as with American identity, regardless of the direction of these differences. In other cases, however, it is either the parents' or the child's acculturation that is linked to family disagreements. In addition, the use of measures of acculturation across multiple domains of acculturation (language, identity, and behavior), as well as with respect to both the new and the native culture, allowed for the pinpointing of specific types of acculturation gaps that were problematic. Such differentiated findings have implications for interventions designed to reduce the acculturation gaps between parents and children.

For example, that adolescents' Russian language competence predicted disagreements suggests that interventions designed to reduce family tension might be aimed at helping immigrant students learn or retain their native language. If a different measure of acculturation had been used, this level of precision would not have been achieved. If a one-dimensional measure of language acculturation were used, the acculturation gap between parents and children would simply reflect their relative knowledge of the English language. If found to be linked to family disagreements, a possible implication of this finding would be to create programs that teach English to parents. However, separating out acculturation to the new from the native culture helped to pinpoint the acculturation gap as relating to the adolescent's native language skills.

Further to this point, the interaction approach (Model 2) to assessing acculturation opens opportunities to identify the relevant main effects as well as interactions. This strategy also has implications for intervention. With respect to American behavior, the interaction model showed that the main effect for *parent* American behavioral acculturation was linked to family disagreements. Yet, prior research with other immigrant groups (Szapocznik et al., 1978) has suggested that it is the "overacculturation" of adolescents to American culture that is responsible for family conflict. However, these findings suggest that interventions aimed to help parents behaviorally engage more with American culture may be helpful.

Finally, the interaction model confirmed findings obtained using Model 1 with respect to American identity, suggesting that the *discrepancy* between parents and children is linked to disagreements regardless of the direction of the differences. Here, interventions that help parents and children discuss their views and attitudes toward American identity may be most effective (Szapocznik, Rio, Perez-Vidal, Kurtines, & Santisteban, 1986). A measurement approach that assesses acculturation to the two cultures independently, considers multiple domains of acculturation, and operationalizes the acculturation gap as the interaction of parent and adolescent acculturation appears to yield richer and more detailed results than the difference score approach.

CONCLUSIONS

This chapter summarizes several issues in conceptualizing, measuring, and computing so-called "acculturation gaps" in immigrant families. As empirical literature on this topic emerges, it is important for researchers to consider the advantages and limitations of different methodological approaches to measuring acculturation and acculturation gaps. Specific suggestions for researchers studying this phenomenon and challenges that remain to be addressed in future research are offered next.

Suggestions for Measurement and Computation of Acculturation Gaps

Two-Dimensional Measures of Acculturation Are Preferable to One-Dimensional Ones

As advocated by many in the field (Berry, 1980; Berry et al., 1986; Birman, 1998; Nguyen et al., 1999; Oetting & Beauvais, 1990), acculturation research is shifting away from using measures that only capture the extent of one's assimilation to the new culture. Instead, two-dimensional measures that assess acculturation to the new as well as the native culture yield more accurate representations of one's acculturation and, as a result, more useful types of acculturation gap descriptions.

Independent Measures of Acculturation to Two Cultures Are Preferable to the "Four-Fold" Measures

The four-fold measurement models that group parents and children into the four categories of acculturative style can be useful and provide informative data with respect to preferences for acculturative styles among parents and adolescents. However, these scales pose questions about how to compute acculturation gaps. As I have illustrated, grouping families into matched and mismatched categories may be useful, but may mask vital information about the nature of the parent–child differences. It is possible to use this type of measure to identify multiple combinations of parent and child acculturation styles. However, given that parents and children would each belong to one of four possible categories of acculturative styles, constructing a matrix of matched and mismatched possibilities seems overly complex, and statistically prohibitive for the kinds of smaller sample studies that are conducted with immigrant families. Thus, use of the four-fold paradigm poses particular challenges that can be avoided by using the "orthogonal" acculturation measurement model that assesses the degree of acculturation to the new and native cultures independently. Researchers can choose from among many such measures that have been developed in the literature (e.g., Birman & Trickett, 2001; Cortes, Rogler, & Malgady, 1994; H. Nguyen et al., 1999; Zea, Asner-Self, Birman, & Buki, 2003).

Conceptualizing Acculturation Interactions of Parents' and Children's Acculturation Levels Is Preferable to Using Difference Scores or Grouping Parents and Children Into "Matched" or "Mismatched" Groups

The interaction model of the acculturation gap provides more information than the difference score, but also allows researchers to ask the same questions asked by difference/discrepancy models. The interaction model allows for the comparison of the impact of each of the four types of gaps illustrated in Table 7.2, and also to consider the impact of main effects of parents' or children's acculturation. Thus, the use of the interaction model provides the greatest flexibility in examining the processes underlying the acculturation gap.

Assessing Multiple Domains of Acculturation Offers Advantages Over Using a Single Index

An additional measurement issue involves the multiple domains of acculturation, such as the ones assessed by LIB measure (Birman & Trickett, 2001). Most studies combine questions about multiple acculturation domains (such as language, choice of friends, preferences for food and music, identity) into a single index, but measures that distinguish between acculturation domains can be used to identify specific acculturation gaps. This kind of specific information can then be used to inform interventions designed to reduce the negative impact of such gaps.

Challenges in Research on Acculturation Gaps

It is important to take note of the many methodological challenges to conducting research in this area that remain and require attention and continued efforts on the part of researchers. The first concerns what acculturation gap studies mean by "parents" because most have used data from only one parent, usually the mother, to determine the presence of an acculturation gap. For example, in "actual gap" studies, Pawliuk et al. (1996), Merali (2002), and Farver, Narang, and Bhadha (2002) collected data from only one parent, the majority mothers. In a "perceived gap" study of parents, Buki et al. (2003) sampled only mothers. In a perceived gap study of adolescents, Lee et al. (2000) asked college students to rate the acculturation of their parents as a pair, and did not distinguish between mothers and fathers. Thus, prior research did not provide guidance with respect to how to analyze data from both mothers and fathers, when available.

In the study described earlier (Birman, in press), parent data were based on responses of mothers in 70% of the families, and fathers in the rest, based on who chose to complete the Problem Solving Checklist that assessed disagreements with their adolescent child at the time of data collection. However, data on acculturation were available from mothers as well as fathers for all two-parent families. This created the opportunity to use both parents' acculturation scores to compute acculturation gaps. Yet this strategy poses a dilemma of how to include both parents in a study. One possibility is to use the average acculturation scores of the two parents, arguing that the acculturation difference between the parents on average and the child is the best indicator of the acculturation gap. Another possibility is to consider identifying the larger acculturation gap between the generations, using the scores of the parent that is more distant from the acculturation level of the child in computing gaps. However, this approach also seemed to have limitations, because the acculturation level of the other parent would be ignored. Ultimately, more sophisticated statistical methods that allow for nesting data in families, such as hierarchical linear modeling, may be required to take into account acculturation levels of both parents, and potentially include multiple siblings, to create a more accurate portrait of acculturation gaps as they occur in families.

Another challenge concerning measurement is that, although measuring actual gaps has advantages over measuring perceived gaps, this approach also raises conceptual concerns. Because acculturation is a developmental construct, the meaning of acculturation scale items may be different for adults than it is for adolescents (e.g., Tsai, Ying, & Lee, 2000). Thus, one potential explanation for why adolescents have been found to have higher levels of ethnic identity than their parents (Birman & Trickett, 2001) is that adolescents' conception of their native culture is different from that of their parents. As a result, the same items on a measure of identification with the native culture may tap different constructs for different generations. If correct, this situation poses special challenges for acculturation gap research and suggests that difference scores in particular can create a misleading view.

The greatest challenge is that research must carefully attend to important methodological and conceptual concerns outlined in this chapter. At the current time, the conceptual and methodological issues surrounding acculturation are viewed as serious enough to permit some (e.g., Escobar & Vega, 2000; Hunt, Schneider, & Comer, 2004) to question the usefulness of the construct. Confronting these concerns in research on acculturation can provide an antidote to these critiques. Greater precision and attention to measurement of the acculturation construct in general and the acculturation gap between parents and children in particular is needed to lend more creditability to this important research area, and advance our knowledge about immigrant parents and children.

ACKNOWLEDGMENTS

The research reported in this chapter was conducted with funding from the Maryland Office for New Americans, Department of Human Services. The author wishes to thank the Office, and Dr. Martin Ford in particular, for making the research possible.

REFERENCES

Berry, J. W. (1980). Acculturation as varieties of adaptation. In A. M. Padilla (Ed.), *Acculturation: Theory, models and some new findings* (pp. 9–25). Boulder, CO: Westview Press.

Berry, J. W., Trimble, J. E., & Olmedo, E. L. (1986). Assessment of acculturation. In W. J. Lonner & J. W. Berry (Eds.), *Field methods in cross-cultural research: Cross-cultural research and methodology series* (Vol. 8, pp. 291–324). Thousand Oaks, CA: Sage.

Birman, D. (1998). Biculturalism and perceived competence of Latino immigrant adolescents. *American Journal of Community Psychology, 26*(3), 335–354.

Birman, D. (in press). Acculturation gap and family adjustment: Findings with Soviet Jewish refugees in the U.S. and implications for measurement. *Journal of Cross-Cultural Psychology.*

Birman, D., & Trickett, E. J. (2001). Cultural transitions in first-generation immigrants: Acculturation of Soviet Jewish refugee adolescents and parents. *Journal of Cross-Cultural Psychology, 32*(4), 456–477.

Birman, D., Trickett, E. J., & Buchanan, R. (2005). A tale of two cities: Replication of a study on the acculturation and adaptation of immigrant adolescents from the former Soviet Union in a different community context. *American Journal of Community Psychology, 35*(1–2), 87–101.

Birman, D., Trickett, E. J., & Vinokurov, A. (2002). Acculturation and adaptation of Soviet Jewish refugee adolescents: Predictors of adjustment across life domains. *American Journal of Community Psychology, 30*(5), 585–607.

Buki, L. P., Ma, T. C., Strom, R. D., & Strom, S. K. (2003). Chinese immigrant mothers of adolescents: Self-perceptions of acculturation effects on parenting. *Cultural Diversity & Ethnic Minority Psychology, 9*(2), 127–140.

Chung, R. H. G. (2001). Gender, ethnicity, and acculturation in intergenerational conflict of Asian American college students. *Cultural Diversity & Ethnic Minority Psychology, 7*(4), 376–386.

Cohen, J., & Cohen, P. (1983). *Applied multiple regression/correlation: Analysis for the behavioral sciences* (2nd ed.). Hillsdale, NJ: Lawrence Erlbaum Associates.

Collins, L., & Horn, J. (Eds.). (1990). *Best methods for the analysis of change: Recent advances, unanswered question, future directions*. Washington, DC: American Psychological Association.

Cortes, D. E., Rogler, L. H., & Malgady, R. G. (1994). Biculturality among Puerto Rican adults in the United States. *American Journal of Community Psychology, 22*(5), 707–721.

Cronbach, L. J., & Furby, L. (1970). How should we measure "change": Or should we? *Psychological Bulletin, 74*(1), 68–80.

Cuellar, I., Arnold, B., & Maldonado, R. (1995). Acculturation Rating Scale for Mexican Americans–II: A revision of the original ARSMA scale. *Hispanic Journal of Behavioral Sciences, 17*, 275–305.

Cuellar, I., Harris, L. C., & Jasso, R. (1980). An acculturation scale for Mexican American normal and clinical populations. *Hispanic Journal of Behavioral Sciences, 2*(3), 199–217.

Delgado-Gaitan, C. (1985). Preparing teachers for inter-ethnic communication. *Equity & Choice, 2*(1), 53–59, 61–65.

Delgado-Gaitan, C. (1994a). *Empowerment in Carpinteria: A five-year study of family, school, and community relationships*. Davis, CA: University of California.

Delgado-Gaitan, C. (1994b). Russian refugee families: Accommodating aspirations through education. *Anthropology & Education Quarterly, 25*(2), 137–155.

Dinh, K. T., Sarason, B. R., & Sarason, I. G. (1994). Parent–child relationships in Vietnamese immigrant families. *Journal of Family Psychology, 8*(4), 471–488.

Escobar, J. I., & Vega, W. A. (2000). Mental health and immigration's AAAs: Where are we and where do we go from here? *Journal of Nervous & Mental Disease, 188*(11), 736–740.

Farver, J. A., Bhadha, B. R., & Narang, S. K. (2002). Acculturation and psychological functioning in Asian Indian adolescents. *Social Development, 11*(1), 11–29.

Farver, J. A., Narang, S. K., & Bhadha, B. R. (2002). East meets west: Ethnic identity, acculturation, and conflict in Asian Indian families. *Journal of Family Psychology, 16*(3), 338–350.

Gil, A. G., & Vega, W. A. (1996). Two different worlds: Acculturation stress and adaptation among Cuban and Nicaraguan families. *Journal of Social & Personal Relationships, 13*(3), 435–456.

Grolnick, W. S., Benjet, C., Kurowski, C. O., & Apostoleris, N. H. (1997). Predictors of parent involvement in children's schooling. *Journal of Educational Psychology, 89*(3), 538–548.

Hao, L., & Bonstead-Bruns, M. (1998). Parent–child differences in educational expectations and the academic achievement of immigrant and native students. *Sociology of Education, 7*, 175–198.

Hunt, L. M., Schneider, S., & Comer, B. (2004). Should "acculturation" be a variable in health research? A critical review of research on U.S. Hispanics. *Social Science and Medicine, 58*, 973–986.

Jones, C. J., & Trickett, E. J. (2005). Immigrant adolescents behaving as culture brokers: A study of families from the former Soviet Union. *Journal of Social Psychology, 145*(4), 405–427.

Kwak, K. (2003). Adolescents and their parents: A review of intergenerational family relations for immigrant and non-immigrant families. *Human Development, 46*(2–3), 15–136.

Kwak, K., & Berry, J. W. (2001). Generational differences in acculturation among Asian families in Canada: A comparison of Vietnamese, Korean, and East-Indian groups. *International Journal of Psychology, 36*(3), 152–162.

Lee, R. M., Choe, J., Kim, G., & Ngo, V. (2000). Construction of the Asian American Family Conflicts Scale. *Journal of Counseling Psychology, 47*(2), 211–222.

Luo, S.-H., & Wiseman, R. L. (2000). Ethnic language maintenance among Chinese immigrant children in the United States. *International Journal of Intercultural Relations, 24*(3), 307–324.

Mau, W.-C. (1997). Parental influences on the high school students' academic achievement: A comparison of Asian immigrants, Asian Americans, and White Americans. *Psychology in the Schools, 34*(3), 267–277.

Merali, N. (2002). Perceived versus actual parent–adolescent assimilation disparity among Hispanic refugee families. *International Journal for the Advancement of Counselling, 24*(1), 57–68.

Nguyen, H., Messe, L. A., & Stollak, G. E. (1999). Toward a more complex understanding of acculturation and adjustment: Cultural involvements and psychosocial functioning in Vietnamese youth. *Journal of Cross-Cultural Psychology, 30*(1), 5–31.

Nguyen, N., & Williams, H. L. (1989). Transition from East to West: Vietnamese adolescents and their parents. *Journal of the American Academy of Child and Adolescent Psychiatry, 28*(4), 505–515.

Oetting, G. R., & Beauvais, F. (1990). Orthogonal cultural identification theory: The cultural identification of minority adolescents. *International Journal of the Addictions, 25*(5-A–6-A), 655–685.

Pawliuk, N., Grizenko, N., Chan-Yip, A., Gantous, P., Mathew, J., & Nguyen, D. (1996). Acculturation style and psychological functioning in children of immigrants. *American Journal of Orthopsychiatry, 66*(1), 111–121.

Portes, A., & Hao, L. (2002). The price of uniformity: Language, family and personality adjustment in the immigrant second generation. *Ethnic & Racial Studies, 25*(6), 889–912.

Portes, A., & Rumbaut, R. G. (1990). *Immigrant America. A portrait.* Berkeley, CA: University of California Press.

Rick, K., & Forward, J. (1992). Acculturation and perceived intergenerational differences among Hmong youth. *Journal of Cross-Cultural Psychology, 23*(1), 85–94.

Rosenthal, D. (1984). Intergenerational conflict and culture: A study of immigrant and nonimmigrant adolescents and their parents. *Genetic Psychology Monographs, 109*(1), 53–75.

Rosenthal, D., Bell, R., Demetriou, A., & Efklides, A. (1989). From collectivism to individualism? The acculturation of Greek immigrants in Australia. *International Journal of Psychology, 24*(1), 57–71.

Rosenthal, D., & Bornholt, L. (1988). Expectations about development in Greek- and Anglo-Australian families. *Journal of Cross-Cultural Psychology, 19*(1), 19–34.

Rueter, M., & Conger, R. (1995). Antecedents of parent–adolescent disagreements. *Journal of Marriage and the Family, 57*(435–448).

Suinn, R. M., Khoo, G., & Ahuna, C. (1995). The Suinn–Lew Asian Self-Identify Acculturation Scale: Cross-cultural information. *Journal of Multicultural Counseling & Development, 23*(3), 139–148.

Szapocznik, J., Kurtines, W., & Fernandez, T. (1980). Bicultural involvement and adjustment in Hispanic-American youths. *International Journal of Intercultural Relations, 4*, 353–365.

Szapocznik, J., Rio, A., Perez-Vidal, A., Kurtines, W. M., & Santisteban, D. A. (1986). Family effectiveness training (FET) for Hispanic families. In H. P. Lefley & P. B. Pedersen (Eds.), *Cross-cultural training for mental health professionals* (pp. 245–261). Springfield, IL: Charles C. Thomas.

Szapocznik, J., Santisteban, D., Kurtines, W. M., Perez-Vidal, A., & Hervis, O. (1984). Bicultural Effectiveness Training: A treatment intervention for enhancing intercultural adjustment in Cuban American families. *Hispanic Journal of Behavioral Sciences, 6*(4), 317–344.

Szapocznik, J., Scopetta, M. A., Kurtines, W., & Aranalde, M. D. (1978). Theory and measurement of acculturation. *Revista Interamericana de Psicologia, 12*(2), 113–130.

Trickett, E. J., Birman, D., & Persky, I. (2004). *Soviet and Vietnamese refugee adults and adolescents in Maryland: A comparative analysis.* Baltimore, MD: Maryland Department of Human Services.

Tsai, J., Ying, Y. W., & Lee, P. (2000). The meaning of "Being Chinese" and "Being American": Variation among Chinese American young adults. *Journal of Cross-Cultural Psychology, 31*, 302–332.

Zea, M. C., Asner-Self, K. K., Birman, D., & Buki, L. P. (2003). The Abbreviated Multidimensional Acculturation Scale: Empirical validation with two Latino/Latina samples. *Cultural Diversity & Ethnic Minority Psychology, 9*(2), 107–126.

8

A Model of Cultural Attachment: A New Approach for Studying Bicultural Experience

Ying-yi Hong
Glenn I. Roisman
Jing Chen
University of Illinois at Urbana-Champaign, U.S.A.

INTRODUCTION

Social groups provide individual members with resources and security. At the same time, with the help of symbols (such as language), groups create norms, conventions, and meaning frameworks that individual members use to interpret and make sense of both their own selves and the external world. As such, the meanings of the self and the world essentially are anchored with reference to the social groups within which individuals live. This notion has raised an interesting question for individuals who have been extensively exposed to the shared knowledge and meanings of two social groups, such as migrants or sojourners. How would these individuals understand the self and the world? Our previous research (Hong, Chiu, & Kung, 1997; Hong, Morris, Chiu, & Benet-Martinez, 2000) has shown that such bicultural individuals[1] are able to switch between cultural frames, a process that is epitomized in the following reflection from Susanna Harrington, a multicultural informant of South American origin in Sparrow's (2000) study:

> I think of myself not as a unified cultural being but as a communion of different cultural beings. Due to the fact that I have spent time in different cultural environments I have developed several cultural identities that diverge and converge according to the need of the moment. (p. 190)

---

[1]Throughout this chapter, "bicultural individuals" is used to refer to people who have been extensively exposed to two cultures and is not limited to people who endorse a particular acculturation strategy.

Importantly, however, Hong and her associates (Hong, Wan, No, & Chiu, in press) also noticed that acquisition of multiple cultural identities can be a mixed blessing. Indeed, in an early analysis of migration and identity, Park (1928) approached the internal conflict and ambivalence arising from identification with multiple cultural groups through the notion of "marginal man," a person who feels simultaneously detached and involved with multiple cultural groups. Identification with multiple cultural groups engenders psychological conflict when values and practices of heritage and mainstream cultural groups are perceived to be too distant or in opposition (see Benet-Martinez, Leu, Lee, & Morris, 2002). Additionally, identity conflict may arise due to exclusion or rejection by desired cultural groups (e.g., Kanno, 2003). Identity ambivalence, marginalization, and alienation may also result from the fluctuating responses of others to multicultural individuals, depending on the salient identity features of a context (Turner, Hogg, Oakes, Reicher, & Wetherell, 1987), as when multicultural individuals are approached with intimacy and familiarity in one context and responded to with fear and distance by the same individuals in another context (Zaharna, 1989). Even within immigrant groups, established immigrants may reject the newly arrived, causing newly arrived immigrants to develop ambivalent and marginal identities. For example, Niemann, Romero, Arredondo, and Rodriguez (1999) found that Mexicans living in the United States perceived more rejection and discrimination from Chicanas/Chicanos (U.S.-born Mexican Americans) than from Anglo Americans. Japanese Peruvians and Japanese Brazilians who traveled to Japan as migrant workers during the late 1980s and throughout the 1990s were treated as Peruvians/Brazilians (an outgroup) by the Japanese, but as Japanese (again an outgroup) in their respective countries of Peru and Brazil, although of mixed blood and being of second- or third-generation status (Takenaka, 1999; Tsuda, 2003).

In short, although multicultural individuals are capable of moving across cultural frames, these individuals also face the challenge of deriving meanings from their multicultural encounters. Oftentimes, these encounters are loaded with a mix of emotions, such as fear (of exclusion and rejection), anxiety (related to acceptance), anger (in response to discrimination), relief (when accepted), and comfort/ "at home" (a feeling of safe haven within the culture). The challenge for acculturation research is to develop a model to capture these experiences. In this chapter, we have sought to meet this challenge by proposing a model of *cultural attachment*. Specifically, we borrowed ideas and methodology from a collection of theories, including attachment theory (Bowlby, 1969/1982), terror management theory (Greenberg, Pyszczynski, & Solomon, 1986; Solomon, Greenberg, & Pyszczynski, 1991, 2000), the dynamic constructivist approach (Hong et al., 2000), and the dialogical self approach (Hermans, 1988; Hermans & Kempen, 1993) to understand the experience of acculturation.

We begin by defining cultural attachment and explaining the approach we have endorsed in understanding the development of bicultural identity. Second, we discuss some rudimentary functions of attachment to culture, drawing support from research on group attachment, terror management theory, and the need for consensual validation. Third, we delineate the basic postulates of our cultural attachment model. Fourth, we introduce a method for assessing individual differences in cultural attachment and report some preliminary results. We conclude by discussing how our cultural attachment model sheds new light on some significant issues on acculturation.

WHAT IS CULTURAL ATTACHMENT?

Attachment theory as originally proposed by Bowlby has underscored the role of relationships in human development from the cradle to the grave (Bowlby, 1969/1982, 1973, 1980).

> For not only young children, it is now clear, but human beings of all ages are found to be at their happiest and to be able to deploy their talents to best advantage when they are confident that, standing behind them, there are one or more trusted persons who will come to their aid should difficulties arise. The person trusted provides a secure base from which his [or her] companion can operate. (Bowlby, 1973, p. 359)

According to Bowlby, relationships with attachment figures play a central role in development because attachment figures provide emotional support and protection that are essential for individuals' survival. Relationships with attachment figures are relevant across the life course. Indeed, attachments have been shown in romantic relationships among adults, although the function of the attachment is more symbolic in nature: (1) the provision of a secure base from which to explore one's environment, and (2) a safe haven in times of uncertainty (Roisman, Tsai, & Chiang, 2004, after Waters & Cummings, 2000).

Extrapolating from attachment theory, we contend that social groups can also serve as attachment bases in that groups can provide emotional support and protection. For instance, Rowell and Hinde (1963) found that rhesus monkeys in isolation were 3 to 50 times more frightened by a masked and cloaked stranger than were monkeys in groups. Similarly, in humans, Schachter (1959) showed that female college students preferred to stay with other participants when they were told that they would be receiving painful electric shocks in an experiment than did college female participants who were not told about the painful electric shocks. As such, a social group (consisting of others who share common experience and fate) seems to provide emotional support to buffer anxiety and fear. In a similar vein, we reason that a social group can play the role of an attachment base. Although we argue that attachment to a social group bears similarities to attachment of infants to primary caregivers, we do not contend that attachments to caregivers and to groups are identical.

Our research focuses on attachment to cultural groups as a particular case of attachment to social groups. In ancient times, cultural groups overlapped greatly with kinship groups, which are paramount in providing individuals with emotional support and protection against adversity in the environment. As a result, individuals had a higher probability of surviving if they stayed in a group rather than by themselves. This tendency increases reproductive fitness and thus was likely to be transmitted from generation to generation. In fact, it has been argued that, just as an infant cannot survive without parental care, our humanoid ancestors could not have survived outside the group (Caporael & Baron, 1997). In modern times, cultural groups are often demarcated by racial and ethnic categorizations and geographical boundaries, and arguably still provide symbolic support for individuals (detailed in the next section) and tangible protection during extreme situations (e.g., war). As such, people can build emotional connections with a cultural group, drawing from it a sense of comfort and safe haven.

Like research on infant–caregiver attachment, we also believe that individuals differ in their attachment relationship with cultural groups. In particular, we intend to differentiate *secure* versus *insecure* patterns of cultural attachment. We are aware that in the literature of attachment theory there are two different approaches in defining attachment security in adulthood. One approach, which follows mainly from the personality and social psychology tradition, examines the styles of relationship with attachment figures often in terms of approaching versus avoiding emotional and physical intimacy with and confiding in adult attachment figures (Fraley & Shaver, 2000; Hazan & Shaver, 1987). This approach, typically using self-report measures, defines secure (vs. insecure) attachment as ease (vs. difficulty) in establishing an intimate, trusting relationship with attachment figures. Research in this tradition has identified some basic dimensions underlying attachment in romantic relationships, including comfort with closeness, the capacity to depend on others in time of need, and anxiety about abandonment and being involved in intimate relationships (Collins & Read, 1990; Griffin & Bartholomew, 1994).

Another approach, which follows mainly from the developmental tradition, examines the emotional connections with attachment figures in terms of the coherence of experience (vs. unresolved emotions) with respect to their relationship with the attachment figures, regardless of the valence of the experience. This approach, using interview methods (e.g., Adult Attachment Interview) typically defines secure (vs. insecure) attachment by way of an adult's ability to be coherent and collaborative in discussing with an unfamiliar person (the interviewer) their experience with attachment figures and the ongoing effects of these relationships in their lives.

There are strengths in both approaches. We reasoned that the former approach would be useful in assessing an approach versus avoidance attachment style, and is compatible with the major theories in acculturation (e.g., Berry's acculturation theory: Berry, 1990, 1997, chapter 2, this volume), which conceptualize accultureation strategies as resulting from maintenance versus rejection and approach versus avoidance of the native and host cultures. However, because our goal is to understand how individuals *resolve* both positive and negative experiences with native and host cultures, the former approach may not be able to provide us with a sufficiently rich picture on the dynamic processes involved in this regard. Instead, the latter approach focuses on how individuals integrate positive and negative emotions relating to the attachment figure, which has been found to show an incremental advantage over the former approach in predicting the quality of attachment in the next generation (van IJzendoorn, 1995) and in alleviating the problem of self-enhancement in self-report measures (Gjerde, Onishi, & Carlson, 2004). By adopting this latter approach, we sought to understand how bicultural individuals manage and resolve negative experiences with cultures, and integrate both positive and negative cultural experiences in their lives. In keeping with this latter approach, we thereby define a secure (vs. insecure) attachment as bicultural individuals' ability to freely evaluate their cultural experiences, and be coherent and collaborative in their narratives about cultural experiences.

It is also important to note that, although forming attachment to our culture may be universal, variation with respect to whether individuals can resolve and integrate negative cultural experiences may only become salient or consequential when they are negotiating a second attachment in a new cultural context (see also Ward, Bochner, & Furnham, 2001). The new culture provides an environment for exploration and at the same time serves as a stressor. As such, we examined our model of cultural attachment with bicultural individuals.

To begin, we compare models of attachment and acculturation. Then we argue how we can extend attachment theory, which deals typically with attachment of an individual to another individual, to cultural attachment theory, which deals with attachment of an individual to a cultural group.

PARALLELS BETWEEN INTERPERSONAL ATTACHMENT AND CULTURAL ATTACHMENT

Based on Bowlby's attachment theory (1969/1982), Bartholomew and Horowitz (1991) proposed four attachment types along the dimension of positive versus negative conception of the self and the dimension of positive versus negative conception of other people. The four types are named *secure* (when individuals hold positive conceptions for both the self and others), *preoccupied or anxious-ambivalent* (when individuals hold negative conceptions of the self but positive conceptions of others), *dismissing-avoidant* (when individuals hold positive conceptions about the self, but negative conceptions about others), and *fearful-avoidant* (when individuals hold negative conceptions for both self and others).

Gaines and Liu (2000) argued that Bartholomew and Horowitz's four attachment types parallel Berry's acculturation strategies. Specifically, Berry, Poortinga, Segall, and Dasen (1992) derived a four-fold typology of acculturation strategies by crossing the dimension of acceptance or rejection of one's native culture and the dimension of seeking or avoiding participation in the host culture. Specifically, the four acculturation strategies are *integration* (when individuals accept their native culture and at the same time seek out the host culture), *assimilation* (when individuals reject their native culture but seek out the host culture), *separation* (when individuals accept their native culture but avoid the host culture), and *marginalization* (when individuals reject their native culture and at the same time avoid the host culture).

Although these parallels are interesting, Gaines and Liu did not discuss further similarities and differences involved in attaching to an individual versus a group. For example, Bartholomew and Horowitz's attachment types, though arguably reflecting the cognitive representations ("working model") of the beholders, are anchored in the relationship between the self and significant others. Significant others take an active role in the relationship. Whether significant others provide resources (tangible or not) to meet the needs of the individual and respond to the demands of the individual affects whether individuals experience acceptance, rejection, or even abandonment by significant others. By contrast, responses from a culture to individuals in similar ways are less obvious. It is thus important first to discuss how culture can serve attachment functions. We propose supportive arguments based on group attachment, terror management, and need for consensual validation.

Attachment to Social Groups

Smith, Murphy, and Coats (1999) argued that attachment to social groups can be understood by borrowing theoretical ideas and measurement methods from research on attachment in close relationships. They pointed out that there is evidence that individuals form close ties with groups as much as they form close ties with significant others. For example, Smith and Henry (1996) showed that individuals incorporate the ingroup into the self, indicating a tendency to seek close proximity to the ingroup. Social groups, similar to attachment figures, may also be viewed as accepting or rejecting the self. As such, the attachment to a group may bear similar patterns as attachment to a significant other. In fact, Smith et al. (1999) found that attachment to groups reflects two basic dimensions: attachment anxiety (extent of worry about acceptance) and avoidance (extent of desire for closeness and dependence), which were also the major dimensions underlying romantic attachment (Brennan, Clark, & Shaver, 1998).

Smith et al.'s (1999) findings provide initial support for extending attachment from the interpersonal level to the group level. However, it is noteworthy that, because they borrowed theoretical ideas and measurement strategies from the personality and social psychology tradition of the attachment literature, they have similarly viewed individual differences in group attachment as reflected by self-reported score differences on basic attachment dimensions (anxiety and avoidance). Although our approach also shares the same goal of extending attachment from the interpersonal level to the group level, as discussed earlier, we borrowed from the developmental tradition of the attachment literature, focusing on the integration of positive and negative experiences with the group instead of the extent to which people report being able to use the group as a safe haven and secure base.

Terror Management

Terror management theory posits that, on one hand, human beings, like other animals, have a biological predisposition toward self-preservation. On the other hand, in contrast to other animals, human beings are capable of abstract temporal representation, which brings the awareness of their own mortality in the future and in turn engenders a potential for paralyzing terror (Greenberg et al., 1986; Solomon et al., 1991; see review by Pyszczynski, Greenberg, Solomon, Arndt, & Schimel, 2004). According to terror management theory, to ward off this terror, people create and participate in culture, thereby deriving a sense of permanence that is extended beyond the individual's lifetime.

> Everything cultural is fabricated and given meaning by the mind, a meaning that was not given by physical nature. Culture is in this sense "supernatural," and all systematizations of culture have in their end the same goal: to raise men [*sic*] above nature to assure them that in some ways their lives count more than merely physical things count. (Becker, 1975, p. 4)

Consistent with this idea, individuals who were made aware of mortality (through manipulation in experiments) were found to be more likely to embrace cultural worldviews (culturally shared conceptions of reality that set standards of values and morals for cultural members) than those without the mortality salience manipulation. It is possible that embracing cultural worldviews helps individuals to feel that they are valued members of the group and thus buffers their fear of mortality (Solomon et al., 1991). According to Pyszczynski et al. (2004):

> In the early stages of development, affection from the parents provides this anxiety buffering function in the absence of any conscious awareness of death or the frightening nature of this ultimate reality. . . . However, with the dawning realization of mortality and the inability of the parents to adequately protect the child from this inevitable threat, the primary basis of security shifts from the parents to a worldview ultimately derived from the deistic and secular figures and constructs of the culture at large. (p. 437)

From the terror management perspective, believing in and living up to internalized standards prescribed by the culture fosters the feeling that "one is an object of primary value in a world of meaningful action" (Becker, 1971, p. 79). As such, culture can provide psychological security for its members.

Need for Consensual Validation

Kruglanski and his associates (Kruglanski, 1989; Kruglanski & Webster, 1996; Webster & Kruglanski, 1994) have shown that people differ in their desire for a definite answer to a question, any firm answer, rather than uncertainty, confusion, or ambiguity. The strength of this desire reflects individuals' need for cognitive closure. Kosic, Kruglanski, Pierro, and Mannetti (2004) extended research on this individual difference to understand the acculturation processes of three immigrant samples in Italy. Their main reasoning is that the process of moving into an unfamiliar and uncertain environment of the host culture motivates people with a high need for closure to seize and freeze on frames of reference that are readily available to them more so than would their low need for closure counterparts. For instance, if individuals with a high need for closure migrate with their family members or close friends, these close others from their native culture could serve as a ready reference group, and thus individuals with a high need for closure would be less motivated to assimilate into the host culture than would their counterparts with a low need for closure. By contrast, if individuals with a high need for closure migrate alone, they would be more motivated to seize the host culture as their reference group, and thus be more likely to assimilate into the host culture. Indeed, Kosic et al. (2004) found supportive evidence in their immigrant samples. These findings, therefore, highlight the referencing function of the cultural group in warding off uncertainty and ambiguity, at least for some individuals (e.g., those with high need for cognitive closure). Consistently, Grieve and Hogg (1999) have proposed that group categorization is motivated by reduction of uncertainty. Both approaches posit that a cultural group can be a source of security by providing consensual validation and cognitive certainty.

In sum, considering the perspectives of group attachment, terror management, and need for consensual validation together, culture can be a source of security. It is therefore possible to extrapolate from attachment to a significant figure to attachment to a culture. Nonetheless, there are two aspects—the dynamic attachment to multiple cultures, and development of cultural attachment—that pertain in particular to attachment of culture, elaborated next.

POSTULATES OF CULTURAL ATTACHMENT

Dynamic Attachment to Multiple Cultures

Hong and her associates (Hong et al., 1997; Hong et al., 2000; Hong, Benet-Martinez, Chiu, & Morris, 2003) have shown that it is possible for bicultural individuals (i.e., people who have been exposed to two cultures extensively) to switch between cultural frames. These researchers primed bicultural individuals (Hong Kong Chinese, Chinese Americans) with either Chinese cultural icons (e.g., the

Chinese dragon) or American cultural icons (Mickey Mouse). When primed with Chinese (vs. American) cultural icons, these bicultural individuals were more inclined to use a group agency model to interpret an ambiguous event; they made more group attributions and fewer individual attributions. This pattern of responses arguably reflects an increased activation of the Chinese (American) cultural knowledge system as a result of the Chinese (American) cultural priming procedures. Analogous culture priming effects have been found on spontaneous self-construal (Ross, Xun, & Wilson, 2002) and cooperative behaviors (Wong & Hong, 2005). In addition, the culture priming effect has also been replicated in studies that used different bicultural samples (Chinese Canadians, Dutch Greek bicultural children), and a variety of cultural primes (e.g., language, experimenter's cultural identity; Ross et al., 2002; Trafimow, Triandis, & Goto, 1991; Verkuyten & Pouliasi, 2002). In sum, the fact that bicultural individuals responded in a culturally typical way as a function of the prior cultural primes they were exposed to suggests that bicultural individuals possess two cultural knowledge systems.

Extending this culture priming research, we argue that bicultural individuals can also form attachment to two cultures. That said, it is an empirical question whether the style of attachment to one culture is correlated with the style of attachment to the other culture. According to attachment theory, the relationship children form with their primary caregiver is represented as a working model, which would then be applied to other close relationships (such as romantic relationships) later in life (e.g., Roisman, Madsen, Hennighausen, Sroufe, & Collins, 2001). Does this model also apply to cultural attachment? That is, is it possible that people who have an insecure (or secure) attachment to their native (heritage) culture are more likely to form a working model that is transferred to the host (mainstream) culture? This may be possible when bicultural individuals encounter two cultures in a distinctively sequential way, such as immigrants or sojourners who enter the host culture after childhood. For bicultural individuals who were born in the host culture (e.g., second or later generations of immigrants), attachment to their native (heritage) culture and the host culture could be independent.

Another unique feature of cultural attachment is that the cultures that individuals possibly attach to may differ in many respects, including level of inclusiveness, relative power and status, and perceived permeability of group boundary. These factors can affect bicultural individuals' motivation to attach to a particular culture in a certain context. To elaborate, Brewer's (1991) optimal distinctiveness theory posited that individuals seek to fulfill both the need to connect and the need to be differentiated. These two needs may act in an antagonistic way that motivates people to identify with a group of higher inclusiveness (i.e., to be connected with a larger ingroup) or to identify with a group of higher exclusiveness (i.e., to be differentiated from a larger outgroup). Brewer and her associates (Brewer & Pickett, 1999; Pickett, Silver, & Brewer, 2002) have shown that people tend to identify with a small group when their sense of distinctiveness is threatened, but tend to identify with a larger group when their sense of connectedness is threatened. To the extent that people may seek to belong to different types of groups (e.g., groups of different inclusiveness) to achieve optimal distinctiveness, minority group members may not identify with the mainstream host culture when the mainstream host culture is too inclusive. For instance, Buriel (1975) found that some Latin Americans living in the United States do not acculturate into the mainstream culture, but instead adopt the norms of their neighborhood ("barrio") with a relatively high proportion of immigrants and minority members, a cultural group that may possibly better meet Latin Americans' need for optimal distinctiveness.

Relative power and status among cultural groups may affect individuals' attachment preference as well. Social identity theory (Tajfel & Turner, 1979) has laid out the conditions under which members from a lower status group would be motivated to "pass" (gain access) into a higher status group. For instance, when the differential power of the two groups is perceived to be legitimate (the status quo is justifiable) and the intergroup boundary is perceived to be permeable (with effort anybody can get access into the higher status group), individuals from the lower status group would be motivated to achieve individual upward mobility and pass into the higher status group. In this case, the individuals may actively seek out the high status group as a source for security while forgoing their lower status group. However, when the differential power of the two groups is perceived to be illegitimate (e.g., the status quo is due to historical injustice) and the intergroup boundary is perceived to be impermeable (exclusion of outgroup members into the higher status group), individuals from the lower status group would be motivated to rebel collectively against the status quo and to reconstruct the social hierarchy. In this case, the individuals may actively seek out their native (heritage) cultural group in opposition to the dominant group of the host (mainstream) culture.

Taken together, research in cultural psychology and social identity literature in general supports our postulation that individuals can form attachments to multiple cultures. In what ways individuals attach to each culture, however, relates to the particular features of the cultural groups (such as inclusiveness, relative status) in different contexts across time.

Development of Cultural Attachment

Bhatia and Ram (2001) observed and criticized that most acculturation models (including Berry's model) assume that acculturation involves a linear trajectory that leads to an end-goal. In response, Hermans (2001) recommended a shift from a focus on the end-states (like "integration" or "competence") to a more process-oriented notion of acculturation that can account for situated, negotiated, and often contested developmental trajectories. To such end, Hermans (2001) applied the "dialogical self" approach to understand the process of acculturation. Specifically, characters or voices are used metaphorically to refer to actual others and the multiple selves, newly generated or established. These voices engage in dialogue within an individual's mind, constantly negotiating and competing for attention and dominance over each other. During the process of acculturation, the voices from the higher status and powerful cultural groups oftentimes dominate the dialogue (Hermans, 2001):

> An increasingly interconnected world society requires attention to dialogical relationships between different cultures, between different selves, and between different cultural positions in the self (e.g., multiple or hyphenated identities). Cultures can be seen as collective voices that function as social positions in the self. Such voices are expressions of embodied and historically situated selves that are constantly involved in dialogical relationships with other voices. At the same time these voices are constantly subjected to differences in power. (p. 272)

Adopting Hermans's "dialogical self" metaphor, we postulate that individuals' self positions in relation to those of the native and host cultures will change through the process of acculturation. These changes facilitate different types of cultural attachment. Moreover, we hypothesize that the processes of acculturation are qualitatively different for first-generation immigrants and later generation ethnic minorities. Consistent with our view, for instance, Tsai, Ying, and Lee (2000) have shown that recent Chinese immigrants (who moved to the United States within the last 6 years) and U.S.-born Chinese Americans attached different meaning to being Chinese and being American. Specifically, "being Chinese" and "being American" were negatively related among recent Chinese immigrants, but were independent among U.S.-born Chinese Americans.

Similarly, Phinney (2002) observed substantial identity difference between the first-generation immigrants and later generation ethnic minorities among a number of ethnic minority groups in the United States:

> The important indicators of identity change are somewhat different for each succeeding generation. For members of the first generation, identity as a member of their culture of origin is secure and unlikely to change substantially. They may or may not develop an "American" identity; the extent to which they begin to feel American seems to be associated, in part, with learning English, developing social networks beyond the group, and becoming culturally competent in the new context (La Fromboise et al., 1993). For members of the second generation, an "American" identity is generally secure, in part because citizenship is granted with birth, and ethnic identity is likely to be associated with retention of ethnic language and social networks. For the third and later generations, the issues become more complex. Various contextual, historical, and political factors unrelated to acculturation influence the extent to which ethnic identity is retained. For non-European ethnic groups, racism and discrimination play a role in the preservation of ethnic identity, perhaps because a strong ethnic identity can provide a sense of group solidarity in the face of discrimination. Until immigrants and their descendants from non-European groups

> are accepted and treated as equals in the United States, as have been later generations of European immigrants (Waters, 1990), ethnic identity will remain important in their lives regardless of their level of acculturation. (p. 78)

In short, acculturation for the first-generation immigrants may involve adding the host culture as a new self position, whereas acculturation for later generation ethnic minorities may involve retention of the native culture or construction of "proxies" for their native culture as possible self positions. In light of this difference, we discuss separately the development of cultural attachment for first-generation immigrants and for later generation ethnic minorities.

Development of Cultural Attachment for First-Generation Immigrants

When immigrants arrive in a new culture, it is easy for them to focus on the differences between the new culture and their native cultures because these are the areas that draw their attention and require new learning. Also, with little knowledge and experience in interacting with the host culture, the position of the self is more likely to align with the native culture. As a result, the difference between the self and the native culture may be attenuated, whereas the difference between the native culture and the host culture are accentuated (as illustrated in the top panel of Figure 8.1). This type of positioning would make it more likely for recent immigrants to use their native culture than the host culture as the source of felt security. The group that possibly violates this prediction is refugees. The trauma that refugees are likely to have experienced in their native culture could lead to unresolved negative feelings associated with the native culture, thus resulting in the refugees displaying a lower likelihood of secure attachment to the native culture than do other types of immigrants.

When the individuals have more exposure to the host culture, they may acquire more accurate knowledge of the attributes of the host culture (Chiu & Chen, 2004). In this context, the difference between the native culture and host culture may then be less accentuated than before. At the same time, the exposure to a different culture may challenge the cultural worldviews prescribed by the native culture. As a result, the position of the self would migrate away from the native culture and move toward the host culture (as illustrated by the middle panel in Figure 8.1). At this time, the individuals may be more likely to form a secure attachment to the host culture than they did previously. However, if prejudice and discrimination against the immigrant's ethnic group is prevalent in the host culture, the likelihood of having unresolved negative experiences with the host culture would be heightened, thus resulting in a lower likelihood of forming a secure attachment with the host culture than would otherwise be the case. This prediction is corroborated by the finding that ethnic minority immigrants who reported more discrimination were less likely to identify themselves as Americans than were those who reported less discrimination (Rumbaut, 1994).

Initial exposure to the host culture

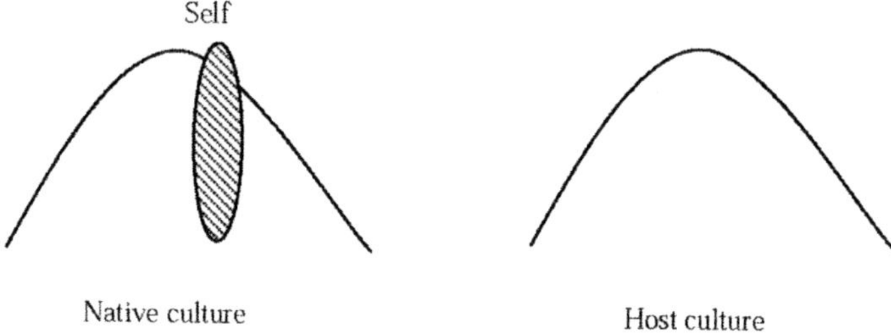

After some exposure to the host culture

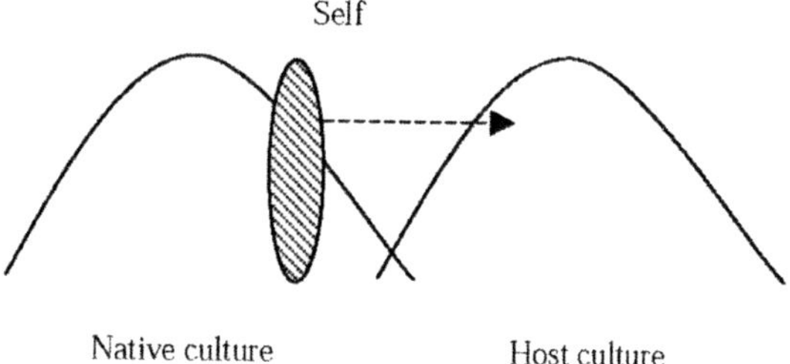

After extensive exposure to the host culture

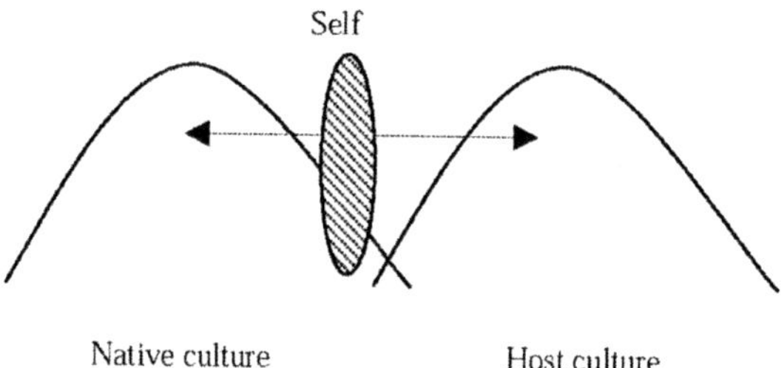

FIGURE 8.1. Idealized development of cultural attachment for first-generation immigrants.

Similarly, we found that some immigrant participants idealized American culture before migrating to the United States. These participants then suffered from emotional distress when they found that their experiences in the United States after migration did not match their prior expectations. As a result, these individuals showed an "illusory" attachment to the host culture before migration, but then displayed insecure attachment to American culture when it fell short of their high expectations.

The host culture can incur prejudice and discrimination against ethnic immigrant groups, and immigrant groups can also incur prejudice and discrimination against the host culture. This may occur, for instance, in colonies where immigrant groups become the elite ruling class of the host society. The superiority feelings of the immigrant group may prevent a secure attachment to the host culture. To the extent that the new immigrant ruling class has political power in reforming the host culture and simulating their native culture in the host society, the immigrant group would not see a need to build a secure attachment to the host culture.

If the immigrants can successfully resolve the negative experiences they encountered in the host culture, they would be able to form a secure attachment with the host culture as well. This process does not require immigrants to forgo their attachment to their native culture. Rather, it is possible that these immigrants have secure attachment to both the native and host cultures. These individuals would be able to switch the position of the self between the two cultural systems (as represented in the bottom panel of Figure 8.1).

Development of Cultural Attachment for Later Generation Ethnic Minorities

As noted, the mainstream culture may be the most immediately available culture for the later generation ethnic minorities to form an attachment. Moreover, as the transmission of the knowledge and skill of the heritage culture wanes across generations, later generation ethnic minorities (especially the third or later generations) may lack the skills (such as language) to access their heritage culture and thus may not be able to form a clear representation of that culture (as presented by a dotted line in the top panel of Figure 8.2). They would thus be more likely to form a secure attachment with the mainstream culture. This would not be problematic if the mainstream culture grants "full" membership to these later generation ethnic minorities, as exemplified by the ease with which descendants of some groups of European immigrants (such as British, German) become mainstream Americans (Hirschman, 1983). However, when descendants of certain ethnic immigrant groups have been continuously seen as minorities and "atypical" members of the culture (Devos & Banaji, 2005), their likelihood of encountering rejection from the culture would be increased. Thus, using the mainstream culture as the sole base of attachment could be risky for these ethnic minorities.

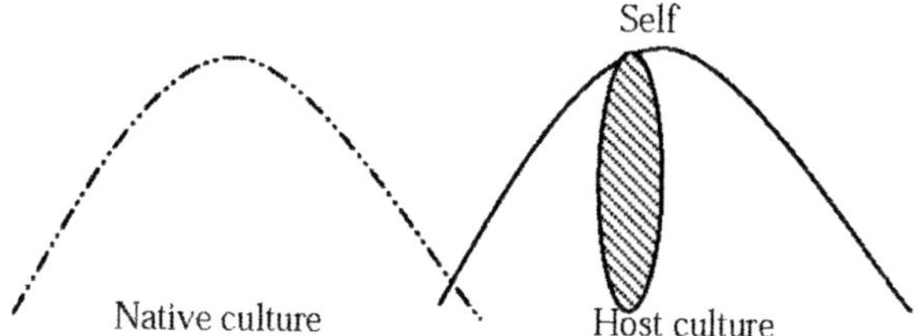

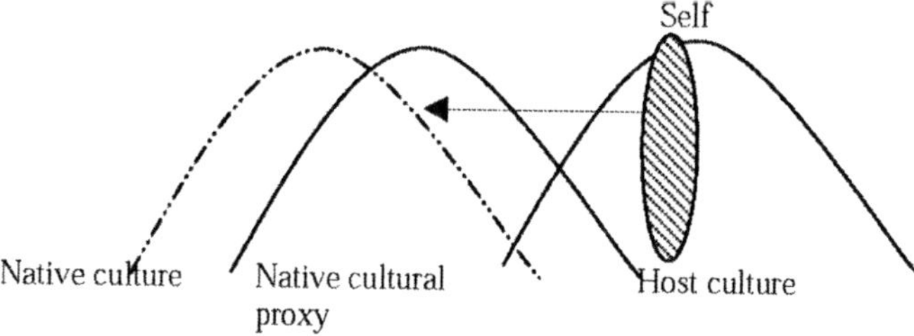

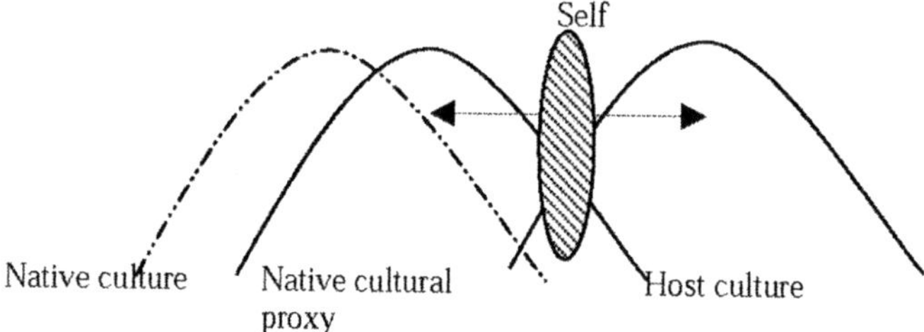

FIGURE 8.2. Idealized development of cultural attachment for later generation ethnic minorities.

As an alternative secure base, the descendants of ethnic minority immigrants may seek out "proxies" of their heritage cultures in the mainstream society. Examples of these cultural "proxies" are pan-ethnic groups such as Asian Americans and Latin Americans. Arguably, these cultural proxies are created within American society and each of the cultural proxies has combined diverse cultural groups.

A case in point is Asian Americans, a category that includes descendants of Filipinos, Chinese, Koreans, Japanese, East Indians, and other Easterners in general (see Hall & Okazaki, 2002). Despite its internal heterogeneity, the cultural "proxy" is represented in later generation ethnic minorities as a contested cultural position (as illustrated in the middle panel of Figure 8.2). With this alternative secure base, it is possible for individuals to switch the self between this pan-ethnic cultural position and the host cultural position, and form two secure bases of attachment (as illustrated in the bottom panel of Figure 8.2).

Individual Differences in the Likelihood of Establishing Bicultural Attachment

We think that there are individual differences in the likelihood of establishing secure cultural attachments. For example, Benet-Martinez, Leu, Lee, and Morris (2002) proposed perceived compatibility as an important factor in determining whether bicultural individuals would view the two cultural identities as complementary or see the two identities as conflicting and thus find it difficult to integrate the two. Moreover, Benet-Martinez et al. (2002) found that participants with high bicultural integration displayed cultural response patterns that were more consistent with the cultural cues in the environment than did those with low bicultural integration, suggesting that viewing the bicultural identities as compatible allows individuals to switch between cultural frames.

No and Hong (2004a, 2004b) further examined whether Korean American participants' beliefs concerning the malleability of race would also moderate their cultural frame switching processes. In particular, the researchers discerned two types of beliefs: Some participants held an essentialist view of race (race is fixed, reflects deep biological essence, and is indicative of abilities and traits), whereas other participants held a social constructivist view of race (race is malleable according to the sociopolitical or economic context, is socially constructed, and racial categories are arbitrary). The researchers further reasoned that believing in race as fixed (vs. malleable) would lead minority members to view the boundary between their own ethnic group and the mainstream group as impermeable. As a result, believing in fixed (vs. malleable) race would create resistance toward cultural frame switching, such that the mainstream American icons would remind Korean Americans of their minority ethnicity (i.e., "I am a Korean."), and thereby elicit contrasting responses (i.e., prototypical Korean responses instead of prototypical American responses) from these individuals. Indeed, in these two studies, a stronger belief in fixed (vs. malleable) race was correlated with more contrasting responses when the Korean American participants were primed with American cultural icons.

In summary, we argue that individuals can form secure attachments to two cultures, and the processes through which such attachments developed could be determined by immigration history, level of prejudice and discrimination in the host society, and the individual's perception and beliefs.

ASSESSING CULTURAL ATTACHMENT

Although rich in data and theory, to this point the psychological study of acculturation has relied almost exclusively on structured questionnaires (see a critique of this practice by Rudmin, 2003). A yet-unexplored alternative to identifying variations in acculturation is to conceptualize bicultural identity as reflected in adults' narratives about their cultural experiences. Such a shift toward analyzing bicultural individuals' discourse related to their cultural experiences reflects an expectation that *how* individuals have come to understand the significance of salient, culturally themed life events may in many cases be more critical than *what* people describe about their experiences (e.g., the positive or negative valence of recalled memories).

A similar distinction has been made in research on adult attachment, examining the fate of earlier childhood experiences. Within this literature, researchers have argued that the foundation for freely evaluating and thereby coherently narrating one's childhood experiences as an adult are supportive experiences with attachment figures in childhood (see, e.g., Roisman, Padrón, Sroufe, & Egeland, 2002). In the developmental literature, such emotionally integrated adults are described as secure/autonomous, an orientation toward prior experiences that seems to confer distinct advantages in terms of successfully engaging adult relationships generally (e.g., with romantic partners; Roisman et al., 2001) and providing effective parenting for the next generation specifically (van IJzendoorn, 1995). Extending from this, we postulate that adults who have formed secure/autonomous attachment to a culture should be able to freely evaluate their experiences with the culture and thereby present a coherent narrative of their cultural experiences when asked to do so. To test this expectation, we adapted a well-validated protocol in developmental research known as the Adult Attachment Interview as the main methodology for our research.

Adapting the Adult Attachment Interview to Measure Cultural Attachment

In childhood, security is generally evidenced in observable responses to separation and reunion, demonstrating that individuals are able to use a primary caregiver as a secure base from which to effectively navigate their immediate environments. Whereas secure infants are able to flexibly explore their environments and use their caregivers as safe havens when distressed (e.g., their relationships allow them to regulate positive and negative affect), insecurity reflects either suppressed (avoidant) or exaggerated (resistant) responses to separation and reunion with implications for secure base behavior.

By adulthood, however, attachment experiences are theorized to become internalized in the form of representations that guide interpersonal behavior (Main, Kaplan, & Cassidy, 1985; Roisman et al., 2001). Perhaps the most widely used and well-validated instrument in developmental research for identifying such adult attachment representations is George, Kaplan, and Main's (1985) Adult Attachment Interview (AAI). In the hour-long AAI, adults are asked emotionally charged questions regarding their childhood experiences, and asked to provide memories relevant to loss, separation, rejection, and trauma. Next, participants' narratives are analyzed according to Grice's (1975) maxims regarding collaborative discourse. Grice (1975) delineated implicit expectations that govern interpersonal communications—namely, that speakers are expected to be truthful (the maxim of quality), succinct and yet complete (the maxim of quantity), relevant (the maxim of relation), and clear and orderly (show good manner). Discourse that is judged to be consistent with these maxims is described as *coherent*. In contrast, significant violations of these rules, as reflected, for example, by incomplete, overly brief, or overly lengthy and unruly narratives, are identified as *incoherent*.

Based on Grice's maxims, participants can be classified into one of three primary attachment categories, which reflect the quality of the discourse they produce: *secure/autonomous*, for individuals who are able to flexibly and freely evaluate their childhood experiences and provide coherent narratives, whether positive or negative in nature; *insecure-dismissing*, for individuals who defensively distance themselves from the emotional content of the interview, either by normalizing harsh early memories or by idealizing their caregivers; and *insecure-preoccupied*, for individuals who are caught up, often angrily, in their prior relationship experiences (Main & Goldwyn, 1998; see Hesse, 1999, for more details).

To examine the degree to which bicultural individuals have come to develop coherent, psychologically integrated narratives about their prior experiences in their native and host cultures, we borrowed extensively from the structure and coding system of AAI and derived the Cultural Attachment Interview (CAI). The CAI is approximately 1 hour in duration and requires participants to generate five words each to characterize their experiences with the native and host cultures, respectively, and provide specific personal stories that support their characterizations of the two cultures. In addition, participants are asked questions related to rejection and discrimination by the native and host cultures. The appendix shows the interview protocol we developed.

Based on the verbatim transcripts of participants' verbal responses from CAI, we evaluated the bicultural participants' extent of secure attachment to their native and host cultures. As already described, individuals rated as more prototypically secure communicate their personal stories, positive or negative, in a coherent manner. In contrast, individuals rated as more prototypically insecure with respect to their cultural experiences are either defensive, as reflected by vague, impersonal, irrelevant, or overidealizing narratives, or angrily/passively overwhelmed by their cultural experiences. (At this stage, we did not attempt to differentiate between dismissing and preoccupied forms of insecurity.)

Empirical Test and Preliminary Findings

Participants

We interviewed 83 Chinese Americans using the CAI. To meet the goal of our study, we specifically recruited participants who had resided in the United States for at least 3 years, and who self-identified as proficient in the English language. The sample was 41% male and 59% female, with an age range from 18 to 59 (*M* age = 26.8, *SD* = 7.62). Fourteen participants were born in the United States, and the rest had resided in the United States from 3 to 21 years (*M* length of residence = 8.1 years). The majority of the participants were graduate or undergraduate students from diverse socioeconomic family backgrounds.

Procedures

The study was conducted in two phases. In the first phase, participants completed structured questionnaires, which included the Adult Self-Report inventory (Achenbach, 1997), assessing participants' psychological adjustment, including anxiety/depression, withdrawal, somatic complains, thought problems, attention problems, aggressive behavior, rule-breaking behaviors, and intrusive behaviors. In addition, participants also filled out a subjective well-being scale (Diener, 1994; Lucas, Diener, & Suh, 1996). About 10 days later, participants completed the Cultural Attachment Interview. All the interviews were conducted by a female, ethnic Chinese interviewer, and English language was used throughout the interviews. The interviews were videotaped. Moreover, the participants were connected to bioamplifiers that measured their skin conductance levels and heart rate throughout the interviews. Because both the videotapes and the physiological data were time coded, we were able to assess participants' physiological changes while they were describing their experiences with the Chinese and American cultures.

Verbatim transcripts of interviews were analyzed in terms of *overall coherence of discourse* according to Grice's maxims. Based on these evaluations, two coders independently rated the extent to which the participants were securely versus insecurely attached to Chinese culture and American culture, respectively, on a 7-point Likert scale.

We were aware of some of the pitfalls of using the Cultural Attachment Interview. For instance, our interview was conducted in English and thus could be affected by the participants' English proficiency. However, all of our participants were either current or former students who were screened for English proficiency when they were admitted into the university. These restrictions safeguarded that our participants were able to communicate in English adequately. In fact, no participants showed language problems likely to inhibit fluent communication with the interviewer in our interviews.

Results

Based on the limited protocols we have analyzed, we found that although there was a slight positive correlation between participants' Chinese and American cultural attachment scores (i.e., coders' ratings of the extent to which participants were securely versus insecurely attached to each culture), the two culture attachments showed different correlations with subjective well-being. Specifically, secure attachment to Chinese culture is not significantly associated with subjective well-being, whereas secure attachment to American culture is associated with higher levels of subjective well-being. It is possible that because the participants were residing in a Midwest, predominately European American community, a secure attachment to American culture would give participants an advantage in adapting to the environment. In future analyses, we plan to consider simultaneously the contributions of Chinese and American cultural attachment, generation status, and length of residency in the United States in predicting participants' psychological adjustment as measured by the Achenbach's Adult Self Report Inventory.

As part of an effort to validate this measure of acculturation, we have also begun to examine the patterns of autonomic response during the administration of the CAI. We expect that individuals who have not been able to successfully resolve negative cultural experiences will find discussion of such memories physiologically distressing. Such expectations are consistent with a small but growing literature demonstrating that adults' narratives about their childhood experiences with caregivers appear to be associated with distinctive patterns of physiological response (Dozier & Kobak, 1992; Roisman, 2004; Roisman, Tsai, & Chiang, 2004). Of particular interest are individuals who seem to systematically misrepresent the reality of their experiences. Such defensive adults have consistently been shown to demonstrate evidence of electrodermal reactivity (i.e., heightened skin conductance), a specific physiological correlate of emotional suppression (Fowles, 1980, 1988). In research using the AAI, adults who become angrily or passively caught up discussing their early lives have, in contrast, shown cardiovascular reactivity (i.e., heightened heart rate), suggesting behavioral activation. The approach outlined earlier emphasizes a growing trend in the study of acculturation focusing on how the development of ethnic identity as a member of a minority culture may play a role in not just psychological adjustment but physical health as well (Williams & Neighbors, 2001; see Guyll, Matthews, & Bromberger, 2001; and Harrell, Hall, & Taliaferro, 2003, for reviews). Such work suggests that the impact of acculturation experiences is inherently multilevel. As such, we believe that research on acculturation should also take a multimethod, multilevel approach, examining psychological as well as potential physiological impacts of acculturation experiences.

Furthermore, we are exploring other useful ways to analyze the narratives. For instance, it would be interesting to examine whether contrasts between Chinese and American cultures were mentioned in the narratives, whether the self was involved as actor versus observer, and whether the stories happened in China or in America. This data would allow us to examine the participants' representation of Chinese and American cultures and how the self is located in relation to the two cultures—the key elements in our postulations on the development of cultural attachment. In addition, we are exploring other analysis schemes as well, such as using interpretive phenomenological analysis (Smith, 1996) to identity major themes in the narratives, and schemes used in the Life Story Interview (McAdams, 1985, 1993) to assess whether the cultural experiences have provided a sense of overall purpose and unity in life for the participants.

ADDED VALUE OF THE CULTURAL ATTACHMENT APPROACH

Many researchers have agreed that the study of acculturation is still in its infancy (e.g., Chun, Organista, & Marin, 2002). There are still many theoretical and methodological gaps in the study of acculturation. In the following, we point out some of these gaps and discuss how our new approach might help to fill these gaps.

Is Acculturation Unidimensional or Multifaceted?

In the preface to their recently edited book on advances in theory, measurement, and applied research on acculturation, Chun et al. (2002, p. xxv) candidly wrote:

> The label acculturation is used by some authors to denote patterns of adaptation that imply only one outcome is possible—assimilation (Vasquez, 1984).... In this sense, many researchers and practitioners assume that certain components of one's culture of origin are lost when a new repertoire of skills and behaviors are learned from another distinct culture. This unidimensional notion of acculturation continues to plague the field despite numerous suggestions by researchers to think of this process as a multifaceted phenomenon.

Echoing this observation, in their extensive content analysis of 21 major measures of acculturation that targeted different ethnic groups, Zane and Mak (2002) concluded that 14 of the measures were constructed in a bipolar manner. That is, acculturation was measured along a continuum representing the native culture at one extreme and the host culture at the other extreme. Endorsement of one orientation entails rejection of the other orientation. "This linear model precludes the possibility that individuals may retain various elements of their culture of origin while simultaneously learning about another culture" (p. 54).

In fact, numerous studies have shown that individual acculturation into the host culture is independent of the retention of their native culture, and thus acculturation is hardly unidimensional. For example, Cuellar, Nyberg, Maldonado, and Roberts (1997) found that ethnic identity change among Mexican Americans was strongly associated with the extent of involvement in Mexican cultural activities and largely independent of their acculturation orientation toward the U.S. culture. That is, respondents' Mexican identity can remain strong without interfering with their participation in the host society, and similarly, respondents' participation in the host society does not necessarily undermine their Mexican identity. Furthermore, Ryder, Alden, and Paulhus (2000) compared the reliability and predictive validity of a unidimensional and a bidimensional measure of acculturation. The bidimensional measure revealed two independent dimensions corresponding to heritage and mainstream cultural identification. Moreover, the two dimensions displayed patterns of correlations with personality, self-identity, and psychosocial adjustment that were more consistent with the theoretical predictions than did the unidimensional measure, suggesting that the bidimensional model is a more valid and functional operationalization of acculturation.

Berry's (1990) typology of acculturation strategies is bidimensional as well. The two dimensions include native cultural maintenance (Is it important to maintain one's ethnic identity and characteristics?) and contact and participation with the host culture (Is it important to get involved with the larger host society?). Crossing the two dimensions gives rise to a four-fold typology, namely integration (maintaining ethnic identity and getting involved with the host culture at the same time), separation (maintaining ethnic identity while avoiding involvement with the host society), assimilation (rejecting ethnic identity but involving the host culture) and marginalization (rejecting ethnic identity culture and avoiding involvement with the host culture).

Our approach bears close resemblance to Berry's model in that we also posit that the types of attachment to the native (heritage) and host (mainstream) culture may be independent. However, unlike Berry, we focused on the psychological integration of experiences in relation to the native and host culture. In our view, the core of acculturation involves incorporating cultural experiences, positive or negative, as a part of life and feeling at peace with the experiences. We do not deny that behavioral manifestations (e.g., food preference, friend or mate selection, language use), which are often the focus of Berry's model, are important indicators of acculturation strategies. However, we worry that such focus could also result from "inauthenticity." That is, individuals who display an integration or assimilation strategy could do so unwillingly because they did not have resources in their environment (e.g., lack of ethnic grocery stores, living in a homogeneously White community in the United States) to support other strategies (e.g., separation).

Moreover, our goal is to examine the process of acculturation rather than typologies of acculturation strategies. We purposely used a Likert rating scale in evaluating participants' states of mind with regard to secure versus insecure attachment and thereby avoided the pitfalls created by typological classifications (see Rudmin, 2003, for criticism of Berry's acculturation typology, and see Fraley & Waller, 1998, for criticism of attachment typologies). As such, our approach may help to change the emphasis of the literature from an end-state to a process orientation.

Which Orientation of Acculturation Is More Adaptive?

After reviewing extensive research on acculturation and adaptation, Berry (1997) concluded that "in recent studies in societies that are more 'melting pot' or assimilationist in orientation, the Integration strategy remained the most adaptive (and conversely marginalization was the least adaptive) strategy" (p. 25). Findings from some recent studies corroborate Berry's conclusion. For example, Ying (1995) examined the link between Berry's four acculturation orientations and depression in a Chinese American sample residing in San Francisco. Participants who endorsed the integration orientation in activities (i.e., those who enjoyed both American and Chinese activities, such as food, movies, and music) reported less depression, more positive and less negative affect (compared to participants who endorsed the separation orientation), and higher life satisfaction (compared to participants who endorsed separation and marginalization orientation). Research on new immigrant families also reveals that integration showed better adaptation. For instance, Nguyen, Messe, and Stollak (1999) found that bicultural Vietnamese American adolescents (i.e., those who are equally involved in Vietnamese and American cultures) reported more positive family relationships compared with adolescents with less bicultural involvement. It is possible that family members who can skillfully switch between cultural systems may be better able to prevent conflicts in the family.

In sharp contrast to these findings, however, other research did not find conclusive evidence that greater integration into the U.S. culture was necessarily associated with better mental health for many ethnic minority groups. For instance, Rogler, Cortes, and Malgady (1991) reviewed 30 empirical studies on Latin Americans' mental health and found that only three studies showed that greater integration was linked with better mental health. Twelve of the remaining studies showed that greater assimilation into the American culture was associated with poorer mental health, 13 studies showed that less assimilation was associated with poorer mental health, and two studies showed mixed results. Similarly, mixed findings were also reported in Ying's (1995) study. She found that participants endorsing the integration and assimilation orientation in the social domain (i.e., those who had both Chinese and American close friends and those who had only

American close friends, respectively) reported more negative affect than participants who endorsed the separation orientation (i.e., those who had only Chinese close friends). In short, the mental health benefits of endorsing the integration or assimilation orientation are inconclusive.

A key issue seems to be the generation cohort of the immigrants. For instance, Furnham and Li (1993) found that second-generation Chinese in Britain, who were more likely to report feeling that they were part of the host community, were significantly more likely than those who did not feel part of the host community to report greater psychological symptoms. Similarly, Robins and Regier (1991) found that the lifetime prevalence of mental illness of U.S.-born Mexican Americans was much higher than that of the first-generation Mexican American immigrants. Organista, Organista, and Kurasaki (2002) thus suggested that the poorer mental health of native-born Mexican Americans, despite their greater assimilation into the U.S. culture than first-generation Mexican Americans, "has to do with their especially stressful experience in America as a devalued and discriminated ethnic minority group" (p. 154).

Our approach might address these mixed findings concerning acculturation and mental health. We believe that developing a secure attachment with at least one culture is vital to a person's mental health because, as we argued earlier, individuals find meaning in their life by referring to the worldviews of the cultural group. For second or later generation ethnic minorities, their ethnic culture may be less likely to support a secure attachment because they do not have ethnic knowledge or skills (e.g., ethnic language skills or knowledge about ethnic practices) and thus would be more likely to turn to the mainstream culture for security. However, descendants of ethnic minorities may face a hard time to be treated as "full" members in the mainstream culture. As a result, the greater likelihood of these descendants to use the host culture as their sole base of secure attachment would paradoxically increase their likelihood of feeling rejected and abandoned, and thus becoming vulnerable to mental problems. This may explain why stronger acculturation has been found to be associated with poorer mental health among third or later generation ethnic minority groups in the United States.

Secure attachment to their native culture can protect individuals' psychological health if the environment affords attachment to their native culture (e.g., having means to practice the native culture, or having an effective voice in the political system). These speculations are consistent with Ethier and Deaux's (1994) longitudinal study of Latin American students during their first year at predominately European American universities. Students with initially strong ethnic identity were more involved in Latin American cultural activities than were students with weaker ethnic identity. As a result, the former group showed heightened ethnic identification after a year. By contrast, without a means to form meaningful relations with their native culture in the new environment, the latter group perceived more threat in the environment and showed decreases in self-esteem associated with group membership and weakened identification with their ethnic group.

Similarly, immigrants who live in their respective ethnic communities in many cities across the United States (e.g., Chinatown, Little Italy) or cities with high concentration of their co-ethnics (e.g., San Francisco for the Asian community) could still adapt well even if they have not formed a secure attachment to American culture (cf. Ying, 1995). These immigrants, however, could become vulnerable if they relocate to an environment that does not allow close connection with their ethnic group (e.g., a predominately White community). Indeed, in our study of a sample of young Chinese American adults who resided in the midwest United States where the population was predominantly European American, participants who were not securely attached to American culture showed poorer subjective well-being than did those who were securely attached to American culture. Consistent with our speculation, these findings suggest that minority members who have unresolved emotion in relating to the mainstream culture could become vulnerable to psychological problems when residing in an environment that does not afford close connection with their native culture.

We also predicted that individuals who do not form a secure attachment to any cultural group (be it the native culture, host culture, or the native cultural "proxies") would be more vulnerable to mental problems than individuals who form secure attachment to at least one cultural group. Conversely, individuals who form a secure attachment with both the native and host cultures would be flexible depending on the context in accessing either cultural group as a reference. This flexibility would increase the competence of coping and, in turn, links to better mental health outcomes.

In short, our approach may help to explain why bicultural attachment is associated with the best mental health outcomes, and separation and assimilation can be adaptive given some favorable conditions. Specifically, separation can be adaptive if the environment affords attachment to the native culture. Assimilation can be adaptive if the immigrant group faces little prejudice and discrimination in the host society.

Is the Rate of Acculturation Uniform in Different Domains and Contexts?

In their extensive content analysis of major measures of acculturation, Zane and Mak (2002) concluded that most measures sampled acculturation orientations in only two to three domains and these domains are often not overlapping across the measures. Among the overlapping domains, language usage and living habits/preferences (such as food and music preferences) were the most frequently sampled domains. Overreliance on a few domains can be problematic if the rate of acculturation is not uniform across domains. In fact, even within the same domain, the rate of acculturation has been shown to vary across contexts. For example, language usage could change according to contexts. Immigrants may prefer to use English in public contexts (e.g., at work or in school) but to use their native language in private contexts (e.g., at home, with close friends). By the same token, Phinney (2002) also found that the link between language use and acculturation was not uniform among different immigrant cohorts. For first-generation immigrants, greater English language proficiency predicted a stronger American identity, but ethnic language was unrelated to their ethnic identity. In contrast, for U.S.-born ethnic minorities, greater ethnic language proficiency predicted stronger ethnic identity, but English was not related to American identity. As such, language use may reflect different acculturation processes for different generation cohorts.

Acculturation can also influence some core values at different rates. For example, Sabogal, Marin, Otero-Sabogal, VanOss Marin, and Perez-Stable (1987) showed that some aspects of the Mexican cultural value of familism (i.e., perceived support from the family) remained strong and personally important regardless of having assimilated into the host culture of the United States. However, other components of familialism (i.e., familial obligations and the power of family members as referents) diminished in importance as acculturation progressed.

Instead of sampling behaviors and preferences in different domains and contexts, our approach focuses on assessing a general state of mind regarding the individual's cultural experience. In the Cultural Attachment Interview, we allow respondents to generate their own stories and select the domains that they deem meaningful. As such, we do not use a nomothetic approach that relies on a preselected set of domains regardless of the meaningfulness of those domains for individual respondents. Instead, we took an idiographic approach that allows individuals to select domains that are meaningful to them. In this way, our approach allows the unique "voices" of respondents to be heard.

CONCLUSIONS

In this chapter, we proposed a model of cultural attachment—a new approach to the process of acculturation. We began with the discussion of the parallels between interpersonal attachment and cultural attachment and the unique functions of cultural attachment (including the need for belongingness, existential need, and need for consensual validation). Then, we argued that bicultural exposure set up a "critical" context in which individuals faced the task of managing their experiences in relating to the native and host cultures. Whether individuals can successfully resolve negative experience and integrate cultural experiences into a meaningful part of their life is consequential for the individuals' mental health and well-being. We also speculated how different generation cohorts (first-generation immigrants and later generations) face different issues in establishing a secure attachment with the native and host cultures and thus have different developmental trajectories of bicultural identity. Throughout the discussion, we emphasized that the environment (e.g., whether the environment allows individuals to practice their native culture) and the attitudes of the mainstream group toward the minority members can alter the developmental trajectory of bicultural identity and the impact of cultural attachment on mental health. To test our model, we constructed the Cultural Attachment Interview and administered it to a group of Chinese American participants. We evaluated the coherence of the participants' narratives with respect to their experience with Chinese and American culture and thereby the extent to which the participants were securely versus insecurely attached to Chinese and American culture. Preliminary results showed that an insecure attachment to American culture was associated with poorer subjective well-being. Finally, we discussed how our new approach sheds light on some key issues in acculturation.

Our model focuses on cultural attachment as defined by emotional integration of bicultural experience, which departs from the focus of acceptance/approach versus rejection/avoidance of native and host cultures of traditional models of acculturation. We believe that it is important to examine the quality of cultural attachment because it reflects how well people can handle and resolve potentially conflicting beliefs, values, and situations of the two cultures and thus should be consequential in the individual's adaptation in the new culture. In our future work, we look forward to empirically testing the incremental advantage of our model over earlier models of acculturation.

ACKNOWLEDGMENTS

The preparation of this chapter was supported in part by Grant # 03143 from the Campus Research Board of the University of Illinois at Urbana-Champaign awarded to the first author. The authors thank the editors, Chris Fraley, John Holmes, Sumie Okazaki, Floyd Rudmin, and Harry Triandis for their comments on an earlier draft of this chapter.

APPENDIX: THE CULTURAL ATTACHMENT INTERVIEW FOR CHINESE-AMERICANS

(The words in bold fonts were the interviewer's script)

This interview focuses on the way bicultural people feel about their primary culture and secondary culture. So, I would like to ask you about your experiences in the two cultures, how you feel about them, and how these cultural experiences may have affected you. And we would encourage you to try to focus on your early experience in each culture as much as possible.

1. **Could you please tell me how long you have been in the U.S.?**

2. At what age did you come to the U.S.?

3. Where did you come from? Have you lived in other countries aside from the U.S. too? Did you stay more than a year there?
(Some of them may come from places other than Mainland China. And we should trace all the way back to the country of origin and all the places where they have spent substantial amount of time, i.e., more than 1 year.)

4. Is that a city or rural area?
(If lived in more than one place, have participant list each separately, indicating how long he or she lived there.)

5. Did you come to the U.S. with your family members or close friends?
If yes, **Who are they?**
(If the subject answers no in Question 5, proceed to Question 6. Otherwise, skip to Question 7.)

6. Did your family members join you in the U.S. later on? When? Did your close friends join you and when? Are they still here with you?

7. Did you come to the U.S. to study or work? Please tell me your major or your job.
ABOVE ARE ALL INTRODUCTORY (WARM UP) QUESTIONS AND MIGHT BE CONSIDERED AS ONE QUESTION WITH MANY PROBES

In the following, we would like to get your view about Chinese and American cultures. We are interested especially in your personal experiences with the two cultures. We will first talk about Chinese culture and then move on to American culture.

8. What do you think about Chinese culture?
(This is a difficult question. Let the interviewee struggle for 2 or 3 minutes.)

9. Now I'd like you to use five adjectives or words to describe your personal experiences with Chinese culture. I want to emphasize that we want the words to be related to your own stories with the Chinese culture rather than just general descriptions of Chinese culture. I know this will take a bit of time, so please take a minute to think about it. I'll write these words down and ask why you chose them.

You have mentioned _____, _____, _____, _____, ______
Among these five words, are they all related to your personal experiences with the Chinese culture?
(If yes, then move on. If no, ask which one is not related to personal experience. Remove the adjective and ask the interviewee to come up with a replacement.)

9. (a) Ok, now let me go through some of your descriptions. First you said ___________. Can you remember a specific time when you experienced Chinese culture as ____________?

(After asking this question, probe the participant at most twice in order to get the full, specific story to the extent that the interviewer would be able to picture the event in mind.)

Possible Probes:

Can you think of a personal experience that makes you feel Chinese culture being _____?

Can you tell me specific incidents that happened to you?

Tell me more about it.

What happened?

How is it related to Chinese culture?

9. (b) Next, you said ____________. Can you remember a specific time when you experienced Chinese culture as ____________?

9. (c) Next, you said ____________. Can you remember a specific time when you experienced Chinese culture as ____________?

9. (d) Next, you said ____________. Can you remember a specific time when you experienced Chinese culture as ____________?

9. (e) Next, you said ____________. Can you remember a specific time when you experienced Chinese culture as ____________?

The main goal of these questions is to probe natural narratives. Thus, probes should aim at getting the interviewees to tell their own personal experiences (versus general definitions of terms), and tie their experiences to the culture.

10. What do you think about American culture?
(This is a difficult question. Let the interviewee struggle for 2 or 3 minutes.)

11. I'd like you to use five adjectives or words to describe your personal experiences in American culture. Again, I want to emphasize that we want the words to be related to your own stories with the American culture rather than just general descriptions of American culture. I know this will take a bit of time, so please take a minute to think about it. I'll write these words down and ask why you chose them.

You have mentioned _____, _____, _____, _____, _____
Among these five words, are they all related to your personal experiences with the American culture?

(If yes, then move on. If no, ask which one is not related to personal experience. Remove the adjective and ask the interviewee to come up with a replacement.)

11. (a) Ok, now let me go through some of your descriptions. First you said ___________. Can you remember a specific time when you experienced American culture as ____________?

(After asking this question, probe the participant at most twice in order to get the full, specific story to the extent that the interviewer would be able to picture the event in mind.)

Possible Probes:

Can you think of a personal experience that makes you feel American culture being _____?

Can you tell me specific incidents that happened to you?

Tell me more about it.

What happened?

How is it related to American culture?

11. (b) Next, you said ____________. Can you remember a specific time when you experienced American culture as ____________?

11. (c) Next, you said ____________. Can you remember a specific time when you experienced American culture as ____________?

11. (d) Next, you said ____________. Can you remember a specific time when you experienced American culture as ____________?

11. (e) Next, you said ____________. Can you remember a specific time when you experienced American culture as ____________?

12. Have you ever felt close to Chinese culture emotionally?
If yes, ask: **When did that happen?**
Can you tell me one incident/time/memory when you felt close to Chinese culture?

13. Have you ever felt discriminated within or rejected from Chinese culture?
If yes, ask: **When did that happen?**
Can you tell me one incident/time/memory when you felt being discriminated / rejected?

14. Have you ever felt close to American culture emotionally?
If yes, ask: **When did that happen?**
Can you tell me one incident/time/memory when you felt close to American culture?

15. Have you ever felt discriminated within or rejected from American culture?
If yes, ask: **When did that happen?**
Can you tell me one incident/time/memory when you felt being discriminated / rejected?

16. If you were born again, would you choose to be a Chinese or an American?
If the interviewee says "American," clarify and ask: **White American? Why?**
The main goal of this question is to understand the reason behind the interviewees' choice. In particular, to see if they substantiate their choice with positive, negative, or balanced experiences in the two cultures.

17. How have your experiences with the Chinese and American cultures affected your personality or the person you are now?

18. Do you have moments when you feel that you don't know whether you are a Chinese or an American?
If yes, ask: **Have you resolved the issue? How?**

19. Is there anything else that you would like to add?
This is the end of the interview. Thank you.

REFERENCES

Achenbach, T. M. (1997). *Manual for the Young Adult Self-Report and Young Adult Behavior Checklist.* Burlington, VT: University of Vermont.

Bartholomew, K., & Horowitz, L. M. (1991). Attachment styles among young adults: A test of a four category model. *Journal of Personality and Social Psychology, 61*, 226–244.

Becker, E. (1971). *The birth and death of meaning* (2nd ed.). New York: Free Press.

Becker, E. (1975). *Escape from evil.* New York: Free Press.

Benet-Martinez, V., Leu, J., Lee, F., & Morris, M. W. (2002). Negotiating biculturalism: Cultural frame switching in biculturals with oppositional versus compatible cultural identities. *Journal of Cross-Cultural Psychology, 33*, 492–516.

Berry, J. W. (1990). Psychology of acculturation. In J. Berman (Ed.), *Cross-cultural perspectives: Nebraska symposium on motivation* (pp. 201–234). Lincoln: University of Nebraska Press.

Berry, J. W. (1997). Immigration, acculturation, and adaptation. *Applied Psychology: An International Review, 46*, 5–34.

Berry, J. W., Poortinga, Y. H., Segall, M. H., & Dasen, P. R. (1992). *Cross-cultural psychology: Research and applications.* Cambridge, England: Cambridge University Press.

Bhatia, D., & Ram, A. (2001). Rethinking "acculturation" in relation to diasporic cultures and postcolonial identities. *Human Development, 44*, 1–18.

Bowlby, J. (1973). *Attachment and loss: Vol. 2. Separation.* New York: Basic Books.

Bowlby, J. (1980). *Attachment and loss: Vol. 3. Loss.* New York: Basic Books.

Bowlby, J. (1982). *Attachment and loss: Vol. 1. Attachment.* New York: Basic Books. (Original work published 1969)

Brennan, K. A., Clark, C. L., & Shaver, P. R. (1998). Self-report measurement of adult attachment: An integrative overview. In J. A. Simpson & W. S. Rholes (Eds.), *Attachment theory and close relationships* (pp. 46–76). New York: Guilford.

Brewer, M. B. (1991). The social self: On being the same and different at the same time. *Personality and Social Psychology Bulletin, 17*, 475–482.

Brewer, M. B., & Pickett, C. L. (1999). Distinctiveness motives as a source of the social self. In T. R. Tyler, R. M. Kramer, & O. P. John (Eds.), *The psychology of the social self: Applied social research* (pp. 71–87). Mahwah, NJ: Lawrence Erlbaum Associates.

Buriel, R. (1975). Cognitive styles among three generations of Mexican American children. *Journal of Cross-Cultural Psychology, 6*, 417–429.

Caporael, L. R., & Baron, R. M. (1997). Groups as the mind's natural environment. In J. A. Simpson & D. Kenrick (Eds.), *Evolutionary social psychology* (pp. 317–344). Mahwah, NJ: Lawrence Erlbaum Associates.

Chiu, C., & Chen, J. (2004). Symbols and interactions: Application of the CCC model to culture, language, and social identity. In S. Ng, C. Candlin, & C. Chiu (Eds.), *Language matters: Communication, culture, and social identity* (pp. 155–173). Hong Kong: City University of Hong Kong Press.

Chun, K. M., Organista, P. B., & Marin, G. (Eds.). (2002). Preface. In K. M. Chun, P. B. Organista, & G. Marin (Eds.), *Acculturation: Advances in theory, measurement, and applied research* (pp. xxiii–xxvii). Washington, DC: American Psychological Association.

Collins, N. L., & Read, S. J. (1990). Adult attachment, working models, and relationship quality in dating couples. *Journal of Personality and Social Psychology, 58*, 810–832.

Cuellar, I., Nyberg, B., Maldonado, R., & Roberts, R. (1997). Ethnic identity and acculturation in a young adult Mexican-origin population. *Journal of Community Psychology, 25*, 535–549.

Devos, T., & Banaji, M. R. (2005). American = White? *Journal of Personality and Social Psychology, 88*, 447–466.

Diener, E. (1994). Assessing subjective well-being: Progress and opportunities. *Social Indicators Research, 31*, 103–157.

Dozier, M., & Kobak, R. R. (1992). Psychophysiology in attachment interviews: Converging evidence for deactivating strategies. *Child Development, 63*, 1473–1480.

Ethier, K. A., & Deaux, K. (1994). Negotiating social identity when contexts change: Maintaining identification and responding to threat. *Journal of Personality and Social Psychology, 67*, 243–251.

Fowles, D. C. (1980). The three arousal model: Implications of Gray's two-factor learning model for heart rate, electrodermal activity, and psychopathy. *Psychophysiology, 17*, 87–104.

Fowles, D. C. (1988). Physiology and psychopathology: A motivational approach. *Psychophysiology, 25*, 373–391.

Fraley, R. C., & Shaver, P. R. (2000). Adult romantic attachment: Theoretical developments, emerging controversies, and unanswered questions. *Review of General Psychology, 4*, 132–154.

Fraley, R. C., & Waller, N. G. (1998). Adult attachment patterns: A test of the typological model. In J. A. Simpson & W. S. Rholes (Eds.), *Attachment theory and close relationships* (pp. 77–114). New York: Guilford.

Furnham, A., & Li, Y. H. (1993). The psychological adjustment of the Chinese community in Britain: A study of two generations. *British Journal of Psychiatry, 162*, 109–113.

Gaines, S. O., Jr., & Liu, J. H. (2000). Multicultural/multiracial relationships. In C. Hendrick & S. S. Hendrick (Eds.), *Close relationships: A sourcebook* (pp. 97–108). Thousand Oaks, CA: Sage.

George, C., Kaplan, N., & Main, M. (1985). *Adult Attachment Interview*. Unpublished manuscript, University of California, Berkeley.

Gjerde, P. F., Onishi, M., & Carlson, K. S. (2004). Personality characteristics associated with romantic attachment: A comparison of interview and self-report methodologies. *Personality and Social Psychology Bulletin, 30*, 1402–1415.

Greenberg, J., Pyszczynski, T., & Solomon, S. (1986). The causes and consequences of a need for self-esteem: A terror management theory. In R. F. Baumeister (Ed.), *Public self and private self* (pp. 189–212). New York: Springer-Verlag.

Grice, H. P. (1975). Logic and conversation. In P. Cole & J. L. Moran (Eds.), *Syntax and semantics III: Speech acts* (pp. 41–58). New York: Academic Press.

Grieve, P. G., & Hogg, M. A. (1999). Subjective uncertainty and intergroup discrimination in the minimal group paradigm. *Personality and Social Psychology Bulletin, 25*, 926–940.

Griffin, D. W., & Bartholomew, K. (1994). Models of the self and other: Fundamental dimensions underlying measures of adult attachment. *Journal of Personality & Social Psychology, 67*, 430–445.

Guyll, M., Matthews, K. A., & Bromberger, J. T. (2001). Discrimination and unfair treatment: Relationship to cardiovascular reactivity among African American and European American women. *Health Psychology, 20*, 315–325.

Hall, N. G. C., & Okazaki, S. (Eds.). (2002). *Asian American psychology: The science of lives in context.* Washington, DC: American Psychological Association.

Harrell, J. P., Hall, S., & Taliaferro, J. (2003). Physiological responses to racism and discrimination: An assessment of the evidence. *American Journal of Public Health, 93*, 248–255.

Hazan, C., & Shaver, P. (1987). Romantic love conceptualized as an attachment process. *Journal of Personality and Social Psychology, 52*, 511–524.

Hermans, H. J. M. (1988). On the integration of nomothetic and idiographic research methods in the study of personal meaning. *Journal of Personality, 56*, 785–812.

Hermans, H. J. M. (2001). The dialogical self: Toward a theory of personal and cultural positioning. *Culture & Psychology, 7*, 243–281.

Hermans, H. J. M., & Kempen, H. J. G. (1993). *The dialogical self: Meaning as movement.* New York: Academic Press.

Hesse, E. (1999). The Adult Attachment Interview: Historical and current perspectives. In J. Cassidy & P. R. Shaver (Eds.), *Handbook of attachment: Theory, research, and clinical applications* (pp. 395–433). New York: Guilford.

Hirschman, C. (1983). America's melting pot reconsidered. *Annual Review of Sociology, 9*, 397–423.

Hong, Y., Benet-Martinez, V., Chiu, C., & Morris, M. W. (2003). Boundaries of cultural influence: Construct activation as a mechanism for cultural differences in social perception. *Journal of Cross-Cultural Psychology, 34*, 453–464.

Hong, Y., Chiu, C., & Kung, M. (1997). Bringing culture out in front: Effects of cultural meaning system activation on social cognition. In K. Leung, U. Kim, S. Yamaguchi, & Y. Kashima (Eds.), *Progress in Asian social psychology* (Vol. 1, pp. 139–150). Singapore: Wiley.

Hong, Y., Morris, M. W., Chiu, C., & Benet-Martinez, V. (2000). Multicultural minds: A dynamic constructivist approach to culture and cognition. *American Psychologist, 55*, 709–720.

Hong, Y., Wan, C., No, S., & Chiu, C. (in press). Multicultural identities. In S. Kitayama & D. Cohen (Eds.), *Handbook of cultural psychology.* New York: Guilford.

Kanno, Y. (2003). *Negotiating bilingual and bicultural identities: Japanese returnees betwixt two worlds.* Mahwah, NJ: Lawrence Erlbaum Associates.

Kosic, A., Kruglanski, A. W., Pierro, A., & Mannetti, L. (2004). The social cognition of immigrants' acculturation: Effects of the need for closure and the reference group at entry. *Journal of Personality and Social Psychology, 86*, 796–813.

Kruglanski, A. W. (1989). *Lay epistemics and human knowledge: Cognitive and motivational bases.* New York: Plenum.

Kruglanski, A. W., & Webster, D. M. (1996). Motivated closing of the mind: "Seizing" and "freezing." *Psychological Review, 103*, 263–283.

La Fromboise, T., Coleman, H. L., & Gerton, J. (1993). Psychological impact of biculturalism: Evidence and theory. *Psychological Bulletin, 114*, 395–412.

Lucas, R. E., Diener, E., & Suh, E. (1996). Discriminant validity of well-being measures. *Journal of Personality & Social Psychology, 71*, 616–628.

Main, M., & Goldwyn, R. (1998). *Adult attachment rating and classification systems, Version 6.0.* Unpublished manuscript, University of California at Berkeley.

Main, M., Kaplan, N., & Cassidy, J. (1985). Security in infancy, childhood, and adulthood: A move to the level of representation. *Monographs of the Society for Research in Child Development, 50*(1–2), 66–104.

McAdams, D. P. (1985). *Power, intimacy, and the life story: Personological inquiries into identity.* New York: Guilford.

McAdams, D. P. (1993). *The stories we live by: Personal myths and the making of the self.* New York: Morrow.

Nguyen, H., Messe, L., & Stollak, G. (1999). Toward a more complex understanding of acculturation and adjustment: Cultural involvements and psychological functioning in Vietnamese youth. *Journal of Cross-Cultural Psychology, 30,* 5–31.

Niemann, Y. F., Romero, A. J., Arredondo, J., & Rodriguez, V. (1999). What does it mean to be "Mexican"? Social construction of an ethnic identity. *Hispanic Journal of Behavioral Sciences, 21,* 47–60.

No, S., & Hong, Y. (2004a). *Negotiating bicultural identity: Contrast and assimilation effects in cultural frame switching.* Poster presented at the 2004 annual conference of the Society for Personality and Social Psychology, Austin, Texas.

No, S., & Hong, Y. (2004b). *Bicultural frame switching: Belief in race as fixed moderates minority reactivity toward cultural primes.* Poster presented at the 2004 annual conference of the American Psychological Society, Chicago, Illinois.

Organista, P. B., Organista, K. C., & Kurasaki, K. (2002). The relationship between acculturation and ethnic minority mental health. In K. M. Chun, P. B. Organista, & G. Marin (Eds.), *Acculturation: Advances in theory, measurement, and applied research* (pp. 139–162). Washington, DC: American Psychological Association.

Park, R. E. (1928). Human migration and the marginal man. *American Journal of Sociology, 33,* 881–893.

Phinney, J. S. (2002). Ethnic identity and acculturation. In K. M. Chun, P. B. Organista, & G. Marin (Eds.), *Acculturation: Advances in theory, measurement, and applied research* (pp. 63–82). Washington, DC: American Psychological Association.

Pickett, C. L., Silver, M. D., & Brewer, M. B. (2002). The impact of assimilation and differentiation needs on perceived group importance and judgments of ingroup size. *Personality & Social Psychology Bulletin, 28,* 546–558.

Pyszczynski, T., Greenberg, J., Solomon, S., Arndt, J., & Schimel, J. (2004). Why do people need self-esteem? A theoretical and empirical review. *Psychological Bulletin, 130,* 435–468.

Robins, L. N., & Regier, D. A. (Eds.). (1991). *Psychiatric disorders in America: The epidemiologic catchment areas study.* New York: Free Press.

Rogler, L. H., Cortes, D. E., & Malgady, R. G. (1991). Acculturation and mental health status among Hispanics: Convergence and new directions for research. *American Psychologist, 46,* 585–597.

Roisman, G. I. (2004). *The psychophysiology of adult attachment relationships: Cardiovascular and electrodermal response of engaged and older married couples in interaction.* Manuscript submitted for publication.

Roisman, G. I., Madsen, S. D., Hennighausen, K. H., Sroufe, L. A., & Collins, W. A. (2001). The coherence of dyadic behavior across parent–child and romantic relationships as mediated by the internalized representation of experience. *Attachment & Human Development, 3,* 156–172.

Roisman, G. I., Padrón, E., Sroufe, L. A., & Egeland, B. (2002). Earned-secure attachment status in retrospect and prospect. *Child Development, 73,* 1204–1219.

Roisman, G. I., Tsai, J. L., & Chiang, K.-H. S. (2004). The emotional integration of childhood experience: Physiological, facial expressive, and self-reported emotional response during the Adult Attachment Interview. *Developmental Psychology, 40,* 776–789.

Ross, M., Xun, W. Q. E., & Wilson, A. E. (2002). Language and the bicultural self. *Personality and Social Psychology Bulletin, 28,* 1040–1050.

Rowell, T. E., & Hinde, R. A. (1963). Responses of rhesus monkeys to mildly stressful situations. *Animal Behavior, 11,* 235–243.

Rudmin, F. W. (2003). Critical history of the acculturation psychology of assimilation, separation, integration, and marginalization. *Review of General Psychology, 7*, 3–37.
Rumbaut, R. (1994). The crucible within: Ethnic identity, self-esteem, and segmented assimilation among children of immigrants. *International Migration Review, 28*, 748–794.
Ryder, A. G., Alden, L. E., & Paulhus, D. L. (2000). Is acculturation unidimensional or bidimensional? A head-to-head comparison in the prediction of personality, self-identity, and adjustment. *Journal of Personality and Social Psychology, 79*, 49–65.
Sabogal, F., Marin, G., Otero-Sabogal, R., VanOss Marin, B., & Perez-Stable, E. J. (1987). Hispanic familialism and acculturation: What changes and what doesn't? *Hispanic Journal of Behavioral Sciences, 9*, 397–412.
Schachter, S. (1959). *The psychology of affiliation: Experimental studies of the sources of gregariousness.* Oxford, England: Stanford University Press.
Smith, E. R., & Henry, S. (1996). An in-group becomes part of the self: Response time evidence. *Personality and Social Psychology Bulletin, 22*, 635–642.
Smith, E. R., Murphy, J., & Coats, S. (1999). Attachment to groups: Theory and measurement. *Journal of Personality and Social Psychology, 77*, 94–110.
Smith, J. A. (1996). Beyond the dividing line between cognition and discourse: Using interpretive phenomenological analysis in health psychology. *Psychological and Health, 11*, 261–271.
Solomon, S., Greenberg, J., & Pyszczynski, T. (1991). A terror management theory of social behavior: The psychological functions of self-esteem and cultural worldviews. In M. E. P. Zanna (Ed.), *Advances in experimental social psychology* (Vol. 24, pp. 93–159). San Diego, CA: Academic Press.
Solomon, S., Greenberg, J., & Pyszczynski, T. (2000). Pride and prejudice: Fear of death and social behavior. *Current Directions in Psychological Science, 9*, 200–204.
Sparrow, L. M. (2000). Beyond multicultural man: Complexities of identity. *International Journal of Intercultural Relations, 24*, 173–201.
Tajfel, H., & Turner, J. C. (1979). An integrative theory of intergroup conflict. In W. G. Austin & S. Worchel (Eds.), *The social psychology of intergroup relations.* Monterey, CA: Brooks-Cole.
Takenaka, A. (1999). Transnational community and its ethnic consequences: The return migration and the transformation of ethnicity of Japanese Peruvians. *American Behavioral Scientist, 42*, 1459–1474.
Trafimow, D., Triandis, H. C., & Goto, S. G. (1991). Some tests of the distinction between the private and the collective self. *Journal of Personality and Social Psychology, 60*, 649–655.
Tsai, J. L., Ying, Y., & Lee, P. A. (2000). The meaning of "being Chinese" and "being American": Variation among Chinese American young adults. *Journal of Cross-Cultural Psychology, 31*, 302–332.
Tsuda, T. (2003). *Strangers in the ethnic homeland: Japanese Brazilian return migration in transnational perspective.* New York: Columbia University Press.
Turner, J. C., Hogg, M., Oakes, P., Reicher, S., & Wetherell, M. (1987). *Rediscovering the social group: A self-categorization theory.* Oxford: Blackwell.
van IJzendoorn, M. H. (1995). Adult attachment representations, parental responsiveness, and infant attachment: A meta-analysis on the predictive validity of the Adult Attachment Interview. *Psychological Bulletin, 117*, 387–403.
Vasquez, A. (1984). Les implications ideologiques du concept d'acculturation [Ideological implications of the concept of acculturation]. *Cahiers de Sociologie Economique et Culturelle, 1*, 83–121.
Verkuyten, M., & Pouliasi, K. (2002). Biculturalism among older children: Cultural frame switching, attributions, self-identification, and attitudes. *Journal of Cross-Cultural Psychology, 33*, 596–609.
Ward, C., Bochner, S., & Furnham, A. (2001). *The psychology of culture shock* (2nd ed.). Philadelphia: Taylor & Francis.
Waters, M. (1990). *Ethnic options: Choosing identities in America.* Berkeley: University of California Press.
Waters, E., & Cummings, E. M. (2000). A secure base from which to explore close relationships. *Child Development, 71*, 164–172.

Webster, D. M., & Kruglanski, A. W. (1994). Individual differences in need for cognitive closure. *Journal of Personality and Social Psychology, 67*, 1049–1062.

Williams, D. R., & Neighbors, H. (2001). Racism and health. In R. C. Gibson & J. S. Jackson (Eds.), *Health in Black America*. Newbury Park, CA: Sage.

Wong, R. Y-M., & Hong, Y. (2005). Dynamic influences of culture on cooperation in the prisoner's dilemma. *Psychological Science, 16*, 429–434.

Ying, Y. (1995). Cultural orientation and psychological well-being in Chinese Americans. *American Journal of Community Psychology, 23*, 893–911.

Zaharna, R. S. (1989). Self-shock: The double-binding challenge of identity. *International Journal of Intercultural Relations, 13*, 501–525.

Zane, N., & Mak, W. (2002). Major approaches to the measurement of acculturation among ethnic minority populations: A content analysis and an alternative empirical strategy. In K. M. Chun, P. B. Organista, & G. Marin (Eds.), *Acculturation: Advances in theory, measurement, and applied research* (pp. 39–60). Washington, DC: American Psychological Association.

III

Development and Acculturation

9

Parenting Cognitions and Practices in the Accultursative Process

Marc H. Bornstein
Linda R. Cote
National Institute of Child Health and Human Development, U.S.A.

INTRODUCTION

An emerging focus of parenting studies is cognitions, that is, parents' beliefs, attitudes, goals, and knowledge. These parenting cognitions are important to study, first, because they are key to understanding parenting in its own right. They help to organize the world of parenting because cognitions affect parents' sense of self and their role as parents. Parents' cognitions are also thought to serve other functions: They generate and shape parenting practices and afford organization and coherence to the tasks of parenting. Parenting cognitions also affect children's development directly and indirectly. More salient in the phenomenology of the child, perhaps, are parents' practices, the actual experiences parents provide children. Most of young children's worldly experience stems directly from interactions they have within the family. The contents of parent–child interactions are dynamic and varied in human beings. Cultural messages are commonly embedded in daily parent–child interactions (Dunn & Brown, 1991), and parenting cognitions and practices are known to vary across cultures. Central to a concept of culture is the expectation that different peoples possess different ideas, as well as behave in different ways, with respect to childrearing (Bornstein, 2005). In a larger sense, parenting cognitions and practices contribute to the "continuity of culture" by helping to define culture and the transmission of culture across generations.

Parenting cognitions are thought to be adopted from one's culture of origin with little modification, as opposed to being the product of individual deliberation. Although parenting cognitions are also thought to resist change (e.g., LeVine, 1982; Ngo & Malz, 1998), at some point parenting cognitions in acculturating peoples probably, some would say must, accommodate those of their culture of origin with those of the culture of destination, assuming the resettlement is perceived by those experiencing it as permanent. However, the genesis of parenting cognitions and practices, and the dynamics of stability and change in parenting cognitions and practices during the acculturation process, are understudied.

To investigate these issues further, we have examined acculturation of different types of parenting cognitions and practices at two levels. At the individual level, we look at whether mothers' acculturation level (when their firstborn children are 5 months old) predicts their later parenting cognitions and practices (when their children are 20 months old). At the group level, we compare parenting cognitions and practices in acculturating mothers to those of mothers in their cultures of origin and destination (when their children are 20 months of age).

IMMIGRANTS AND ACCULTURATION

Altogether, 317 mothers of 20-month-old children from five cultural groups have so far participated in our studies. Participants were drawn from this pool of 317 mothers for each of the research studies we summarize based on whether they had complete data for a particular measure (see Bornstein & Cote, 2003, 2004; Bornstein, Hahn, Suizzo, Cote, & Haynes, 2004; Cote & Bornstein, 2004, 2005; for sample specifics). Japanese mothers were from Tokyo, Japan; Argentine mothers were from Buenos Aires, Argentina; and the Japanese immigrant, South American immigrant, and European American mothers were from the Washington, DC, environs. Mothers in all five cultural groups were recruited to be demographically similar to each other yet representative of middle-class mothers in their country of origin or, for the United States samples, their particular ethnic or immigrant group (U.S. Census Bureau, 2001). Nearly all mothers were married to their baby's father, and the majority lived in nuclear families. Their children were firstborn, healthy, and term; approximately equal numbers of boys and girls participated in each group. Sociodemographic information for the participants and sample sizes appear in Table 9.1.

Acculturating mothers self-identified as Japanese American or South American (Marín & Marín, 1991), and they or their ancestors were immigrants and not sojourners or refugees (Berry & Sam, 1997).[1] Our Japanese American and South

[1]We refer to mothers of Japanese or South American ethnicity living in the United States as Japanese American or South American mothers and also as acculturating mothers. To avoid confusion, we refer to mothers living in Argentina as Argentine mothers. Although one could correctly argue that all mothers in our study are acculturating because all cultures are continuously in flux, this is more of an issue for our Japanese American and South American mothers because the vast majority of them are either immigrants or the children of immigrants (see Arends-Tóth & van de Vijver, chapter 3, this volume).

TABLE 9.1
Participant Demographic Data

	Japanese (n = 80)	*Argentine (n = 56)*	*Japanese American (n = 40)*	*South American (n = 41)*	*European American (n = 100)*
Age	30.09	28.95	33.30	32.87	31.03
	(3.68)	(4.14)	(4.05)	(4.93)	(4.86)
Education[a]	4.99	4.86	5.68	5.90	5.84
	(1.13)	(1.30)	(0.76)	(0.84)	(1.00)
Hours worked (per week)	8.96	16.53	11.86	17.51	18.81
	(17.40)	(18.95)	(18.60)	(18.88)	(18.47)

Note. *M* (*SD*).
[a]Hollingshead 1–7 point scale.

American mothers were primarily first- and second-generation Americans (i.e., they were born outside the United States and immigrated to the United States or they were born in the United States but their parents were not, respectively). In contrast, European American participants were either fourth- or fifth-generation (i.e., most or all grandparents were born in the United States). In terms of nativity, our immigrant participants were overwhelmingly born outside the United States. The South American mothers tended to be younger at the time of immigration and thus had lived in the United States longer than the Japanese American mothers. There were no differences between acculturating mothers on any sociodemographic variables, including generation level and nativity. Japanese mothers' first language was either Japanese or English. South American mothers' first language was either Spanish or English, and they were primarily from Argentina, Colombia, and Peru (differences within the South American cultural group on the dependent variables did not exceed chance). With the exception of the Japanese American and South American mothers, mothers in all of our samples were married to fathers of the same ethnicity. Approximately one-half of the Japanese American and South American immigrant mothers were married to men of the same ethnicity, and the remainder were married to European American men. However, no differences on any of the dependent variables were found based on spousal ethnicity.

We focused on Japanese American and South American families acculturating to the United States for several reasons. Theoretically, it is interesting to compare Japanese American and South American families because they spring from different parts of the globe but are arriving on the same shores. At the same time, previous research shows that Japanese Americans and South Americans share generally collectivist views of social relationships, whereas European Americans are individualists (Hofstede, 1991; Marín & Marín, 1991; Markus & Kitayama, 1991; Parke & Buriel, 1998). Individualist cultures tend to stress independence, psychological and behavioral autonomy, and social assertiveness, whereas collectivist cultures value and expect social interdependence, connectedness, and mutual deference in interpersonal interactions. The degree of societal and personal individualism or collectivism is believed to affect a variety of psychological variables and to contribute to differences in childrearing goals and thus parenting behaviors (e.g., Benedict, 1938; Bornstein, Haynes, Pascual, Painter, & Galperín, 1999; Caudill & Schooler, 1973; Tamis-LeMonda, Bornstein, Cyphers, Toda, & Ogino, 1992), including, on the individualist side, parental socialization for self-reliance, exploration, and independence in children versus, on the collectivist side, parental socialization for sensitivity to others, obedience, and duty; independence versus dependence on social support; and adoption of a "self" versus an "others" orientation (see Greenfield & Suzuki, 1998; Markus & Kitayama, 1991; Triandis, 1989). We administered immigrant mothers in our study Triandis' Individualism–Collectivism Scale questionnaire. Both immigrant groups scored more collectivist than individualist, which is identical to what other researchers have found (Hofstede, 1991; Marín & Marín, 1991). Mothers' collectivism scores did not change in mean level from 5 to 20 months and were highly stable.

On a practical level, it is interesting to compare Japanese American and South American immigrant families because one in five children under the age of 18 in the United States is a child of immigrants or is an immigrant her- or himself (Federal Interagency Forum on Child and Family Statistics, 2002). Yet, most of our information about "American" parenting and children's development comes from studies of European American families. We know too little about Asian and Latin American immigrant families' caregiving cognitions and practices (Parke & Buriel, 1998). Figure 9.1 shows trends by decade in immigration to the United States. Today, unlike in the past, most immigrants to the United States come from Asia or Latin America. Asians and Latinos are currently the majority immigrant groups to the United States (Jacoby, 2004). Our research shows that it is incorrect to assume that ideas about parenting and children's development held by European American families are also held by other cultural groups in the United States.

We studied different ethnic groups migrating to the same culture of destination at the same historic period for two reasons. First, relatively little is known about parenting among immigrant families (e.g., Garcia Coll & Pachter, 2002), and their increasing numbers (U.S. Census Bureau, 2001) make it imperative to learn more about them so that psychologists, educators, and practitioners can effectively promote children's development. Second, two sets of comparisons allowed us to examine generalities and specificities in the acculturation of parenting among immigrant groups. Moreover, because there are childrearing differences among both Asians and Latinos (e.g., Field & Widmayer, 1981; Uba, 1994), we studied specific subsamples of each.

Measurement of Acculturation

We appropriately adapted a 21-item acculturation scale from existing acculturation scales (the Suinn-Lew Asian Self-identity Acculturation Scale by Suinn & Lew, 1987; and the Acculturation Rating Scale for Mexican-Americans by

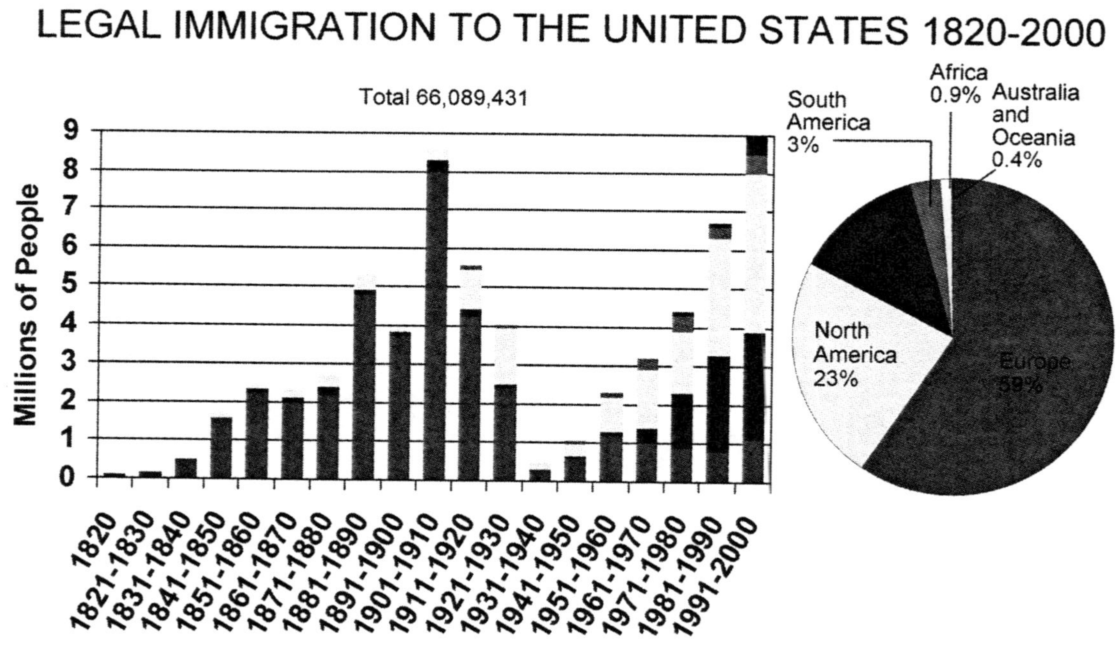

FIGURE 9.1. Legal immigration to the United States 1820–2000.

Cuellar, Harris, & Jasso, 1980) for Japanese and South American immigrants. The items cover topics such as language, identity, friendship, behavior, and attitudes. Sample items include: "How do you identify yourself?", "What language can you speak?", "What is your food preference at home?", and "Do you participate in Japanese/South American occasions, holidays, traditions, etc.?" Japanese participants rated each item on a scale from 1 (Japanese) to 5 (U.S. American); for the South American participants, the scale ranged from 1 (South American) to 5 (U.S. American). On the scale we used, "3" indicated *bicultural: about equally Japanese and American*. We calculated acculturation level by taking the mean of mothers' ratings on all 21 items. The acculturation scales had high internal reliability (αs = .90 to .96) and good construct validity (our scales were positively correlated with the number of years the mothers had lived in the United States and negatively correlated with age at immigration).

On average, mothers were bicultural (scoring about 2.5 on the 5-point scale), and the two groups did not differ in acculturation level. Their acculturation level also remained the same from 5 to 20 months. The continuity of mothers' acculturation might reflect the fact that 15 months is too short a time to detect group-level change in acculturation. However, as Hofstede (1991) and Oyserman, Coon, and Kemmelmeier (2002) suggested, cultural beliefs are typically continuous, and group-level changes can be expected to occur only very slowly. It may also be that, for our immigrant samples, biculturalism is the desired endpoint of individual-level acculturation, and because our participants were already bicultural as a group by the time their infants were 5 months of age, their cultural identity remained the same (Berry, 1990). Mothers' acculturation scores were also highly stable over the 15-month period.

To summarize immigrant mothers' demographic characteristics: Mothers were equivalently acculturated and demographically similar. Acculturation, individualism, and collectivism were continuous and stable over time.

PARENTING COGNITIONS

We investigated four types of parenting cognitions at the individual and group levels: mothers' attributions for their parenting behavior, their self-perceptions of parenting, their parenting knowledge, and their parenting style. We took several steps to promote the validity and cultural appropriateness of all the instruments we used for we aimed to arrive at versions that had "adapted equivalence" (in van de Vijver & Leung's, 1997, terms) across cultures from a psychological perspective. The questionnaires, originally constructed and written in English, were first forward-translated into Japanese and Spanish and then back-translated by bilingual bicultural Japanese and Argentine natives using standard back-translation techniques (Brislin, 1980, 1986). The translated instruments were next checked for preservation of meaning and cultural appropriateness by psychologists or professionals from each country. Then, professionals and bilingual mothers from each culture, who lived in the United States and were not participants in the study, were interviewed regarding the cultural validity of items in the instruments. Finally, pilot testing was undertaken to ensure that the instruments were comprehensible and ethnographically valid. All measures had good reliability (Bornstein et al., 1998; Cote & Bornstein, 2003).

Constructs and Instruments

Attributions are important to study because they are believed to influence our behaviors and reactions toward others. How parents interpret their successes and failures at parenting, for example, inform how they behave as parents. The Parental Attributions Questionnaire (MacPhee, Seybold, & Fritz, personal communication; Sirignano & Lachman, 1985) asks mothers to rate each of five causal attributions to explain success and failure in seven parenting activities using a 5-point Likert-type rating scale. This is an example of successful parenting behavior: "When I am able to get my child to take a bath, it is because. . . ." The five causal attributions we studied were ability, task, child behavior, effort, and mothers' mood. Mothers' scores were the average for each subscale (range = 1–5). Thus, 10 dependent variables were generated from the attributions questionnaire. For parenting success and failure situations, mothers rated each of the five attributions separately.

Second, *self-perceptions* of parenting have to do with parents' discrete feelings of competence in the role of caregiver, satisfaction gained from caregiving relationships, investment in caregiving, and ability to balance caregiving with other social roles. Functionally, for example, perceptions of parenting competence are associated with parents' use of more effective childrearing strategies. The Self-Perceptions of the Parental Role (MacPhee, Benson, & Bullock, 1986) instrument contains 22 items that assess mothers' competence, satisfaction, investment, and role balance. Each item has a pair of statements that describe contrasting endpoints of the dimension in question in order to minimize socially desirable responses. This example is from the competence subscale: "Some mothers and fathers aren't sure they were suited to be parents." BUT "Parenting comes easily and naturally to other parents." Mothers were asked to check one statement from the pair then decide whether that statement was "really true for me" or "sort of true for me." The four response possibilities were weighted 1, 2, 4, and 5, similar to Harter's self-esteem scale. Mothers' scores were the average for each subscale (range = 1–5). Four dependent variables were generated from the self-perceptions measure. They were competence, satisfaction, investment, and role balance in parenting.

Third, the general state of *knowledge* that parents have constitutes an important frame of reference from which they interpret their children's behavior and growth. Knowledgeable parents have more realistic expectations and are more likely to behave in developmentally appropriate ways with their children, whereas parents who harbor unrealistic developmental expectations, or whose expectations are not informed by accurate knowledge of child development, experience greater stress as a result of mismatches between expectations and actual child behaviors. Parents' knowledge about child development and childrearing is relevant to parenting, parent–child interactions, and child development as well as to clinical practice. The Knowledge of Infant Development Inventory (MacPhee, 1981) uses 75 items that ask about developmental norms and milestones, developmental processes, parenting strategies, and health and safety guidelines for the first 2 years of life. An example is, "The newborn can see a face 6 feet away as well as an adult can." Mothers are either asked to choose the correct response among several options or to indicate whether a statement is true or false. The dependent variable was the percentage of items that mothers answered correctly.

Finally, we were interested in mothers' reports about their own parenting *style* in three different domains: social interaction, didactic exchange, and limit setting. Social interactions consist of physical and verbal strategies parents use to engage their child in affective interpersonal dyadic interchanges. In didactic exchanges, parents stimulate their child's attention to objects, properties, or events in the environment. Limit setting consists of the parent's attempts to teach their children self-control. The Maternal Style Questionnaire (Bornstein et al., 1996) is a 16-item instrument that asks mothers to rate, on 5-point Likert-type scales, how frequently they engage in social, didactic, and limit setting behaviors with their children. This example is from the social subscale: "I provide my child with positive affectionate displays of warmth and attention." Mothers' scores were the average for each domain (range = 1–5). Thus, three dependent variables were generated from the Maternal Style Questionnaire—mothers' reports of their social, didactic, and limit setting behavior.

In addition to these measures, mothers also filled out a Social Desirability Scale (Crowne & Marlowe, 1960) and a demographic questionnaire about their family. Mothers' demographic characteristics and their social desirability scores were used as covariates in the following analyses as necessary.

Analytic Plan

In order to assess the acculturation of parenting cognitions at the individual level, we first computed Pearson correlations to examine the covariation of mothers' acculturation level at 5 months with their parenting cognitions at 20 months (attributions, self-perceptions, knowledge, and style), separately for Japanese American and South American mothers. Then, when significant relations were obtained, we performed sequential multiple regressions in which covariates (if any) were entered on Step 1 and acculturation level was entered on Step 2. Acculturation at the group level was assessed by comparing the parenting cognitions of our acculturating mothers to mothers in their cultures of origin and culture of destination using multivariate analyses of variance (MANOVAs) followed by analysis of simple effects or univariate analyses of variance (ANOVAs) and Tukey HSD tests (or *t*-tests with Bonferroni's correction in the case of parental style). One set of MANOVAs was performed for the Japanese comparison and one set for the South American comparison. For all analyses, we report only findings that remained significant after covariates were controlled. For all analyses reported in this chapter, the alpha level was set at .05.

Acculturation of Parenting Cognitions at the Individual Level

Very few relations between mothers' acculturation level and parenting cognitions were obtained for either Japanese American or South American mothers. In fact, of the 18 parenting cognitions we examined, only four significant relations between Japanese American mothers' acculturation level when their infants were 5 months old and their parenting cognitions when their infants were 20 months old emerged (i.e., attributions to ability and task in success situations, feelings of competence, and knowledge of child development); and of these, only one remained significant after covariates were controlled: Japanese American mothers' acculturation level positively covaried with and predicted their knowledge of parenting. No significant relations between mothers' acculturation level and parenting cognitions were found for South American mothers.

Because mothers' acculturation level was highly stable from 5 to 20 months (*r*s ≥ .82 even after covariates were controlled; see Cote & Bornstein, 2003), this result cannot be explained by differences in when acculturation level and parenting cognitions were measured. Perhaps our acculturation scale targeted "behavioral acculturation" (i.e., the adoption of observable aspects of the new culture, such as language and habits) more than "value acculturation" (i.e., adoption of less observable aspects of culture, such as basic value orientations; Szapocznik, Scopetta, Kurtines, & Aranalde, 1978). Thus, behavioral and value acculturation may have been disconcordant in the current study because, in more private spheres such as parenting and family life, more cultural maintenance is sought even though the individual may be acculturating to the culture of destination in other, more overt ways (e.g., Berry & Sam, 1997). From Arends-Tóth and van de Vijver's perspective (chapter 3, this volume), our acculturation measure was domain aspecific (Level 1 in their typology), and our parenting cognitions were Level 3 (beliefs about childrearing). Perhaps if we had measured acculturation at Level 2 (public vs. private), we would have obtained different results.

A number of theorists and researchers have suggested that it is important to measure acculturation at the individual level (i.e., individual variability within a population; e.g., Berry, 1990, 1997; Berry, Trimble, & Olmedo, 1986; Szapocznik et al., 1978), but our results suggest that individual differences in acculturation are not as evident as group level differences (e.g., differences among groups who vary in generation level) in acculturating families (Bornstein & Cote, 2004). That said, it is possible that, if our groups had been more diverse in terms of cultural or demographic characteristics or generation level, stronger predictive relations between acculturation in infancy and parenting cognitions in early childhood might have emerged. Although acculturation may relate to other kinds of cognitions, it appears that its influence is not pervasive.

Acculturation of Parenting Cognitions at the Group Level

We investigated acculturation at the group level by comparing Japanese and South American immigrant mothers' parenting cognitions to those of mothers in their cultures of origin (Japan, Argentina) and to those of mothers in their culture of destination. We chose to study European American mothers in the culture of destination because this is currently the majority cultural group in the United States, on whom most research on parenting is based. We do *not* believe that European American mothers' cognitions are either normative or the ideal end point for our acculturating mothers. We only discuss parenting cognitions for which immigrant mothers differed significantly from mothers in either their culture of origin or destination.

Attributions

Immigrant mothers differed from mothers in their cultures of origin or destination for three of the five parenting success attributions (Figure 9.2). Specifically, Japanese immigrant mothers' ability attributions were stronger than those of Japanese mothers but weaker than those of European American mothers. This confirms that ability attributions are characteristic of European American mothers' cultural cognitions (Holloway, 1988; Machida, 1996) and suggests that they are somewhat resistant to change. Japanese immigrant mothers were similar to Japanese mothers, and made weaker task attributions than European American mothers, suggesting that task attributions are also resistant to change. South American immigrant mothers were similar to European American mothers and made stronger child behavior attributions than Argentine mothers, suggesting that child behavior attributions are amenable to change in this cultural group.

For attributions in unsuccessful parenting situations, Japanese immigrant mothers' ability attributions were similar to mothers in Japan and stronger than those of European American mothers (Figure 9.3). Conversely, Japanese immigrant mothers' effort attributions were not as strong as those of Japanese mothers and were similar to those of European American mothers. This suggests that Japanese immigrant mothers may have retained Japanese cultural beliefs about the role of ability in unsuccessful outcomes but adopted the face-saving attributional style of European Americans with respect to effort. Argentine mothers agreed with ability and task attributions more strongly than South American immigrant

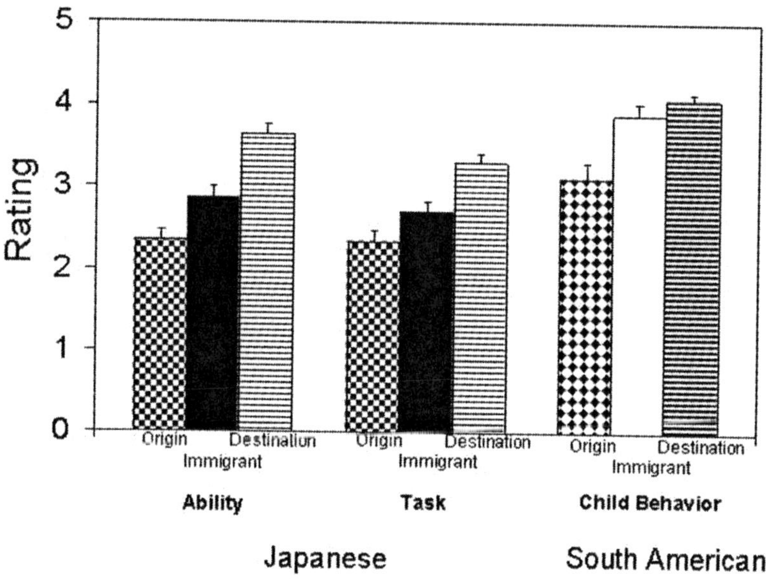

FIGURE 9.2. Attributions for parenting success.

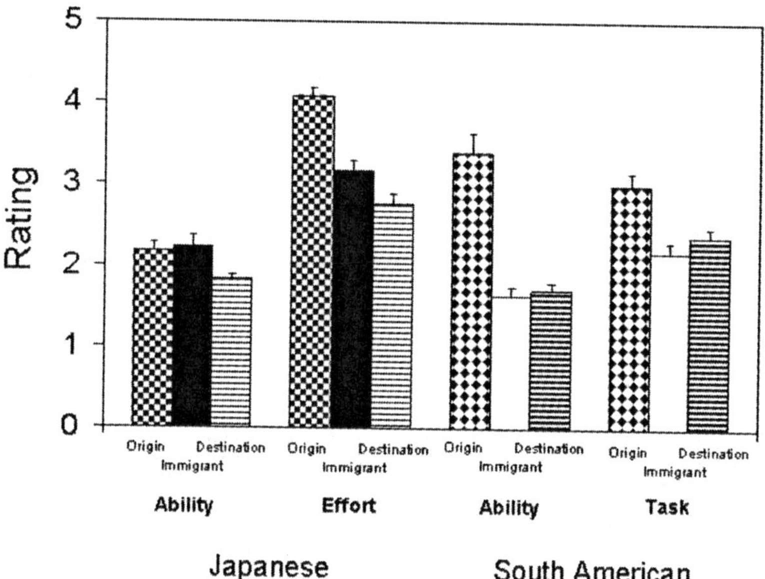

FIGURE 9.3. Attributions for parenting failures.

mothers, suggesting that these attributions are amenable to change in this cultural group (Figure 9.3). Now that they are in the United States, South American mothers appear to resist attributing their lack of parenting success to themselves, as native Argentine mothers have been found to do (Bornstein et al., 1998).

Self-Perceptions

Three of the four self-perceptions of parenting differed between immigrant mothers and mothers in their cultures of origin or destination (Figure 9.4). Specifically, Japanese American immigrant mothers felt more competent about parenting than mothers in Japan, but not as competent as European American mothers. This suggests that acculturating mothers of Japanese ethnicity might engage less in abasement (Connor, 1974) or modesty (Gjerde, 1996) than mothers in their home country. South American immigrant mothers felt more competent about their parenting and were more satisfied with and more balanced in parenting than Argentine mothers. South American immigrant mothers may feel more confident when they are in a society where a woman's role as mother is esteemed yet balanced with other responsibilities.

Knowledge

Japanese immigrant mothers knew less about parenting than European American mothers, but were similar to mothers in Japan (Figure 9.5). It may be that mothers who are more acculturated to U.S. society are more likely to learn about

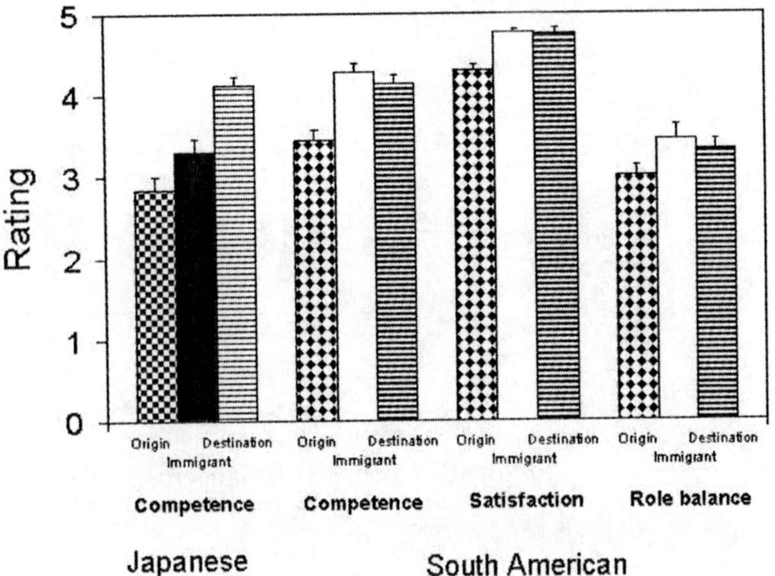

FIGURE 9.4. Self-perceptions of parenting.

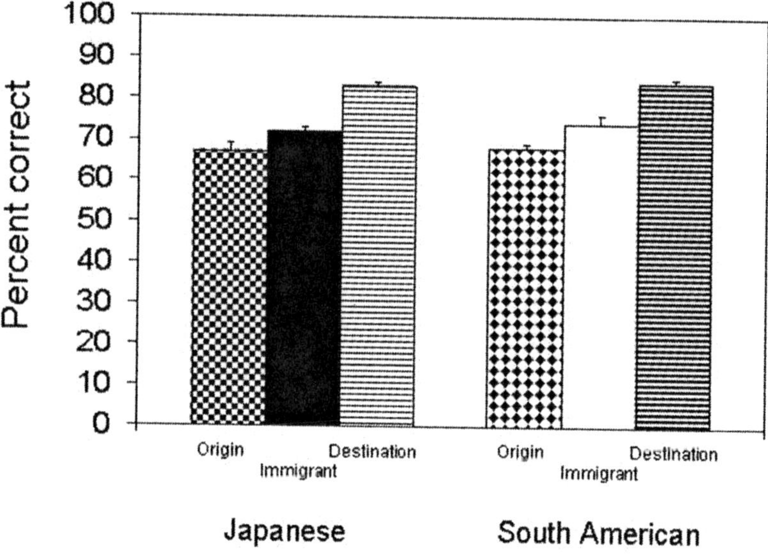

FIGURE 9.5. Parenting knowledge.

childrearing and child development (Harkness, Super, & Keefer, 1992). South American immigrant mothers were intermediate to mothers in Argentina and the United States. In the United States, it is the parents' responsibility to notice their children's behavior, monitor their well-being, and bring them to a specialist on their own initiative if they observe a problem with their child's health or development. "Well baby" visits in the United States typically involve inoculations rather than developmental assessments, and it is usually the parents' responsibility to raise any developmental concerns they may have with their physician. In Japan, in contrast, mothers depend on clinics for regular developmental screening and not simply assessment of physical health.

Style

Immigrant mothers differed from mothers in their cultures of origin or destination in all three parenting style domains (Figure 9.6). Both Japanese immigrant and South American immigrant mothers reported that they engaged in more social exchanges with their toddlers than mothers in their cultures of origin. This suggests that these immigrant mothers maintain this culturally valued parenting behavior (Bornstein et al., 1996; Caudill & Frost, 1972).

Specifically, consistent with research comparing mothers in Japan and the United States (Tamis-LeMonda et al., 1992), Japanese immigrant mothers reported that they engaged in less didactic interaction with their toddlers than European American mothers. South American immigrant mothers, in contrast, re-

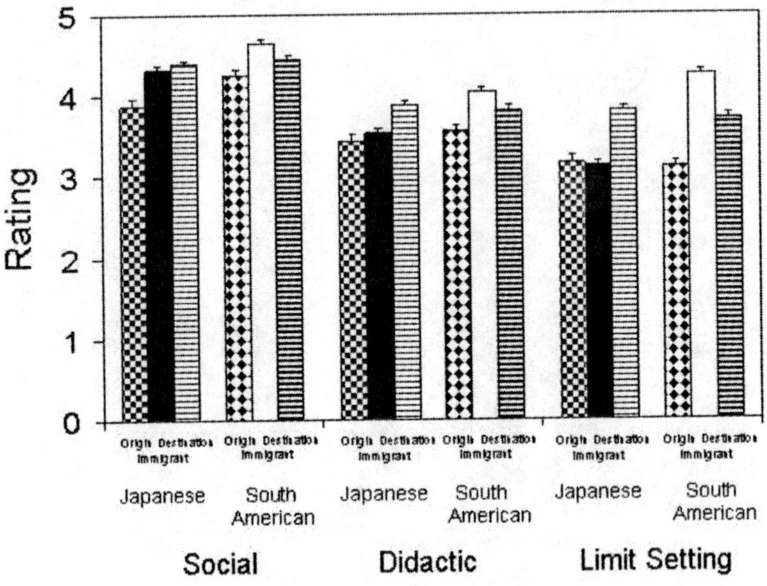

FIGURE 9.6. Parenting style.

ported that they engaged in more didactic interaction with their toddlers than mothers in Argentina, and thus are more similar to European American mothers (Bornstein et al., 1996; Bornstein et al., 1999). These results suggest that, like European American mothers, South American immigrant parents value and engage their children in didactic interaction. Similar to mothers in Japan, Japanese immigrant mothers reported that they engaged in less limit setting than European American mothers, which is consonant with Japanese and American cultural views. Specifically, the cultural norm for mothers in Japan is to be permissive and indulgent with young infants (e.g., Hara & Minagawa, 1996; Lanham & Garrick, 1996), perhaps because it is believed that infants are born spiritually pure and are only gradually corrupted ("spoiled") by their general exposure to adults (whose characters have been corrupted by daily living). In contrast, European Americans believe that spoiling is typically caused by parental indulgence (Hara & Minagawa, 1996). South American immigrant mothers reported that they engaged in more limit setting than Argentine mothers, consonant with American cultural views (Bornstein et al., 1996).

Summary

Acculturation did not appear to predict parenting cognitions at the individual level. However, at the group level, for the majority of cognitions we examined, immigrant mothers differed from mothers of similar middle-class socioeconomic circumstances in their cultures of origin or destination. This was equally true for Japanese immigrant and South American immigrant mothers. Overall, however, Japanese immigrant mothers' cognitions tended to be more similar to mothers in Japan or intermediate to mothers in Japan and the United States. In contrast, South American mothers' cognitions tended to be similar to those of European American mothers, and different from mothers in Argentina. Thus, different patterns of results were found for Japanese immigrant and South American immigrant mothers even though their cognitions and socioeconomic circumstances were very similar to each other. This may be because South America and the United States share many Western traditions not shared by Japan. Previous research supports the idea that South American and European American mothers' cognitions about parenting are more similar for many, but not all, of the cognitions for which we found differences (i.e., ability and child behavior attributions in success situations, competence, and satisfaction; Bornstein et al., 1998).

This general pattern suggests that the acculturation of parenting cognitions may be more relaxed for South American immigrant mothers than for Japanese immigrant mothers, who appear to retain deeply held cultural beliefs about mothering and a woman's social role. These findings accord with previous research that has reported that Asian immigrant parents tend to maintain traditional beliefs when in new cultural environments (Chun & Akutsu, 2003; Uba, 1994).

Regardless of why these patterns of differences for the Japanese and South American comparisons obtain, their existence highlights the inadequacy of simply taking generation level into account when attempting to understand the psychology of immigrant parents from different lands. Nor can one assume equality across immigrant groups, or across different parenting cognitions for that matter. It will certainly be the case that future research in the acculturation of parenting needs to be more differentiated and nuanced.

Parental cognitions (i.e., attributions, self-perceptions, knowledge, and style) constitute significant forces at work for self-definition among adults *and* in the development of children. Seeing oneself in a particular way may lead to certain affect, thinking, and behavior in childrearing situations: Parents who rate themselves as higher in competence (versus parents who feel negatively about their competence) act with their children in more optimal and effective ways (i.e., warm, sensitive, and responsive), and these self-evaluations in turn may color their perceptions of child behavior. Seeing one's children in a particular way can have similar consequences: Parents who regard their children as being difficult may respond to them in less optimal ways, which in turn may interfere with the child's healthy adaptation and development. Finally, seeing childhood in a particular way has its general consequences as well: Parents who believe that they can or cannot affect their child's temperament, intelligence, or other characteristics may modify their parenting accordingly. Parents' cognitions help to explain how and why parents parent, and provide further insight into the broader cultural contexts of children's development.

PARENTING PRACTICES

Because some researchers have suggested that parenting behaviors acculturate more quickly and readily than cognitions, we examined the acculturation of parenting practices in addition to parenting cognitions. Thus, we asked whether mothers' acculturation at 5 months predicted their play behavior with their toddlers (when they were 20 months old), and we compared mothers' play behavior in cultures of origin, acculturating cultures, and cultures of destination. We chose to study mothers' play because, during the first years of life, children's representational abilities develop rapidly. As a prime example, children's play gradually moves from being object-oriented (exploratory) to pretend (symbolic). Play is an important developmental activity for young children (Piaget, 1962; Vygotsky, 1978).

Although exploratory and symbolic play are developmentally continuous and culturally universal, cross-cultural differences exist in their relative emphasis. Cultural differences in parenting practices sometimes correspond to the degree of individualism or collectivism in a society. For example, research shows that middle-class European American childrearing stresses individual achievement, autonomy in children, and exploration of the environment. These findings are consistent with an individualist perspective. Although all mothers engage their children in both exploratory and symbolic play, consistent with these cultural values, mothers from individualist cultures have been found to encourage their children's exploratory play in particular. Research shows that Japanese culture emphasizes interdependence and sensitivity to nonverbal signals. South American culture also emphasizes interpersonal relationships. Mothers in both of these collectivist cultures have been found to encourage their young children's symbolic play more than exploratory play; the reverse is true for European American mothers in the United States.

Procedures

Mother–child dyads were visited in their homes when the children were 20 months old. Visits were scheduled at a time when the children were awake and alert, and no one was home except the child, mother, and observer. A standard set of toys (i.e., doll, blanket, tea set, telephone, train, two picture books, foam rubber ball, and nesting barrels) that allowed for a variety of different play behaviors was placed on the floor in front of the child. After a period of acclimation (20 minutes), the child and mother were videotaped for 10 minutes. Pilot testing ensured the ecological validity of the observation.

Mothers' play demonstrations (i.e., mothers model an action for their children, for example, by dialing a toy telephone) and solicitations (i.e., mothers encourage their children's participation in a specific activity, for example, by moving the telephone toward the child and suggesting that the child dial) were coded separately. Mothers' play was coded using an eight-level mutually exclusive and ex-

TABLE 9.2
Play Categories and Levels

Play Level	*Definition*	*Example*
Exploratory play		
1. Unitary functional activity	Production of an effect that is unique to a single object	Throw a ball
2. Inappropriate combinatorial activity	Inappropriate juxtaposition of two or more objects	Put a ball into a teacup
3. Appropriate combinatorial activity	Appropriate juxtaposition of two or more objects	Put the cup on the saucer
4. Transitional play	Approximation of pretense without confirmatory evidence	Put the telephone receiver to the ear
Symbolic play		
5. Self-directed pretense	Clear pretense activity directed toward self	Drink from a cup
6. Other-directed pretense	Clear pretense activity directed toward another	Pretend telephone rings
7. Sequential pretense	Linking of two or more pretense actions	Dial and speak into the telephone
8. Substitution pretense	Pretend activity involving one or more object substitutions	Pretend a block is a telephone

haustive coding system (Table 9.2). Frequency and duration data for these eight play levels were recorded. Levels 1–4 were summed into an exploratory play score, and levels 5–8 were summed into a symbolic play score. Because frequency and duration scores were highly intercorrelated, absolute and proportional frequency and duration scores were aggregated into mean *z*-scores. Interrater reliability for this coding system was excellent (see Cote & Bornstein, 2005).

Analytic Plan

Similar to our analysis of the acculturation of parenting cognitions at the individual and group levels, first we computed Pearson correlations to examine the covariation of mothers' acculturation level at 5 months with their parenting practices at 20 months (demonstrations and solicitations of exploratory and symbolic play), separately for Japanese American and South American mothers. Then sequential multiple regressions were performed when significant relations were obtained. MANOVAs, followed by ANOVAs and Tukey HSD tests, were performed to investigate group differences in mothers' parenting practices. Similar to our analysis of the acculturation of parenting cognitions at the group level, immigrant mothers' play was compared to the play of mothers in cultures of origin and destination. Demographic variables were used as covariates in all analyses as necessary; for all analyses, only findings that remained significant after covariates were controlled are reported.

Acculturation of Parenting Practices at the Individual Level

No significant relations between mothers' acculturation level and play behaviors were found for either Japanese American or South American mothers.

Acculturation of Parenting Practices at the Group Level

Immigrant mothers differed from mothers in their cultures of origin or destination in all four play behaviors we examined (exploratory and symbolic play demonstrations and solicitations).

Exploratory Play

South American immigrant and European American mothers demonstrated *and* solicited more exploratory play than Argentine mothers (Figure 9.7).

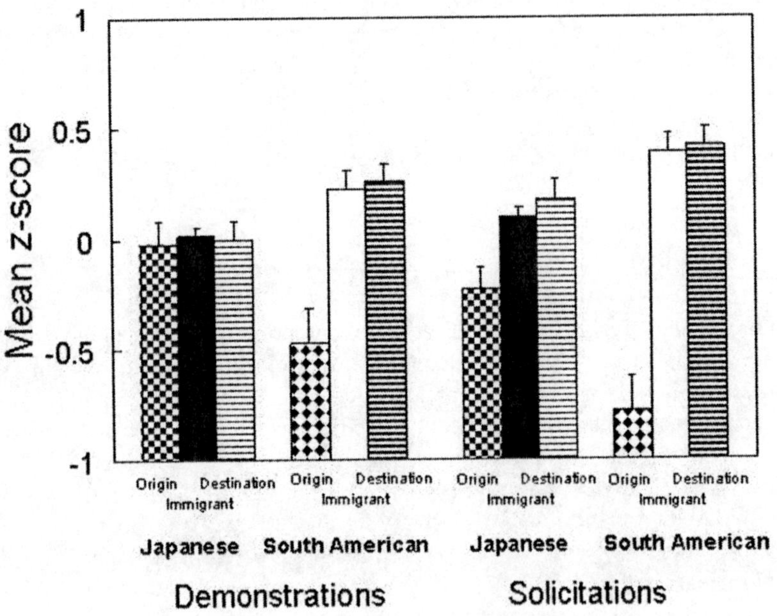

FIGURE 9.7. Maternal exploratory play.

Symbolic Play

Japanese mothers demonstrated more symbolic play than European American mothers (Figure 9.8). Japanese mothers solicited more symbolic play than Japanese immigrant mothers. Argentine mothers demonstrated more symbolic play than either South American immigrant or European American mothers.

Summary

As with parenting cognitions, we found few relations between acculturation at the individual level and parenting practices. Instead, we found that the acculturation of parenting practices was more apparent at the group level. Specifically, overall, European American and immigrant mothers in the United States tended to highlight exploratory object play, whereas Japanese and Argentine mothers tended to stress symbolic play. These contrasting dyadic emphases are consistent with larger cultural concerns and styles. In the United States, the play session sets the stage, and the toys were typically the objects of communication. In contrast, in Argentina and Japan, the play session and toys seemed predominantly to mediate dyadic interaction for itself. U.S. mothers encouraged exploratory play activities such as throwing the ball or putting the cup on the saucer, whereas Japanese and Argentine mothers encouraged interactive, symbolic play, such as feeding the doll. Thus parenting practices seem to acculturate more readily at the group than

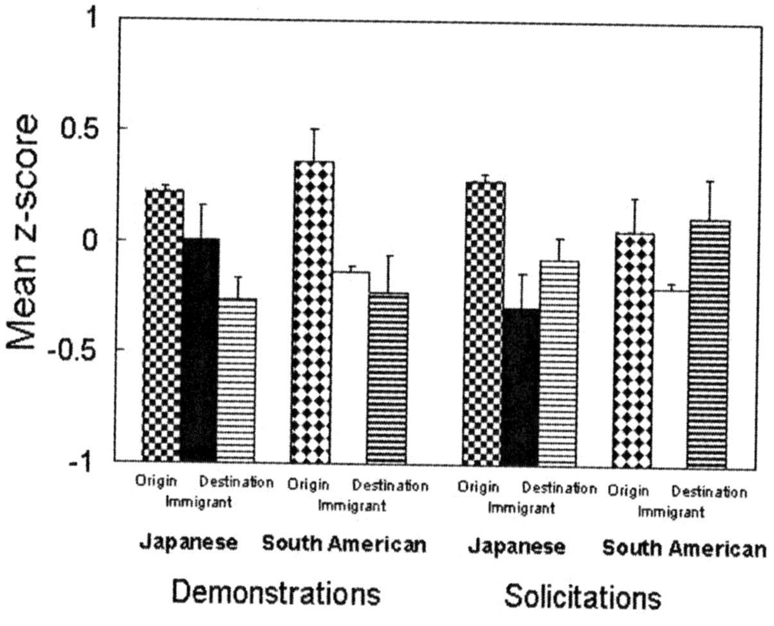

FIGURE 9.8. Maternal symbolic play.

at the individual level, perhaps because assimilation is sought in more public spheres (such as parenting behavior) whereas cultural maintenance is sought in more private spheres (such as parenting beliefs; e.g., Arends-Tóth & van de Vijver, chapter 3, this volume; Berry & Sam, 1997).

CONCLUSIONS AND FUTURE DIRECTIONS

Our findings address three issues with respect to the acculturation of parenting. First, the acculturation of parenting cognitions and practices appears to be more evident at the group than at the individual level (at least for the cognitions and practices we examined). For this reason, both levels must be assessed. However, it is important to point out that our failure to find associations between acculturation and parenting could be ascribable to the acculturation measure we used, which was unidimensional (and domain aspecific). At the time we began our study, such unidimensional measures of acculturation were widely used (Ward, 2001), and because they index psychological acculturation and can capture individual differences, they are certainly superior to using demographic descriptors such as generation level to index individual acculturation. Moreover, previous researchers have found that measures of acculturation based on uni- and bidimensional models of acculturation are highly related (Cuéllar, Arnold, & Maldonado's, 1995, ARSMA II), and both uni- and bidimensional acculturation measures have been found to have good psychometric characteristics (Arends-Tóth & van de Vijver, chapter 3, this volume). Although many researchers currently favor Berry's (see, e.g., Berry, Kim, & Boski, 1987) four-category conceptualization of acculturation, few measures have been able to capture his conceptualization reliably (Rudmin, 2003; Ward, 1999). Thus, investigators who study acculturating families still struggle to find conceptually *and* psychometrically adequate acculturation measures.

Second, our findings indicate that Japanese American mothers' parenting cognitions acculturate more slowly than those of South American mothers, despite the fact that these groups were sociodemographically similar. Our results, therefore, suggest that a uniform model of acculturation for parenting cognitions is inappropriate (Berry et al., 1987; Lightfoot & Valsiner, 1992). Diverse cultural groups do not necessarily share the childrearing beliefs of parents in the majority cultural group. Rather, complexity appears to be the rule: The acculturation process for parenting appears to be influenced (at least) by which cognitions and practices are evaluated and which cultures are compared.

Third, our findings address the issue of whether parenting cognitions and behaviors acculturate at similar or different rates. It seems as if behaviors change, but cognitions are like possessions, we cling to them. Alternatively, it may be that behaviors are more under our conscious control. Or perhaps we assimilate what others can see (public sphere), but not what they cannot (private sphere). Our finding that parenting behaviors seem to acculturate more readily than parenting cognitions at the group level is consistent with previous research that has suggested that, in general, cultural practices acculturate more readily than attitudes (Nagata, 1994). Moreover, our finding that parenting practices seem to acculturate more speedily than cognitions may exemplify differential acculturation between public (practices) and private (cognitions) domains. For example, research on Dutch immigrants suggests that they prefer to adopt Dutch culture (e.g., or integrate it with their culture of origin) in the public domain but prefer cultural maintenance in the private domain (e.g., Arends-Tóth & van de Vijver, chapter 3, this volume).

In the future, we plan to examine the acculturation of additional types of parenting practices at the individual and group levels when our acculturating mothers' firstborn children are 5 years old. In addition, we are currently recruiting a sample of Korean American families to extend our work on acculturating families in the United States. In this new study, we use a revised acculturation scale, modeled on Cuellar et al.'s (1995) revised acculturation measure (the ARSMA II). This acculturation scale separates the dimensions of Korean cultural maintenance and American cultural adoption, and allows for both numerical representation of acculturation level and the assignment of Berry's (Berry et al., 1987) four-way typology of acculturation. Unfortunately, although studies of immigration and acculturation are becoming more common, as Arends-Tóth and van de Vijver (chapter 3, this volume) point out, a large gap yawns between the substantial number of research studies on acculturation and the relatively modest developments in acculturation theory and methodology.

ACKNOWLEDGMENTS

This research was supported by the Intramural Research Program of the NIH, National Institute of Child Health and Human Development. This chapter summarizes selected aspects of our research, and portions of the text have appeared in our published research. We thank H. Azuma, C. Galperín, O. M. Haynes, E. Hunter, J. Lampard, M. Ogino, N. Okazaki, K. Painter, L. Pascual, K. Schulthess, W. Smith, S. Toda, and C. Varron for comments and assistance.

REFERENCES

Benedict, R. (1938). Continuities and discontinuities in cultural conditioning. *Psychiatry, 1*, 161–167.

Berry, J. W. (1990). Psychology of acculturation: Understanding individuals moving between cultures. In R. W. Brislin (Ed.), *Applied cross-cultural psychology: Cross-cultural research and methodology series* (pp. 232–253). Newbury Park, CA: Sage.

Berry, J. W. (1997). Immigration, acculturation, and adaptation. *Applied Psychology, An International Review, 46*, 5–34.

Berry, J. W., Kim, U., & Boski, P. (1987). Psychological acculturation of immigrants. In Y. Y. Kim & W. B. Gudykunst (Eds.), *International and intercultural communication annual: Vol. 11. Cross-cultural adaptation: Current approaches* (pp. 62–89). Newbury Park, CA: Sage.

Berry, J. W., & Sam, D. L. (1997). Acculturation and adaptation. In J. W. Berry, M. H. Segall, & C. Kagitçibasi (Eds.), *Handbook of cross-cultural psychology: Vol. 3. Social behavior and applications* (2nd ed., pp. 291–326). Boston: Allyn & Bacon.

Berry, J. W., Trimble, J. E., & Olmedo, E. L. (1986). Assessment of acculturation. In W. J. Lonner & J. W. Berry (Eds.), *Cross-cultural research and methodology series: Vol. 8. Field methods in cross-cultural research* (pp. 291–324). Beverly Hills, CA: Sage.

Bornstein, M. H. (2005). Some metatheoretical issues in culture, parenting, and developmental science. In Q. Jing, M. Rosenzweig, G. d'Ydewalle, H. Zhang, & H. C. Chen (Eds.), *Proceedings of the XVIIIth international congress of psychology*. East Sussex, UK: Psychology Press.

Bornstein, M. H., & Cote, L. R. (2003). Cultural and parenting cognitions in acculturating cultures: II. Patterns of prediction and structural coherence. *Journal of Cross-Cultural Psychology, 34*, 350–373.

Bornstein, M. H., & Cote, L. R. (2004). Mothers' parenting cognitions in cultures of origin, acculturating cultures, and cultures of destination. *Child Development, 75*, 221–235.

Bornstein, M. H., Hahn, C., Suizzo, M., Cote, L. R., & Haynes, O. M. (2004). *Experiential, sociodemographic, and cultural factors predicting mothers' knowledge about child development and childrearing: National, immigrant, and cross-national studies*. Manuscript in preparation.

Bornstein, M. H., Haynes, O. M., Azuma, H., Galperín, C., Maital, S., Ogino, M., et al. (1998). A cross-national study of self-evaluations and attributions in parenting: Argentina, Belgium, France, Israel, Italy, Japan, and the United States. *Developmental Psychology, 34*, 662–676.

Bornstein, M. H., Haynes, O. M., Pascual, L., Painter, K. M., & Galperín, C. (1999). Play in two societies: Pervasiveness of process, specificity of structure. *Child Development, 70*, 317–331.

Bornstein, M. H., Tamis-LeMonda, C. S., Pascual, L., Haynes, O. M., Painter, K. M., Galperín, C. Z., et al. (1996). Ideas about parenting in Argentina, France, and the United States. *International Journal of Behavioral Development, 19*, 347–367.

Brislin, R. W. (1980). Translation and content analysis of oral and written material. In H. C. Triandis & J. W. Berry (Eds.), *Handbook of cross-cultural psychology* (Vol. 1, pp. 389–444). Boston: Allyn & Bacon.

Brislin, R. W. (1986). The wording and translation of research instruments. In W. J. Lonner & J. W. Berry (Eds.), *Field methods in cross-cultural research* (pp. 137–164). Newbury Park, CA: Sage.

Caudill, W., & Frost, L. (1972). A comparison of maternal care and infant behavior in Japanese-American, American, and Japanese Families. In U. Bronfenbrenner (Ed.), *Influences on human development* (pp. 329–342). Hinsdale, IL: Dryden.

Caudill, W. A., & Schooler, C. (1973). Child behavior and child rearing in Japan and the United States: An interim report. *The Journal of Nervous and Mental Disease, 157*, 323–338.

Chun, K. M., & Akutsu, P. D. (2003). Acculturation among ethnic minority families. In K. Chun, P. B. Organista, & G. Marín (Eds.), *Acculturation: Advances in theory, measurement, and applied research* (pp. 95–114). Washington, DC: American Psychological Association.

Connor, J. W. (1974). Acculturation and changing need patterns in Japanese-American and Caucasian-American college students. *The Journal of Social Psychology, 92*, 293–294.

Crowne, D. P., & Marlowe, D. (1960). A new scale of social desirability independent of psychopathology. *Journal of Consulting Psychology, 24*, 349–354.

Cote, L. R., & Bornstein, M. H. (2003). Cultural and parenting cognitions in acculturating cultures: I. Cultural comparisons and developmental continuity and stability. *Journal of Cross-Cultural Psychology, 34*, 323–349.

Cote, L. R., & Bornstein, M. H. (2004). *Mothers' perceptions of their own and their spouses' parenting styles in cultures of origin, acculturating cultures, and cultures of destination*. Manuscript submitted for publication.

Cote, L. R., & Bornstein, M. H. (2005). Child and mother play in cultures of origin, acculturating cultures, and cultures of destination. Special issue, *International Journal of Behavioral Development, 29*, 479–488.

Cuéllar, I., Arnold, B., & Maldonado, R. (1995). Acculturation Rating Scale for Mexican Americans II: A revision of the original ARSMA Scale. *Hispanic Journal of Behavioral Sciences, 17*, 275–304.

Cuellar, I., Harris, L. C., & Jasso, R. (1980). An acculturation scale for Mexican American normal and clinical populations. *Hispanic Journal of Behavioral Sciences, 2*, 199–217.

Dunn, J., & Brown, J. (1991). Becoming American or English? Talking about the social world in England and the United States. In M. H. Bornstein (Ed.), *Cultural approaches to parenting* (pp. 155–172). Hillsdale, NJ: Lawrence Erlbaum Associates.

Federal Interagency Forum on Child and Family Statistics. (2002). *America's children: Key national indicators of well-being.* Washington, DC: U.S. Government Printing Office.

Field, T. M., & Widmayer, S. M. (1981). Mother–infant interactions among lower SES Black, Cuban, Puerto Rican and South American immigrants. In D. S. Palermo (Series Ed.) and T. M. Field, A. M. Sostek, P. Vietze, & P. H. Leiderman (Vol. Eds.), *Child psychology: Cultural and early interactions* (pp. 41–62). Hillsdale, NJ: Lawrence Erlbaum Associates.

Garcia Coll, C. T., & Pachter, L. M. (2002). Ethnic and minority parenting. In M. H. Bornstein (Ed.), *Handbook of parenting: Vol. 4. Applied parenting* (2nd ed., pp. 1–20). Mahwah, NJ: Lawrence Erlbaum Associates.

Gjerde, P. F. (1996). Longitudinal research in a cultural context: Reflections, prospects, challenges. In D. W. Shwalb & B. J. Shwalb (Eds.), *Culture and human development. Japanese childrearing: Two generations of scholarship* (pp. 279–299). New York: Guilford.

Greenfield, P. M., & Suzuki, L. K. (1998). Culture and human development: Implications for parenting, education, pediatrics, and mental health. In W. Damon (Series Ed.), and I. E. Sigel & K. A. Renninger (Vol. Eds.), *Handbook of child psychology: Vol. 4. Child psychology in practice* (5th ed., pp. 1059–1109). New York: Wiley.

Hara, H., & Minagawa, M. (1996). From productive dependents to precious guests: Historical changes in Japanese children. In D. W. Shwalb & B. J. Shwalb (Eds.), *Culture and human development. Japanese childrearing: Two generations of scholarship* (pp. 9–30). New York: Guilford.

Harkness, S., Super, C. M., & Keefer, C. H. (1992). Learning to be an American parent: How cultural models gain directive force. In R. A. Paul & R. A. Shweder (Series Eds.) and R. G. D'Andrade & C. Strauss (Vol. Eds.), *Publications of the Society for Psychological Anthropology: Human motives and cultural models* (Vol. 1, pp. 163–178). Cambridge: Cambridge University Press.

Hofstede, G. (1991). *Cultures and organizations: Software of the mind.* London: McGraw-Hill.

Holloway, S. D. (1988). Concepts of ability and effort in Japan and the United States. *Review of Educational Research, 58*, 327–345.

Jacoby, T. (Ed.). (2004). *Reinventing the melting pot: The new immigrants and what it means to be American.* New York: Basic Books.

Lanham, B. B., & Garrick, R. J. (1996). Adult to child in Japan: Interaction and relations. In D. W. Shwalb & B. J. Shwalb (Eds.), *Culture and human development. Japanese childrearing: Two generations of scholarship* (pp. 97–124). New York: Guilford.

LeVine, R. A. (1982). *Culture, behavior, and personality: An introduction to the comparative study of psychosocial adaptation* (2nd ed., pp. 15–39). New York: Aldine.

Lightfoot, C., & Valsiner, J. (1992). Parental beliefs about developmental processes. *Human Development, 25*, 192–200.

Machida, S. (1996). Maternal and cultural socialization for schooling: Lessons learned and prospects ahead. In D. W. Shwalb & B. J. Shwalb (Eds.), *Culture and human development. Japanese childrearing: Two generations of scholarship* (pp. 241–259). New York: Guilford.

MacPhee, D. (1981). *Manual: Knowledge of Infant Development Inventory.* Unpublished manuscript, University of North Carolina, Chapel Hill, NC.

MacPhee, D., Benson, J. B., & Bullock, D. (1986, April). *Influences on maternal self-perceptions*. Paper presented at the Fifth Biennial International Conference on Infant Studies, Los Angeles.

Marín, G., & Marín, B. V. (1991). *Applied Social Research Methods Series: Vol. 23. Research with Hispanic populations*. Newbury Park, CA: Sage.

Markus, H. R., & Kitayama, S. (1991). Culture and the self: Implications for cognition, emotion, and motivation. *Psychological Review, 98*, 224–253.

Nagata, D. K. (1994). Assessing Asian American acculturation and ethnic identity: The need for a multidimensional framework. *Asian American and Pacific Islander Journal of Health, 2*, 109–121.

Ngo, P. Y. L., & Malz, T. A. (1998). Cross-cultural and cross-generational differences in Asian Americans' cultural and familial systems and their impact on academic striving. In H. I. McCubbin & E. A. Thompson (Eds.), *Resiliency in Family Series: Vol. 2. Resiliency in Native American and immigrant families* (pp. 265–274). Thousand Oaks, CA: Sage.

Oyserman, D., Coon, H., & Kemmelmeier, M. (2002). Rethinking individualism and collectivism: Evaluation of theoretical assumptions and meta-analyses. *Psychological Bulletin, 128*, 3–72.

Parke, R. D., & Buriel, R. (1998). Socialization in the family: Ethnic and ecological perspectives. In W. Damon (Series Ed.) & N. Eisenberg (Vol. Ed.), *Handbook of child psychology: Vol. 3. Social, emotional, and personality development* (5th ed., pp. 463–552). New York: Wiley.

Piaget, J. (1962). *Play, dreams, and imitation in childhood* (C. Gattegno & F. M. Hodgson, Trans.). New York: W. W. Norton. (Original work published 1951)

Rudmin, F. W. (2003). Critical history of the acculturation psychology of assimilation, separation, integration, and marginalization. *Review of General Psychology, 7*, 3–37.

Sirignano, S. W., & Lachman, M. E. (1985). Personality change during the transition to parenthood: The role of perceived infant temperament. *Developmental Psychology, 21*, 558–567.

Suinn, R. M., & Lew, S. (1987). *Suinn-Lew Asian Self-identity Acculturation Scale*. Unpublished manuscript, Colorado State University, Fort Collins, CO.

Szapocznik, J., Scopetta, M. A., Kurtines, W., & Aranalde, M. (1978). Theory and measurement of acculturation. *Interamerican Journal of Psychology, 12*, 113–130.

Tamis-LeMonda, C. S., Bornstein, M. H., Cyphers, L., Toda, S., & Ogino, M. (1992). Language and play at one year: A comparison of toddlers and mothers in the United States and Japan. *International Journal of Behavioral Development, 15*, 19–42.

Triandis, H. C. (1989). The self and social behavior in differing cultural contexts. *Psychological Review, 96*, 506–520.

Uba, L. (1994). *Asian Americans: Personality patterns, identity, and mental health*. New York: Guilford.

United States Census Bureau. (2001). *Profile of the foreign-born population in the United States: 2000* (Current Population Reports, Series P23-206) [Electronic version]. Washington, DC: Government Printing Office.

van de Vijver, F. J. R., & Leung, K. (1997). *Methods and data analysis for cross-cultural research*. Thousand Oaks, CA: Sage.

Vygotsky, L. (1978). *Mind in society*. Cambridge, MA: Harvard University Press.

Ward, C. (1999). Models and measures of acculturation. In W. J. Lonner, D. L. Dinnel, D. K. Forgays, & S. A. Hayes (Eds.), *Merging past, present, and future in cross-cultural psychology: Selected papers from the Fourteenth International Congress of the International Association for Cross-Cultural Psychology* (pp. 221–230). Lisse, The Netherlands: Swets & Zeitlinger B. V.

Ward, C. (2001). The A, B, Cs of acculturation. In D. Matsumoto (Ed.), *The handbook of culture & psychology* (pp. 411–445). New York: Oxford University Press.

10

Studying Acculturation Among Latinos in the United States

Robin L. Harwood
Ruhr University, Bochum, Germany

Xin Feng
University of Connecticut, U.S.A.

INTRODUCTION

Changing Demographic Trends in the United States

In the 1990s, roughly 40% of the United States' total population growth was due to net immigration (that is, the number of incoming minus the number of outgoing migrations). This relative growth rate through immigration is equalled in U.S. history only by the decade 1901–1910. In the 2000 Census, a total of 31.1 million foreigners was counted, comprising the largest immigrant population in modern history. According to Camarota (Center for Immigration Studies, 2002), these new figures "indicate that we are currently in the midst of a huge social experiment," in which the United States must find a way to "incorporate and assimilate 31 million newcomers into its society."

In addition to a dramatic increase in the volume of immigration, the demographic profile of U.S. immigrants has also changed dramatically in the past few decades. In 1940, only 13% of immigrants were from Asia and Latin America, whereas 86% came from Europe and Canada. By 1990, this pattern had reversed, with 84% coming from Asia and Latin America, and less than 13% from Europe and Canada (U.S. Bureau of the Census, 1992; Rumbaut, 1994). Due to these shifting immigration patterns and to differential fertility rates among these populations, one out of four U.S. residents identified themselves in a category other than "White, non-Hispanic" in 1990. Consistent with these statistics, only 62% of children born in the United States in 1995 were White non-Latinos whose parents had also been born in the United States (Hernandez, 1997).

It is clear that the United States is entering a time of ethnic diversity unprecedented in its history. Hernandez (1997) called this an era of "revolutionary demographic transformations . . . in the nature of childhood" (p. 159). For example, between 1900 and 1970, White non-Latinos accounted for 85% to 89% of the U.S. child population. By 1995, this proportion had fallen to 69% and is projected to decline to 42% by 2050. Also by this date, Latino children are expected to be the largest minority group, comprising roughly 29% of the U.S. child population.

Latinos in the United States

Currently, Latinos are one of the fastest growing minority groups within the United States. Between 1990 and 2000, the Latino population grew by 58%, compared to a single-digit growth rate in the nation as a whole. The 2000 Census counted 35.3 million Latinos living in the United States, or roughly one out of every 8 Americans. By 2002, this figure had increased nearly 10% to 38.8 million. Also in 2002, the Census Bureau officially declared Latinos the largest minority group in the United States, accounting for just over 13% of the total population. Given the relative youth of the Latino population (nearly 40% are under age 20), and assuming a continuation of current migratory and fertility trends, this number is expected to rise to one in four by 2050 (U.S. Census Bureau, 2001; Marotta & Garcia, 2003).

The term "Latino" is itself an umbrella term used to refer to people who have their origins in Mexico, Central or South America, and the Spanish-speaking Caribbean. Although this label represents a group of people who share a history of colonization by Spain, it is important to keep in mind that Latinos are a diverse people with diverse reasons for being in the United States. First, Latinos differ by their place of origin. In 2000 the largest percentage (58%) claimed Mexican heritage, followed by Puerto Rican (10%), and Cuban (4%; Marotta & Garcia, 2003). The remaining 28% of Latinos represent all Central and South American countries, as well as the remainder of the Spanish-speaking Caribbean. Thus, some 20 countries of origin are represented by the broad term "Latino."

Second, Latinos differ substantially among themselves with regard to the historical and personal circumstances of their arrival in the United States. Large numbers of Latinos in the Southwest were "acquired" as citizens due to the annexation of a large portion of Mexico in 1848. In 1917, Puerto Ricans became U.S. citizens nearly two decades after the island was won from Spain in 1898. Among both Mexicans and Puerto Ricans, several waves of migration can be identified based on periods of economic unrest in the homeland or renewed labor opportunities in the States. In Cuba, internal revolution resulted in the exodus of members of the elite classes following Castro's takeover in 1959; three distinct phases of migration from Cuba have been identified since then (Cauce & Rodríguez, 2002).

Among Central and South Americans, migrants have included people fleeing homelands ravaged by war and poverty as well as educated professionals seeking employment opportunities. Latinos thus vary widely in terms of their historical and personal reasons for being in the United States, including those who are citizens by virtue of conquest, political refugees seeking asylum, both documented and undocumented laborers attempting to find jobs, family members seeking to be reunited with loved ones, students pursuing higher education, and professionals in search of employment opportunities.

A third and related source of internal diversity among Latinos is socioeconomic status. Although 27% of Latinos in the United States live below the poverty line, the majority do not. Within-group differences also arise on this index, with Cubans having the lowest (11%) and Puerto Ricans the highest (30%) poverty rate. In terms of educational attainment, internal diversity is also present, with 70% of Cubans, 64% of Puerto Ricans and Central Americans, but only 50% of Mexicans over the age of 25 having finished high school (U.S. Census Bureau, 1999). Although a great deal of attention has been focused on Latinos as a high-risk group living in poverty, it is important to keep in mind that the majority of Latinos are in the United States legally, complete high school, obtain employment, and live above the poverty line. An almost exclusive focus on low-SES Latino groups in the research literature not only makes it difficult to disentangle culture from SES as a source of influence on behavior (Betancourt & Regeser López, 1993), but also perpetuates the "stereotypic view that ethnic families are monolithic . . . and generally 'different' than the 'normative middle-class white families,' as well as the unsupported assumption that with educational and occupational mobility, ethnic minorities will become indistinguishable from white middle-class families" (Fisher, Jackson, & Villarruel, 1998, p. 1151). It is thus crucial to highlight and be sensitive to diversity among Latinos with regard to socioeconomic status.

A fourth source of diversity is level of acculturation. In 2000, roughly 40% of Latinos in the United States were not born here (Therrien & Ramirez, 2000). Among these, researchers typically define the first or immigrant generation as individuals who migrated after the age of 12. Second-generation Latinos are comprised of individuals who were born here, but whose parents were not, whereas the third generation has parents who were born in the United States, but grandparents who were not. Each of these generational groups is likely to have had different opportunities for exposure to both the culture of origin and U.S. culture.

Moreover, fifth, the differential geographical distribution of Latinos across the United States creates different local environments for the relative preservation of the culture of origin. For example, in 2000, nearly two thirds of U.S. Latinos lived in just four states (California, Texas, New York, and Florida). However, the states with the highest concentration of Latinos were New Mexico, Texas, California, and Arizona, where they were respectively 42%, 32%, 32%, and 25% of the total state populations (Marotta & Garcia, 2003; U.S. Census Bureau, 2000). These differential distributions suggest the existence of ethnic enclaves in which cultural preservation is more or less likely to occur across generations. In addition, individuals differ among themselves with regard to the family and personal experiences that led them to either strengthen or attenuate ties to Latino culture within their own lives.

Given these various sources of diversity, it is imperative to become more sensitive to the fact that "Latinos" are a heterogeneous group of people differing among themselves in terms of their country of origin, historical and personal reasons for being in the United States, socioeconomic status, and level of acculturation (Cauce & Rodríguez, 2002; Roosa, Morgan-Lopez, Cree, & Specter, 2002). As Wolf (1994) observed, we must "recognize that ethnicities come in many varieties and to call a social entity an 'ethnic' group is merely the beginning of the inquiry" (p. 7).

PUERTO RICANS IN THE UNITED STATES

Puerto Ricans are the second largest Latino group in the United States (in 2000, Mexican Americans comprised 58% and Puerto Ricans 10% of all Latinos). However, in the Northeast United States, Puerto Ricans are the largest group, accounting for nearly 40% of the total Latino population in 2000. In Connecticut, where Latinos now constitute nearly 10% of the total population, Puerto Ricans represent nearly 61% of all Latinos.

In addition, migratory levels from Puerto Rico to the mainland have remained high throughout the past two decades, with a net migration of over 130,000 during the period of 1995–2000 alone (U.S. Census Bureau, 2000). It is estimated that, sometime in 2004, the number of Puerto Ricans living on the mainland United States equalled and then surpassed the number of Puerto Ricans living on the island.

Migration To and From Puerto Rico

Migration to and from the mainland constitutes a critical element of Puerto Rican life today. As Alarcón, Erkut, García Coll, and Vázquez García (1994) observed, Puerto Ricans "have the unique status of being native born Americans who are immigrants because of culture and geography, not legal status. Having no restrictions, they travel back and forth from the island to the mainland" (p. 2). The 2000 Census counted over 7 million Puerto Ricans, nearly one half (48%) of whom lived on the mainland United States (U.S. Census Bureau, 2000). On the island itself, one out of every four Puerto Ricans is estimated to have undergone some sort of migratory experience (Lucca Irizarry & Pacheco, 1992). Vasquez Calzada (1979) observed that "migration has been one of the population topics that has received the least attention [from social scientists]. . . . in spite of the fact that today migration is the most important variable of the population equation [in Puerto Rico]" (p. 223). Lucca Irizarry and Pacheco (1992) similarly asserted that "Puerto Rican migration to and from the United States is one of the world's most sustained population displacements" (p. 226). This circular migration, although understudied, is likely to affect patterns of acculturation (Alarcón et al., 1994).

Studying the Migratory Experience

The most frequently studied aspect of the migratory experience has been acculturation, defined briefly as "the process through which immigrants and their offspring acquire the values, behavioral norms, and attitudes of the host society" (Cortes, Rogler, & Malgady, 1994, p. 708). In particular, researchers studying processes of migration have focused primarily on two dimensions: attempts to measure acculturation, and examinations of the relation between acculturative stress and mental health. Briefly, these studies have yielded conflicting results, with some researchers finding a positive and other researchers finding a negative relation between acculturation and a variety of mental health outcomes. In a meta-analytic study of the relevant literature, Moyerman and Forman (1992) concluded that "there does not appear to be a consistent unidirectional effect of acculturation on adjustment" (p. 177). The authors go on to suggest that acculturation cannot be understood without attention to specific factors that appear to influence the quality of the migratory experience, such as particular sociodemographic and familial circumstances.

Studying Acculturation

Researchers have emphasized the need to broaden examination of acculturation and the migratory experience (García Coll et al., 1996; Phinney, 1996; Rogler, 1994). In particular, they have noted: (1) past investigations have tended to view migration from a deficit perspective, viewing it as a stressor and examining its relation to mental health outcomes (Cohen, 1987; García Coll, Meyer, & Brillon, 1995); normative processes of cultural change and the migratory experience have not been studied; (2) we know relatively little regarding the ways in which specific aspects of the migratory experience, such as socioeconomic status or the composition of one's social networks, may relate to the adoption of the host country's beliefs and practices (Rogler, 1994); and (3) most past research has tended to assume a "bipolar" view of ethnic identity, in which "the adoption of the new culture occurs at the expense of a corresponding rejection of the culture of origin" (Cortes et al., 1994, p. 718; Rogler, Cortes, & Malgady, 1991). The development of a bicultural identity, as well as the delineation of processes involving selective rather than wholesale cultural change, remain unexamined. As Wolf (1982) noted, "It is an error to envisage the migrant as the protagonist of a homogeneously integrated culture that he either retains or yields up as a whole" (p. 361).

Several researchers have therefore urged that future studies of migrant families focus on: (1) competencies rather than deficits (García Coll et al., 1995; Werner, 1997); (2) specific circumstances that may influence the nature of the migratory experience, such as changes in social networks and in socioeconomic status (Rogler, 1994; Tilly, 1990); and (3) the development of a bicultural identity from a perspective that eschews the notion that ethnic identity is either discrete or static (Vega, 1990).

Theoretical Models of Acculturation

One of the difficulties in the acculturation literature has been a lack of theoretical models within which to frame questions and interpret research findings. One model that has received recent attention is that proposed by Berry (1997). In this model, Berry builds on the need for a more complex understanding of the acculturation process, including a rejection of the "bipolar" view of ethnic identity. In particular, he puts forward a model that views the migrant as potentially maintaining and adopting beliefs, values, and behaviors from more than one culture. In this model, migrating individuals can be either low or high in their identification with both the culture of origin and the host culture, thus yielding four categories of ethnic identity status: marginalization, in which the person professes low participation in both cultures; separation, in which the migrant retains high attachment to the culture of origin combined with low involvement in the host culture; assimilation, in which the person yields identification with the culture of origin in preference for the host culture; and integration, or biculturalism, in which the migrant incorporates components from both cultures into his or her identity. This fourth category is considered to be the most potentially enriching identity status for the migrant to adopt.

Contributions of the Present Study

The present study addresses the need for research on normative processes of cultural change by exploring: (1) the development of monocultural versus bicultural orientations across two generations of migrating mothers; (2) the complexity of cultural change and preservation (e.g., Which aspects of the original culture do mothers wish to preserve in their children and under what circumstances? Which aspects of the host culture do they consider important for their children to adopt?); and (3) specific life circumstances that may relate to the development of monocultural versus bicultural orientations.

In addition to its theoretical contribution to our understanding of processes of cultural change following migration, the present research has at least three implications for social policy in the United States. First, as the number of Latino families and children continues to rise, it becomes increasingly imperative for teachers, health care providers, and other professionals to understand normative patterns of migratory experience and cultural change within this population. For example, in order to be successful, primary prevention efforts such as school-based social competence promotion and parenting programs must be grounded on a solid knowledge of normative patterns within a variety of minority groups, including Latinos. Second, as the United States becomes increasingly multicultural, the importance of addressing and correcting popular (mis)conceptions of Latino culture and processes of cultural change can only grow. Jimenez de Wagenheim (as cited in Rodriguez, Sanchez Korrol, & Alers, 1980) described Puerto Ricans as "a people forever travelling between two realities, two cultures, two worlds." Such observations have fed popular debates regarding the assimilation of Latinos into contemporary American society. For example, Sutton (1992) noted that "rather than becoming hyphenated Americans, [current Latino migrants] operate with a transnational dual-place identity" that "once again confront[s] Americans with questions about how American society is held together . . . and what becoming 'americanized' means today" (p. 231). Examining current patterns of cultural change among a population of Latino migrants can aid us in our attempts to understand what it means to live in an increasingly multicultural society. Finally, in this age of expanded global interdependence and mobility, the likelihood of encountering migrant families and their children in a variety of personal and professional contexts multiplies for all people, highlighting the value of a deeper comprehension of both universal and group-specific aspects of cultural change and the migratory experience.

METHODS IN THE STUDY OF ACCULTURATION AMONG LATINOS

The research was conducted with working-class first- and second-generation migrant Puerto Rican mothers of children aged 18 to 36 months. The rationale for choosing these groups as the study population includes:

(1) Puerto Rican mothers represent a rapidly growing minority group within the United States that has often appeared ethnically and culturally distinctive to members of the mainstream population; in particular, they represent a culture that has generally been considered to be more sociocentric (Harwood, Miller, & Lucca Irizarry, 1995), thus contrasting sharply with the individualism of their host setting, and heightening the potential for cultural conflict and change that this migrant group may experience.

(2) First-generation migrant mothers were anticipated to afford a glimpse into normative childrearing beliefs by examining parenting values and beliefs among Puerto Rican mothers within a few years of their arrival in the United States.

(3) Second-generation migrant mothers were expected to contribute deeper insight into factors associated with cultural change by investigating the extent to which the childrearing beliefs and values of this group are similar to and/or different from both first-generation migrant and host-culture mothers. Working-class rather than middle-class mothers were sampled because the majority of migrant Puerto Rican mothers in the United States are working-class, and thereby comprise the most representative population from which to draw these mothers.

Sampling

The sample was comprised of women with at least a 10th-grade education who were from families in which the household head was employed in skilled, semi-skilled, or unskilled labor (Levels III, IV, and V on the Hollingshead, 1975, index). First-generation Puerto Rican mothers (n = 26) were reared and educated primarily in Puerto Rico and spoke Puerto Rican Spanish as their first language; second-generation mothers (n = 38) were reared and educated primarily in the United States, with no more than 6 years spent living in Puerto Rico. Each mother had at least one child between the ages of 18 to 36 months, enabling us to examine childrearing beliefs and values using target children who were mobile and verbal enough to elicit parental concerns regarding appropriate socialization, but too young to have encountered the significant external socializing influences that exist in school and preschool settings (Tobin, Wu, & Davidson, 1989).

Information was obtained from all participants on a variety of sociodemographic variables, both in the host country and the country of origin, and effects of these variables were assessed. Similar recruitment procedures were employed for both groups. Specifically, mothers were obtained through WIC offices, family resource centers, and other agencies servicing Puerto Rican families in the greater Hartford, CT, area. As can be seen in Table 10.1, the resulting samples of mothers were similar on 17 sociodemographic indices.

Because of the history of circular migration between the United States and Puerto Rico, it was expected that the determination of generational status would be complicated. With this in mind, the following generational criteria were developed for inclusion in the study:

(1) Migration age 12 or older, no more than six years spent in the United States, and primarily schooled in Puerto Rico.
(2) Parents first generation, no more than six years spent in Puerto Rico, and primarily schooled in the United States.

As can be seen in Table 10.2, the variable that distinguished the two generational groups the most reliably was the place where mothers were primarily schooled, with 100% of the first-generation mothers having spent their school years in

TABLE 10.1
Demographic Characteristics

	PR 1st Gen (*n* = 26)	*PR 2nd Gen* (*n* = 38)	*p*
Mother's age	26.38	25.26	*ns*
Mother's education	11.73	12.14	*ns*
Religious background (%)			*ns*
None	7.69	10.53	
Protestant	46.15	15.79	
Catholic	30.80	55.26	
Other	15.38	18.42	
Total number children	2.07	1.97	*ns*
% Firstborn	34.62	44.74	*ns*
% Female	46.15	42.11	*ns*
Total household size	3.88	4.00	*ns*
% Mothers employed	50.00	55.26	*ns*
No. hours work/week	33.88	31.24	*ns*
% Mothers living w/partner	65.38	63.16	*ns*
% Married	38.46	23.68	
Partner's education	11.82	11.96	*ns*
Partner's age	29.35	29.00	*ns*
% Partners unemployed	17.65	20.83	*ns*
No. hours work/week	43.11	40.47	*ns*
Household Hollingshead	27.38	27.93	*ns*
Family composition			*ns*
% Nuclear family	65.38	47.39	
% Single parent	23.08	18.42	
% Extended family	11.54	18.42	
% Living w/other adults	0.00	15.79	
% Government aid	69.23	50.00	*ns*
No. rooms in house	2.31	2.49	*ns*

$^*p < .05$. $^{**}p < .01$. $^{***}p < .001$.

TABLE 10.2
Migration Characteristics of Puerto Rican Mothers

	1st Generation	*2nd Generation*	*p*
% Born in Puerto Rico	84.62	28.95	**
Age first migration	17.88	3.13	**
Range	0.00–27.00	0.00–7.00	
% Return migration	38.46	34.21	
Length (Yrs)	10.75	1.92	**
Total yrs in Puerto Rico	19.63	1.75	**
Total yrs in U.S.	6.73	23.51	**
% Schooled in Puerto Rico	100.00	0.00	**
% Schooled in U.S.	0.00	100.00	**

$^*p < .05$. $^{**}p < .01$.

Puerto Rico, and 100% of the second-generation mothers having spent their school years in the United States.

Procedures to Promote Cross-Cultural Validity

We interviewed all mothers in their preferred language (i.e., Puerto Rican Spanish or English), and took several steps to promote the cultural appropriateness of the research materials in the Puerto Rican context. First, we examined all research protocols for cultural suitability in consultation with Puerto Rican cultural consultants and revised the protocols on the basis of their comments. We then undertook complete translations by bilingual, bicultural Puerto Ricans, and checked them for preservation of meaning and cultural appropriateness. Finally, pilot testing ensured that all materials were readily comprehensible and ethnographically valid.

Testing, Control, and Reliability Procedures

Trained interviewers who were fluent in the mother's preferred language and blind to the study hypotheses conducted interviews in mothers' homes. To ensure comprehension of the protocol, the interviewers read all interview items to mothers. Mothers' oral responses were written down verbatim for the majority of interview items; however, in order to facilitate mothers' open-ended responses to the questions regarding their socialization goals and migratory experiences, these portions of the interviews were audiotaped for later transcription. All naturalistic observations were videotaped. Trained research assistants who were blind to the study hypotheses coded oral interviews and videotaped observations. At least two different people coded independently 50% of all the open-ended interviews, and 20% of the videotaped observations to ensure reliability; an agreement level of at least .70 (Cohen's kappa) was achieved across all coding categories.

Specific Goals

The present study examined: (1) the development of monocultural versus bicultural orientations across two generations of migrating mothers; (2) the complexity of cultural change and preservation (e.g., which aspects of the original culture do mothers wish to preserve in their children and under what circumstances? Which aspects of the host culture do they consider important for their children to adopt?); and (3) specific life circumstances that may relate to the development of monocultural versus bicultural orientations, including the composition of social networks, socioeconomic success in the host country, and negative versus positive perceptions of and experiences within the host country.

Study Procedures

We administered procedures in mothers' homes in three sessions, each lasting 2 hours or less, scheduled within a 4-week time period. The first session included interviews regarding mothers' social networks. The second session involved observations of the target child's activities. The final session investigated mothers' socioeconomic circumstances and perceptions of the migratory experience. In addition, in the final session mothers completed a standardized acculturation instrument.

Social Networks Inventory

Social networks appear to be important to the study of cultural change for a variety of reasons. First, family stability and social support have been linked to more positive experiences and greater socioeconomic success among migrant families (Rumbaut, 1997). In addition, the ethnic composition of social networks may reflect greater or lesser insulation from the host culture, thus providing insight into factors associated with cultural change. Finally, research indicates that cultural values regarding familism versus individualism may be related to social network composition (Miller & Harwood, 2001). Social networks may thus serve to (1) support individuals through the potential stresses associated with migration by providing greater access to important social and financial resources; (2) facilitate or inhibit cultural change through exposure to meaningful cross-ethnic relationships; and (3) reflect values regarding the role played in one's social network by family members versus friendships.

We used the methods outlined in Maguire (1983) to investigate group differences in mothers' social networks. Specifically, we asked mothers to provide the following information regarding their relationships: (1) number; (2) type (e.g., neighbor, family, friend); (3) ethnic composition; (4) frequency of contact (e.g., daily, weekly, monthly); (5) geographical proximity (e.g., whether the contact is local or long distance via phone or mail); (6) degree of psychological intimacy, including duration of relationship; and (7) what sorts of information, support, or aid mothers feel they can obtain from each relationship. We examined social networks rather than social support more narrowly defined because social network mapping constitutes a broader and more normative consideration of a person's support system than do standardized social support questionnaires (Maguire, 1983), which have primarily been used in studies of stress and coping.

Naturalistic Observations

The second session was devoted to naturalistic observations of the target child's evening meal, free time, and play activities. In this paper, the naturalistic observations provided us with a direct measure of maternal language (i.e., Spanish or English) directed toward the child.

Migratory Experiences Interview

The Migratory Experiences Interview was used to gather qualitative information and develop indices for three primary types of data for each of the first and second generation migrant mothers: (1) history of migration back and forth between the two cultures; (2) positive versus negative perceptions of the two cultures; and (3) the development of a bicultural identity. In particular, both first- and second-generation migrant mothers were interviewed regarding: (1) the history of their migration between the culture of origin and the host culture, including frequency of visits and length of stays; (2) how much of their immediate and extended family is currently living in the two settings, and whether they feel family relationships have changed as a result of migration; (3) their reasons for migrating; (4) what their initial and ongoing experiences in the host culture have been like, and what it is like for them now when they visit the culture of origin; and (5) what they like most and least about living in each setting. Both first- and second-generation mothers were also asked whether they: (1) have personally observed differences in the way children are brought up in the two settings and, if so, what some of those differences are; (2) think their own childrearing beliefs and practices are more reflective of those in the culture of origin or those in the host culture; (3) see behaviors or qualities displayed in both the host culture and the culture of origin that they particularly either want or do not want their own child to develop; (4) think there are differences in what makes a person competent in each culture; and (5) believe it is important that their child be competent in both cultures and why or why not, and if so, whether they have personally made any adjustments to help their child be competent in both cultures.

In addition, mothers were asked: (1) how traditional they believe their upbringing was with regard to the culture of origin; (2) whether any values they were taught from their culture of origin conflicted with values they encountered in the host culture, and if so, what effect that had on them; (3) to what extent they have personally adopted values and behaviors from both cultures versus simply knowing about them; (4) whether they feel equally comfortable and competent in both cultural settings across all contexts (e.g., home, work, school, friendships, family), or whether they feel more or less comfortable in specific contexts; (5) whether they feel that their own personal ethnic identity is more similar to the culture of origin, the host culture, or a unique combination of both; (6) whether they have dated/married within or outside of the culture of origin; and (7) if married, how open the spouse is to both cultures.

Coding of MEI

Culturally relevant coding schemes for the content analysis of mothers' open-ended responses to the Migratory Experiences Interview were created inductively, based on mothers' own responses (Harwood, 1992; Harwood et al., 1995; Harwood, Schoelmerich, Ventura-Cook, Schulze, & Wilson, 1996). In particular, the data were used to provide descriptive information and to examine group differences among the first- and second-generation mothers regarding: (1) patterns of migration back and forth between the host culture and the culture of origin; (2) positive versus negative experiences within and perceptions of both the original and host cultures; and (3) mothers' relative comfort in, preference for, and acceptance of the two cultures, with particular attention to cultural beliefs and practices regarding childrearing.

Standardized Acculturation Instrument

As a final part of the Migratory Experiences Interview, mothers completed a standardized acculturation measure. This provided: information regarding linguistic skills and preferences; a baseline for comparison with previous studies on acculturation; and a convergent measure for the open-ended questions regarding mothers' relative comfort in, preference for, and acceptance of the two cultures. We used the bicultural measure created by Cortes et al. (1994) specifically for use with Puerto Rican populations. Researchers (Cortes et al., 1994; Rogler, 1994) have argued that involvement in the host culture and the culture of origin should be studied as independent phenomena, rather than along a single scale. Specifically, the single scale measurement tool has been criticized for assuming that greater involvement in one culture must correspond with lesser involvement in the other. By assessing involvement in the two cultures independently, Cortes et al.'s Bicultural Involvement Scale allows researchers to assess the extent to which an individual feels competent in and enjoys specific aspects of both cultures.

The Bicultural Involvement Questionnaire contains 36 items, 18 measuring involvement in Puerto Rican culture, and 18 measuring involvement in European American culture. These items use a 4-point Likert scale to rate comfort with the two languages in a variety of settings, as well as enjoyment of and relative preference for a variety of culturally specific activities, including food, the media, holiday celebrations, and entertainment. There is a possible range from 18 to 72 for each scale, with 18 representing low cultural involvement, and 72 representing high involvement. In this study, the alpha coefficient for the 18 items measuring involvement in European American culture was .95 and for the 18 items measuring involvement in Puerto Rican culture was .91.

CULTURAL INVOLVEMENT

One-way ANOVAs on the Bicultural Involvement Scales yielded significant group differences on both the Puerto Rican, $F(1, 63) = 18.4$, $p < .001$, and European American, $F(1, 63) = 65.8$, $p < .001$, scales, with first- compared to second-generation mothers having higher scores on the Puerto Rican Cultural Involvement Scale (respective $M = 69.3, 61.2$), and lower scores on the European American Cultural Involvement Scale (respective $M = 47.2, 64.2$).

We performed stepwise regression analyses on a variety of demographic and migration characteristics to determine significant predictors of mothers' scores on the two cultural involvement scales. The total number of years lived in Puerto Rico significantly ($R^2 = .27, p < .01$) predicted Puerto Rican cultural involvement. In contrast, spending the school years primarily in the United States significantly ($R^2 = .54, p < .01$) predicted involvement in European American culture.

MAINTENANCE OF PUERTO RICAN CULTURE

Mothers' Own Upbringing

We performed a chi-square analysis on mothers' responses to the open-ended question regarding whether they perceived that their own upbringing was traditionally Puerto Rican or not. More first-generation mothers compared to second generation described themselves as having had a "traditional" Puerto Rican upbringing (percentages 68% and 37.8%), and fewer said that their upbringing was not entirely traditional, but did include observation of customs involving holidays and food (percentages = 28% and 51.4%), Fisher's exact test = 12.3, $p < .01$. Fisher's exact test instead of Pearson's chi-square was reported because the smallest cell had expected counts less than 5.

Values and Customs

We performed a chi-square analysis on mothers' responses to the open-ended question regarding the maintenance of Puerto Rican culture in her current life. First-generation compared to second-generation mothers were more likely to say that they were maintaining both traditional values and customs, and less likely to say they were not maintaining any of their Puerto Rican heritage in their current life, $\chi^2(3) = 8.5, p < .05$ (see Table 10.3).

Spanish Language

We performed chi-square analyses on the mothers' stated language preference (English vs. Spanish), as well as their observed language use during the interview. More first-generation mothers, compared to second-generation mothers, stated a preference for Spanish, $\chi^2\,(2) = 34.9, p < .01$, and also actually spoke Spanish exclusively or almost exclusively during the interview, $\chi^2\,(2) = 20.4, p < .01$ (see Table 10.3).

TABLE 10.3
Maintenance of Puerto Rican Culture

	1st Generation	*2nd Generation*	*p*
% Maintenance of values & customs			*
Both values & customs	30.77	13.51	
Values only	23.08	29.73	
Customs only	46.15	35.14	
No maintenance	0.00	21.62	
% Stated language preference			**
Spanish	96.15	21.05	
Bilingual	0.00	15.79	
English	3.85	63.16	
% Observed language use during interview			**
Spanish only/mostly	48.00	5.41	
Both Spanish & English	52.00	62.16	
English only/mostly	0.00	32.43	
% Relatives in household	3.85	23.68	*
% Visit PR since migration	65.38	86.49	*
% Felt treated like PR	88.24	45.45	**
% Close to family in PR	84.62	51.35	**

$^*p < .05$. $^{**}p < .01$.

Contact With Relatives

We performed chi-square analyses on whether mothers had relatives living in the same household, had visited Puerto Rico since migration, felt treated like a Puerto Rican during visits to the island, and felt close to family in Puerto Rico. Compared to second-generation mothers, fewer first-generation mothers had relatives living in the same household, χ^2 (1) = 4.6, $p < .05$, or had visited Puerto Rico since their migration, χ^2 (1) = 3.9, $p < .05$, but more reported feeling treated like a Puerto Rican while visiting the island, χ^2 (2) = 9.9, $p < .01$, and to state that they felt close to family on the island, χ^2 (1) = 7.4, $p < .01$ (see Table 10.3).

ADOPTION OF U.S. CULTURE

U.S. Values

We performed a chi-square analysis on mothers' responses to the open-ended question regarding whether they felt they had adopted any U.S. values or customs. More first-generation mothers, compared to second generation, stated that they had not adopted any U.S. values or customs, χ^2 (3) = 12.2, $p < .01$ (see Table 10.4).

TABLE 10.4
Adoption of U.S. Culture

	1st Generation	*2nd Generation*	*p*
Adoption of U.S. values & customs			**
% Values	11.54	35.14	
% Customs only	30.77	29.73	
No adoption	46.15	10.81	
Uncertain	11.54	24.32	

$^*p < .05$. $^{**}p < .01$.

Social Contacts

Chi-square analyses indicated that fewer first-generation mothers compared to second-generation mothers had: (1) European American friends, χ^2 (1) = 4.5, $p <$ .05, respective percentages = 0%, 15.8%), (2) friends from other ethnic backgrounds, such as African American or other Latino groups, χ^2 (1) = 11.6, $p < .01$, respective percentages = 3.8%, 42.1%, or (3) ever been in a relationship with a non-Puerto Rican, χ^2 (1) = 12.2, $p < .01$, respective percentages = 20.8%, 69%. There were no group differences with regard to neighborhood composition.

ETHNIC IDENTITY

Mother's Identity

The overwhelming majority of mothers in both generations indicated that their Puerto Rican ethnic heritage was "very important" to them (first generation, 88.5%, and second generation, 89.2%). The majority in both groups also indicated that "Puerto Rican" was their preferred ethnic identity label (first generation, 76.9% and second generation, 56.8%), although a significant percentage of second-generation mothers chose other labels, such as "Latino," "Hispanic," "Latino American," "American," and so on (see Table 10.5). However, when asked where they feel most at home, more second-generation mothers, compared to first-generation mothers, indicated that they felt most at home in the United States (Fisher's exact test = 5.6, $p < .05$).

Child's Identity

As can be seen in Table 10.5, chi-square analysis was significant, χ^2 (3) = 13.6, $p < .01$, with more first-generation mothers, compared to second-generation, reporting that they wanted a Puerto Rican identity for their child. There were no group

TABLE 10.5
Ethnic Identity

	1st Generation	*2nd Generation*	*p*
% Very important	88.46	89.19	
% Puerto Rican label	76.92	56.76	
Where mother feels at home (%)			*
Puerto Rico	37.50	16.67	
Connecticut	37.50	73.33	
Both places	25.00	10.00	
Child's ethnic identity (%)			**
Puerto Rican	80.77	34.21	
Bicultural	11.54	34.21	
American	3.85	21.05	
Child decides	3.85	10.53	

$^*p < .05$. $^{**}p < .01$.

differences with regard to wanting their child to feel comfortable in both cultural settings.

CULTURAL IDENTITY STATUS

A mean-split on the two cultural *involvement* scales was used to categorize the two groups of mothers according to Berry's (1997) cultural identity status framework. In particular, mothers: below the mean on both the Puerto Rican and European American cultural involvement scales were classified as Marginalized; above the mean on Puerto Rican involvement but below the mean on Anglo involvement were classified as Separate; below the mean on Puerto Rican but above the mean on Anglo involvement were classified as Assimilated; and above the mean on both scales were classified as Bicultural. As can be seen in Table 10.6, a chi-square analysis performed on mothers' cultural identity status classification by group membership yielded a significant group difference in cultural identity

TABLE 10.6
Cultural Identity

	1st Generation	*2nd Generation*	*p*
Classification (number of people, with % in parentheses)			**
Marginalized	2 (7.69)	1 (2.63)	
Separate	21 (80.77)	3 (7.89)	
Assimilated	1 (3.85)	20 (52.63)	
Bicultural	2 (7.69)	14 (36.84)	

$^*p < .05$. $^{**}p < .01$.

classification, $\chi^2(3) = 39.2, p < .01$, with more first-generation compared to second-generation mothers falling into the Separate category, but fewer falling into the Assimilated or Bicultural categories.

INFLUENCES ON CULTURAL IDENTITY STATUS

Demographic and Migration Characteristics

To identify influences on mother's ethnic identity status, we performed MANOVA and chi-square analyses by generation on 17 demographic variables. Only one of these reached significance, $\chi^2 (9) = 17.5, p < .05$, with mothers falling into the Separate and Bicultural categories more likely to identify themselves as Protestant than mothers falling into the Assimilated category (respective percentages = 54.2%, 25.0%, and 4.8%). In addition, we performed univariate and chi-square analyses on seven migration characteristics: birthplace, age of first migration, total years lived in Puerto Rico and the United States, where the mother was primarily schooled, whether or not she had made a return migration to Puerto Rico, and whether or not she was from a rural area. As can be seen in Table 10.7, differences arose on six of the seven migration variables by cultural identity status, with mothers in the Separate category, compared to mothers in the Assimilated and Bicultural categories ($p < .01$): (1) having spent more years in Puerto Rico and fewer years in the United States, including the formative school years, (2) been older at the time of their first migration to the United States, and (3) more likely to have grown up in a rural area. In addition, mothers in the Assimilated categories, compared to mothers in the Separate or Bicultural categories, were more likely to have been born in the United States ($p < .01$). There were no differences with regard to whether or not mothers had made a return migration to Puerto Rico.

TABLE 10.7
Significant Demographic & Migration Differences by Cultural Identity Status

	Marginalized $n = 3$	*Separate* $n = 24$	*Assimilated* $n = 21$	*Bicultural* $n = 16$	*p*
Protestant (%)	0.00	54.17	4.76	25.00	*
Born U.S. (%)	0.00	20.83	85.71	50.00	**
Age first migration†	5.33	18.09	7.87	6.33	**
Total # years U.S.	13.83	8.56	22.57	21.66	**
Total # years Puerto Rico	11.83	17.25	1.71	5.72	**
Primarily schooled P.R. (%)	66.67	87.50	4.76	12.50	**
Return migration (%)	66.67	29.17	28.57	50.00	
Grew up in rural area (%)	66.67	37.50	0.00	0.00	**

†Respective *ns* for this variable = 3, 22, 4, 9.
$^*p < .05$. $^{**}p < .01$.

Multinomial logistic regression analyses examined associations between the categorical variable regarding Cultural Identity Status and variables regarding mothers' maintenance of Puerto Rican culture, adoption of U.S. values, social networks, and ethnic labeling of themselves and their children. For the following analyses, the category Marginalization of the ethnic identity was not included due to the extremely small sample size ($n = 3$).

Maintenance of Puerto Rican Culture

A multinomial logistic regression model was estimated to assess the association between mothers' cultural identity status and their maintenance of Puerto Rican values. The overall model for cultural maintenance was marginally significant, χ^2 $(4) = 8.21, p = .08$. Parameter estimates (see Table 10.8) indicated that, compared with the Separate group, more mothers in the Assimilated group reported having maintained Puerto Rican values. There was no difference between Bicultural and Separate groups with regard to the maintenance of Puerto Rican values.

In addition, a multinomial logistic regression model was used to examine the association between mothers' cultural identity status and variables related to mothers' maintenance of connections with Puerto Rico (i.e., whether they felt emotionally close to family in Puerto Rico, whether they felt they were treated like a Puerto Rican when visiting the island, and whether they had relatives living in the same household). The overall model was significant, $\chi^2\,(6) = 18.13, p < .01$. Mothers who kept a close relationship with their families in Puerto Rico were more likely to be Separate or Bicultural than Assimilated in their cultural identity

TABLE 10.8
Parameter Estimates for Multinomial Logistic Regression Models Relating Cultural Identity Status to Mothers' Maintenance of Puerto Rican Culture

Significant Contrast	*Wald χ^2*	*B*	*SE*	*Odds Ratio*
Assimilated vs. separate				
Maintenance of PR values	4.96*	−2.64	1.19	.07
Maintenance of PR customs only	ns			
Bicultural vs. separate				
Maintenance of PR values	ns			
Maintenance of PR customs only	ns			
Assimilated vs. separate				
Close to family in PR	6.93**	−2.56	.97	.08
Relatives in house	ns			
Treated like PR	4.18*	−1.85	.90	.04
Bicultural vs. assimilated				
Close to family in PR	5.89*	2.42	1.00	11.20
Relatives in house	ns			
Treated like PR	ns			

*$p < .05$. **$p < .01$.

status. Similarly, mothers who felt they were treated like Puerto Ricans when visiting the island were also less likely to have an Assimilated than a Separate identity status. Whether mothers had relatives living in the same household did not contribute significantly to the explanation of their identity status.

Adoption of U.S. Values

A multinomial logistic regression model was estimated to assess the relation between mothers' cultural identity status and their adoption of U.S. values and customs. The overall model was significant, χ^2 (6) = 16.51, p < .05. Mothers who stated that they had adopted U.S. values and customs were more likely to have an Assimilated than a Separate orientation, and mothers who were uncertain about whether they had adopted U.S. values were more likely to be in the Bicultural rather than the Separate group (see Table 10.9).

Social Networks

To examine the influences of social networks on mothers' ethnic identity status, a multinomial logistic regression model was estimated with four social network variables as predictors, and cultural identity status as the response variable. The overall model was significant, χ^2 (8) = 36.06, $p < .001$, and all but one predictor variable was significant: Living in a Puerto Rican Neighborhood, χ^2 (2) = 9.32, $p < .01$; Having a Non-Puerto Rican Partner, $\chi^2 = 7.30$, $p < .05$; and Number of Relatives Living Within Walking Distance, χ^2 (2) = 8.06, $p < .05$. The parameter estimates for each of the significant contrasts are presented in Table 10.10. Mothers who had relatives within walking distance and who had ever had partners who

TABLE 10.9

Parameter Estimates for Multinomial Logistic Regression Model Relating Cultural Identity Status to Mothers' Adoption of U.S. Values

Significant Contrast	*Wald* χ^2	*B*	*SE*	*Odds Ratio*
Assimilated vs. separate				
Maintenance of PR values	8.26**	2.91	1.02	18.33
Maintenance of PR customs only	ns			
Uncertain	ns			
Bicultural vs. separate				
Maintenance of PR values	ns			
Maintenance of PR customs only	3.94*	1.84	.93	6.29
Uncertain	ns			

*$p < .05$. **$p < .01$.

TABLE 10.10
Parameter Estimates for Multinomial Logistic Regression Model Relating Cultural Identity Status to Mothers' Social Networks

Significant Contrast	*Wald* χ^2	*B*	*SE*	*Odds Ratio*
Assimilated vs. separate				
Has had non-PR partner	5.96*	2.42	.99	11.21
Non-PR friends	3.04	2.32	1.33	10.15
Living in PR neighborhood	5.73*	−3.09	1.29	.04
Relatives within walking distance	4.85*	2.25	1.02	9.53
Bicultural vs. separate				
Has had non-PR partner	3.38	1.54	.84	4.68
Non-PR friends	3.25	2.27	1.26	9.71
Living in PR neighborhood	ns			
Relatives within walking distance	5.48*	2.15	.92	8.62
Bicultural vs. assimilated				
Has had non-PR partner	ns			
Non-PR friends	ns			
Living in PR neighborhood	4.58*	2.54	1.19	12.73
Relatives within walking distance	ns			

*$p < .05$.

were not Puerto Rican were more likely to be Assimilated than Separate in their cultural identity status. Mothers who had relatives within walking distance were also more likely to be Bicultural than Separate. Mothers who were living in a Puerto Rican neighborhood were more likely to be in the Separate or Bicultural group than in the Assimilated group. Mothers who had Non-Puerto Rican friends were marginally more likely to be Assimilated and Bicultural than Separate.

Ethnic Identity

We also examined mothers' cultural identity status derived from the acculturation questionnaire regarding its relations to mothers' self-identification as Puerto Rican, as well as the ethnic identity they wished their children to have. The overall multinomial logistic regression model was significant, χ^2 (6) = 24.06, p = .001, and the likelihood ratio tests indicated that both Puerto Rican Label, χ^2 (2) = 6.58, $p < .04$, and Child Identity, χ^2 (4) = 15.11, $p < .01$, were significant predictors. Mothers who wanted their child to develop a primarily Puerto Rican identity were less likely to have an Assimilated than a Separate status and were marginally less likely ($p < .07$) to have a Bicultural than a Separate status. Mothers were more likely to be Separate or Bicultural in their orientation when they labeled themselves as Puerto Ricans (see Table 10.11).

TABLE 10.11
Parameter Estimates for Multinomial Logistic Regression Model Relating Cultural Identity Status to the Identity Labels Mothers Used for Self and Child

Significant Contrast	*Wald* χ^2	*B*	*SE*	*Odds Ratio*
Assimilated vs. separate				
Mother identifies as PR	ns			
Child identity: Mostly Puerto Rican	8.97**	−2.83	.95	.06
Mostly American	ns			
Bicultural vs. separate				
Mother identifies as PR	5.88*	−2.07	.86	.13
Child identity: Mostly Puerto Rican	3.50	−1.861	1.00	.16
Mostly American	ns			

$^*p < .05$. $^{**}p < .01$.

THE COMPLEX PICTURE OF FIRST- AND SECOND-GENERATION MIGRATING MOTHERS

Our findings support the idea that acculturation is a complex, uneven process, in which many migrating individuals may follow the traditional idea of unilinear or bipolar culture change, but others do not. With regard to generational differences, compared to first-generation mothers, second-generation mothers were more likely to indicate that (1) English was their preferred language, (2) they were not maintaining traditional Puerto Rican values and customs but (3) were adopting U.S. values in their lives, (4) did not feel close to family in Puerto Rico, (5) did not feel they were treated like Puerto Ricans when they visited the island, (6) felt more at home in Connecticut than in Puerto Rico, and were more likely to (7) include European Americans and other non-Puerto Ricans in their social networks, and (8) also to have had a non-Puerto Rican male partner.

However, second-generation mothers still had active attachments to Puerto Rican culture, as indicated by their continued use of Spanish during the interview, relatively high scores on the Puerto Rican Cultural Involvement Scale, the presence of relatives living with them in their homes, tendencies to identify themselves predominantly as Puerto Rican and to state that their ethnic heritage was very important to them, and their stated desire for their children to retain a Puerto Rican identity and to feel comfortable in both cultural contexts.

Our examination of mothers by cultural identity status confirmed the presence of a more complex picture. Although first-generation mothers fell overwhelmingly (over 80%) into the category of Separate, the second-generation was less clearcut, with just over half falling into the Assimilated category and over a third into the Bicultural category. Analyses examining factors that may influence cultural identity status indicated that, compared to Assimilated mothers, Bicultural mothers did not appear to have spent more time in the United States or to have spent a larger number of formative years in Puerto Rico. However, they did appear to have retained a greater attachment to Puerto Rican culture as indexed by their social networks. In particular, Assimilated mothers were less likely than Bicultural mothers to live in a primarily Puerto Rican neighborhood and to report having close family ties on the island.

These findings highlight the crucial role played by social networks in the development of bicultural as opposed to monocultural identities. Surprisingly, demographic variables did not predict cultural identity status, with the exception that Separate mothers were more likely to have grown up in rural areas, and that Assimilated mothers were more likely to be Catholic. These significant differences with regard to religious background are particularly intriguing, and may reflect either cohort differences with regard to time of migration from the island or social network differences with regard to neighborhood settlement patterns. Further study is needed investigating the intersection between social networks and religious affiliations.

It is noteworthy that only three mothers in this sample were identified as relatively low in both Puerto Rican and European American cultural involvement. This is consistent with Berry's (1997) hypothesis that a marginalized identity status would be relatively rare and would most likely reflect some troubles or confusion in the acculturation process. Although three mothers is too small a sample on which to base any generalizations, it is interesting to note that these mothers were relatively unlikely to describe their ethnic heritage as "very important," while at the same time, they had spent on average a relatively large number of years in Puerto Rico. Further research is needed with a larger group of migrating individuals who might be described as Marginalized in their cultural identity process to further determine characteristics associated with this group.

Strickland (2000) asked, "How do we avoid using psychology, both overtly and more subtly, to label and punish those who are different from ourselves?" (p. 332). First, it is imperative that future research on Latino parents recognize the diversity that characterizes this group of people who share what is essentially a label of convenience, but that includes individuals from some 20 countries of origin, with widely differing reasons for being in the United States, a full range of socioeconomic status, and varying levels of acculturation. On a related note, the study of culture itself needs to move beyond a simple equation of culture with ethnic group membership. Although it is important to recognize the power of ethnicity in parents' lives, it is nonetheless true that ethnic group membership does not perfectly predict a parent's beliefs and practices. More careful delineation of sources of influence on within-group heterogeneity is necessary (Harwood, Handwerker, Schoelmerich, & Leyendecker, 2001).

Second, there continues to be a need for normative research that is based on participants' own indigenous meaning systems (Harwood et al., 1995). This is particularly important for Latino parents, many of whom are first-generation immigrants from a variety of different countries (Harwood, Leyendecker, Carlson, Asencio, & Miller, 2002). The preponderance of problem-focused research using inner city samples not only perpetuates negative stereotypes, but also limits our understanding of normative development among what is projected to become a quarter of the U.S. population by 2050.

Third, it is important to examine the effects of acculturation on childrearing beliefs and practices among Latinos from a perspective that acknowledges that it is a bicultural, socially embedded process that unfolds over time (Gonzales, Knight, Morgan-Lopez, Saenz, & Sirolli, 2003). The use of measures that examine more complex changes in cultural identity status rather than global measures of linguistic competence will enable us to move forward in our understanding of the complexity of the acculturation process.

As Strickland (2000) observed:

> Excluded from our theories, ignored by our methods, and punished by our conclusions, the others, especially women and minorities, have often turned away from us, knowing that our idiosyncratic notions of psychological need and normality do not represent them. . . . We must expand our boundaries by remembering that our theories and methods were designed to be replaced. . . . We cannot continue to push our notions of normality and psychological well-being without regard and respect for the dignity of every individual and the contributions of every culture. (p. 336)

These would seem to be wise words of warning as we stand at the start of the 21st century, poised to continue our efforts to understand parenting and normative development in all its complexity among Latinos in the United States (Betancourt & Regeser López, 1993).

ACKNOWLEDGMENTS

This research was made possible through a grant to the first author from the National Institute of Child Health and Human Development (HD37515). We are grateful to M. Singer of the Hispanic Health Council in Hartford, CT, for making the Council's research resources available for the collection of the Puerto Rican data, and to L. Comparini and A. Yalcinkaya for their coordination of this site, including assistance with translation. We also thank A. Schölmerich and B. Leyendecker for their immense help as co-investigators of the project. Finally, we express appreciation to D. Weakliem for his feedback regarding data analyses, and to B. Muller, M. Idzelis, C. Johnston, E. Kublay, and K. Ripoll for their assistance with data collection, entry, and coding.

REFERENCES

Alarcón, O., Erkut, S., García Coll, C., & Vázquez García, H. (1994). *An approach to engaging in culturally-sensitive research on Puerto Rican youth* (Working Papers Series No. 275). Wellesley, MA: Center for Research on Women.

Berry, J. W. (1997). Immigration, acculturation, and adaptation. *Applied Psychology: An International Review, 16*, 5–62.

Betancourt, H., & Regeser López, S. (1993). The study of culture, ethnicity, and race in American psychology. *American Psychologist, 48*, 629–637.

Cauce, A. M., & Rodríguez, M. D. (2002). Latino families: Myths and realities. In J. M. Contreras, K. A. Kerns, & A. M. Neal-Barnett (Eds.), *Latino children and families in the United States: Current research and future directions* (pp. 3–26). Westport, CT: Praeger.

Center for Immigration Studies (2002, June). *Census releases immigrant numbers for year 2000.* Available online at www.cis.org/articles/2002/censuspr.html

Cohen, R. E. (1987). Stressors: Migration and acculturation to American society. In M. Gaviria & J. D. Arana (Eds.), *Health and behavior: Research agenda for Hispanics* (pp. 59–71). Chicago, IL: University of Illinois.

Cortes, D. E., Rogler, L. H., & Malgady, R. G. (1994). Biculturality among Puerto Rican adults in the United States. *American Journal of Community Psychology, 22*, 707–721.

Fisher, C. B., Jackson, J. F., & Villarruel, F. A. (1998). The study of African American and Latin American children and youth. In W. Damon (Series Ed.), *Handbook of child psychology, 5th ed., Vol. 1: Theoretical models of human development* (pp. 1145–1207). New York: Wiley.

García Coll, C., Lamberty, G., Jenkins, R., McAdoo, H. P., Crnic, K., Wasik, B. H., et al. (1996). An integrative model for the study of developmental competencies in minority children. *Child Development, 67*, 1891–1914.

García Coll, C., Meyer, E. C., & Brillon, L. (1995). Ethnic and minority parenting. In M. H. Bornstein (Ed.), *Handbook of parenting: Vol. 2. Biology and ecology of parenting* (pp. 189–209). Mahwah, NJ: Lawrence Erlbaum Associates.

Gonzales, N. A., Knight, G. P., Morgan-Lopez, A., Saenz, D., & Sirolli, A. (2002). Acculturation and the mental health of Latino youths: An integration and critique of the literature. In J. M. Contreras, K. A. Kerns, & A. M. Neal-Barnett (Eds.), *Latino children and families in the United States: Current research and future directions* (pp. 45–74). Westport, CT: Praeger.

Harwood, R. L. (1992). The influence of culturally derived values on Anglo and Puerto Rican mothers' perceptions of attachment behavior. *Child Development, 63*, 822–839.

Harwood, R. L., Handwerker, W. P., Schoelmerich, A., & Leyendecker, B. (2001). Ethnic category labels, parental beliefs, and the contextualized individual: An exploration of the individualism–sociocentrism debate. *Parenting: Science and Practice, 1*, 217–236.

Harwood, R. L., Leyendecker, B., Carlson, V. J., Asencio, M., & Miller, A. M. (2002). Parenting among Latino families in the U.S. In M. H. Bornstein (Ed.), *Handbook of parenting, Vol. 4: Social conditions and applied parenting* (2nd ed., pp. 21–46). Mahwah, NJ: Lawrence Erlbaum Associates.

Harwood, R. L., Miller, J. G., & Lucca Irizarry, N. (1995). *Culture and attachment: Perceptions of the child in context.* New York: Guilford.

Harwood, R. L., Schoelmerich, A., Ventura-Cook, E., Schulze, P. A., & Wilson, S. P. (1996). Culture and class influences on Anglo and Puerto Rican mothers' beliefs regarding long-term socialization goals and child behavior. *Child Development, 67*, 2446–2461.

Hernandez, D. J. (1997). Child development and the social demography of childhood. *Child Development, 68*, 149–169.

Hollingshead, A. B. (1975). *Four factor index of social status.* Unpublished manuscript, Yale University, New Haven, CT.

Lucca Irizarry, N., & Pacheco, A. M. (1992). Intercultural encounters of Puerto Rican migrants. *Environment and Behavior, 24*, 226–238.

Maguire, L. (1983). *Understanding social networks.* Beverly Hills, CA: Sage.

Marotta, S. A., & Garcia, J. G. (2003). Latinos in the United States in 2000. *Hispanic Journal of Behavioral Sciences, 25*, 13–34.

Miller, A. M., & Harwood, R. L. (2001). Long-term socialization goals and the construction of infants' social networks among middle-class Anglo and Puerto Rican mothers. *International Journal of Behavioral Development, 25*, 450–457.

Moyerman, D. R., & Forman, B. D. (1992). Acculturation and adjustment: A meta-analytic study. *Hispanic Journal of Behavioral Sciences, 14*, 163–200.

Phinney, J. S. (1996). When we talk about American ethnic groups, what do we mean? *American Psychologist, 51*, 918–927.

Rodriguez, C. E., Sanchez Korrol, V., & Alers, J. O. (1980). The Puerto Rican struggle: To survive in the United States. In C. E. Rodriguez, V. Sanchez Korrol, & J. O. Alers (Eds.), *The Puerto Rican struggle: Essays on survival in the U.S.* (pp. 1–10). Maplewood, NJ: Waterfront Press.

Rogler, L. H. (1994). International migrations: A framework for directing research. *American Psychologist, 49*, 701–708.

Rogler, L. H., Cortes, D. E., & Malgady, R. G. (1991). Acculturation and mental health status among Hispanics: Convergence and new directions for research. *American Psychologist, 46*, 585–597.

Roosa, M. W., Morgan-Lopez, A. A., Cree, W. K., & Specter, M. M. (2002). Ethnic culture, poverty, and context: Sources of influence on Latino families and children. In J. Contreras, K. Kerns, & A. Neal-Barnett (Eds.), *Latino children and families in the United States* (pp. 27–44). Westport, CT: Praeger.

Rumbaut, R. G. (1994). Origins and destinies: Immigration to the United States since World War II. *Sociological Forum, 9*, 583–621.

Rumbaut, R. G. (1997). Paradoxes (and orthodoxies) of assimilation. *Sociological Perspectives, 40*, 483–511.

Strickland, B. R. (2000). Misassumptions, misadventures, and the misuse of psychology. *American Psychologist, 55*, 331–338.

Sutton, C. R. (1992). Transnational identities and cultures: Caribbean immigrants in the United States. In M. D'Innocenzo & J. P. Sirefman (Eds.), *Immigration and ethnicity: American society—"melting pot" or "salad bowl"?* (pp. 231–241). Westport, CT: Greenwood Press.

Therrien, M., & Ramirez, R. R. (2000). *The Hispanic population in the United States: March 2000* (Current Population Reports, P20-535). Washington, DC: U.S. Census Bureau.

Tilly, C. (1990). Transplanted networks. In V. Yans-McLaughlin (Ed.), *Immigration reconsidered: History, sociology, and politics* (pp. 79–95). New York: Oxford University Press.

Tobin, J. J., Wu, D. Y. H., & Davidson, D. H. (1989). *Preschool in three cultures*. New Haven, CT: Yale University Press.

U.S. Census Bureau. (1992). *General population characteristics: United States* (Current Population Reports CP-1-1). Washington, DC: Department of Commerce.

U.S. Census Bureau. (1999). *Current population survey, ethnic and Hispanic statistics branch, population division*. Available online at www.census.gov/population/socdemo/hispanic/cps99/tab05-2.txt

U.S. Census Bureau. (2000). *The Hispanic population: Census 2000 brief*. Available online at: www.census.gov/population/socdemo/race/ombdir15.html

U.S. Census Bureau. (2001). *Overview of race and Hispanic origin: Census 2000 Brief (CENBR/01-1)*. Available online at www.census.gov/population/www/cen2000/briefs.html

Vasquez Calzada, J. L. (1979). Demographic aspects of migration. In *Labor migration under capitalism: The Puerto Rican experience* (Publication of the History Task Force: Centro de Estudios Puertorriquenos, pp. 223–236). New York: Monthly Review Press.

Vega, W. (1990). Hispanic families in the 1980s: A decade of research. *Journal of Marriage and the Family, 52*, 1015–1024.

Werner, E. E. (1997, April). Conceptual and methodological issues in studying minority children: An international perspective. In S. Feldman (Chair), *Conditions that facilitate the well-being of minority children around the world*. Symposium conducted at the biennial meeting of the Society for Research in Child Development, Washington, DC.

Wolf, E. R. (1982). *Europe and the people without history*. Berkeley, CA: University of California Press.

Wolf, E. R. (1994). Perilous ideas: Race, culture, people. *Current Anthropology, 35*, 1–11.

11

Acculturation and Family Characteristics That Facilitate Literacy Development Among Latino Children

JoAnn M. Farver
Stefanie Eppe
Daniel Ballon
University of Southern California, U.S.A.

INTRODUCTION

Over the past 30 years, there has been a dramatic increase in immigration to the United States. Individuals who trace their ancestry to Latin America currently make up 13% of the overall population, with 44% concentrated in the western United States (U.S. Census Bureau, 2002). Accompanying this increase in the Latino population has been a rise in the number of young children who are enrolled in preschool programs and public schools (U.S. Department of Education, 1994). If the current immigration pattern continues, it is estimated that by 2010 Latinos will number more than 40 million, and by 2030 one fourth of all school-age children will be Latino (Rosenblatt, 1996).

Adults enter the United States with great hope and high aspirations for a better life for themselves. But the children who accompany them, or who are later born in the United States, often face considerable challenges to their school readiness and later academic achievement. To some extent, these challenges are related to the psychological impact of immigration and the acculturation process on adult behavior, which, in turn, affects overall family functioning and child outcomes. Within the family setting, parents and children influence each other in a bidirectional shaping process. Contextual factors, such as acculturation, social class background, parent psychological functioning, and perceived stress and social support, exert their impact on children through the effects on parents' behavior and characteristics of the home environment.

For many children, these challenges are further compounded by risk factors that characterize many Latino immigrant families, such as poverty, low parental education, adult illiteracy, and lack of English language skills (Walker, Greenwood, Hart, & Carter, 1994). As these risk factors accumulate, the chances increase that there will be a mismatch between what children bring to their kindergarten and first grade experiences and what schools expect of them if they are to succeed (Bowman, Donovan, & Burns, 2001). Overall, children of immigrants from Mexico and Central America do poorly in school. According to the U.S. National Assessment of Educational Progress (National Center for Educational Statistics, 1999), Latino students consistently performed below their non-Latino peers in reading, writing, mathematics, and science by age 9, and these disparities begin as early as kindergarten and remain stable through age 17.

Although teachers are important in developing children's literacy skills, the foundations of literacy lie in the home environment. Past research has shown that home environments can support children's facility with oral language and literacy achievement. In homes where adults converse and read with children, there are ample reading materials and books, and adults value literate activities, children develop literacy skills earlier and maintain more positive attitudes toward reading than do children whose homes do not provide such opportunities (Burgess, Hecht, & Lonigan, 2002; Leseman & de Jong, 1998; Lonigan, 1994; Sénéchal, LeFevre, Thomas, & Daley, 1998).

There is evidence to suggest that immigrant families provide opportunities and experiences that support their children's early skill development (Delgado-Gaitan, 1992; Reese & Gallimore, 2000). Unfortunately, little is known about how the unique aspects of the Latino immigration experience may relate to literacy outcomes for their children. Our study, therefore, was undertaken to explore the influence of acculturation on the home environments of Latino families, with a specific focus on young children's emergent literacy skills.

ACCULTURATION

In the past, acculturation was conceptualized as a group-level linear phenomenon (Redfield, Linton, & Herskovits, 1936) where individuals were viewed as ranging on a continuum from "unacculturated" to "assimilated" (e.g., Gordon, 1964). More recently, research with Asian, Latin American, and Middle Eastern immigrants (Bond & Yang, 1982; Rueschenberg & Buriel, 1989; Triandis, Kashima, Shimada, & Villareal, 1986) has led to a more complex model where acculturation is regarded as a multidimensional process that includes an orientation toward one's own ethnic group, the larger society, and other ethnic groups (Berry, chapter 2, this volume; Berry, Kim, Power, Young, & Bujaki, 1989). Accordingly, Phinney (1996) defined acculturation as "the extent to which individuals have maintained their culture of origin or adapted to the larger society" (p. 921). Acculturation may be more stressful for some ethnic groups than for others (Berry & Kim, 1988; Keefe & Padilla, 1987). Generally, the greater the difference between the natal and the new culture, the higher is the stress level (Heras & Revilla, 1994; Thomas, 1995), and the more difficulty individuals experience in their psychological functioning (La Fromboise, Coleman, & Gerton, 1993; Padilla, Cervantes, Maldonado, & Garcia, 1988; Phinney, 1990). According to Berry's model of acculturation (i.e., Berry, chapter 2, this volume; Berry & Kim, 1988; Berry et al., 1989), there are four ways ethnic group members can associate with their host culture. Individuals can *assimilate* (identify solely with the dominant culture and sever ties with their own culture); *marginalize* (reject both their own and the host culture), *separate* (identify solely with their own group and reject the host culture); and *integrate* (become bicultural by maintaining characteristics of their own ethnic group, while selectively acquiring those of the host culture).

One line of research investigated the psychological impact of immigration and acculturation on individual behavior and family functioning (e.g., Booth, Crouter, & Lansdale, 1997). The work of Berry and his colleagues (Berry, Kim, Minde, & Mok, 1987; Berry & Kim, 1988; Sam & Berry, 1995) assessing the acculturation strategies of various immigrant groups in North America has demonstrated that integration is the most psychologically adaptive pattern. Integrated or bicultural individuals experienced less acculturative stress and anxiety and manifested fewer psychological problems than individuals who were marginalized, separated, or assimilated. Overall, marginalized individuals suffered the most distress, including problems with self-identification and cultural alienation, which adversely affected their overall psychological well-being. Some researchers have shown that children whose immigrant parents did not adapt to the host culture (i.e., preferred separation) had more psychological problems than children whose parents were integrated or assimilated (Barankin, Konstantareas, & deBosset, 1989; Koplow & Messinger, 1990; Minde & Minde, 1976). Similarly, in families where the immigrant parents were overly identified with their ethnic group, their strong ties to the natal culture served to marginalize the family from the host culture (Keefe & Padilla, 1987).

A second line of research focused on modes or individual styles of acculturation to delineate within-group cultural differences. This approach assumes that the acculturation process produces common patterns of experience among immigrants as they adapt to life in the United States. Therefore, acculturation has been studied with respect to how it may affect individual immigrant families, and how culture influences children's early socialization and development to produce variations in child outcomes. For example, in a comparison of monocultural and bicultural Mexican mothers' reasoning about child development, Gutierrez and Sameroff (1990) found bicultural mothers developed a more objective understanding of their children's behavior, which, in turn, enhanced their parenting behavior and children's developmental outcomes. In a study of Asian Indian families, Patel, Power, and Bhavnagri (1996) found that parents who were more acculturated adopted relatively Americanized childrearing attitudes and behaviors and were more likely to encourage American characteristics in their children than were parents who were less acculturated. Likewise, in a study of Korean American immigrant families, Farver and Lee-Shin (2000) found that mothers who had an assimilated or integrated acculturation style began to resemble mainstream European American families in their childrearing attitudes and in their preference for play and creativity over academic activities in their preschoolers.

These studies suggest that there are distinct cultures of family life and childhood that manifest themselves as immigrant families individually adopt the U.S. lifestyle. An implication of these findings is that acculturation may exert an influence on children's overall developmental functioning and in particular their literacy skills, through parents' behavior and their structuring of the home environment.

EMERGENT LITERACY AND READING

Although most children learn to read without significant problems, many nevertheless experience considerable difficulty. In contrast to the outdated *reading readiness* perspective, the emergent literacy approach maintains that literacy acquisition proceeds along a continuum that originates in infancy and develops across the early school years (Teale, 1986). Thus, there is strong continuity between the skills children possess when they enter school and their later academic performance. This pattern has been apparent in longitudinal studies that have demonstrated that children who experience problems in reading early on often fall behind their more literate peers, rarely catch up, and continue to experience difficulties throughout their school years and beyond (Stanovich, 1986).

Three Key Emergent Literacy Skills

Emergent literacy is defined as the knowledge, skills, and attitudes that are the precursors to conventional reading and writing (Teale, 1986). Research carried out with preschoolers has shown that skilled reading requires three component emergent literacy skills: oral language (vocabulary), phonological processing abilities, and print knowledge (Lonigan, Burgess, & Anthony, 2000; Whitehurst & Lonigan, 1998). Children who have more of these key emergent literacy skills profit more from their reading instruction, they learn to read sooner, and they read better than children who have less of these skills (Adams, 1990; Walker et al., 1994).

Oral language skills are linked to vocabulary, oral linguistic skills, and all levels of a child's reading development. Children who have larger vocabularies and greater understanding of spoken language have higher reading scores later (Adams, 1990; Walker et al., 1994). Children with larger vocabularies also have well-developed phonological sensitivity (Wagner, Torgesen, & Rashotte, 1994; Wagner et al., 1997), and this relation begins in the preschool period (Lonigan, Burgess, Anthony, & Barker, 1998; Lonigan et al., 2000). In most interventions designed to enhance children's emergent literacy, efforts to improve their oral language skills are targeted early in a sequenced approach (Lonigan et al., 1998, 2000). Moreover, as Snow, Burns, and Griffin (1998) have maintained, most reading problems could be prevented by, among other things, enhancing children's oral language skills.

Phonological processing also plays a key role in the acquisition of reading and spelling in alphabetic languages (Adams, 1990; Wagner & Torgesen, 1987). Phonological sensitivity is the ability to detect and manipulate the sounds in oral language. This is apparent in a child's skill in identifying words that rhyme, blending spoken syllables or phonemes together to form a word, deleting syllables or phonemes from spoken words to form a new word, or counting the number of phonemes in a spoken word. Children who cannot perceive the individual sounds in spoken words have difficulty in identifying the correspondence between print and the language it represents.

Print knowledge is one of the single best predictors of eventual reading achievement (Adams, 1990; Stevenson & Newman, 1986). In alphabetic writing systems, decoding text involves the translation of units of print (graphemes) to units of sound (phonemes), and writing involves translating units of sound into units of print. At the most basic level, this task requires the ability to distinguish letters. A beginning reader who cannot recognize and distinguish letters of the alphabet will have difficulty in learning the sounds those letters represent (Bond & Dykstra, 1967). In our study we assessed children's key emergent literacy skills in both Spanish and English.

Parent Behavior

During early childhood, preschoolers begin to acquire knowledge about letters, words, and books as well as some fundamental beliefs, attitudes, and practices regarding literacy. Although children receive direct instruction in these skills in school settings, many theorists and practitioners believe that these skills originate much earlier through intentional and incidental interactions with adults in their home environment. Most importantly, it has been argued that children derive their attitudes toward literacy based on their parents' direct teaching efforts and their modeling of literacy related behaviors. For example, past research has shown that supportive home environments, characterized by the frequency of parents' literacy activities in the home, the provision of literacy related materials, and positive attitudes and beliefs toward literacy, can strengthen children's oral language skills (Moon & Wells, 1979), particularly among low-income Latino preschoolers (Farver, Xu, Eppe, & Lonigan, 2005).

Moreover, despite some controversy over the relative effects of shared storybook reading on children's reading skills in first grade and beyond (Scarborough

& Dobrich, 1994; Bus, van IJzendoorn, & Pelligrini, 1995), most researchers agree that the time parents spend reading to their preschoolers makes a significant contribution to their oral language development (Snow et al., 1998; Whitehurst & Lonigan, 1998). In a series of studies, Sénéchal and her colleagues (Sénéchal, LeFevre, Hudson, & Lawson, 1996; Sénéchal, Thomas, & Monker, 1995) found that children's shared storybook reading with adults was associated with increases in their expressive and receptive vocabulary. Similarly, Burgess et al. (2002) examined the relation between parents' ability and inclination to provide home literacy opportunities (determined in part, by their access to resources, modeling of literate behavior, and efforts to directly engage their preschoolers in literacy activities) and children's oral language and emergent literacy skills. Their results showed that, for this middle-class sample, parents' direct teaching and structuring of home learning environments produced the strongest effects on children's oral language and other emergent literacy skills, such as phonological sensitivity and print knowledge.

Opportunities for children to participate in educational activities in their homes may also be closely related to parents' own literacy habits (e.g., Heath, 1982, 1983). Early studies showed that parents' frequency of reading for pleasure, the quality of their reading materials, and their value and enjoyment of reading were associated with children's oral vocabulary and reading skills (Clark, 1976; Durkin, 1966; Hansen, 1969). More recent research has found that the combination of parents' own literacy habits and the types of literacy related materials (magazine, books, newspapers, children's books) provided in the home are associated with the development of children's literacy skills (Elliot & Hewison, 1994). In a study of Mexican American children, Okagaki, Frensch, and Gordon (1995) found a similar pattern. Parents of high-achieving children modeled literacy activities in the home (i.e., read magazines, checked for information in a book, and so forth) more often than did the parents of low achievers, and these effects remained robust after controlling for mothers' education.

Child Interest

Parent behavior has a significant impact on shaping children's home literacy environments, but there are also data to suggest that children's interest in educational activities contributes to their school readiness and to parents' inclination to engage in these kinds of activities with their children. Children who are more interested in literacy activities may persuade their parents to read with them more frequently. It is also possible that children who are frequently read to develop more interest in literacy activities. There are data to support both possibilities. In an analysis of parents' reports, Lonigan, Anthony, Arnold, and Whitehurst (1994) found that children's interest in literacy was correlated with measures of receptive and expressive language in samples of 2- to 4-year-olds and 4- to 5-year-olds. In addition, based on data collected in an intervention study, Lonigan (1994) found children who were read to from an earlier age read more frequently, were more likely to initiate reading sessions, were more interested during reading episodes, enjoyed reading episodes more, and were less likely to lose interest in the middle of a reading episode than children who were not read to at an early age.

Affective Climate of the Home

Bus et al. (1995) suggested that the affective climate of the home, and especially the quality of the parent–child relationship, also contributes to the development of children's early literacy skills. When these interactions are positive and rewarding, research has confirmed that they can promote parent–child cooperation and the enjoyment of shared reading activities, which enhances children's performance on various school readiness tests, oral vocabulary (Britto, 2001), and other emergent literacy skills (de Jong & Leseman, 2001). However, the quality of the parent–child relationship and the overall affective climate of the home may be compromised by high levels of parental stress. Mothers' perceptions of the stress associated with economic hardship, mental health, and parenting may directly influence the extent to which they are sensitive and responsive to their children and the likelihood they can provide a home environment that is supportive of and conducive to developing children's school readiness skills (Saracho, 1997).

Clearly, the stress associated with the process of adapting to a new culture may have direct effects on parents' psychological functioning. In a literature review, Rogler, Cortés, and Malgady (1991) noted that Latino immigrants face considerable stress-inducing challenges when adjusting to a new language, customs, norms for social interaction, unfamiliar laws, and in some cases extreme lifestyle changes (e.g., from rural Mexico or Central America to large metropolitan cities).

LATINO FAMILIES

Although Latino families may be heterogenous (Harwood & Feng, chapter 10, this volume), they are generally portrayed as traditional in their value orientation. That is, fathers are revered as the absolute authority, mothers and other female family members are submissive, and children are socialized to be unquestioning and obedient (Marin, 1993). Whether these customary patterns of behavior and childrearing continue to exist remains an open question (Buriel & De Ment, 1997). However, based on ethnographic accounts (Delgado-Gaitan, 1992; Valdés, 1996), interventions (Goldenberg & Sullivan, 1994), and recent interviews (Lieber, Davis, & Weisner, 2004) carried out with Latino immigrant families, it appears that most tend to retain the basic value system associated with the agrarian culture of Latin America. This includes an identification with and attachment to the family (i.e., familism) as well as a sense of interdependence and strong connection to members of the wider community, which contribute to and support the family unit.

Although educational reform has been a priority in recent times, Mexico and other Central American countries have not been highly successful in educating their populations. Thus, many Latino immigrants enter the United States with low levels of education and few material resources, and when compared with their native-born counterparts, many are more likely to be living in poverty (U.S. Bureau of the Census, 2002). At the same time, studies that have examined Latino home environments while controlling for social class, report that the educational aspects of the environments parents created in their homes are differentially associated with children's facility with oral language and literacy and their socioemotional functioning (e.g., Farver et al., 2004). A commonly cited explanation for these variations is the extent to which Latino families emphasize *educación* and the importance of *bien educado. Educación*, which differs from the English word education, refers to a basic childrearing goal of rearing a moral, responsible, and socially competent child who will become *un persona de bien* (a good person) who is *bien educado* (well brought up), respectful of adults, and on *el buen camino* (the good path; Delgado-Gaitan, 1992; Reese, 2002; Reese & Gallimore, 2000). Thus, in many Latino households, learning to read may be valued, but education is more than book learning, and a child must also learn to be respectful and well-mannered. Latino parents' preoccupation with their children's behavior rather than their academic functioning has been noted in several studies (Delgado-Gaitan, 1992; Greenfield, Quiroz, & Raeff, 2000; Valdés, 1996).

ACCULTURATION AND THE HOME LITERACY ENVIRONMENTS OF LATINO FAMILIES

To our knowledge, there are no existing studies that have examined relations among acculturation styles, characteristics of family environments, and children's literacy skills. However, it seems reasonable to argue that how parents relate to their natal as well as to the host culture would influence their attempts to create a home environment that is conducive to their children's literacy acquisition. Accordingly, we had two primary objectives: to examine how Latino mothers' acculturation styles relate to characteristics of their home environments and to their children's emergent literacy skills, and to determine how aspects of home environments might be associated with children's emergent literacy skills.

Participants

The sample was recruited from 25 Head Start preschool classrooms located in several inner city neighborhoods of Los Angeles, California. Parents were informed about the project and their written consent was obtained during meetings held at the preschools. The preschool staff and parents were told that we wanted to learn about the families' home environments and children's school readiness skills and that their participation in the study was voluntary.

Three hundred and thirty-nine parents who traced their ancestry to Latin America were identified from a larger sample of approximately 532 families. Of these families, 304 (135 girls, 169 boys) children aged 48 to 66 months ($M = 57.82$, $SD = 4.59$) and their mothers agreed to participate. Ten percent of the mothers declined to participate due to time constraints and conflicting work schedules. As shown in Table 11.1, all of the children were born in the United States, whereas most of their mothers (88%) and fathers (73%) were not. Parents immigrated to the United States primarily as young adults between 1969 and 2001 from Mexico (63%), El Salvador (14%), Guatemala (9%), and Honduras (2%). To our knowledge, none of the immigrant families were refugees. For parents who were foreign-born, the average length of residence in the United States was about 13 years

TABLE 11.1
Sample Description ($N = 304$)

Variable	*Range*		*M*	*SD*
Children's age in months	48–66		57.82	(4.59)
Mothers' age in years	20–52		31.15	(6.23)
Fathers' age in years	17–53		33.65	(6.72)
Mothers' birth place	U.S.	12%		
	Mexico	63%		
	Central America	25%		
Fathers' birth place	U.S.	27%		
	Mexico	53%		
	Central America	20%		
Mothers' education	1 = 7th grade or less		2.40	(1.38)
	2 = some high school			
	3 = high school or GED			
	4 = partial college or training			
	5 = college degree			
Fathers' education	6 = professional training		2.22	(1.35)
Mothers' employment	Unemployed	70%		
	Unskilled	16%		
	Semiskilled	13%		
	Skilled	1%		
	Managerial	0%		
Fathers' employment	Unemployed	12%		
	Unskilled	45%		
	Semiskilled	27%		
	Skilled	14%		
	Managerial	2%		
Family size	2–14		5.28	(2.01)
Foreign-born father's age at immigration	1–45		19.46	(6.44)
Foreign-born mothers' age at immigration	1–35		18.28	(6.90)

for both parents. Family size ranged from 2 to 14 individuals (M = 5.28, SD = 2.01), reflecting some single parent (n = 40) and extended family households containing grandparents, paternal siblings, or other relations. Fifty-seven percent of the families spoke only Spanish in the home, 3% spoke primarily English, and 40% were bilingual households. The majority of the foreign-born parents completed at least primary school in their country of origin. Most mothers were unemployed, whereas most fathers held full time semiskilled positions.

Measures and Procedures

Trained researchers who were all bilingual collected the data. Prior to the data collection, team members spent time in the preschool settings establishing rapport and trust with the staff, families, and children. Mothers completed several questionnaires in the language they felt the most comfortable with. The child assessments were separated into short sessions administered in a game-like format in a quiet, familiar area in the preschools. Each child was assessed in both Spanish and English.

Parent Questionnaires

Family Demography

A family demographic questionnaire included items about the parents' education, language use in the home, employment status, and family composition.

Parent Stress

The Parent Stress Index (PSI/SF; Abidin, 1995) contains 36 items rated on a 5-point scale (1 = *strongly agree*; 5 = *strongly disagree*) and yields three subscales: *parental distress* (i.e., parent has an impaired sense of parenting competence and perceived restrictions on other life roles; α = .87); *difficult child* (i.e., the parents' perception of the child's basic characteristics that make him or her either easy or difficult to manage; α = .88); and *mother–child dysfunctional interaction* (i.e., parents' perception that the child does not meet expectations and interactions with the child are not reinforcing to the parent; α = .86).

Acculturation

The Acculturation Rating Scale (Cuellar, Arnold, & Maldonado, 1995) consists of 30 items, rated on a 5-point scale (1 = *not at all*; 5 = *extremely often*), that indicate an orientation toward the Latino or European American culture (e.g., predominant language use; language skills in English and Spanish; degree, frequency, and intensity of contact with European American or Latino culture, and so forth). The scale yields two subscales: Cultural orientation to Latino (17 items) and to European American culture (13 items). To provide an orthogonal model of acculturation, we used median splits to calculate four possible combinations of cultural orientation referred to as acculturation styles: *integrated* (high American/ high Latino orientation), *assimilated* (high American/low Latino orientation), marginalized (low American/low Latino), or *separated* (low American/high Latino). Reliability for the Anglo orientation was alpha = .83, and for the Latino orientation alpha = .88.

Home Environment

Aspects of families' home literacy environments were assessed using the Home Literacy Environment Questionnaire (HLEQ; Lonigan & Farver, 2002). The HLEQ was adapted from a survey developed by Whitehurst and colleagues (Payne, Whitehurst, & Angell, 1994). During the pilot phases of our work, the wording of the items and the structure of the questionnaire were simplified to facilitate comprehension by adults with limited education, and a Spanish language version was developed. The resulting questionnaire does not represent a conceptual or empirical advance over the prior measure but was optimized for use with this specific sample.

Mothers rated their own reading skills and those of their husband/partner on a 4-point scale (1 = *poor*; 4 = *outstanding*) and 13 items concerning the frequency of their literacy habits, parent–child home literacy activities, and their children's interest in literacy, using a 7-point scale (1 = *never*; 7 = *daily*). To reduce the number of variables, we created subscales based on prior factor analysis of the HLEQ (Farver et al., 2005). *Parent literacy habits* was the sum of three items (frequency mother and father read for pleasure and how often the child sees either parent reading for pleasure); *parents' literacy involvement* was the sum of five items (frequency mother reads to child per week; teaches the alphabet (letters); takes child to the library per month, plays rhyming games, and points out words and tells the child what they say); and *child interest* was the sum of five items (frequency child asks to be read to; child reads by him- or herself; child asks about printed words; child attempts to write words; and child plays with alphabet games, puzzles, or materials).

Child Emergent Literacy Skill Assessments

Oral Language

Children's oral language skills were assessed in both English and Spanish using the Preschool Language Scale (PLS-4; Zimmerman, Steiner, & Evatt Pond, 1993). This scale, which is available in Spanish and English, focuses on development of syntax, morphology, vocabulary, concepts, and integrative thinking skills and has two components: receptive and expressive language. In our analyses we used the total scores for children's expressive language in Spanish and English as indicators of their oral language skills.

Phonological Sensitivity

Children's phonological sensitivity was assessed in English using the Preschool Comprehensive Test of Phonological and Print Processing (P-CTOPPP; Lonigan, Wagner, Torgesen, & Rashotte, 2003) and in Spanish using the P-CTOPPP-S (Lonigan, Farver, & Eppe, 2003). The Pre-CTOPPP is a downward extension of the Comprehensive Test of Phonological Processing (CTOPPP; Wagner, Torgesen, & Rashotte, 1999). Phonological sensitivity was measured with two subtests of the P-CTOPPP/P-CTOPPP-S: blending (the child is asked to blend sound units together) and elision (the child is asked to separate sound units). Both subtests begin with blending or separating compound words and then two- and three-syllable words (i.e., units that are blended or separated become smaller). Total scores for the number of correct items provided an index of children's blending and elision skills.

Print Knowledge

Children's print knowledge was measured using a subtest of the P-CTOPPP/P-CTOPPP-S that assessed knowledge of print concepts, letter discrimination, word discrimination, letter-name knowledge, and letter-sound knowledge. Total scores for the number of correct items provided an index of children's print knowledge.

Preliminary Analyses

We computed correlations to examine relations among the independent variables. As shown in Table 11.2, mothers' education was positively correlated with parents' literacy habits and their involvement in home literacy activities and children's oral vocabulary scores. Frequency of home literacy activities, parents' literacy habits, and children's interest in literacy activities were negatively correlated with the parenting stress items. Children's emergent literacy assessments in Spanish and English were positively correlated with parents' literacy habits and involvement in home literacy activities.

MOTHERS' ACCULTURATION STYLES AND THEIR HOME LITERACY ENVIRONMENTS

As shown in Table 11.3, 90 mothers were categorized as integrated, 52 assimilated, 94 separated, and 68 marginalized. Analysis of variance tests showed that assimilated and integrated mothers had higher levels of education and had lived in the United States longer than did the separated and marginalized mothers. Inte-

TABLE 11.2
Correlations Among the Variables ($N = 304$)

Variable	*1*	*2*	*3*	*4*	*5*	*6*	*7*	*8*	*9*	*10*	*11*	*12*	*13*	*14*	*15*	*16*	*17*
1. Children's age	—																
2. Mothers' education	–.08	—															
3. Mothers' years in U.S.	–.01	.26**	—														
4. Literacy habits	.14*	.16**	.15*	—													
5. Literacy involvement	–.11	.21**	.15*	.68**	—												
6. Children's interest	.08	.01	–.01	.14*	.23**	3**	*	—									
7. Spanish oral language	.13*	.12*	.11	.50**	.51**	.12*	—										
8. Spanish blending	.17**	.05	.02	.23**	.21**	.10	.31**	—									
9. Spanish elision	.19**	.07	.15*	.05	.01	.05	.10	.15*	—								
10. Spanish print knowledge	.24**	.06	.04	.24**	.26**	.15*	.38**	.36**	.26**	—							
11. English oral language	.03	.18**	.34**	.48**	.54**	.06	.21**	.23**	.08	.34**	—						
12. English blending	.25**	.11	.15*	.24**	.29**	.13*	.14*	.38**	.09	.34**	.53**	—					
13. English elision	.20**	.10	.25**	.26**	.32**	.05	.08	.32**	.25**	.36**	.45**	.41**	—				
14. English print knowledge	.24**	.04	.06	.22**	.30**	.21**	.22**	.29**	.18**	.77**	.44**	.41**	.41**	—			
15. Mother–child dysfunctional interaction	–.11*	–.15**	–.05	–.13*	–.16**	–.12*	–.09	–.01	–.06	–.09	–.09	–.09	–.08	–.15*	—		
16. Parent distress	.01	–.12*	.01	–.16**	–.19**	–.13*	–.11	–.03	–.01	–.04	–.03	–.02	–.08	–.07	.66**	—	
17. Difficult child	–.07	–.17**	–.05	–.11	–.11	–.14*	–.01	–.01	–.02	–.05	–.14*	–.17**	–.07	–.16**	.68**	.41**	—

*$p < .05$. **$p < .01$. ***$p < .001$.

TABLE 11.3
Sample Characteristics by Mothers' Acculturation Style ($N = 304$)

	Acculturation								
	Integrated ($n = 90$)		*Assimilated* ($n = 52$)		*Separated* ($n = 94$)		*Marginalized* ($n = 68$)		
Sample characteristics	*M*	*SD*	*M*	*SD*	*M*	*SD*	*M*	*SD*	*F*
Mothers' education	2.74	(1.40)	2.96	(1.54)	1.94	(1.07)	2.15	(1.32)	9.33***
Fathers' education	2.38	(1.26)	2.98	(1.60)	1.95	(1.22)	1.96	(1.35)	8.16***
Family size	5.13	(1.68)	4.90	(1.88)	5.32	(2.13)	5.74	(2.19)	2.04
Years at current address	5.05	(3.35)	5.66	(4.99)	3.35	(2.64)	3.83	(3.78)	6.34***
Mother years in U.S.	16.91	(7.31)	19.28	(7.88)	10.93	(5.69)	14.63	(7.25)	17.34***
Father years in U.S.	17.76	(8.33)	20.09	(8.26)	12.94	(7.12)	14.30	(7.18)	8.14***
Parent literacy habits	17.61	(3.44)	14.30	(3.67)	11.89	(4.24)	9.75	(3.85)	62.36***
Parent involvement	23.38	(6.11)	18.63	(5.78)	15.62	(4.40)	11.44	(3.74)	77.39***
Child interest	26.99	(5.76)	26.02	(5.20)	26.21	(6.11)	25.28	(5.97)	1.13
Mothers' reading skill	2.76	(.82)	2.75	(.76)	2.53	(.88)	2.47	(.89)	2.21
Fathers' reading skill	2.68	(.88)	2.48	(1.01)	2.46	(.90)	2.37	(.85)	1.71
Parental distress	2.26	(.64)	2.24	(.49)	2.29	(.63)	2.60	(.68)	4.97**
Difficult child	2.40	(.76)	2.23	(.66)	2.50	(.74)	2.67	(.66)	4.16**
Parent–child dysfunctional interaction	2.04	(.70)	2.05	(.72)	2.21	(.79)	2.46	(.82)	4.80**

$^{*}p < .05$. $^{**}p < .01$. $^{***}p < .001$.

grated mothers had higher frequencies of involvement in home literacy activities and literacy habits than did mothers in the other three groups. Marginalized mothers had the highest scores on the parenting stress items. There were no differences in mothers' acculturation style for family size, child interest in literacy activities, or parent's reading skills.

Acculturation, the Home Literacy Environment, and Children's Emergent Literacy Skills

We conducted multivariate analysis of covariance tests (MANCOVAs) to compare children's Spanish and English emergent literacy skills by acculturation, mothers' education level, literacy habits, and involvement in literacy activities. Separate MANOVAs were carried out for the two languages, and mothers' education level, literacy habits, and involvement in literacy activities were entered into the analyses as covariates.

For the Spanish language assessments, there was a significant multivariate effect for acculturation, Wilks' $\Lambda = .880$, $F(12, 677) = 2.80$, $p = .001$, and for the covariates for parents' literacy habits, Wilks' $\Lambda = .933$, $F(4, 256) = 4.63$, $p = .001$, and parent's literacy involvement, Wilks' $\Lambda = .932$, $F(4, 256) = 4.64$, $p = .001$. There were no significant results for mothers' education. Analysis of covariance tests, which were conducted on each dependent variable as follow-up to the MANCOVA, are displayed in Table 11.4. Children's Spanish oral language scores were significant for acculturation, parents' literacy habits, and involvement in home literacy activities. More specifically, children's Spanish oral language scores were highest when mothers had an integrated or separated acculturation style and reported frequent literacy habits and involvement in home literacy activities. Children's Spanish language elision scores were highest when parents reported frequent literacy habits. There were no significant results for children's Spanish blending or print knowledge scores.

For the English language assessments, there was a significant multivariate effect for acculturation, Wilks' $\Lambda = .931$, $F(12, 746) = 1.72$, $p = .05$, parents' literacy habits, Wilks' $\Lambda = .966$, $F(4, 282) = 2.50$, $p = .04$, parent's literacy involvement, Wilks' $\Lambda = .971$, $F(4, 282) = 2.43$, $p = .05$, and the interaction of acculturation and the three covariates, Wilks' $\Lambda = .883$, $F(16, 862) = 2.25$, $p = .003$. There were no significant results for mothers' education. Analysis of covariance tests, which were conducted on each dependent variable as follow-up to the MANCOVA, are displayed in Table 11.5. Children's English oral language scores were significant for acculturation, parents' literacy habits, and involvement in home literacy activities. Children's blending scores were significant for parent involvement, their print knowledge scores were significant for acculturation, and their elision scores were significant for parent involvement and the interaction of the covariates with acculturation. More specifically, children's English oral language and print knowledge scores were highest when mothers had an inte-

TABLE 11.4

Children's Spanish Language Literacy Assessment Scores by Mothers' Acculturation Style, Education Level, Literacy Habits, and Involvement in Literacy Activities in the Home ($N = 304$)

	Acculturation Style												
	Integrated (*n* = 90)		*Assimilated* (*n* = 52)		*Separated* (*n* = 94)		*Marginalized* (*n* = 68)		*F*	*F*	*F*	*F*	*F*
Spanish assessments	*M*	*SD*	*M*	*SD*	*M*	*SD*	*M*	*SD*	*Acculturation*	*Mother Education*	*Lit. Habits*	*Lit. Involvement*	*Interact*
Oral language	104.31	(14.32)	79.81	(17.20)	99.17	(15.21)	75.46	(15.08)	8.58***	2.07	13.63***	17.87***	1.04
Blending	12.63	(3.43)	10.89	(5.13)	11.61	(3.66)	10.71	(3.63)	.75	.23	1.51	2.17	1.36
Print knowledge	12.71	(5.83)	10.87	(5.20)	11.70	(6.12)	8.00	(3.85)	1.40	.17	.57	1.15	.67
Elision	8.56	(3.88)	7.22	(3.52)	9.04	(3.77)	8.51	(3.39)	1.87	1.20	4.44*	.30	.92

*$p < .05$. **$p < .01$. ***$p < .001$.

TABLE 11.5
Children's English Language Literacy Assessment Scores by Mothers' Acculturation Style, Education Level, Literacy Habits, and Involvement in Literacy Activities in the Home ($N = 304$)

	Acculturation Style												
	Integrated ($n = 90$)		*Assimilated* ($n = 52$)		*Separated* ($n = 94$)		*Marginalized* ($n = 68$)		*F*	*F*	*F*	*F*	*F*
English assessments	*M*	*SD*	*M*	*SD*	*M*	*SD*	*M*	*SD*	*Acculturation*	*Mother Ed.*	*Lit. Habits*	*Lit. Involvement*	*Interact*
Oral language	87.31	(13.73)	85.33	(13.15)	67.73	(13.47)	65.96	(13.73)	3.52*	.03	3.73*	5.94**	3.78*
Blending	13.11	(4.61)	13.09	(4.12)	10.82	(4.51)	9.75	(4.23)	2.17	.19	.05	3.71*	1.92
Print knowledge	17.09	(8.48)	15.63	(9.22)	13.10	(7.75)	9.50	(4.58)	4.68*	1.56	2.29	.55	1.68
Elision	7.23	(3.16)	7.52	(3.39)	5.75	(1.98)	5.14	(1.95)	.45	.34	.78	4.31*	3.56*

$*p < .05$. $**p < .01$. $***p < .001$.

grated or assimilated acculturation style. Children's oral language scores were also highest in homes where mothers reported frequent literacy habits and involvement in home literacy activities. Children's English language blending and elision scores were highest when parents reported frequent involvement in home literacy activities.

In summary, children whose mothers had an integrated or separated style of acculturation had higher Spanish oral language scores, whereas children whose mothers had an integrated or assimilated style had higher English oral language and print knowledge scores. Children whose parents reported more frequent literacy habits and involvement in home literacy activities had higher Spanish and English oral language scores.

CONCLUSIONS

The United States is currently experiencing an influx of immigrants akin to the historic boom at the beginning of the 20th century (Fuligni, 1997). Moreover, one quarter of the foreign-born now live in the New York and Los Angeles metropolitan areas (Rumbaut, 1995). As these families become part of our communities, schools, and society, the need to understand how they adapt to the American lifestyle and the problems they encounter becomes ever more apparent (Booth et al., 1999). Abundant research suggests that acculturation is influenced by a variety of factors, many of which stress the importance of the family. Therefore, our primary objective was to explore the influence of mother's level of acculturation on the family environment and their children's emergent literacy skills.

Consistent with prior work that has contended that an integrated acculturation style is the most adaptive (Berry & Sam, 1997; Phinney, 2003), in the homes where mothers had an integrated style of acculturation, children had the best outcomes. Parents were more likely to model and engage in literacy activities in the home, and their children had high scores on the emergent literacy assessments in both Spanish and English. As might be expected, the children of separated mothers had high oral language skills in Spanish, but not in English, whereas the reverse was true for the children of assimilated mothers—they had higher language emergent literacy skills in English than in Spanish. The children of the marginalized mothers fared the worst of the four groups in terms of their English language emergent literacy skills. To some extent these findings are related to the language spoken in the home. Statistics on English language learners (ELLs) reported that children whose first language was Spanish were at risk for poor literacy outcomes and were twice as likely than non-Latino Whites to read below grade level in English (Federal Interagency Forum on Child and Family Statistics, 2002). However, in a study of Puerto Rican ELLs, Hammer, Miccio, and Wagstaff (2003) found that mothers of children who were learning English simultaneously (rather than sequentially) with Spanish were more likely to teach their children preacademic and literacy skills and to have a stronger orientation toward achievement than mothers of sequential ELLs who emphasized the development of social skills. These differences were attributed, in part, to the number of years the mothers had lived in the United States and the gradual shift in their child-rearing goals and values as they became more familiar with the American school system and lifestyle.

Currently, in California there are no bilingual public school programs. Therefore, most preschool curricula are designed to introduce and strengthen children's English rather than their Spanish language skills. There is considerable controversy about bilingual education theory and research (see Crawford, 1991, for a review). Those who advocate using the child's home language in the schools argue that children learn most readily in a language they know best; what they learn in the first language is still known when they learn a second language, and the skills that are learned in the first language transfer to the second language (Goldenberg, 1996). Thus, it is not all together clear whether the language of the home hinders children's development of emergent literacy skills in either language. However, an examination of the correlations for children's Spanish and English emergent literacy assessments suggests that the skills do transfer across the two languages and learning one language does not detract from learning another (Crawford, 1991; Goldenberg, 1996).

Clearly, conditions in the home, such as family size, parent education, and income, can be limiting factors that potentially restrict the possibilities for children's development in general. The mothers who had a marginalized style of acculturation reported the highest parenting stress levels, were the least involved in creating a literacy environment in the home, and their children had the lowest English language emergent literacy skills.

At the same time, these objective conditions should not obscure the influences that may help to define alternative and promising paths for children's school success. For example, our results also showed that parents' direct involvement in and encouragement of literacy-related activities were associated with children's emergent literacy skills. These findings illustrate how parents can be instrumental in preparing their young children for school by being proactive in their efforts and by altering aspects of their home environment that are within their capability to change. During qualitative interviews with participating families, all parents endorsed the value of "academic" education (i.e., reading, writing, and mathematics) to help their children get ahead in life. However, as prior studies have shown, simply valuing education may not be enough to support and prepare children for school (Okagaki et al., 1995). Instead, parents need to take an active approach by modeling educational practices, monitoring their children's activities, and supporting their children's efforts.

Moreover, given the promise of preschool programs to reduce ethnic group-related inequalities in children's emergent literacy skills as they begin public school, a key issue is how these early programs fit with immigrant parents' beliefs, values, and goals for socializing and educating their children. Because parents' expectations for children's development vary across cultural and social class backgrounds, and with differing acculturation styles, it is important to understand how early childhood programs and parent values can be mutually adapted to support young children's school readiness.

Our findings should be interpreted with some caution. Although our measures of children's emergent literacy skills were objective independent assessments, the evaluation of the home literacy environment relied solely on responses from the parents. Mothers might have had trouble estimating the frequencies of their own behavior and that of their children. Furthermore, social desirability is always an issue. Because most mothers (and even immigrant families) know that they are *supposed* to read to their children, parents may have overreported the frequencies of their literacy behaviors. Certainly, it would have been more optimal to cross-validate parents' reports with observations of some kind. At the same time, the use of surveys can be justified. Survey reports significantly correlate with observational and diary assessments (Lonigan, Anthony, Arnold, & Whitehurst, 1994; Moon & Wells, 1979) and with parents' knowledge of children's storybooks (Burgess, 1999; Sénéchal et al., 1996), and the reliability of survey estimates has been shown to be moderate (Burgess, 1999). For instance, Leseman and de Jong (1998) reported a mean intercorrelation of .69 for survey reports of the home literacy environment obtained on three separate occasions over a 2-year period. Overall, the various critiques of self-reports and surveys to assess the home literacy environment should result in an underestimation (rather than an overestimation) of its relation to developmental outcomes.

There was significant variability in the family environments that were studied here. Reasons for these differences are complex and varied, and may be related, in part, to basic limitations in resources. Because our sample was drawn from inner city neighborhoods located in the Los Angeles metropolitan area, which has a high concentration of immigrants from Latin America, these variations may take different forms when examined in other urban or suburban areas and among different ethnic groups. For example, SES may be expressed differently in rural settings in terms of families' capacities to provide safe housing, nutritious food, high quality preschool experiences, and all the other opportunities that foster learning and adaptation. These demographic aspects should be taken into account in future studies. Also, it is difficult to determine the extent to which the stress associated with immigration and acculturation override the stress of living in inner city neighborhoods that are often characterized by high crime and violence rates.

We measured acculturation at only one point in time and only with mothers. This process is highly dynamic, and individuals' styles or levels are likely to vary over time as a function of experience with the host culture. Therefore, to adequately examine acculturation, it would be helpful to measure fathers' acculturation and to use a longitudinal study with several data points.

Finally, our findings could be a reflection of the community where we collected the data. Southern California is a highly diverse urban environment where immigrants from around the world take up residence. Therefore, there is an abundance of multicultural communities that provide individuals with a range of choice as to how much they wish to participate in the wider society. They can buy items from their country of origin and converse entirely in their own language if they choose to do so. Recently, attitudes toward immigrants have become increasingly tense in the United States. However, Southern California has retained a somewhat a higher degree of tolerance and acceptance for diversity, whereas in relatively "monocultural" communities, immigrant families have fewer choices of how to associate with the host culture.

Despite these shortcomings, the results of our study provide a beginning step for future research on this topic. Attitudes toward immigrants, and among immigrant themselves, have changed from a "melting pot" ethos. Although many families and individuals still immigrate to the United States for educational and economic opportunities, few wish for the cultural assimilation once expected of immigrants (Zigler & Hall, 2000). Rather, most desire to retain their cultural heritage while becoming uniquely American. Although this diversity has the potential to enrich the United States, the policies and practices related to the provision of services for immigrants have been slow to change. This is most notably felt in the response (or lack of response) by the American educational system. In the 21st century, as the European American population becomes a minority, these policies and practices will need to shift. How best to respond to the changing face of America requires a better understanding of the process of adaptation to the American lifestyle; and specifically what is it that determines whether the process is positive or negative.

ACKNOWLEDGMENTS

We thank the participating preschool program staff, the families, and their children. This work was supported by a grant from the National Science Foundation (REC-0128970) awarded to the first author. Views expressed herein are the authors' and have not been cleared by the grantors.

REFERENCES

Abidin, R. R. (1995). *Parenting Stress Index* (3rd ed.). Odessa, FL: Psychological Assessment Resources.

Adams, M. J. (1990). *Beginning to read: Thinking and learning about print.* Cambridge, MA: MIT Press.

Barankin, T., Konstantareas, M., & deBosset, F. (1989). Adaptation of Soviet Jewish immigrants and their children to Toronto. *Canadian Journal of Psychiatry, 34*, 512–518.

Berry, J. W., Kim, U., Minde, T., & Mok, D. (1987). Acculturative stress in Canada. *International Migration Review, Special Issue on Migration and Health, 21*, 491–511.

Berry, J. W., & Kim, U. (1988). Acculturation and mental health. In P. Dansen, J. W. Berry, & N. Sartorius (Eds.), *Health and cross-cultural psychology: Towards applications* (pp. 207–238). London: Sage.

Berry, J. W., Kim, U., Power, S., Young, M., & Bujaki, M. (1989). Acculturation attitudes in plural societies. *Applied Psychology, 38*, 185–206.

Berry, J. W., & Sam, D. L. (1997). Acculturation and adaption. In J. W. Berry, M. H. Segal, & C. Kagitcibasi (Eds.), *Handbook of cross-cultural psychology* (2nd ed., pp. 292–326). Toronto: Allyn & Bacon.

Booth, A., Crouter, A., & Lansdale, N. (1999). *Immigration and the family: Research and policy on U.S. immigrants*. Mahwah, NJ: Lawrence Erlbaum Associates.

Bond, G. L., & Dykstra, R. (1967). The cooperative research program in first-grade reading instruction. *Reading Research Quarterly, 2*, 5–142.

Bond, M., & Yang, K. (1982). Ethnic affirmation versus cross-cultural accommodation: The variable impact of questionnaire language on Chinese bilinguals in Hong Kong. *Journal of Cross-Cultural Psychology, 13*, 169–185.

Bowman, B. T., Donovan, M. S., & Burns, M. S. (2001). *Eager to learn*. Washington, DC: Academy Press.

Britto, P. R. (2001). Family literacy environments and young children's emerging literacy skills. *Reading Research Quarterly, 36*, 346–348.

Burgess, S. R. (1999, April). *Parental characteristics that predict children's home literacy environment*. Poster presented at the annual meeting of the Southwestern Psychological Association, Albuquerque, NM.

Burgess, S. R., Hecht, S. A., & Lonigan, C. J. (2002). Relations of home literacy environment (HLE) to the development of reading-related abilities: A one-year study. *Reading Research Quarterly, 37*, 408–426.

Buriel, R., & De Ment, T. (1997). Immigration and sociocultural change in Mexican, Chinese, and Vietnamese American Families. In A. Booth, A. Crouter, & N. Lansdale (Eds.), *Immigration and the family*. Mahwah, NJ: Lawrence Erlbaum Associates.

Bus, A. G., van IJzendoorn, M. H., & Pelligrini, A. (1995). Joint book reading makes for success in learning to read: A meta-analysis on intergenerational transmission of literacy. *Review of Educational Research, 65*, 1–21.

Clark, M. M. (1976). *Young fluent readers: What can they teach us?* London: Heinemann.

Crawford, J. (1991). *Bilingual education; History, politics, theory and practice* (2nd ed.). Los Angeles, CA: Bilingual Services.

Cuellar, I., Arnold, B., & Maldonado, R. (1995). Acculturation Rating Scale for Mexican Americans–II: A revision of the original ARSMA scale. *Hispanic Journal of Behavioral Sciences, 17*, 275–304.

Delgado-Gaitan, C. (1992). School matters in the Mexican-American home: Socializing children to education. *American Educational Research Journal, 29*, 495–513.

de Jong, P. F., & Leseman, P. M.(2001). Lasting effects of home literacy on reading achievement in school. *Journal of School Psychology, 39*, 389–414.

Durkin, D. (1966). *Children who read early*. New York: Teacher's College Press.

Elliot, J. A., & Hewison, J. (1994). Comprehension and interest in home reading. *British Journal of Educational Psychology, 64*, 203–220.

Farver, J. M., & Lee-Shin, Y. (2000). Acculturation and Korean-American children's social and play behavior. *Social Development, 10*, 316–336.

Farver, J. M., Xu, Y., Eppe, S., & Lonigan, C. (2005). *Home environments and young Latino children's school readiness*. Manuscript submitted for publication.

Fuligni, A. (1997). The academic achievement of adolescents from immigrant families: The roles of family background, attitudes, and behavior. *Child Development, 68*, 351–363.

Goldenberg, C. (1996). *Latin American immigration and U.S. schools. Society for Research in Child Development.* Social Policy Report. Vol X. No. 1.

Goldenberg, C., & Sullivan, J. (1994). *Making change happen in a language-minority school: A search for coherence.* (EPR # 13). Washington, DC: Center for Applied Linguistics.

Gordon, M. M. (1964). *Assimilation in American life.* New York: Oxford Press.

Greenfield, P., Quiroz, B., & Raeff, C. (2000). Cross cultural conflict and harmony in the social construction of the child. In S. Harkness, C. Raeff, & C. Super (Eds.), *New directions for child development: Vol. 87. Variability in the social construction of the child.* San Francisco: Jossey-Bass.

Gutierrez, J., & Sameroff, A. (1990). Determinants of complexity in Mexican-American mothers' conceptions of child development. *Child Development, 61*, 384–394.

Hammer, C. S., Miccio, A. W., & Wagstaff, D. A. (2003). Home literacy experiences and their relationship to bilingual preschoolers' developing English literacy abilities: An initial investigation. *Language, Speech and Hearing Services in the Schools, 34*, 20–30.

Hansen, H. S. (1969). The impact of home literacy environment on reading attitude. *Elementary English, 46*, 17–24.

Heath, S. B. (1982). What no bedtime story means: Narrative at home and school. *Language in Society, 11*, 49–78.

Heath, S. B. (1983). *Ways with words: Language, life, and work in communities and classrooms.* Cambridge: Cambridge University Press.

Heras, P., & Revilla, L. A. (1994). Acculturation, generational status and family environment of Filipino Americans. *Family Therapy, 21*, 129–138.

Keefe, S., & Padilla, A. (1987). *Chicano identity.* Albuquerque: University of New Mexico Press.

Koplow, L., & Messinger, E. (1990). Developmental dilemmas of young children of immigrant parents. *Child and Adolescent Social Work, 7*, 121–134.

La Fromboise, T., Coleman, H., & Gerton, J. (1993). Psychological impact of biculturalism: Evidence and theory. *Psychological Bulletin, 114*, 395–412.

Leseman, P., & de Jong, P. F. (1998). Home literacy: Opportunity, instruction, cooperation, and social-emotional quality predicting early reading achievement. *Reading Research Quarterly, 33*, 294–319.

Lieber, E., Davis, H., & Weisner, T. (2004, November). *Preliteracy practices in Head Start families: Qualitative and mixed methods in the study of children's literacy preparedness.* Paper presented at the symposium of the National Association for the Education of the Young Child, Anaheim, CA.

Lonigan, C. J. (1994). Reading to preschoolers exposed: Is the emperor really naked? *Developmental Review, 14*, 303–323.

Lonigan, C. J., Anthony, J. A., Arnold, D. H., & Whitehurst, G. J. (1994, August). *Children's interest in literacy: Compounded daily*? Paper presented at the 102nd annual convention of the American Psychological Association, Los Angeles, CA.

Lonigan, C. J., Burgess, S. R., & Anthony, J. A. (2000). Development of emergent literacy and reading skills in preschool children: Evidence from a latent variable longitudinal study. *Developmental Psychology, 36*, 596–613.

Lonigan, C. J., Burgess, S. R., Anthony, J. L., & Barker, T. A. (1998). Development of phonological sensitivity in 2- to 5-year-old children. *Educational Psychology, 90*, 294–311.

Lonigan, C. J., & Farver, J. M. (2002). *Home Literacy Environment Questionnaire (HLEQ).* Unpublished measure.

Lonigan, C. J., Farver, J. M., & Eppe, S. (2003). *Preschool Comprehensive Test of Phonological and Print Processing—Spanish Language Version.* Unpublished measure.

Marin, G. (1993). Influence of acculturation on familialism and self-identification among Hispanics. In M. E. Bernal & G. P. Knight (Eds.), *Ethnic identity: Formation and transmission among Hispanics and other minorities* (pp. 181–196). Albany: State University of New York Press.

Minde, K., & Minde, R. (1976). Children of immigrants: The adjustment of Ugandan Asian primary school children in Canada. *Canadian Psychiatric Association Journal, 21*, 371–381.

Moon, C., & Wells, G. (1979). The influence of the home on learning to read. *Journal of Research in Reading, 2*, 53–62.

National Center for Education Statistics. (1999). *Home literacy activities and signs of children's emerging literacy, 1993 and 1999*. Washington, DC: U.S. Department of Education.

Okagaki, L., Frensch, P. A., & Gordon, E. W. (1995). Encouraging school achievement in Mexican American children. *Hispanic Journal of Behavioral Sciences, 17*, 160–179.

Padilla, A. M., Cervantes, R. C., Maldonado, M., & Garcia, R. E. (1988). Coping responses to psychosocial distress among Mexican and Central American immigrants. *Journal of Community Psychology, 16*, 418–427.

Patel, N., Power, T., & Bhavnagri, N. (1996). Socialization vales and practices of Indian immigrant parents: Correlates of modernity and acculturation. *Child Development, 67*, 302–313.

Payne, A. C., Whitehurst, G. J., & Angell, A. L. (1994). The role of the home literacy environment in the development of language ability in preschool children from low-income families. *Early Child Research Quarterly, 9*, 427–440.

Phinney, J. (1990). Ethnic identity in adolescents and adults: A review of research. *Psychological Bulletin, 108*, 499–514.

Phinney, J. (1996). When we talk about American ethnic groups, what do we mean? *American Psychologist, 51*, 918–917.

Phinney, J. (2003). Ethnic identity and acculturation. In K. M. Chun, P. B. Organista, & G. Marin (Eds.), *Acculturation: Advances in theory, measurement, and applied research* (pp. 63–81). Washington, DC: American Psychological Association.

Reese, L. (2002). Parental strategies in contrasting cultural settings: Families in México and *El Norte*. *Anthropology and Education Quarterly, 33*, 30–59.

Reese, L., & Gallimore, R. (2000). Immigrant Latinos' cultural model of literacy development. *American Journal of Education, 108*, 103–134.

Redfield, R., Linton, R., & Herskovits, M. (1936). Memorandum on the study of acculturation. *American Anthropologist, 38*, 149–152.

Rogler, L. H., Cortés, D. E., & Malgady, R. G. (1991). Acculturation and mental health status among Hispanics: Convergence and new directions for research. *American Psychologist, 46*, 585–597.

Rosenblatt, R. (1996, March 14). Latinos, Asians to lead rise in U.S. population. *Los Angeles Times*, pp. A1, A4.

Rueschenberg, E., & Buriel, R. (1989). Mexican American family functioning and acculturation: A family systems perspective. *Hispanic Journal of Behavioral Sciences, 1*, 232–244.

Rumbaut, R. (1995). The new Californians: Comparative research findings on the educational progress of immigrant children. In R. Rumbaut & W. Cornelius (Eds.), *California's immigrant children* (pp. 111–135). San Diego, CA: Center for U.S. Mexican Studies.

Sam, D. L., & Berry, J. W. (1995). Acculturative stress among young immigrants in Norway. *Scandinavian Journal of Psychology, 36*, 10–24.

Saracho, O. N. (1997). Perspectives on family literacy. *Early Child Development and Care, 127*, 3–11.

Scarborough, H. S., & Dobrich, W. (1994). On the efficacy of reading to preschoolers. *Developmental Review, 14*, 145–302.

Sénéchal, M., LeFevre, J., Hudson, E., & Lawson, E. P. (1996). Knowledge of storybooks as a predictor of young children's vocabulary. *Journal of Educational Psychology, 88*, 520–536.

Sénéchal, M., LeFevre, J., Thomas, E. M., & Daley, K. E. (1998). Differential effects of home literacy experiences on the development of oral and written language. *Reading Research Quarterly, 33*, 96–116.

Sénéchal, M., Thomas, E., & Monker, J. A. (1995). Individual differences in vocabulary acquisition. *Journal of Educational Psychology, 87*, 218–229.

Snow, C., Burns, S., & Griffin, P. (Eds.). (1998). *Preventing reading difficulties in young children*. Washington, DC: National Academy Press.

Stanovich, K. E. (1986). Matthew effects in reading: Some consequences of individual differences in the acquisition of literacy. *Reading Research Quarterly, 21*, 360–407.

Stevenson, H. W., & Newman, R. S. (1986). Long-term prediction of achievement and attitudes in mathematics and reading. *Child Development, 57*, 646–659.

Teale, W. H. (1986). Home background and young children's literacy development. In W. H. Teale & E. Sulzby (Eds.), *Emergent literacy: Writing and reading* (pp. 173–206). Norwood, NJ: Ablex.

Thomas, T. (1995). Acculturative stress in the adjustment of immigrant families. Special issue: A psychological view of mental illness. *Journal of Social Distress and the Homeless, 41*, 131–142.

Triandis, H. C., Kashima, Y., Shimada, E., & Villareal, M. (1986). Acculturation indices as a means of confirming cultural differences. *Journal of Psychology, 21*, 43–70.

U.S. Census Bureau. (2002). *The Hispanic population in the U.S., March 2002*. Washington, DC: U.S. Department of Commerce.

U.S. Department of Education. (1994). *Mini-digest of educational statistics* (NCES 94-131). Washington, DC: U.S. Government Printing Office.

Valdés, G. (1996). *Con respecto* [With respect]. New York: Columbia Teachers' College Press.

Walker, D., Greenwood, C., Hart, B., & Carter, J. (1994). Prediction of school outcomes based on early language production and socioeconomic factors. *Child Development, 65*, 606–621.

Wagner, R. K., & Torgesen, J. K. (1987). The natural of phonological processing and its causal role in the acquisition of reading skills. *Psychological Bulletin, 101*, 192–212.

Wagner, R. K., Torgesen, J. K., & Rashotte, C. A. (1994). Development of reading-related phonological processing abilities: New evidence of bidirectional causality from a latent variable longitudinal study. *Developmental Psychology, 30*, 73–87.

Wagner, R. K., Torgesen, J. K., & Rashotte, C. (1999). *Comprehensive test of phonological processing*. San Antonio, TX: The Psychological Corporation.

Wagner, R. K., Torgesen, J. K., Rashotte, C. A., Hecht, S. A., Barker, T. A., Burgess, S. R., et al. (1997). Changing relations between phonological processing abilities and word level reading as children develop from beginning to skilled readers: A 5-year longitudinal study. *Developmental Psychology, 33*, 468–479.

Whitehurst, G. J., & Lonigan, C. J. (1998). Child development and emergent literacy. *Child Development, 69*, 848–872.

Zigler, E., & Hall, N. (2000). *Child development and social policy: Theory and applications*. Monterey, CA: McGraw Hill.

Zimmerman, I., Steiner, V., & Evatt Pond, R. (2002). *Preschool Language Scale* (4th ed.). San Antonio, TX: The Psychological Corporation.

12

The Relation of Language Brokering to Depression and Parent–Child Bonding Among Latino Adolescents

Raymond Buriel
Pomona College, U.S.A.

Julia A. Love
Terri L. De Ment
Claremont Graduate University, U.S.A.

INTRODUCTION

Because most immigrant parents do not speak English, they often rely on their children to interpret for them. Children who act as interpreters for their non-English speaking parents are referred to as *language brokers* (Buriel, Perez, De Ment, Chavez, & Moran, 1998; McQuillan & Tse, 1995; Shannon, 1990; Tse, 1995). Because these children are often the first members of their families to attend school in the United States, they also serve as *cultural brokers* or information links between European American culture and their parents' native culture. As a result of their greater linguistic and cultural knowledge of U.S. society, language brokers are often delegated adult-like responsibilities by their parents for making decisions with English-speaking agents that affect the entire family (Kibria, 1993; McQuillan & Tse, 1995; Vasquez, Pease-Alvarez, & Shannon, 1994; Zhou & Bankston, 1998). Consequently, traditional parent–child authority relationships within families are altered as children assume responsibility for cross-cultural transactions such as arranging medical appointments and filling out job applications for parents, disputing telephone, credit card, and rental charges, and dealing with schools and the legal system (McQuillan & Tse, 1995; Olsen & Chen, 1988; Tse, 1995; Weisskirch & Alva, 2002). The many adult-like responsibilities assigned to language brokers strongly suggest that they experience more developmental challenges and stressors than children who do not interpret and translate for their parents.

In this chapter we seek to explain language brokering and its relation to parent–child bonding and depression among Latino adolescents. In so doing we examine how language brokering and academically related characteristics of adolescents affect the parent–child bond, and, in turn, how all these variables relate to depression. An additional aim of the chapter is to shed more light on the gendered nature of language brokering among Latino adolescents. Our examination of language brokering focuses on outcomes for adolescents. The outcomes for parents are examined by Chao (chapter 13, this volume).

BACKGROUND LITERATURE ON LANGUAGE BROKERING

Among Latino and Asian American populations, language brokering begins at about age 10 and often continues into adulthood, even after brokers are living away from home (Buriel et al., 1998; De Ment, Buriel, & Villanueva, 2005; Tse, 1995). Although the number of children who serve as language brokers in the United States is not known, there are currently thousands of children who are in a position to act as interpreters and translators for their immigrant parents and extended family members. A recent federal report indicates that nearly 1 in 5 children live with at least one parent who was born outside the United States (Federal Interagency Forum on Child and Family Statistics, n.d.). Moreover, because the non-English-speaking population in the United States is growing at a much faster rate for adults than children, the need for child language brokers will increase in the future. For example, for every new Spanish-speaking child of school age, there were four new adults who spoke Spanish in 1990 (Macias, 1993).

The many adult-like responsibilities of children who broker on a regular basis suggest that these children's cognitive and socioemotional development may be accelerated relative to children of immigrant families who broker infrequently or not at all. Furthermore, language brokers acquire the social skills not only to negotiate sensitive situations, such as disputes over telephone bills, but also to serve as mediators in the adult world. In an ethnographic study of Mexican and Central American immigrant children, Shannon (1990) found that children who acted as language brokers acquired adult sociolinguistic skills. These children knew how to address and speak with professionals such as doctors, and also how to advocate for their parents, while at the same time maintaining the dignity of their parents. More recently, Buriel et al. (1998) found a positive correlation between language brokering and social self-efficacy for high school language brokers. Adolescents who brokered felt more in control in interactions with adults. We also found that the number of different places where children brokered was positively associated with high school grade point averages. In addition, academic self-efficacy and biculturalism was higher for children with more language brokering experience (Buriel et al., 1998).

STRESS AND LANGUAGE BROKERING

The studies by Buriel et al. (1998) and Shannon (1990) describe some of the social and cognitive advantages associated with language brokering. However, language brokering experiences may also be associated with disadvantages for younger language brokers. Weisskirch and Alva (2002) found that fifth-grade Latino children who reported language brokering said that they were uncomfortable in their role as language broker. In addition, a handful of clinical case studies suggest that the responsibilities of language brokering may be overwhelming for some children and lead to psychological distress (Baptiste, 1993; Hardy-Fanta & Montana, 1982). For example, Baptiste (1993) noted that the role of family interpreter risks greater criticism and harsher treatment from parents because it is associated with more opportunities for error in sensitive situations having implications for the entire family. Others claim that language brokering creates a "status inconsistency for the child—a situation in which a person occupies two or more distinct social statuses with incompatible social expectations leading to chronic stress" (Athey & Ahearn, 1991, p. 12). A major aim of the study we report here was to examine the relation of language brokering to depression. We believe that the role of language broker may be especially precarious during adolescence as children attempt to assert their autonomy (Love & Buriel, 2005) while at the same time being drawn closer into family matters by their parents, who depend on them for interpreting. The ability to fulfill the role of language broker without significant psychological distress, especially during adolescence, may depend on the quality of the parent–child relationship.

LANGUAGE BROKERING AND PARENT–CHILD RELATIONSHIPS

College students who served successfully as language brokers recalled that as adolescents they felt close to their parents and wanted to help them and their families in their adjustment to U.S. society (De Ment et al., 2005). Although many college students admitted to feeling annoyed, and sometimes burdened, by their brokering responsibilities, most felt that the role of language broker gave them insight and appreciation for the sacrifices their parents made in coming to this country. As a result, they felt they were more "bonded" with their parents than their siblings. Feeling bonded with parents is an aspect of familism that is an important socialization goal among immigrant families from Asia and Latin America (Buriel & De Ment, 1997; Harrison, Wilson, Pine, Chan, & Buriel, 1990). Familism involves several dimensions, including physical and affective closeness to family members (Chao, 2001; Keefe & Padilla, 1987), obligation to family (Fuligni, Tseng, & Lam, 1999), and family pride (Gil, Vega, & Dimas, 1994). Various studies have shown that familism, in its various forms, helps minimize acculturative stress and its negative consequences among members of immigrant families (Gil et al., 1994; Hovey, 2000; Rogler, Cortes, & Malgady, 1991). In addition, a breakdown of familism, as manifested in parent–child conflict, has been associated with higher depression and lower self-esteem among adolescent children of immigrants (Rumbaut, 1994). Whether or not children feel bonded or connected to their parents, however, has implications for how the language brokering role will affect their psychological well-being. Children who feel more bonded with their parents may derive greater satisfaction from their brokering responsibilities, which enhances their psychological well-being. On the other hand, children who are more disconnected from their parents may feel resentful about their brokering role and as a result experience greater psychological distress. One aspect of our study was to examine how language brokering is related to parent–child bonding.

Successful language brokering requires children to become bilingually competent in English and their parents' native language in order to facilitate communication between adults who speak different languages (Valdes, 2003). Zambrana and Silva-Palacios (1989) found that perceived limited English proficiency was related to elevated stress among Mexican immigrant adolescents. These researchers concluded that the adolescents' perceived stress was heightened by their need to learn a new language, not only for their own self-expression, but also to negotiate the external environment for their families. Research also shows that as children of immigrants learn English at school, there is often simultaneous loss of their native language (Wong-Fillmore, 1991). Because English is taught formally in school whereas the native language is learned informally at home and in the community, there is likely to be an uneven development in the two languages of immigrant children (Valdes, 2003). This situation may handicap the language brokering abilities of some children for three reasons. First, children may be at a loss for words, syntax, and meaning to communicate effectively between two languages. Second, loss of the native language can impair meaningful parent–child communication and thus weaken affective intergenerational bonds between family members (Baptiste, 1993). Third, children's poor command of the native language can also diminish parental control and authority and lead to parent–child conflict in immigrant families (Rumbaut, 1994). To date, the relation of language proficiency to both parent–child bonding and the psychological well-being of language brokers has not been examined. It seems likely that children's English and Spanish proficiency are important personal resources that can reduce stress that is related to the language-brokering role. At the same time, Spanish language proficiency facilitates communication between Latino adolescents and their parents and may strengthen the affective bond between them.

LANGUAGE BROKERING AND ACADEMIC SUCCESS

Many children from immigrant families are motivated to do well in school in order to demonstrate appreciation for their parents' sacrifices and also to bring honor to their family (Chao, 1996; Fuligni et al., 1999; Suarez-Orozco & Suarez-Orozco, 1995). Studies have consistently shown that Latino immigrant youths have higher educational aspirations, expectations, and grades than their native-born peers (Buriel, 1984, 1994; Kao & Tienda, 1995; Suarez-Orozco & Suarez-Orozco, 1995; Valenzuela, 1999). Valdes (2003) argued that the advanced linguistic and cognitive skills of language brokers constitute a form of "giftedness" that is overlooked by most practitioners and researchers. Under optimum conditions, language brokers may have an academically related advantage over the children of immigrants in general. Heath (1986) theorized that the more opportunities language-minority children have to use language in diverse community settings, the greater the likelihood they develop the linguistic competencies necessary for school success. Buriel et al. (1998) found that brokering in more places was positively related to adolescents' high school grade point averages. Academic success relates to higher self-esteem and lower depression among adolescent children of immigrants (Rumbaut, 1994). In the present study, adolescents' level of depression was examined in relation to their educational aspirations and expectations, and their language brokering experiences. Because academic success is one way children express appreciation for their immigrant parents' sacrifices, we also examined the relation of educational aspirations and expectations to parent–child bonding.

GENDER AND LANGUAGE BROKERING

Among adolescents from immigrant families, girls broker more than boys (Buriel et al., 1998; Kibria, 1993), and girls exhibit more depression than boys (Hovey & King, 1996; Rumbaut, 1994). However, the hypothesis that language brokering contributes to girls' higher depression has not been tested. Gender role socialization often results in girls being assigned more responsibility for helping their families than boys (Goodnow, 1988). The stress of assisting family members with language brokering, coupled with the attendant stress of adolescence as a transition period, may increase the risk of depression for girls. Given the striking gender differences described in the literature, we compared boys and girls on all variables, and we examined the relation of language brokering, parent–child bonding, and other variables to depression separately for boys and girls.

RESEARCH QUESTIONS

The primary aim of our study was to better understand the relation of language brokering to depression among Latino adolescents, and how the bond between adolescents and their parents affects this relation. In view of the literature we reviewed, we hypothesized that: (1) girls would report more language brokering activities and higher levels of depression than boys; (2) parent–child bonding would be predicted by language brokering, English and Spanish proficiency, and educational aspiration and expectations; (3) depression would be predicted by parent–child bonding, English and Spanish proficiency, and educational aspiration and expectations; and (4) depression would be predicted by language brokering after taking into account the contributions of parent–child bonding, English and Spanish proficiency, and educational aspirations.

DATA COLLECTION METHODS

Participants

The participants were 157 10th- and 11th-grade Latino students (93 females, 64 males) attending a predominately Latino high school in eastern Los Angeles County. The average age of the students was 15.29 years (*SD* = 1.17 years). The community served by the high school is predominately Latino and includes a large number of immigrant families. According to the 2000 census, 55 % of households in the community speak Spanish, and 31.8 % include people who speak English less than “very well” (United States Census Bureau, 2000). As a condition for inclusion in the study, all students were from immigrant households where both parents were foreign-born. The nativity of the students was 36.3% foreign-born and 63.7% native-born. The average length of U.S. residence for foreign-born students was 7.36 years (*SD* = 4.11 years). Students of Mexican descent made up the majority (85%) of the sample, with the remaining students coming primarily from Central American families. Questionnaires were administered during general English classes. All students spoke English well enough to be in regular English classrooms, and none were in English Language Learner (ELL) programs. A bilingual research assistant read the questions out loud to the participants in English as they followed along on their own questionnaires. This class administration procedure was used to compensate for possible differences in reading abilities among the participants. All students included in the study reported having some Spanish/English language brokering experience based on their responses to the language brokering items in the questionnaire they completed. Data for students without language brokering experience was excluded from the analysis.

Measures

Language Brokering

Participants completed the Language Brokering Scale (LBS) developed by Tse (1995) and revised by Buriel et al. (1998). The LBS measures four language brokering dimensions, including persons for whom one has brokered (*persons*), places where one has brokered (*places*), things (usually documents) translated (*things*), and one's feelings about brokering (*feelings*). The *persons* dimension consists of 10 questions that ask respondents to indicate how often they language broker for family members, friends, neighbors, teachers, and strangers. Responses are scored 1 (*never*), 2 (*a little bit*), 3 (*a lot*), and 4 (*always*). The *persons* dimension is a measure of the frequency of language brokering. Examples of items in the *persons* dimension include "How often do you translate for your parents?" and "How often do you translate for teachers?" The *places* dimension asks respondents to check either *yes* or *no* to 12 places where they may have brokered. Because translating in some places is considered more difficult than in other places (De Ment, Buriel, & Villanueva, 2005), a *yes* response was weighted on a scale of 1 to 3 by the level of difficulty involved. Thus, for example, a *yes* response for translating at home was given a score of 1; translating at school was given a score of 2; and translating at the hospital or doctor's office was given a score of 3. The *things* dimension asks respondents to check either *yes* or *no* to 12 things they may have translated during brokering situations. Because things translated also vary by level of difficulty, a *yes* response was weighted on a scale of 1 to 3. Thus, for example, translating flyers left by door-to-door salespeople was given a score of 1; translating phone bills and credit card bills at home was given a score of 2; and translating insurance forms or rental contracts was given a score of 3. The *feelings* dimension asks respondents to evaluate their personal satisfaction with their brokering experiences. The *feelings* dimension includes 12 items that are scored on a 4-point scale ranging from (4) *always* to (1) *never*. Due to wording, four of these items were scored in the opposite direction. Examples of items in the *feelings* dimension include: "I like to translate." and "I feel embarrassed when I translate for others." The items for each dimension were summed to derive a subscore for *persons*, *places*, *things*, and *feelings*. Previous research (Buriel et al., 1998) indicated that these subscores yield stronger and more theoretically interesting relations to various dependent variables than a total score that combines all dimensions of the LBS. The full LBS has a test–retest reliability (3-week interval) of .84 with Latino adolescents (Diaz-Lazaro, 2002).

Depression

The depression scale used was taken from the psychological impairment measure developed by Warheit (Warheit, Holzer, & Arey, 1974; Warheit, Holzer, & Schwab, 1973) for his extensive epidemiological surveys of diverse ethnic and social class groups that included Latinos. The psychological impairment measure consists of six scales, each measuring a specific aspect of psychopathological symptomology, including depression. The Depression Scale consists of 18 items that assess psychological symptoms of depression (feelings of dejection, despair, meaninglessness, self-blame, helplessness, loneliness, suicide ideation, and powerlessness). Responses to all items were on either a 3-point or 5-point Likert scale. The 3-point scale included six items with the following response alternatives: *never* (1), *sometimes* (2), and *often* (3). The 5-point scale included 12 items with the following response alternatives: *never* (1), *seldom* (2), *sometimes* (3), *often* (4), and *all the time* (5). Both scales were averaged separately and then added together, yielding a possible range of scores from 2 to 8. In the present sample of adolescents, depression scores ranged from 2.42 to 7.08. Higher scores are in the direction of more depression symptoms. According to the criteria of Warheit et al. (1974), scores that are one standard deviation above the sample mean are considered more "at risk" for clinical depression. For the present sample, 6 boys (3.8%) and 19 girls (12.1%) scored one or more standard deviations above the mean. Therefore, the majority of the sample is not at risk. In addition to the epidemiological studies of Warheit, this same Depression Scale was used by Griffith (1983) in a study of acculturation and psychological impairment in Mexican Americans. In both sets of studies, the reliability of the Depression Scale was above .80, and Warheit et al. (1974) provided evidence for the validity of the Depression Scale.

Parent–Child Bonding

The Parent–Child Bonding Scale (PCBS) was used to measure closeness of students to their parents. The PCBS was developed from the assumption that children in collectivist cultures are encouraged early in life to form a strong relationship, or bond, with their parents and to maintain and strengthen it throughout their lives (Kim, 1989). In this regard, Parental Bonding is akin to family obligation (Fuligni et al., 1999) and parent–adolescent relationship closeness (Chao, 2001), which are core values in Latino and Asian cultures. The PCBS was originally developed for work with Korean American college students (Kim, 1989), but has also been used with Mexican American, Vietnamese American, and European American adolescents (De Ment, 1998). The PCBS consists of 10 items utilizing a 4-point Likert ranging from (4) *strongly agree* to (1) *strongly disagree*, with higher scores indicating greater parent–child bonding. Due to wording, three of these items were scored in the opposite direction. Examples of items from the PCBS include: "If I have a choice, I prefer to spend my time with my parents rather than my friends." "I feel I have the responsibility to take care of my parents after they get older." and "My parents are the most important people in my life." In previous research (Kim, 1989), the PCBS has been shown to have good reliability (alpha = .92) and validity (negatively correlated with acculturation).

Educational Aspirations and Expectations

A 4-item scale was used to measure students' educational aspirations and expectations. Each item in the scale consisted of two corresponding questions. The first question asked students to rate the personal importance they attached to the educational goal described in the question. Students rated the importance on a 4-point Likert scale ranging from (4) *very important* to (1) *not at all important*. This rating was used as a measure of students' educational aspirations. Each aspiration question was followed by a question that asked students to rate the personal likelihood of attaining the educational goal described in the previous question. Students made their rating on a 4-point Likert scale ranging from (4) *very likely* to (1) *very unlikely*. This rating was used as a measure of students' educational expectations. The four items in the scale included the importance and likelihood of the following educational behaviors: receiving good grades in school, being prepared for class in the morning, studying hard before a test, and getting along with the teacher. The internal consistency of the scale was .76 in previous research with Mexican American adolescents (Buriel, Calzada, & Vasquez, 1982). Respondents' responses were summed to derive separate aspiration and expectation scores.

English and Spanish Proficiency

Language brokering involves both interpreting oral communications (oral skills) and translating written documents (literacy skills). Therefore, English and Spanish proficiency was assessed with four self-report questions for each language: "How well do you understand English/Spanish?" "How well do you speak English/Spanish?" "How well do you read English/Spanish?" and "How well do you write English/Spanish?" The possible responses to these questions consisted of a 4-point Likert scale ranging from (1) *not at all* to (4) *very well*. This self-report measure has been used successfully in previous research (Buriel & Cardoza, 1988; Buriel & Reigadas, 1994; Cardoza & Hirano-Nakanishi, 1984).

Parental Education

Students reported the highest grade in school completed by their fathers and mothers. A scale with years of schooling ranging from 1 year to more than 18 years was used for students to report their parents' level of education. This grade-by-grade method of measuring parents' education is advantageous because it can detect small, but important, differences in years of schooling even within a population having, on average, very limited education. The average years of schooling for fathers and mothers was 8.1 years and 8.4 years, respectively.

Demographic Information

Students answered a series of questions to collect demographic information about themselves and their parents. Student data included gender, age, ethnicity, generation, and years living in the United States. Parental information included country of origin and years of schooling.

STATISTICAL ANALYSES OF THE RESEARCH QUESTIONS

A preliminary correlation analysis was carried out between all of the variables in the study. This analysis showed that for foreign-born students there were no correlations between years of U.S. residence and any of the language brokering subscales. In addition, years of U.S. residence were unrelated to depression. Years of U.S. residence were therefore dropped from subsequent analyses. In addition, fathers' and mothers' years of schooling were uncorrelated with the other variables in the study. For this reason, and in order to reduce the number of missing values, fathers' and mothers' education were not used in subsequent analyses. Earlier research has shown higher levels of depression among native-born Latino adolescents (Swanson, Linskey, Quintero-Salinas, Pumariega, & Holzer, 1992). However, another set of preliminary analyses revealed no difference in depression between foreign- and native-born youths in our sample. Generation was therefore not used in subsequent analyses.

GENDER

We used Hotellings' multivariate analysis to test the first hypothesis by comparing boys and girls on all variables. The multivariate test showed a significant overall difference, $F(10, 146) = 4.10$, $p < .001$. Table 12.1 presents means and standard deviations for boys and girls as well as the results of univariate tests. Girls reported significantly more language brokering for persons, places, and things. Girls also reported feeling more favorable about language brokering than boys. In addition, girls reported significantly more depression than boys. Overall, the hypothesis that girls would language broker more and report more depression than boys was supported.

PARENT–CHILD BONDING

We computed a three-step hierarchical regression analysis separately for boys and girls to test the hypothesis concerning the expected relation of language brokering, English and Spanish proficiency, and educational aspirations and expectations to parent–child bonding. Because language brokering involves chil-

TABLE 12.1
Means, Standard Deviations, and Comparisons Between Boys and Girls

	Boys	*Girls*	*Univariate F*
Brokering: person	12.29 (.33)	12.49 (.43)	9.55**
Brokering: place	8.23 (5.64)	12.36 (6.56)	16.80***
Brokering: thing	7.06 (6.93)	11.67 (7.83)	14.42***
Brokering: feeling	35.76 (5.55)	37.74 (5.72)	4.62*
Depression	4.04 (.73)	4.59 (.86)	17.18***
Bonding	29.15 (4.05)	29.37 (4.36)	.10
Educational aspirations	12.68 (2.09)	13.05 (2.17)	1.10
Educational expectations	11.48 (1.99)	11.96 (2.16)	2.00
English proficiency	13.07 (2.84)	13.26 (2.60)	.18
Spanish proficiency	12.71 (2.54)	13.38 (2.28)	2.94

Note. All analyses are based on an n of 157. Numbers in parentheses are standard deviations.
$^*p < .05$. $^{**}p < .01$. $^{***}p < .001$.

dren directly assisting their parents, it is likely to have a stronger relation to parent–child bonding than language and education variables. The four language brokering variables were therefore entered as a set in Step 1. Because English and Spanish are used in language brokering, they were entered together in Step 2. Educational aspirations and expectations were entered as a set in Step 3. Results of the hierarchical regression analyses are presented in Table 12.2. Results for boys show that feelings about language brokering was the only variable to explain significant variance in parent–child bonding. Boys who feel more favorable about language brokering are more bonded with their parents. For girls, two variables are related to parent–child bonding, both in a positive direction. Feelings about language brokering and educational expectations both explained significant variance in parent–child bonding for girls. Girls who feel better about language brokering, and who hold higher educational expectations, are more bonded with their parents. The second hypothesis was supported only for feelings about language brokering for both boys and girls, and educational expectations for girls only. Language was unrelated to language brokering for both boys and girls.

DEPRESSION

We tested Hypotheses 3 and 4 in the same hierarchical regression analysis using depression as the criterion variable, using the four dimensions of language brokering separately. Less is known about the effects of language brokering on depression relative to the other predictor variables. Thus, in order to examine the unique contribution of language brokering to depression, it was entered last in the hierarchical regressions for both boys and girls. The order of entry was as follows: parent–child bonding in Step 1, English and Spanish proficiency in Step 2, educa-

TABLE 12.2
Hierarchical Regression Analysis of Parent–Child Bonding for Boys ($n = 64$) and Girls ($n = 93$) with Language Brokering, Language, and Educational Variables as Predictors

		Boys					Girls				
Step	*Variables*	*B*	*SE B*	β	R^2 *Change*	*F Change*	*B*	*SE B*	β	R^2 *Change*	*F Change*
1	Language brokering				0.15	2.73				0.12	3.20*
	Person	−0.06	0.16	−0.04			0.28	0.11	−0.02		
	Places	0.00	0.11	0.10			0.00	0.01	0.05		
	Things	−0.00	0.00	−0.02			0.00	0.00	0.07		
	Feelings	0.39	0.14	0.36**			0.35	0.12	0.31**		
2	Language				0.02	0.71				0.02	0.51
	English	0.00	0.19	−0.07			0.00	0.01	0.03		
	Spanish	0.02	0.02	0.16			0.04	0.01	0.16		
3	Education				0.05	0.62				0.09	5.10**
	Aspirations	0.04	0.27	0.22			0.03	0.02	0.15		
	Expectations	0.03	0.28	0.18			0.05	0.02	0.28*		

Note. For boys: $R^2 = 0.23$ (adjusted $R^2 = 0.12$); $F(8, 55) = 2.07$; $p < .10$. For girls: $R^2 = 0.23$ (adjusted $R^2 = 0.16$); $F(8, 84) = 3.31$; $p < .01$.
$^*p < .05$. $^{**}p < .01$.

tional aspirations and expectations in Step 3, and language brokering in Step 4. Table 12.3 presents the results of these analyses. For boys, parental bonding entered in Step 1 and was negatively related to depression. Hence, the closer boys felt to their parents, the less depression they reported. The only other variable to explain significant variance in depression for boys was language brokering, particularly as it pertained to places. This relation was in a positive direction, indicating that brokering in a wider variety of settings is associated with greater depression for boys. Neither language nor education contributed significant variance in depression for boys. Thus, Hypothesis 3 was supported only with respect to parent–child bonding, and Hypothesis 4 was supported only with respect to the places where boys language brokered.

Results for girls showed that parent–child bonding and English proficiency were the only variables showing a significant relation to depression. In both cases, the direction of this relationship was negative. Thus, more parent–child bonding and more English proficiency were both related to less depression for girls. Therefore, Hypothesis 3 was partially supported with respect to parent–child bonding and English proficiency for girls. Contrary to Hypothesis 4, language brokering was completely unrelated to depression for girls.

IMPLICATIONS OF THE FINDINGS

Adolescence is a time often fraught with stressful parent–child relationships that can contribute to adolescent depression. The frequency of stressful parent–child relationships is potentially greater when children must act as language brokers between their parents and the external environment. The responsibilities associated with language brokering may either positively or negatively affect the quality of the parent–child relationship, and in turn, the adolescent's level of depression. In addition, personal resources of adolescents such as language proficiency and educational goals can affect both the strength of the parent–child bond and adolescents' ability to cope with the demands of their language brokering role. Our study sought to better understand the relation between language brokering and depression, and their mutual relation to parent–child bonding, English/Spanish proficiency, and educational aspirations and expectations.

THE GENDERED NATURE OF LANGUAGE BROKERING

Results of this study provide further evidence of the gendered nature of language brokering. Girls consistently scored higher on all three behavioral subscales of the language brokering measure. They also reported more positive feelings about brokering than boys. There are at least three possible explanations for the greater brokering activities of girls. First, girls are typically more verbal in childhood and

TABLE 12.3

Hierarchical Regression Analysis of Depression for Boys (n = 64) and Girls (n = 93) with Parent–Child Bonding, Language, and Educational Variables as Predictors

		Boys					Girls				
Step	*Variables*	*B*	*SE B*	β	R^2 *Change*	*F Change*	*B*	*SE B*	β	R^2 *Change*	*F Change*
1	Bonding	−0.58	0.21	−.032**	0.10	7.21**	−0.81	0.18	−0.40**	0.16	18.22***
2	Language				0.08	3.00				0.06	7.03**
	English	−0.07	0.03	−0.27			−0.06	0.31	−0.20*		
	Spanish	0.00	0.03	0.02			0.03	0.03	0.10		
3	Education				0.04	1.18				0.04	1.83
	Aspirations	−0.01	0.04	−0.05			0.06	0.05	0.16		
	Expectations	−0.07	0.05	−0.19			−0.12	0.05	−0.32		
4	Language brokering				0.16	3.60*				0.02	0.77
	Person	0.32	0.27	0.14			−0.12	0.22	−0.06		
	Places	0.04	0.01	0.32*			−0.00	0.01	−0.01		
	Things	−0.01	0.01	−0.13			0.02	0.14	0.19		
	Feelings	0.33	0.25	0.17			0.06	0.25	−0.03		

Note. For boys: $R^2 = 0.39$ (adjusted $R^2 = 0.29$); $F(9,54) = 3.89$; $p < .001$. For girls: $R^2 = 0.29$ (adjusted $R^2 = 0.22$); $F(9,83) = 3.93$; $p < .001$.
$^*p < .05$. $^{**}p < .01$. $^{***}p < .001$.

adolescence than boys, which may lead parents to think they are better suited to language brokering than their male siblings. The verbal superiority of girls is most obvious at about age 11 and after (Clarke-Stewart, Friedman, & Koch, 1985), which coincides with the time many children report as the beginning of their language brokering responsibility (Buriel et al., 1998; Tse, 1995). Second, the nature of gender status and roles in Latino immigrant families may afford boys more freedom from responsibilities that can be shared with their sisters. The inconvenience, and potential embarrassment, associated with language brokering may motivate boys to suggest to parents that their sisters should language broker instead of them. Research by Kibria (1993), with Vietnamese immigrant families, suggests that threats to male pride associated with speaking broken English in public discourages some men from assuming the role of language broker. A third reason girls may language broker more is because they are more available than boys. In traditional Latino families, gender role socialization encourages girls to spend more time with parents and family members (Ginorio, Gutierrez, & Cauce, 1996; Ramirez & Castaneda, 1974). As a result, girls may be on hand more often when their parents need someone to language broker and eventually they may come to accept this responsibility as part of their role in the family. This may explain why the girls in this study reported feeling better about language brokering than boys.

LANGUAGE BROKERING AND PARENT–CHILD BONDING: ONLY FEELINGS MATTER

It was hypothesized that language brokering helps adolescents fulfill their family obligation and become more closely bonded with their parents. Because girls language broker more than boys, they might also be expected to report stronger parent–child bonding. However, there was no difference between boys and girls in their level of parent–child bonding. Furthermore, our analyses showed that neither the frequency nor type of language brokering was related to parent–child bonding for either boys or girls. Instead, only feelings about language brokering was positively related to parent–child bonding for both boys and girls. Thus, it appears that the act of language brokering per se is not as instrumental to parent–child bonding as the perception of satisfaction derived from this activity. Former language brokers have reported feeling ambivalent about their responsibilities because, on one hand, they created inconveniences and embarrassments, while, on the other hand, they were a source of great personal satisfaction for helping their parents (De Ment et al., 2005). On reflection, however, they felt the satisfaction associated with language brokering outweighed the inconvenience and embarrassment, consistent with the results of our study. The importance of language brokering in the daily activities in the Latino immigrant community undoubtedly invests this behavior with the potential for great personal satisfaction regardless of its attendant inconveniences. The importance of language brokering suggests that it can be a source of satisfaction whether one language brokers a little or a lot. In addition, because language brokering is usually done in the service of parents, who are held in high esteem in the Latino immigrant community, it may be perceived as a means of strengthening the bond with parents. Yet, an alternative explanation to the observed relation is that parent–child bonding contributes to the level of satisfaction children derive from language brokering. Children who have developed a secure and rewarding relationship with their parents early in life may derive more satisfaction from their language brokering responsibilities later on. Viewed from this perspective, the parent–child bond may serve as a social support that makes language brokering a less taxing and more personally satisfying experience for children.

THE RELATION OF LANGUAGE BROKERING TO ACADEMIC AND LANGUAGE VARIABLES

In this study, the educational expectations of girls, but not boys, related to parent–child bonding. Girls with higher educational expectations report a stronger parent–child bond. Previous research, with the same measures used in this study, indicated that Mexican American parents hold higher educational expectations for their daughters than for their sons (Buriel & Reigadas, 1994). Parents may convey these expectations to their daughters, who in turn, internalize them as a way of bonding with their parents. Girls may perceive higher parental expectations as a form of caring, which they reciprocate by also holding higher educational expectations of themselves. The previous research showed that Mexican American parents held equal educational aspirations for their sons and daughters, but higher expectations that these aspirations would be fulfilled by their daughters (Buriel & Reigadas, 1994).

The hypothesis that Spanish proficiency would be positively related to parent–child bonding was not supported for either boys or girls. Perhaps Spanish is so pervasive and expected on the part of language brokers in Latino immigrant families that the use of this language, by children, does not evoke for them a stronger parent–child bond. However, an avenue for future research is parents' own reaction to their children's retention or loss of Spanish. That is, Latino immigrant parents are appreciative of their children's efforts to retain Spanish in the face of social and educational pressures to replace their native language with English (Valdes, 2003), and this may strengthen their bond with their children.

FACTORS IMPACTING DEPRESSION AMONG LANGUAGE BROKERS

The parental support and positive family relationships inherent in parent–child bonding have been shown to serve as protective factors against depression among Latino adolescents from immigrant families (Hovey & King, 1996). It is to be expected, therefore, that parent–child bonding is negatively related to depression for both boys and girls in this study. This finding highlights the importance of family cohesion in immigrant households, which are faced with many acculturative stressors. Fortunately, research shows that in the absence of extended family support, Mexican immigrant families often turn inward for support, thus strengthening family relationships and bonding (Buriel, 1993). Future research might focus on whether bonding with the parent of the same sex is more important than bonding with both parents. This line of inquiry is suggested by the work of Ge, Lorenz, Conger, Elder, and Simons (1994), who found that girls with less supportive mothers are more vulnerable to negative life changes as compared to boys.

A major aim of this study was to examine the possible relation of language brokering to depression. From a mainstream developmental perspective, language brokering might be perceived as an at-risk behavior due to the allocation of potentially stressful adult-like responsibilities to children. The only documented detrimental effects of language brokering involve clinical case studies where extreme situations were reported (Baptiste, 1993), and a small sample of fifth-grade language brokers who may have reported negative feelings about language brokering due to their immature cognitive, linguistic, and social skills (Weisskirch & Alva, 2002). In contrast, the present study used a representative sample of Latino adolescents who language broker to a greater or lesser degree in Southern California. If language brokering is a risk behavior, then those who language broker more, such as girls, would seem to be most at risk. However, although girls reported more depression, their depression was unrelated to their language brokering activities. Perhaps girls do not get as depressed about language brokering because their gender role socialization leads them to expect this family obligation more than boys. Although language brokering may be burdensome for girls, their appraisal of their language brokering role may be more consistent with their gender role expectations and thus less stressful. In immigrant Latino culture, girls are expected to spend more time with parents, which means they will normally be more available, and expected to serve as language brokers more than boys. This same gender role expectation of being closer to parents also suggests that deviations from it may be a source of tension for girls. This is probably why girls who are less bonded with parents report more depression. For girls, language brokering may help fulfill their gender role expectation of being close to their parents, thereby reducing gender role inconsistency and its attendant stress.

Boys' language brokering, on the other hand, did show a relation to depression having to do with the places where they language brokered. Unlike the persons for whom one language brokers and the things one interprets, translating in different places necessitates being in diverse public settings. Because accompanying parents in public is less expected of Latino male adolescents, language brokering in different settings may be more stressful for them than girls. In addition, boys may be more adversely affected in their language brokering role when it brings them in contact with situations that disclose their family's economic hardships. Research with European American (Conger et al., 1992) and Latino adolescents (Dennis, Parke, Coltrane, Blacher, & Borthwick-Duffy, 2003) indicates that family economic stress negatively impacts the adjustment of boys more than girls. In the course of language brokering in different places, children may sometimes have to be made aware of their family's limited economic resources and their implications.

For children of immigrant parents in the United States, acquiring fluency in the second language of English is critically important for academic success and adaptation to society. The necessity to learn English is universal to children of immigrants, not just those who language broker. It is understandable, therefore, that higher English proficiency is associated with less depression in girls because they carry out more language brokering activities than boys. Because English is the privileged public language necessary for children of immigrants to achieve in school, and thus bring recognition to their families, it carries more implications for their feelings of personal self-worth than the family's native language.

CONCLUSIONS

Language brokering is an important and expected responsibility for many children from non-English-speaking immigrant communities living in the United States. Although research on language brokering is just starting, the role of children as language brokers is part of the history of European immigration to this country since before the beginning of the 20th century. Through their language brokering activities, children have played a pivotal role in their families' adaptation to life in this country. Today, emerging research with Asian and Latino children is beginning to describe the activities of language brokers and their implications for healthy child development. The results of this study show that girls are more likely than boys to serve as language brokers for their families, but that this added responsibility is not associated with symptoms of depression. Boys, however, experience depression in relation to the places where they are required to language broker. What is common for both boys and girls is the protective role that parent–child bonding plays against depression. In addition, the more English-proficient girls become, the less likely they are to experience depression. The findings point to the importance of home and school factors in the adjustment of children of immigrant families who serve as language brokers.

The findings need to be considered in light of the small sample size relative to the number of independent variables, and the age of the participants. To date, most language brokering research has focused on college and high school students, many of whom have been language brokering for years. Children who have not coped well with their language brokering responsibilities may have experienced family conflicts and psychological problems that forced them to leave school. Consequently, they would not have appeared in samples drawn from college and high school populations. Future research should include elementary school age children who are just assuming language brokering responsibilities and whose cognitive and social development are in their early stages. Such research could provide a better understanding of the developmental impact that language brokering has on the lives of growing children, and help to clarify the directionality of the findings. Future research should also compare children from different immigrant language minority groups in order to investigate possible culturally related differences in language brokering and its relationship to important mental health outcomes.

REFERENCES

Athey, J. L., & Ahearn, F. L. (1991). The mental health of refugee children: An overview. In J. L. Athey & F. L. Ahearn (Eds.), *Refugee children: Theory, research and services* (pp. 1–19). Baltimore: The John Hopkins University Press.

Baptiste, D. A. (1993). Immigrant families, adolescents and acculturation: Insights for therapists. *Marriage & Family Review, 19*, 341–346.

Booth, A., Crouter, A. C., & Lansdale, N. (Eds.). (1997). *Immigration and the family: Research and policy on U.S. immigrants*. Mahwah, NJ: Lawrence Erlbaum Associates.

Buriel, R. (1984). Integration with traditional Mexican American culture and sociocultural adjustment. In J. L. Martinez & R. Mendoza (Eds.), *Chicano psychology* (2nd ed., pp. 95–130). New York: Academic Press.

Buriel, R. (1993). Childrearing orientations in Mexican American families: The influence of generation and sociocultural factors. *The Journal of Marriage and the Family, 55*, 987–1000.

Buriel, R. (1994). Immigration and education of Mexican Americans. In A. Hurtado & E. E. Garcia (Eds.), *The educational achievement of Latinos: Barriers and success* (pp. 197–226). Santa Cruz, CA: Regents of the University of California.

Buriel, R., Calzada, S., & Vasquez, R. (1982). The relationship of traditional Mexican American culture to adjustment and delinquency among three generations of Mexican American male adolescents. *Hispanic Journal of Behavioral Sciences, 4*, 41–55.

Buriel, R., & Cardoza, D. (1988). Sociocultural correlates of achievement among three generations of Mexican American high school seniors. *American Educational Research Journal, 25*, 177–192.

Buriel, R., & De Ment, T. (1997). Immigration and sociocultural change in Mexican, Chinese, and Vietnamese American families. In A. Booth, A. C. Crouter, & N. Landale (Eds.), *Immigration and the family: Research and policy on U.S. immigrants* (pp. 165–200). Mahwah, NJ: Lawrence Erlbaum Associates.

Buriel, R., Perez, W., De Ment, T., Chavez, D. V., & Moran, V. R. (1998). The relationship of language brokering to academic performance, biculturalism and self-efficacy among Latino adolescents. *Hispanic Journal of Behavioral Sciences, 20*, 283–297.

Buriel, R., & Reigadas, E. (1994, October). *Gender differences among Mexican American parents in their academic aspirations and expectations and desired level of education for their children*. Paper presented at the 5th Mexican Conference of Social Psychology, Merida, Mexico.

Cardoza, D., & Hirano-Nakanishi, M. (1984). *Conceptualizing language factors in survey data: A look at high school and beyond*. (Research Report No. R-24). Los Alamitos, CA: National Center for Bilingual Research.

Chao, R. K. (1996). Chinese and European American mothers' beliefs about the role of parenting in children's school success. *Journal of Cross-Cultural Psychology, 27*, 403–423.

Chao, R. K. (2001). Extending research on the consequences of parenting style for Chinese Americans and European Americans. *Child Development, 72*, 1832–1843.

Clarke-Stewart, A., Friedman, S., & Koch, J. (1985). *Child development: A topical approach*. New York: John Wiley & Sons.

Conger, R. D., Conger, K. J., Elder, G. H. Jr., Lorenz, F. O., Simons, R. L., & Whitbeck, L. B. (1992). A family process model of economic hardship and adjustment of early adolescent boys. *Child Development, 63*, 526–541.

De Ment, T. (1998). *Age expectations of autonomy and parental bonding in Mexican American, Vietnamese American, and Euro American adolescents*. Unpublished doctoral dissertation, Claremont Graduate University, Claremont, CA.

De Ment, T. L., Buriel, R., & Villanueva, C. M. (2005). Children as language brokers: A narrative of the recollections of college students. In F. Salili & R. Hoosain (Eds.), *Language in multicultural education* (pp. 255–272). Greenwich, CT: Information Age Publishing.

Dennis, J., Parke, R., Coltrane, S., Blacher, J., & Borthwick-Duffy, S. (2003). Economic stress, maternal depression, and child adjustment in Latino families. *Journal of Family and Economic Issues, 24*, 183–202.

Diaz-Lazaro, C. M. (2002). *The effects of language brokering on perceptions of family authority structures, problem solving abilities, and parental locus of control in Latino adolescents and their parents*. Unpublished doctoral dissertation, Graduate School of the State University of New York at Buffalo.

Federal Interagency Forum on Child and Family Statistics. (2002). *America's Children: Key National Indicators of Well-Being, 2002* (Federal Interagency Forum on Child and Family Statistics). Washington, DC: U.S. Government Printing Office.

Fuligni, A. J., Tseng, V., & Lam, M. (1999). Attitudes toward family obligations among American adolescents with Asian, Latin American, and European backgrounds. *Child Development, 70*, 1031–1044.

Ge, X., Lorenz, F. O., Conger, R. D., Elder, G. H., & Simons, R. L. (1994). Trajectories of stressful life events and depressive symptoms during adolescence. *Developmental Psychology, 30*, 467–483.

Gil, A. G., Vega, W. A., & Dimas, J. M. (1994). Acculturative stress and personal adjustment among Hispanic adolescent boys. *Journal of Community Psychology, 22*, 43–54.

Ginorio, A., Gutierrez, L., & Cauce, A. (1996). Psychological issues for Latinas. In H. Landrine (Ed.), *Bringing cultural diversity to feminist psychology* (pp. 241–264). Washington, DC: American Psychological Association.

Goodnow, J. J. (1988). Children's household work: Its nature and functions. *Psychological Bulletin, 103*, 5–26.

Griffith, J. (1983). Relationship between acculturation and psychological impairment in adult Mexican Americans. *Hispanic Journal of Behavioral Sciences, 5*, 431–459.

Hardy-Fanta, C., & Montana, P. (1982). The Hispanic female adolescent: A group therapy model. *Journal of Group Psychotherapy, 32*, 351–366.

Harrison, A. O., Wilson, M., Pine, C. J., Chan, S., & Buriel, R. (1990). Family ecologies of ethnic minority children. *Child Development, 61*, 347–367.

Heath, S. B. (1986). Sociocultural contexts of language development. In *Beyond language: Social and cultural factors in schooling language minority students* (pp. 143–186). Los Angeles: California State University, Los Angeles, Evaluation Dissemination and Assessment Center (EDAC).

Hovey, J. D. (2000). Acculturative stress, depression, and suicidal ideation in Mexican immigrants. *Cultural Diversity and Ethnic Minority Psychology, 6*, 134–151.

Hovey, J. D., & King, C. A. (1996). Acculturative stress, depression, and suicidal ideation among immigrant and second-generation Latino adolescents. *Journal of the American Academy of Child and Adolescent Psychiatry, 35*, 1183–1192.

Kao, G., & Tienda, M. (1995). Optimism and achievement: The educational performance of immigrant youth. *Social Science Quarterly, 76*, 1–19.

Keefe, S. E., & Padilla, A. M. (1987). *Chicano ethnicity*. Albuquerque, NM: University of New Mexico Press.

Kibria, N. (1993). *Family tightrope: The changing lives of Vietnamese Americans*. Princeton, NJ: Princeton University Press.

Kim, S. (1989). *Acculturation of Korean-American college students: Implications for mental health*. Unpublished master's thesis, Claremont Graduate University, Claremont, CA.

Lonigan, C. J., Anthony, J. A., Arnold, D. H., & Whitehurst, G. J. (1994, August). *Children's interest in literacy: Compounded daily?* Paper presented at the 102nd Annual Convention of the American Psychological Association, Los Angeles, CA.

Lonigan, C. J., Wagner, R. K., Torgesen, J. K., & Rashotte, C. A. (2003). *Preschool Comprehensive Test of Phonological and Print Processing*. Austin, TX: PROED.

Love, J., & Buriel, R. (2005). *Language brokering, autonomy, parent–child bonding, biculturalism, and depression: A study of Mexican American adolescents from immigrant families*. Manuscript submitted for publication.

Macias, R. F. (1993). Language and ethnic classification of language minorities: Chicano and Latino Students in the 1990s. *Hispanic Journal of Behavioral Sciences, 15*, 230–257.

McQuillan, J., & Tse, L. (1995). Child language brokering in linguistic minority communities: Effect of cultural interaction, cognition and literacy. *Language and Education, 9*, 195–215.

Olsen, L., & Chen, M. T. (1988). *Crossing the schoolhouse border: Immigrant students and the California public schools*. San Francisco: California Tomorrow Policy Research Report.

Ramirez, M., & Castaneda, A. (1974). *Cultural democracy, bicognitive development, and education*. New York: Academic Press.

Rogler, L. H., Cortes, D. E., & Malgady, R. G. (1991). Acculturation and mental health status among Hispanics. *American Psychologist, 46*, 585–597.

Rumbaut, R. G. (1994). The crucible within: Ethnic identity, self-esteem, and segmented assimilation among children of immigrants. *International Migration Review, 28*, 748–794.

Shannon, S. M. (1990). English in the barrio: The quality of contact among immigrant children. *Hispanic Journal of Behavioral Sciences, 12*, 256–276.

Suarez-Orozco, M. M., & Suarez-Orozco, C. E. (1995). The cultural patterning of achievement motivation: A comparison of Mexican, Mexican immigrant, Mexican American, and non-Latino White American students. In R. G. Rumbaut & W. A. Cornelius (Eds.), *California's immigrant children: Theory, research, and implications for educational policy* (pp. 161–190). San Diego: University of California, San Diego.

Swanson, J. W., Linskey, A. O., Quintero-Salinas, R., Pumariega, A. J., & Holzer, C. E. (1992). A binational school survey of depressive symptom, drug use, and suicidal ideation. *Journal of the American Academy of Child and Adolescent Psychiatry, 31*, 669–678.

Tse, L. (1995). Language brokering among Latino adolescents: Prevalence, attitudes, and school performance. *Hispanic Journal of Behavioral Sciences, 17*, 180–193.

U.S. Census Bureau. (2000). *United States Census 2000*. Retrieved June, 2003, from http://factfinder.census.gov/bf/_lang=en_vt_name=DEC_2000_SF3_U_DP2_geo_id=16000US0658072.html

U.S. Census Bureau. (2002). *The Hispanic population of the U.S., March 2002*. Washington, DC: U.S. Department of Commerce.

Valdes, G. (2003). *Expanding definitions of giftedness: The case of young interpreters from immigrant communities*. Mahwah, NJ: Lawrence Erlbaum Associates.

Valenzuela, A. (1999). *Subtractive schooling: U.S.-Mexican youth and the politics of caring*. Albany: State University of New York Press.

Vasquez, O. A., Pease-Alvarez, L., & Shannon, S. M. (1994). *Pushing boundaries: language and culture in the Mexicano community*. Cambridge, UK: Cambridge University Press.

Warheit, G. J., Holzer, C. E., & Arey, S. A. (1974). Race and mental illness: An epidemiologic update. *Journal of Health and Social Behavior, 16*, 243–256.

Warheit, G. J., Holzer, C. E., & Schwab, J. (1973). An analysis of social class and racial difference in depressive symptomatology: A community study. *Journal of Health and Social Behavior, 4*, 291–299.

Weisskirch, R. S., & Alva, S. A. (2002). Language brokering and the acculturation of Latino children. *Hispanic Journal of Behavioral Sciences, 24*, 369–378.

Wong-Fillmore, L. (1991). When learning a second language means losing a first. *Early Childhood Research Quarterly, 6*, 323–347.

Zambrana, R. E., & Silva-Palacios, V. (1989). Gender differences in stress among Mexican immigrant adolescents in Los Angeles, California. *Journal of Adolescent Research, 4*, 426–442.

Zhou, M., & Bankston, C. L. (1998). *Growing up American: How Vietnamese children adapt to life in the United States*. New York: Russell Sage.

13

The Prevalence and Consequences of Adolescents' Language Brokering for Their Immigrant Parents

Ruth K. Chao
University of California, Riverside, U.S.A.

INTRODUCTION

Researchers have recently begun to recognize the salience and importance of children's contributions to the functioning of families in the United States. Some of this research has focused on work contributions that children make in the form of chores or household work (Crouter, Head, Bumpas, & McHale, 2001; Goodnow, 1998; Goodnow & Delaney, 1989; Goodnow & Warton, 1992). In the United States, one of the most striking examples of children's contributions to the family is among youth from immigrant families. These youth are often placed in the role of cultural brokers, acting as cross-cultural intermediaries between their parents and the world outside the family. Because children often acculturate and acquire fluency in English at a faster rate than their parents, they are expected to broker for their parents by translating for them. Through their role as language brokers, these children contribute to the acculturation of their parents by transmitting important cultural information to them (Parke et al., 2005; Valenzuela, 1999). However, parents' reliance on their children for such brokering may have consequences for parent–child relationships and children's adjustment.

There is some initial, descriptive evidence that parents' authority or status may be undermined by having to rely on their children for this linguistic support (Menjivar, 2000; Olsen, 1988). Reciprocally, children's participation in brokering may lead to better parent–child relationships because brokering provides more opportunities for communication and understanding of parents' acculturation experiences. There is also some initial evidence that brokering may create additional stress for these youth (McQuillan & Tse, 1995). Additionally, although language translation or brokering has been found to be prevalent for children of immigrants, we know very little about whether it is more prevalent for some children than others (Buriel, Perez, De Ment, Chavez, & Moran, 1998; McQuillan & Tse, 1995; Tse, 1995, 1996a, 1996b). In studies with Latino immigrants, eldest siblings and also girls provided more brokering than boys (Buriel et al., 1998; Orellana, Dorner, & Pulido, 2003a; Valenzuela, 1999). Based on samples of Mexican, Chinese, and Korean American adolescents with immigrant parents, my study was undertaken to determine not only the prevalence of adolescents' brokering for their parents, but also the youth and family characteristics that are associated with brokering. Ultimately, this study will examine whether adolescents' brokering for parents has consequences for adolescents' respect for parents and for their psychological adjustment.

CHILDREN'S CONTRIBUTIONS TO THE FAMILY

There has been a resurgence in research focusing on children's contributions to the family. Goodnow and Lawrence (2001) clarify what is meant by contributions, including not only work such as chores and household tasks, but also the sustenance and general functioning of the family. The former distinction of children's work is based on extensive changes in the United States regarding the elimination of economic roles for children and the relegation of children's work to noninstrumental household tasks or chores. In historical descriptions of child labor reforms and societal changes in the meaning of childhood occurring in the United States in the 19th and 20th centuries, Zelizer (1985) described how such transformations in the economic roles of children ultimately led to the "economically useless" but "emotionally valued child." The notion of children's work shifted from instrumental to instructional, as parents sought to use household chores as "lessons in helpfulness, order, and unselfishness" (p. 99).

However, Zelizer (1985) discussed a shift in more thinking among some researchers that warns against the negative consequences of "unproductive" children. Some psychologists argued that, when children are not allowed to derive a sense of self-worth from their contributions to the family, they become more focused on their psychological qualities and overly dependent on their parents for self-validation. Zelizer also highlighted evidence from anthropologists and sociologists that suggests that, when children contributed to the family's subsistence, they were more responsible, helpful, and concerned about the welfare of others, and had gained a sense of belonging and being needed. In contrast, less instrumental work, in the form of household chores, seems to have only limited benefits for fostering children's helping in that these behaviors did not generalize to others outside the family (Grusec, Goodnow, & Cohen, 1996).

Similar notions of family obligations have also been found among Chinese immigrants in the United States. Their notions of family obligations are consequences of culturally defined roles of family interdependence, and of support and assistance to each other. Chao and Tseng (2002) described the importance of filial piety in fostering family interdependence among Chinese. Filial piety traditionally entails a hierarchical system of age veneration and patriarchy where parents and elders wield greater authority and respect, and children often continue to seek their parents' advice and guidance throughout their adulthood. Fuligni, Yip, and Tseng (2002) found that the family obligations of Chinese immigrants included contributions throughout childhood and into adulthood. Contributions during childhood ranged from helping parents at their jobs, helping with household chores and caring for younger siblings, and spending time with the family. They also found that obligations were not associated with psychological distress, but instead were associated with a greater belief in the importance and utility of education.

In a study of how immigrant children facilitate the initial permanent settlement of their families in the United States, Valenzuela (1999) found that one of the primary types of assistance that children provide is through acting as translators, or "tutors." Through in-depth interviews with Mexican immigrant children and their parents, he found that children often translated for their parents from English to Spanish, in addition to providing more extensive and complex interpretation or explanation of details or issues surrounding the translation. Also, immigrant children often act as "advocates" by intervening, mediating, or advocating for their families involving financial, legal, or other complicated difficulties. Another contribution that these children made to their family's settlement process was in caring for younger siblings and in household tasks, including cooking, dressing, bathing, and baby-sitting for younger siblings. Children were also consulted by parents about dealing with the disciplinary or behavioral problems of their younger siblings. Not only do the contributions that immigrant youth make to their families extend beyond the typical type of household work or chores found for other families, their language brokering or translating is one of the most common types of assistance they provide.

LANGUAGE BROKERING AMONG CHILDREN OF IMMIGRANTS

Although only a handful of studies has focused explicitly on the topic of language brokering, these studies have found that not only is brokering or translating common for children of immigrants, children most often translated for their own parents (Grosjean, 1982; McQuillan & Tse, 1995; Orellana et al., 2003a; Orellana,

Reynolds, Dorner, & Meza, 2003b; Tse, 1995, 1996a; Vasquez, Pease-Alvarez, & Shannon, 1994). Based on Latino, Chinese, and Vietnamese American adolescents who reported English as their second language, Tse (1995, 1996a) found that at least 90% had brokered at least once in their lifetime and continued to broker. The largest majority of these youth reported brokering for parents (91 to 92%), compared to friends (almost 63%), relatives (56%), siblings (50%), neighbors (over 37%), teachers (34 to 37%), and other school officials (21 to 26%). Orellana et al. (2003a) also found with Latino youth that a greater proportion reported brokering for their mothers (over 70%) than fathers (55%), followed by 49% who brokered for their grandparents. However, these studies were mostly qualitative in nature and based on small samples. Large-scale, systematic studies have not been conducted of the prevalence and levels of brokering provided by children for their immigrant parents.

These initial studies also indicate that brokering involves a great deal of complexity, much more than just the translation and interpretation of communication between different linguistic and cultural agents (Buriel et al., 1998; Grosjean, 1982; McQuillan & Tse, 1995; Orellana et al., 2003a, 2003b; Shannon, 1990; Tse, 1995, 1996a, 1996b; Vasquez et al., 1994). Not only do children serve as negotiators for their parents and other parties, they also advocate on behalf of these individuals across a range of different institutions and settings (McQuillan & Tse, 1995; Orellana et al., 2003a, 2003b; Valenzuela, 1999). These researchers also stress the additional complexity of this role for youth in that they are often involved in an unequal power relationship between themselves, as brokers, and the agents (i.e., parents and other adults) because the agents are usually in some position of authority or supervision to the child brokers.

Brokers possess certain qualities that enable them to be effective (Buriel et al., 1998; Shannon, 1990; Vasquez et al., 1994). For instance, Buriel et al. found that brokering was associated with perceived biculturalism. Studies with Latino youth have found that females reported brokering more than males and eldest siblings more than younger siblings (Buriel et al., 1998; Orellana et al., 2003a; Valenzuela, 1999). However, these latter studies must also consider the number of children in the family. As the number of siblings in the family increases, the demands of brokering are likely to be distributed across siblings and less likely to fall on any single child. Other family characteristics may also be important in that parents with higher education and more fluency in English may require less brokering, whereas single parents may require more. Finally, the parent's age at immigration or arrival in the United States may be especially important, as parents who came to the United States at younger ages may not only be more fluent in English, but may also be more acculturated and thus require less brokering. The few studies that have explicitly focused on language brokering were not specific to parents, but instead were based on the total brokering provided across different people. Studies are needed to determine the characteristics of youth and families that are most associated with brokering for *parents*.

CONSEQUENCES OF CHILDREN'S BROKERING

The few studies that have examined children's language brokering have found both negative and positive consequences for children's well-being. McQuillan and Tse (1995) found that brokers felt they were more mature and independent, relative to other age-mates, and that they had gained a sophistication and cultural understanding of the larger world through their brokering experiences. Tse (1995, 1996a) also found that a greater proportion of adolescent brokers reported positive feelings about brokering compared to those that reported negative feelings: The majority either liked brokering (52% and 54%) or were proud to broker (46% and 48%), whereas only 17% and 23% reported they did not like it, that it was a burden (17% and 9%), or that they were embarrassed (9% and 11%). McQuillan and Tse (1995) also found that brokers reported additional stress. However, their study did not directly examine the association between psychological adjustment and brokering.

Their feelings of embarrassment, frustration, and resentment toward parents may be indicative of the potential role reversals that child and adolescent brokers experience with parents. These role reversals may lead to brokers having a diminished respect for and identification with parents as authority figures and role models (Olsen, 1988). On the other hand, McQuillan and Tse (1995) found that brokers feel they have more trusting relationships with parents because of the brokering responsibilities expected of them by their parents. Such trusting relationships may indicate that brokering fosters better understanding of parents, and even increased respect. Although these studies have primarily focused on adolescents, there have been no studies that have examined the consequences of brokering for parent–adolescent relationships. As adolescents seek to establish their own identity and autonomy from parents, their feelings and respect for parents may become more intensified, either diminishing or increasing. Studies of adolescents are also important because brokering may become more pronounced as youth gain more maturity and language fluency (Vasquez et al., 1994).

Based on survey data involving a large sample of adolescents with immigrant parents, my study examines not only the prevalence, but also the frequency of brokering provided by adolescents for both mothers and fathers. This study also examines the characteristics of adolescents and their families that are most associated with brokering, above and beyond those related to language fluency. The consequences of brokering for adolescents' respect for mothers and fathers, and for their psychological adjustment, are also examined. Two generations of immigrants—adolescents who are foreign-born or first-generation immigrants, and those who are born in the United States to foreign-born parents or second-generation descent—from three ethnic groups (Mexican, Chinese, and Korean) are included. Latinos and Asians are the most predominant immigrant groups in the United States, with Mexicans and Chinese representing the largest ethnic subgroups among Latinos and Asians, respectively (U.S. Census Bureau, 2002).

Thus, this study examines ethnic-generational differences in the characteristics (i.e., being female and bilingual) that were found to be related to brokering among Latino adolescents, and also differences in the consequences of brokering for adolescents' respect for parents and their psychological adjustment.

Specifically, I addressed four research questions: What is the prevalence and extent of brokering by adolescents for their immigrant parents? What youth and family characteristics are most associated with brokering for both mother and father? What are the consequences of brokering for parental respect and for adolescents' psychological adjustment? Are there ethnic-generational differences in the key characteristics associated with brokering, and in how brokering is associated with adolescents' respect for mothers and fathers, and their own adjustment?

METHODS FOR STUDYING LANGUAGE BROKERING IN IMMIGRANT ADOLESCENTS

Participants

Adolescents in the ninth grade were drawn from eight high schools in the Los Angeles area. The sample consisted of 463 Mexican, 581 Chinese, and 557 Korean American youth with immigrant parents. Of the Mexican American youth, 122 were first-generation immigrants (i.e., foreign-born) and 341 were second-generation (U.S.-born with foreign-born parents). Of the Chinese American youth, 193 were first-generation and 388 were second-generation. Of the first-generation Chinese immigrants, 25% were from Taiwan, 36.8% were from People's Republic of China (P.R.C.), 3.6% were from Hong Kong, and 4.6% were from other parts of Asia. Of the Korean immigrant youth, 170 were first-generation and 387 were second-generation (U.S.-born with foreign-born parents). The first-generation youth arrived in or immigrated to the United States at an average age of 6.53 years (4.95 years for Mexicans, 7.31 years for Chinese, and 8.76 years for Koreans). An overall significant difference was found across the ethnic groups for adolescents' age of arrival, $F(2, 432) = 28.29, p < .01$. Based on the post hoc comparisons, the Mexican youth immigrated at much younger ages than the Korean and Chinese youth, and the Chinese immigrated at a younger age than the Korean.

Slightly less than 7% of the adolescents were only children (just over 0.2% and 0.4% among first- and second-generation Mexicans, respectively; 2.2% and 1.5% among first- and second-generation Chinese; and 0.6% and 1.7% among first- and second-generation Koreans). Tests for differences across the ethnic-generational groups in the proportion of only children were conducted. An overall test of mean differences in the proportion of only children across the ethnic-generational groups was significant, $F(5, 1595) = 11.27, p < .01$. There was a significantly ($p < .01$) greater proportion of only children among first-generation Chinese than among the other ethnic-generational groups. Means/proportions and standard deviations of additional youth and family characteristics are presented in Table 13.1 for the overall sample and for each ethnic-generational group.

Measures and Procedure

In order to allow adolescents' participation in the study, consent from both parents and adolescents were required. A passive consent procedure was used with parents, asking that they respond to or send back consent forms only if they did *not* wish their children to participate. All parents received copies of the consent letter in English, Spanish, Chinese, and Korean along with a postage paid, preaddressed envelope for returning the forms. The participation rate was high, at 80.6%. Of all adolescents eligible to participate, fewer than 9.3% either refused to participate or did not have parental consent; another 10.1% were either absent on the day of the study or did not receive their parental consent forms.

Adolescents were given 50 minutes (the whole class period) to complete paper-and-pencil surveys that included the following measures in English:

Language Brokering

The measures for language brokering consisted of (1) one item for whether the adolescent has *ever* translated for either parent, including spoken or written words, phrases, or sentences, and (2) nine items for the frequency of translation provided for mother and father separately. The latter nine items consisted of translating for homework/assignments, materials from school (notices, letters, permission slips, report card/progress reports), meetings or conversations between parents and school staff, household bills/financial materials, household matters not related to money (chores, siblings, or relatives), medical or health-related issues (doctor visits, medication), immigration/naturalization papers, media (TV programs, news, newspapers, etc.), and issues around parent's work or business. Frequency of translation was coded on a 5-point scale (0 as *not at all*, 1 as *at least once*, 2 as *a few times*, 3 as *weekly*, and 4 as *daily*). Scale scores for frequency of translation were created by averaging the nine items for each parent. These scales possessed strong internal consistency with alphas of .90 for translating for mother among the overall sample (alphas for each of the ethnic-generational groups ranged from .88 to .92), and .92 for translating for father (alphas for the ethnic-generational groups ranged from .91 to .95).

Respect for Mother and Father

Respect was assessed using eight items created for this study based on the Parental Identification measure derived by Bowerman and Bahr (1973). The new measure not only captures adolescents' identification with parents (e.g., "I have a high regard for my parent."), but also their respect for and obedience to mothers

TABLE 13.1
Means or Proportions, and Standard Deviations/Standard Errors on Youth and Family Characteristics

	Whole Sample	*Chinese* 1st Generation	*Chinese* 2nd Generation	*Koreans* 1st Generation	*Koreans* 2nd Generation	*Mexicans* 1st Generation	*Mexicans* 2nd Generation	*Differences Across Groups*
Eldest sibling	.44	.49	.45	.49	.44	.41	.40	—
	(.50)	(.50)	(.50)	(.50)	(.50)	(.49)	(.49)	
No. of siblings	1.67	1.27	1.44	1.16	1.27	2.64	2.55	c1, c2, k1, k2 < m1, m2
	(1.19)	(.94)	(.92)	(.57)	(.70)	(1.55)	(1.42)	
Age	15.72	15.81	15.57	15.95	15.71	15.81	15.68	c2 < c1, k1, m1; c2, k2, m2 < k1
	(.64)	(.70)	(.56)	(.67)	(.62)	(.71)	(.62)	
Gender (female)	.53	.54	.51	.48	.50	.59	.56	—
	(.50)	(.50)	(.50)	(.50)	(.50)	(.49)	(.50)	
Bilingual	.17	.19	.11	.29	.17	.16	.17	c2, k2, m2 < k1
	(.38)	(.39)	(.31)	(.45)	(.38)	(.37)	(.37)	
Mother's English fluency	3.12	2.85	3.38	2.64	3.22	2.39	3.29	c1, k1, m1 < c2, k2, m2
	(1.11)	(1.03)	(.97)	(.96)	(1.08)	(1.26)	(1.27)	
Father's English fluency	3.35	3.02	3.55	2.97	3.46	2.97	3.51	c1, k1 < c2, k2, m2; m1 < c2
	(1.11)	(1.14)	(1.02)	(1.06)	(1.04)	(1.32)	(1.19)	
Mother's education	6.53	6.70	6.99	6.78	6.86	5.47	5.77	m1, m2 < c1, c2, k1, k2
	(1.95)	(1.78)	(1.76)	(1.35)	(1.49)	(2.36)	(2.40)	
Father's education	6.82	7.11	7.31	7.22	7.15	5.92	5.82	m1, m2 < c1, c2, k1, k2
	(1.94)	(1.59)	(1.54)	(1.16)	(1.40)	(2.41)	(2.60)	
Mother's age of arrival	25.52	31.55	23.96	32.66	24.36	24.65	20.60	c2, k2, m1 < c1, k1; m2 < c1, k1, k2, m2
	(7.06)	(7.29)	(4.91)	(7.26)	(4.93)	(6.58)	(6.26)	
Father's age of arrival	26.68	32.58	25.46	33.52	25.79	26.13	21.59	c2, k2, m1 < c1, k1; m2 < c1, c2, k1, k2, m1
	(7.37)	(7.69)	(5.00)	(8.05)	(5.33)	(6.39)	(6.61)	
Single-parent household	.15	.15	.10	.18	.12	.11	.21	—
	(.35)	(.35)	(.30)	(.39)	(.33)	(.31)	(.41)	

Note. c1 = first-generation Chinese, c2 = second-generation Chinese, k1= first-generation Korean, k2 = second-generation Korean, m1 = first-generation Mexican, and m2 = second-generation Mexican; the findings for the across-group differences were based on an alpha level of .05.

and fathers (e.g., "I respect my parent's opinions about important things in my life." "I try to be obedient to my parent."). Responses were coded on a 5-point scale ranging from 1 = *strongly disagree* to 5 = *strongly agree*. Separate scale scores were created for mothers and fathers by averaging the eight items for each parent. These scales possessed strong internal consistency with alphas of .89 for respect for mother (alphas for each of the ethnic-generational groups ranged from .84 to .93), and .90 for respect for father (alphas for each of the ethnic-generational groups ranged from .84 to .93).

Psychological Adjustment

Adolescents' psychological adjustment was assessed by the internalizing and externalizing scales of the Youth Self-Report Form (YSR) of the Child Behavioral Checklist (CBCL; Achenbach, 1991). The *internalizing scale* consists of subscales for Depression-Anxiety, Somatic Complaints, and Withdrawal. The Depression-Anxiety subscale contains 20 items such as "I cry a lot" and "I feel lonely." The Somatic Complaint subscale consists of nine items such as "I feel dizzy" and "I feel overtired." Another seven items such as "I am shy" comprise the Withdrawal subscale. The *externalizing scale* consists of two subscales, Aggression and Delinquency. Twenty items such as "I am mean to others" and "I try to get a lot of attention" comprised the Aggression subscale. The Delinquency subscale contains 11 items such as "I lie or cheat." Responses for all the items of the internalizing and externalizing scales were coded on a 3-point scale ranging from 0 (*not true*) to 2 (*very true or often true*). Separate scale scores were created for internalizing and externalizing symptoms by averaging all the items comprising each scale. The two scales possessed good internal consistency for all the ethnic-generational groups of adolescents. The alpha for the internalizing scale was .90 for overall sample (ranging from .89 to .92 for each of the ethnic-generational groups). The alpha for the externalizing scale was .89 for overall sample (ranging from .87 to .93 for each of the ethnic-generational groups).

Youth and Family Characteristics

Eldest is a dichotomous variable, based on two items asking for the number of older and younger siblings. Those youth who indicted they have no older siblings were coded as eldest. Additional characteristics of *number of siblings* (based on the total derived from items asking for the number of older and younger siblings) and *adolescents' age* were also assessed. The measure for *bilingualism* was based on the following two items, each assessing adolescents' fluency in their heritage language and in English: How well do you (1) speak and understand the heritage language/English when others speak it to you, and (2) read and write the heritage language/English? All responses were based on a 5-point scale with 1 as *not at all well*, 3 as *moderately well*, and 5 as *extremely well*. A dichotomous variable was then created in which youth who scored a 3 or greater on all items were coded as bilingual. *Mothers' and fathers' English fluency levels* were measured based on two items each for how well each parent speaks/understands and reads/writes English. Scale scores were created by averaging the two items for each parent; strong internal consistencies were found with alphas of .91 for mother's English fluency (ranging from .84 to .93 among the ethnic-generational groups), and .91 for father's English fluency (ranging from .85 to .93). *Mothers'* and *fathers' education* were measured based on an item asking what is the highest level of education completed for each parent that included the following eight options: 1 = *no formal schooling*, 2 = *some elementary school*, 3 = *finished elementary school*, 4 = *finished middle school*, 5 = *finished high school*, 6 = *some vocational or college training*, 7 = *finished four-year college degree*, and 8 = *finished graduate degree*. *Mothers'* and *fathers' age of arrival in the United States* were measured based on an item asking for age at which each parent arrived or immigrated to the United States. *Single-parent household* was assessed through an item asking whom the youth lived with that included nine options. The options of "only my mother" and "only my father" were coded as single-parent households.

PREVALENCE AND EXTENT OF LANGUAGE BROKERING

In addressing the question of the prevalence and frequency of language brokering, percentages of those who have ever translated for either parent and means and standard deviations for frequency levels of translation for both mothers and fathers are presented in Table 13.2. Analyses were conducted to test whether there were ethnic-generational differences in the proportions of those that have ever translated (for either parent) using chi-square tests and in mean frequency levels of translation for each parent, using one-way ANOVAs and then Scheffé post hoc tests. Post hoc comparisons are also presented in Table 13.2.

Ever Translated for Either Parent

Almost 70% of adolescents have provided translation for their parents, with first-generation Mexicans reporting the highest proportion, followed by first-generation Koreans and first-generation Chinese. An overall difference was found across the ethnic-generational groups for those that have ever translated, $\chi^2(5, 1065) = 57.48$, $p < .01$.

Frequency of Translation for Mother and Father

An overall test of mean differences in translation for mother across the ethnic-generational groups was significant, $F(5, 1018) = 20.64$, $p < .01$. Significant group differences in translation for father were also found, $F(5, 989) = 18.35$, $p <$

TABLE 13.2

Means/Proportions and Standard Deviations for Ever Translated, Translation for Mother and Father, and Respect for Mother and Father

		Chinese		*Korean*		*Mexican*		
	Whole Sample %	*1st Generation %*	*2nd Generation %*	*1st Generation %*	*2nd Generation %*	*1st Generation %*	*2nd Generation %*	*Differences Across Groups*
Ever translated (mother or father)	N = 1,065 69.70	N = 147 78.90	N = 300 57.00	N = 122 87.70	N = 320 66.90	N = 52 88.50	N = 124 71.00	
	Mean (SD)	*Mean (SD)*	*Mean (SD)*	*Mean (SD)*	*Mean (SD)*	*Mean (SD)*	*Mean (SD)*	
Translation mother	N = 991 .95 (1.03)	N = 139 1.16 (.98)	N = 294 .66 (.90)	N = 116 1.45 (1.04)	N = 311 .86 (.95)	N = 48 1.82 (1.13)	N = 116 1.06 (1.13)	c1 < m1; c2 < c1, k1, m1, m2; k2 < k1, m1; m2 < m1
Translation father	N = 991 .75 (.95)	N = 134 .84 (.90)	N = 291 .49 (.84)	N = 111 1.15 (1.00)	N = 304 .64 (.85)	N = 46 1.61 (1.21)	N = 109 .91 (1.10)	c1 < m1; c2 < c1, k1, m1, m2; k2 < k1, m1; m2 < m1
Respect for mother	N = 1,136 3.89 (.74)	N = 152 3.91 (.76)	N = 323 3.85 (.74)	N = 130 3.80 (.69)	N = 330 3.90 (.71)	N = 62 3.76 (.88)	N = 193 3.99 (.77)	—
Respect for father	N = 1,136 3.76 (.85)	N = 149 3.79 (.87)	N = 312 3.70 (.83)	N = 123 3.81 (.69)	N = 322 3.80 (.85)	N = 59 3.58 (.97)	N = 176 3.79 (.95)	—

Note. c1 = first-generation Chinese, c2 = second-generation Chinese, k1 = first-generation Korean, k2 = second-generation Korean, m1 = first-generation Mexican, and m2 = second-generation Mexican; the findings for the across-group differences were based on an alpha level of .05.

.01. For all three ethnic groups, first-generation immigrants reported higher levels of translation for both parents than their second-generation counterparts. Also, first-generation Mexicans translated more for their mothers and fathers than first-generation Chinese. Additional analyses (i.e., paired *t-tests*) were also conducted to determine whether adolescents provided more translating for mothers than fathers. Adolescents provided significantly more brokering for mothers than fathers, $t(990) = 11.29, p < .01, M = .95, SD = 1.03; M = .75, SD = .95$, respectively. In looking within each ethnic-generational group, these higher levels of translating for mother were also found among each group ($p < .01$, but only at $p < .05$ among second-generation Mexicans).

CHARACTERISTICS ASSOCIATED WITH LANGUAGE BROKERING/TRANSLATING

In order to examine which youth characteristics are associated with translating, as well as parental respect and internalizing/externalizing, Pearson's correlations were first conducted among all variables. These are presented in Table 13.3, for Chinese and Koreans, and Table 13.4 for Mexicans. Then also for each ethnic group, these associations were also examined *net of* other youth and family characteristics by including all the characteristics together in regression models with translation for mother and for father as the outcomes. The estimates are presented in Table 13.5 for each ethnic group. Generational differences in the associations between youth characteristics and translating were tested by estimating two-way interactions between generation (dummy-coded as first-generation) and each characteristic in separate regression models.

Translating for Mother

Among the Chinese, being in a single-parent household was related to higher levels of translating for mother *net of* all other factors, whereas mothers' English fluency and educational levels were negatively related. Also, as mothers' age of arrival in the United States increased, the levels of translating increased. For the Koreans, being bilingual was related to higher levels of translating for mother *net of* all other factors, whereas mother's English fluency and education were negatively related. Also, just as with the Chinese, as mothers' age of arrival or immigration increased, translating increased. Among the Mexicans, being first-generation and bilingual were related to higher levels of translating for mother *net of* all other factors, whereas mothers' fluency in English was negatively related.

Among the Chinese and the Mexicans, a two-way interaction between immigrant status and being a female was found for translating for mothers, $B = .44, SE = .18, p = .02$, and $B = .91, SE = .37, p = .02$, respectively. Being a female was more positively associated with translation for mother among first- than second-

TABLE 13.3

Bivariate Associations (r) All Variables for Chinese Americans (Upper Half) and Korean Americans (Lower Half)

	1	*2*	*3*	*4*	*5*	*6*	*7*	*8*	*9*	*10*	*11*	*12*	*13*	*14*	*15*	*16*	*17*	*18*	*19*
1 Immigrant		.04	–.09*	.18**	.02	.11**	–.24**	–.23**	–.08	–.06	.51**	.46**	.06	.24**	.18**	.04	.05	.05	–.03
2 Eldest	.05		–.35**	–.06	.03	.05	.06	.02	.03	.02	–.07	–.07	–.08	.03	.04	.06	.09	–.08	–.04
3 No. of Siblings	–.08	–.34**		.03	.01	–.04	–.08	.01	–.09*	–.09*	–.06	–.04	–.06	.02	–.01	.00	.03	.11**	.05
4 Age	.17**	–.05	.03		–.04	.08	.06	–.05	.10*	.06	.10*	.11**	.04	.05	.05	–.05	–.09	–.00	.02
5 Female	–.02	.10*	.08	–.05		.05	–.03	–.05	–.08	–.06	.01	–.01	.01	.09	.05	.12**	.09	.06	–.14**
6 Bilingual	.13**	.03	–.07	–.03	.06		.06	–.00	–.02	.03	.11**	.09*	.01	.08	.12*	.09	.09	–.00	–.02
7 Mother English fluency	–.24**	.05	.08	–.08	.04	–.07		.47**	.16**	.13**	–.21**	–.15**	.03	–.37**	–.24**	.21**	.08	–.12**	–.11*
8 Father English fluency	–.20**	.03	.08	–.02	–.01	–.02	.56**		.15**	.20**	–.21**	–.23**	–.08	–.34**	–.36**	.06	.11*	–.04	–.07
9 Mother educ.	–.03	.01	.00	–.06	.01	–.01	.12**	.11*		.46**	–.03	–.06	.03	–.17**	–.16**	–.07	–.06	–.04	.01
10 Father educ.	.02	.04	–.01	.04	.07	–.01	.18**	.16**	.39**		–.07	–.11**	.07	–.17**	–.21**	–.03	–.02	–.06	–.02
11 Mother age of arrival	.56**	–.06	–.14**	.16**	–.13**	.08	–.40**	–.26**	–.05	–.03		.76**	.07	.25**	.16**	.03	.00	.06	.01
12 Father age of arrival	.49**	–.03	–.12**	.14**	–.08	.10*	–.30**	–.29**	–.12**	–.03	.76**		.03	.24**	.23**	.03	–.01	.05	.04
13 Single parent	.08	–.01	–.04	–.03	–.03	–.03	.00	.01	.04	.09*	.16**	.02		.10*	–.09	.04	–.10*	.05	.03
14 Translating mother	.26**	.02	–.10*	.08	.01	.18**	–.38**	–.18**	–.13**	–.19**	.32**	.24**	–.02		.81**	.10*	.07	.18**	.05
15 Translating father	.25**	.01	–.05	.04	.06	.15**	–.30**	–.23**	–.14**	–.18**	.31**	.29**	–.09	.82**		.03	.09	.17**	.06
16 Respect for mother	–.06	.03	.01	.07	.09	.12*	.16**	.13*	–.05	–.03	–.04	–.05	–.11*	.03	.11*		.73**	–.11*	–.35**
17 Respect for father	.01	.05	–.03	.08	.04	.12*	.07	.11*	–.05	–.09*	.02	–.04	–.16**	.05	.15**	.79**		–.13**	–.36**
18 Internalizing	–.03	–.03	.13**	–.04	.20**	–.03	–.05	–.02	–.04	.00	.04	.04	.06	.16**	.14**	–.16**	–.13**		.54**
19 Externalizing	–.04	–.05	.04	–.06	–.05	–.04	–.02	–.03	–.06	–.02	–.04	–.03	.13**	.08	.06	–.36**	–.28**	.56**	

*$p < .05$. **$p < .01$.

TABLE 13.4
Bivariate Associations (*r*) All Variables for Mexican Americans

	1	*2*	*3*	*4*	*5*	*6*	*7*	*8*	*9*	*10*	*11*	*12*	*13*	*14*	*15*	*16*	*17*	*18*	*19*
1 Immigrant		.01	.03	.09*	.03	–.00	–.31**	–.20**	–.06	.02	.26**	.28**	–.12*	.29**	.27**	–.12	–.10	.04	.03
2 Eldest			–.39**	.00	–.09	–.06	.22**	.24**	.08	.09	–.17**	–.12**	–.01	–.07	–.09	.10	–.06	.07	–.05
3 No. of siblings				.11*	.02	–.02	–.17*	–.26**	–.02	–.07	.01	.07	–.03	.12	.13	–.04	.03	–.01	–.01
4 Age					–.01	–.04	–.13	–.04	–.03	.08	.01	.07	–.04	.10	.09	–.04	–.05	.02	–.03
5 Female						.05	–.02	–.04	–.11*	–.01	–.10*	–.04	–.03	.00	–.02	.05	.01	.26**	.04
6 Bilingual							.08	.05	.00	–.01	–.05	–.09	–.10*	.11	.17*	.18**	.17**	–.03	–.05
7 Mother English fluency								.64**	.29**	.24**	–.37**	–.30**	.08	–.48**	–.40**	.10	.04	.05	.11
8 Father English fluency									.22**	.25**	–.22**	–.17*	.10	–.37**	–.43**	.06	.05	–.01	.05
9 Mother educ.										.43**	.08	.03	.02	–.09	–.09	.04	.00	.01	–.00
10 Father educ.											.06	.08	.01	–.04	–.09	–.05	–.02	.05	–.00
11 Mother age of arrival												.59**	–.09	.22**	.16*	–.04	–.03	–.05	.01
12 Father age of arrival													–.02	.21**	.13	–.05	.00	.00	–.03
13 Single parent														–.15	–.23**	–.02	–.15*	.09	.06
14 Translating mother															.88**	.13	.05	–.01	–.05
15 Translating father																.18*	.13	–.01	–.08
16 Respect for mother																	.71**	–.14*	–.43**
17 Respect for father																		–.26**	–.45**
18 Internalizing																			.52**
19 Externalizing																			

*$p < .05$. **$p < .01$.

TABLE 13.5

Relations Between Child Characteristics, and Translation for Mother and Father (Unstandardized Coefficients & S.E. (B))

	Translation for Mother						*Translation for Father*					
	Chinese		*Korean*		*Mexican*		*Chinese*		*Korean*		*Mexican*	
	B	*S.E.*	*B*	*S.E.*	*B*	*S.E.*	*B*	*S.E.*	*B*	*S.E.*	*B*	*S.E.*
Immigrant (1st gen.)	–.05	.11	.22	.12	.42*	.20	.04	.10	.28*	.11	.48*	.22
Eldest sibling	.17	.09	.07	.10	.13	.19	.09	.09	.03	.09	.02	.20
No. of siblings	.03	.05	–.07	.07	.06	.06	.01	.05	–.04	.07	–.00	.07
Age	.06	.07	.02	.07	–.04	.14	.04	.07	–.02	.07	.13	.14
Gender (female)	.14	.08	.09	.09	.04	.17	.03	.08	.17	.09	–.12	.18
Bilingual	.14	.11	.24*	.10	.41*	.18	.23*	.11	.14	.10	.42*	.18
Mother's English fluency	–.30**	.04	–.24**	.04	–.42**	.08	—	—	—	—	—	—
Father's English fluency	—	—	—	—	—	—	–.26**	.04	–.08	.04	–.39**	.08
Mother's education	–.07**	.02	–.08**	.03	.03	.04	—	—	—	—	—	—
Father's education	—	—	—	—	—	—	–.07**	.03	–.13**	.03	.01	.04
Mother's age of arrival	.02**	.01	.03**	.01	.01	.01	—	—	—	—	—	—
Father's age of arrival	—	—	—	—	—	—	.02*	.01	.03**	.01	.01	.01
Single parent	.33*	.14	–.11	.13	–.28	.23	–.35*	.14	–.22	.14	–.53	.28
	$N = 422, R^2 = .22, F(11, 410) = 10.34, p = .001$		$N = 421, R^2 = .24, F(11, 409) = 11.58, p = .001$		$N = 156, R^2 = .31, F(11, 144) = 5.81, p = .001$		$N = 409, R^2 = .20, F(11, 397) = 9.18, p = .001$		$N = 406, R^2 = .19, F(11, 394) = 8.21, p = .001$		$N = 145, R^2 = .29, F(11, 133) = 4.81, p = .001$	

$^*p < .05.$ $^{**}p < .01.$

generation immigrants. Among the Koreans, a two-way interaction between immigrant status and mother's education, $B = -.14$, $SE = .07$, $p = .05$, was found such that mothers' level of education was more negatively associated with translation among first- than second-generation.

Translating for Father

Among the Chinese, being bilingual, and increases in fathers' age of arrival in the United States were related to more translation, *net of* all other factors, whereas living in a single-parent household was related to less translation for father. Also, net of all other factors, as fathers' English fluency and education increased, translating for father decreased. For the Koreans, being first generation, and increases in fathers' age of arrival were related to more translation, net of all other factors. Also, as fathers' education increased, translating for father decreased. Among the Mexicans, being first generation and bilingual were related to more translation, whereas increases in fathers' English fluency were related to less translation for father *net of* all other factors.

Among the Chinese and Mexicans, a two-way interaction between immigrant status and being a female was found for translating for fathers, $B = .57$, $SE = .17$, $p = .001$ and $B = .83$, $SE = .40$, $p = .04$, respectively. Females provided more translation for father than males among first- than second-generation immigrants. For the Chinese and Koreans, a two-way interaction between immigrant status and being bilingual were found for translating for fathers, $B = .41$, $SE = .21$, $p = .05$, and $B = -.58$, $SE = .21$, $p = .001$. For the Chinese, being a bilingual was more positively associated with translation for father among first- than second-generation immigrants, whereas among the Koreans being bilingual was more positively associated with translation for father among second- than first-generation. Also, for the Chinese, a two-way interaction between immigrant status and fathers' education was found, $B = .12$, $SE = .06$, $p = .03$. There was a less negative relation between fathers' level of education and translation among first- than second-generation Chinese.

CONSEQUENCES OF LANGUAGE BROKERING/ TRANSLATING FOR PARENTAL RESPECT

To examine the consequences of adolescents' translating for parental respect within each ethnic group, regression analyses were conducted separately for respect for each parent. Youth and family characteristics were also included as covariates in each model. These analyses are presented in Table 13.6. Generational differences in the associations between translating and parental respect were also tested by estimating two-way interactions between generational status (described earlier) and frequency of translation for each parent.

TABLE 13.6

Relations Between Translation for Mother and Father, and Respect for Mother and Father (Unstandardized Coefficients & S.E. (B))

	Respect for Mother						Respect for Father					
	Chinese		Korean		Mexican		Chinese		Korean		Mexican	
	B	*S.E.*	*B*	*S.E.*	*B*	*S.E.*	*B*	*S.E.*	*B*	*S.E.*	*B*	*S.E.*
Immigrant (1st gen.)	.12	.09	−.10	.09	−.16	.16	.19	.11	.09	.10	−.30	.20
Eldest sibling	.04	.08	−.01	.08	.40	.15	.14	.09	.00	.09	.25	.18
No. of siblings	.04	.04	−.03	.05	.07	.05	.08	.05	−.08	.06	.10	.06
Age	−.08	.06	.11*	.06	−.09	.11	−.08	.07	.10	.06	−.14	.13
Gender (female)	.12	.07	.09	.07	.03	.14	.08	.08	.04	.08	−.01	.16
Bilingual	.06	.10	.17*	.08	.37*	.14	.10	.11	.21*	.09	.34*	.17
Mother's English fluency	.22**	.04	.13**	.04	.09	.07	—	—	—	—	—	—
Father's English fluency	—	—	—	—	—	—	.12*	.04	.11**	.04	.16*	.08
Mother's education	−.03	.02	−.01	.02	.01	.03	—	—	—	—	—	—
Father's education	—	—	—	—	—	—	.00	.03	−.05	.03	−.04	.04
Mother's age of arrival	.01	.01	.01	.01	−.00	.01	—	—	—	—	—	—
Father's age of arrival	—	—	—	—	—	—	.00	.01	−.01	.01	.02	.01
Single parent	.06	.11	−.24*	.10	−.07	.17	−.12	.15	−.43**	.13	−.41	.26
Translation for mother	.13**	.04	.05	.04	.17*	.07	—	—	—	—	—	—
Translation for father	—	—	—	—	—	—	.10	.05	.13**	.05	.15*	.08
	$N = 403$, $R^2 = .11$, $F(12, 390) = 4.13$, $p = .001$		$N = 405$, $R^2 = .08$, $F(12, 392) = 2.74$, $p = .001$		$N = 147$, $R^2 = .20$, $F(12, 134) = 2.75$, $p = .01$		$N = 386$, $R^2 = .07$, $F(12, 373) = 2.20$, $p = .001$		$N = 390$, $R^2 = .11$, $F(12, 377) = 3.71$, $p = .001$		$N = 135$, $R^2 = .15$, $F(12, 122) = 1.74$, $p = .07$	

$^{*}p < .05$. $^{**}p < .01$.

Respect for Mother

Among the Chinese, translation for mother was associated with adolescents' respect for mother. Also, as mothers' English fluency increased, youth's respect for mother was enhanced. For the Koreans, translation for mother was not associated with respect for mother. Of the characteristics associated with respect for mother among Koreans, being a bilingual youth and increases in adolescents' age and mothers' English fluency were related to more respect for mother, whereas living in a single-parent household was related to less respect. For the Mexicans, similar to what was found among the Chinese, as translation for mother increased, respect for mother was enhanced. Being bilingual was also related to more respect for mother. In addition, no generational differences were found among any of the ethnic groups in the association between translation for mother and respect for mother, $p > .05$.

Respect for Father

Among the Chinese, translation for father was only marginally ($p = .06$) related to adolescents' respect for father. Also, as fathers' English fluency increased, respect for father increased. Among the Koreans, translation for father was positively related to adolescents' respect for father. Also, being bilingual and increases in fathers' English fluency were positively associated with respect for father, whereas living in a single-parent household was negatively related to respect for father. For the Mexicans, similar to what was found for the Koreans, translation for father was related to more respect for father. Of the characteristics associated with respect for father, being bilingual and increases in fathers' English fluency were related to increases in respect for father. Finally, there were no generational differences in the association between translating and respect for either mother or father.

CONSEQUENCES OF BROKERING FOR ADOLESCENTS' PSYCHOLOGICAL ADJUSTMENT

To examine the consequences of adolescents' brokering for their psychological adjustment, similar regression analyses for adolescents' adjustment were conducted as for the outcome of parental respect. That is, for each ethnic group, regression analyses were conducted separately for the outcomes of internalizing and externalizing, also controlling for the youth and family characteristics previously described. These results are presented in Tables 13.7 and 13.8, respectively, for internalizing and externalizing.

TABLE 13.7
Relations Between Translation for Mother (First Half of Columns) and Father (Latter Half of Columns), and Adolescents' Internalizing Symptoms (Unstandardized Coefficients & S.E. (B))

	Adolescents' Internalizing											
	Chinese		*Korean*		*Mexican*		*Chinese*		*Korean*		*Mexican*	
	B	*S.E.*	*B*	*S.E.*	*B*	*S.E.*	*B*	*S.E.*	*B*	*S.E.*	*B*	*S.E.*
Immigrant (1st gen.)	.01	.04	–.10**	.04	.05	.07	.01	.04	–.09**	.04	.13	.07
Eldest sibling	–.05	.03	.02	.03	.01	.06	–.07*	.03	.02	.03	.04	.06
No. of siblings	.03	.02	.09**	.02	–.01	.02	.02	.02	.08**	.02	.01	.02
Age	–.01	.02	–.02	.02	–.01	.05	–.02	.02	–.01	.02	–.05	.05
Gender (female)	.05	.03	.11**	.03	.25**	.06	.04	.03	.11**	.03	.27**	.06
Bilingual	–.01	.04	–.02	.03	–.07	.06	–.03	.04	–.01	.03	–.04	.06
Mother's English fluency	–.02	.02	.01	.01	.03	.03	—	—	—	—	—	—
Father's English fluency	—	—	—	—	—	—	.02	.02	.01	.01	.02	.03
Mother's education	.01	.01	–.01	.01	.10	.01	—	—	—	—	—	—
Father's education	—	—	—	—	—	—	.01	.01	.01	.01	–.01	.01
Mother's age of arrival	.01	.01	.01	.03	–.01	.01	—	—	—	—	—	—
Father's age of arrival	—	—	—	—	—	—	.01	.01	.01	.01	–.01**	.01
Single parent	.05	.05	.08*	.04	.13	.08	.07	.05	.08	.05	.10	.09
Translation for mother	.05**	.02	.06**	.02	.02	.03	—	—	—	—	—	—
Translation for father	—	—	—	—	—	—	.07**	.02	.05**	.02	.02	.03
	$N = 422, R^2 = .06$, $F(12, 409) = 2.33$, $p = .001$		$N = 421, R^2 = .14$, $F(12, 408) = 5.42$, $p = .001$		$N = 156, R^2 = .15$, $F(12, 143) = 2.10$, $p = .02$		$N = 409, R^2 = .06$, $F(12, 396) = 2.19$, $p = .001$		$N = 406, R^2 = .12$, $F(12, 393) = 4.52$, $p = .001$		$N = 145, R^2 = .21$, $F(12, 132) = 2.94$, $p = .001$	

$^*p < .05$. $^{**}p < .01$.

TABLE 13.8

Relations Between Translation for Mother (First Half of Columns) and Father (Latter Half of Columns), and Adolescents' Externalizing Symptoms (Unstandardized Coefficients & S.E. (B))

	Adolescents' Externalizing											
	Chinese		*Korean*		*Mexican*		*Chinese*		*Korean*		*Mexican*	
	B	*S.E.*	*B*	*S.E.*	*B*	*S.E.*	*B*	*S.E.*	*B*	*S.E.*	*B*	*S.E.*
Immigrant (1st gen.)	–.04	.03	–.02	.03	.07	.06	–.03	.03	–.05	.03	.17**	.07
Eldest sibling	–.01	.03	–.03	.03	–.08	.06	–.02	.03	–.02	.03	–.05	.06
No. of siblings	–.00	.01	.03	.02	–.00	.02	–.01	.02	.03	.02	–.01	.02
Age	.01	.02	–.01	.02	–.01	.04	.00	.02	–.01	.02	–.04	.04
Gender (female)	–.05*	.02	–.02	.02	–.02	.05	–.05*	.02	–.03	.02	–.04	.05
Bilingual	–.01	.03	–.01	.03	–.09	.06	–.02	.03	–.01	.03	–.05	.05
Mother's English fluency	–.03*	.01	.00	.01	.05	.03	—	—	—	—	—	—
Father's English fluency	—	—	—	—	—	—	.01	.01	–.00	.01	.02	.03
Mother's education	.01	.01	–.00	.01	.01	.01	—	—	—	—	—	—
Father' education	—	—	—	—	—	—	.00	.01	.00	.01	–.01	.01
Mother's age of arrival	.00	.00	–.01	.00	–.00	.00	—	—	—	—	—	—
Father's age of arrival	—	—	—	—	—	—	.00	.00	.00	.00	–.01**	.00
Single parent	.05	.04	.13**	.04	.07	.07	.03	.04	.11**	.04	.05	.08
Translation for mother	.01	.01	.04**	.01	.01	.03	—	—	—	—	—	—
Translation for father	—	—	—	—	—	—	.02	.01	.03*	.01	–.02	.03
	$N = 422$, $R^2 = .05$, $F(12, 409) = 1.65$, $p = .08$		$N = 421$, $R^2 = .07$, $F(12, 408) = 2.41$, $p = .001$		$N = 156$, $R^2 = .07$, $F(12, 143) = .92$, $p = .53$		$N = 409$, $R^2 = .03$, $F(12, 396) = 1.01$ $p = .44$		$N = 406$, $R^2 = .05$, $F(12, 393) = 1.63$, $p = .08$		$N = 145$, $R^2 = .12$, $F(12, 132) = 1.43$, $p = .16$	

$*p < .05$. $**p < .01$.

Internalizing Symptoms Related to Translating for Mother

Among Chinese, as adolescents' translating for mother increased, their internalizing symptoms also increased. Among Koreans, similar to what was found among the Chinese, a positive association was found between translating for mother and internalizing symptoms. Additionally, among Koreans, being a female, living in a single-parent household, and increases in the number of siblings were related to higher levels of internalizing symptoms, whereas being first-generation was negatively related to internalizing symptoms. Among Mexicans, there was no association between translating for mother and adolescents' reports of their internalizing symptoms, but being a female was positively related to internalizing symptoms. No generational differences were found among any of the ethnic groups in the association between translating for mother and perceived internalizing symptoms.

Internalizing Symptoms Related to Translating for Father

For the Chinese, as translating for father increased, internalizing symptoms increased, net of all other factors, and being an eldest sibling was negatively associated with internalizing. For Koreans, similar to the findings for the Chinese, a positive association was found between translating for father and internalizing symptoms, net of all other factors. Also net of all other factors, being a female and increases in the number of siblings were positively related to internalizing symptoms, whereas being a first-generation immigrant was negatively related to internalizing symptoms. For the Mexicans, there was no association between translating for father and internalizing symptoms, but just as with Chinese and Koreans, females reported higher levels of internalizing symptoms, and as fathers' age of arrival in the United States increased, adolescents' internalizing symptoms decreased. No generational differences were found among any of the ethnic groups in the association between translating for father and perceived internalizing symptoms.

Externalizing Symptoms Related to Translating for Mother

Among Chinese, no association was found between translating for mother and adolescents' externalizing symptoms, but being a female and increases in mothers' English fluency were related to lower levels of externalizing, net of all other factors. For Koreans, a positive association between translating for mother and externalizing was found, and also living in a single-parent household was positively associated with higher levels of externalizing symptoms, net of all other factors. For Mexicans, no significant association between translating for mother and externalizing symptoms was found. Finally, there were no generational differences among any of the ethnic groups in the association between translating for mother and adolescents' externalizing symptoms.

Externalizing Symptoms Related to Translating for Father

Among Chinese, no association between translating for father and externalizing was found, but being a female was related to lower levels of externalizing, net of all other factors. Among Koreans, net of all other factors, a positive association between translating for father and externalizing was found. In addition, living in a single-parent household was positively related to higher levels of externalizing symptoms, net of all other factors. Among Mexicans, no significant association between translating for father and externalizing symptoms was found. However, net of all other factors, being a first-generation immigrant was associated with higher levels of externalizing symptoms, whereas increases in father's age of arrival in the United States was associated with lower levels of externalizing. Once again, no generational differences were found among any of the ethnic groups in the association between translating for father and externalizing symptoms.

BROKERING FOSTERS RESPECT FOR PARENTS

The main purpose of this study was to examine a very salient and important phenomenon among immigrant families involving the language brokering that youth provide for their parents. This study first addressed the prevalence and frequency of language brokering among a large, diverse sample of youth with immigrant parents, and then examined the characteristics of youth that are associated with higher levels of brokering. Ultimately, this study was interested in determining whether adolescents' language brokering has consequences for their relationships with parents, in terms of either diminishing or increasing their respect for parents, and for their psychological adjustment. This is the first large-scale, systematic study of the prevalence and consequences of youth's language brokering for their immigrant parents.

Brokering not only appears to be highly prevalent among adolescents with immigrant parents, it also seems to occur fairly frequently. A large majority (almost 84%) of first-generation immigrant youth have brokered for their parents at least once during their lifetime. Moreover, for each of the ethnic groups, first-generation youth broker more frequently for both parents than second-generation youth. Of the first-generation, Mexican youth report higher frequencies of brokering than Chinese, but not significantly more than Korean youth. Youth also broker more frequently for their mothers than fathers.

This study has revealed that the characteristics most consistently related to brokering for both mothers and fathers was parents' English fluency, followed by their education and age of immigration or arrival in the United States. Immigrant parents with higher English fluency and educational levels required less brokering from their adolescents, and parents who arrived in the United States at younger ages also required less brokering. The latter association may be due to the increased acculturation levels of those parents that have been in the United States for a greater number of years. Adolescents' immigrant status and bilingualism were also associated with translating for mothers and fathers, but somewhat less consistently than the parental characteristics previously mentioned. Because bilingualism is a component of language acculturation, its positive association with brokering is not surprising. This association was also found by Buriel et al. (1998) with Latino adolescents. However, *generational* differences were found in this association for translation for fathers such that among Koreans, being bilingual increased translation more so among second-generation youth than first-generation, whereas among Chinese, being bilingual increased translation more among first- than second-generation immigrants. Also, just as Buriel et al. (1998) found that among Latinos, females provided more brokering than males, in the current study, this was also found among the Mexicans and Chinese, regardless of the gender of the parent.

In looking at the consequences of brokering for adolescents' respect for parents, there is support for positive consequences in that translation is positively related to respect for mothers and fathers, net of other youth and family characteristics. Although this was found for both mothers and fathers among Mexican American youth, brokering was related to respect for father only among Korean American youth, and for mother only among Chinese American youth. Although adolescents' brokering responsibilities may create more opportunities for trust with both parents (McQuillan & Tse, 1995), the consequences of brokering for fathers may be more profound because of the roles that fathers have in Asian immigrant families. The Korean culture in particular may espouse more traditional authoritarian and disciplinarian roles for fathers than other Asian cultures. This traditional role for fathers also entails more emotional distance between themselves and their children, compared to mothers. When adolescents in these families are provided with brokering experiences with their fathers, the emotional distance between fathers and their children is perhaps diminished.

These underlying mechanisms for explaining how brokering impacts adolescents' respect for parents need to be examined in further studies. As argued earlier, when adolescents broker for parents, it may create more opportunities for communication and trust between adolescents and parents that may mediate the effects of brokering on parental respect. Additionally, as Zelizer (1985) discussed, adolescents may experience a sense of self-validation from being valued and needed by their parents. Through the process of brokering for parents, adolescents may also gain a deeper understanding of the impact of acculturation on their parents. These mediating mechanisms should be explored in further studies.

One limitation of the current study, though, is the difficulty of capturing the full extent of brokering through survey items. In her ethnographies and qualitative interviews, Orellana (2003) found that translation for parents is often "taken-for-granted household work" that youth and families are sometimes not conscious or aware of. Translating for parents is often a spontaneous activity so embedded in the everyday lives of immigrant families that it is often overlooked as being an important experience for children. This study attempted to address this problem by explicitly including in the instructions for respondents that translating includes "spoken or written words, phrases, or sentences." However, attempts to capture such experiences, and especially the frequency of its occurrence, through survey items may still result in underreporting. Perhaps the frequencies of brokering reported in this study represent a more conservative estimate of adolescents' brokering. Nonetheless, even as a conservative estimate, the frequencies of brokering reported in this study covary with other important factors, both family characteristics and adolescent outcomes that point to important avenues of future study. Finally, reports from parents or others (e.g., teachers) are also needed to address possible source variation when relying solely on adolescents' reports on all variables.

In examinations for whether brokering causes increased psychological symptoms for youth, brokering for mothers and fathers appears to be related to higher levels of internalization and externalization among Korean youth, whereas higher internalization was found among Chinese as translating for both mothers and fathers increased. Although it appears that youth from Mexican immigrant families are not identifying with parents at the expense of their own psychological well-being, this does appear to the be case among Korean youth, and somewhat the case among Chinese youth from immigrant families.

Children's contributions to the family are a relatively understudied area because they have not been regarded as significant to the functioning of families in the United States. The brokering provided by immigrant youth offers a striking example of how some children in the United States do make important contributions to the family. However, some clinical psychologists argue that parental reliance on children for family functioning may cause what they identify as "childhood parentification," or parent–child role reversal (Wells & Jones, 2000). This role reversal represents the child's premature identification with the parent's expectations and needs at the expense of the child's development. This role reversal may to some extent explain the elevation of internalizing and externalizing symptoms as brokering demands increase among Koreans and somewhat among Chinese. However, this explanation does not account for why we did not find negative consequences for brokering among the Mexican Americans. Perhaps brokering may be more normative for the latter group than the Asian immigrant groups, or there may not have been sufficient power for the Mexican Americans (due to small sample sizes) to detect smaller effect sizes.

CONCLUSIONS

This study helps to provide an understanding not only of the salience of children's contribution to their families in the form of brokering, but also of its consequences for parent–adolescent relationships and adolescent adjustment. The results suggest that the brokering provided by adolescents may provide opportunities for communication and contact with parents that may contribute to adolescents feeling trusted and needed by parents. Not only may brokering foster a greater trust and respect between adolescents and their immigrant parents, it may also be an important source of support for their parents that may help facilitate parents' acculturation to the host society. However, for some immigrant families, particularly Korean immigrants, this may come at the cost of the adolescents' own psychological well-being.

ACKNOWLEDGMENTS

This research was supported by a grant from the National Institutes of Health (NIH/NICHD) (R01 HD38949-02) awarded to Ruth K. Chao. The author thanks Dr. Thomas L. Hanson for his editing and assistance in data analyses, and also Dr. Inna Padmawidjaja for her assistance in running some of the analyses.

REFERENCES

Achenbach, T. M. (1991). *Manual for the Youth Self Report and 1991 profile*. Burlington, VT: University of Vermont.

Bowerman, C. E., & Bahr, S. J. (1973). Conjugal power and adolescent identification with parents. *Sociometry, 36*, 366–377.

Buriel, R., Perez, W., De Ment, T. L., Chavez, D. V., & Moran, V. R. (1998). The relationship of language brokering to academic performance, biculturalism, and self-efficacy among Latino adolescents. *Hispanic Journal of Behavioral Sciences, 20*, 283–297.

Chao, R., & Tseng, V. (2002). Parenting of Asians. In M. H. Bornstein (Series Ed.), *Handbook of parenting: Vol. 4, Social conditions and applied parenting* (2nd ed., pp. 59–93). Mahwah, NJ: Lawrence Erlbaum Associates.

Crouter, A. C., Head, M. R., Bumpas, M. F., & McHale, S. M. (2001). Household chores: Under what conditions do mothers lean on daughters. In A. Fuligni (Ed.), *Family obligation and assistance during adolescence: Contextual variations and developmental implications* (pp. 23–42). San Francisco: Jossey-Bass.

Fuligni, A. J., Yip, T., & Tseng, V. (2002). The impact of family obligation on the daily activities and psychological well-being of Chinese American adolescents. *Child Development, 73*, 302–314.

Goodnow, J. J. (1998). Beyond the overall balance: The significance of particular tasks and procedures for perceptions of fairness in distributions of household work. *Social Justice Research, 11*, 359–376.

Goodnow, J. J., & Delaney, S. (1989). Children's household work: Task differences, styles of assignment, and links to family relationships. *Journal of Applied Developmental Psychology, 10*, 209–226.

Goodnow, J. J., & Lawrence, J. A. (2001). Work contributions to the family: Developing a conceptual and research framework. In A. Fuligni (Ed.), *New directions for youth development: Theory, practice and research, Special issue on Family obligation and assistance during adolescence: Contextual variations and developmental implications* (pp. 5–22). San Francisco: Jossey-Bass.

Goodnow, J. J., & Warton, P. M. (1992). Understanding responsibility: Adolescents' views of delegation and follow-through within the family. *Social Development, 1*, 89–106.

Grosjean, F. (1982). *Life with two languages: An introduction to bilingualism*. Cambridge, MA: Harvard University Press.

Grusec, J. E., Goodnow, J. J., & Cohen, L. (1996). Household work and the development of concern for others. *Developmental Psychology, 32*, 999–1007.

McQuillan, J., & Tse, L. (1995). Child language brokering in linguistic minority communities: Effects on cultural interaction, cognition, and literacy. *Language and Education, 9*, 195–215.

Menjivar, C. (2000). *Fragmented ties: Salvadorian immigrant networks in America*. Berkeley, CA: University of California Press.

Olsen, L. (1988). *Crossing the schoolhouse border: Immigrant students and the California public schools: A California Tomorrow policy research report*. San Francisco: California Tomorrow.

Orellana, M. F. (2003). Responsibilities of children in Latino immigrant homes. In A. Fuligni (Ed.), *New directions for youth development: Theory, practice and research, special issue on social influences in the positive development of immigrant youth* (pp. 25–39). San Francisco, CA: Jossey-Bass.

Orellana, M. F., Dorner, L., & Pulido, L. (2003a). Accessing assets: Immigrant youth's work as family translators or "para-phrasers." *Social Problems, 50*, 505–524.

Orellana, M. F., Reynolds, J., Dorner, L., & Meza, M. (2003b). In other words: Translating or "para-phrasing" as a family literacy practice in immigrant households. *Reading Research Quarterly, 38*(1), 12–34.

Parke, R. D., Killian, C., Dennis, J., Flyr, M., McDowell, D., Simpkins, S., et al. (2005). Managing the external environment: The parent and child as active agents in the system. In L. Kucznyski (Ed.), *Handbook of the dynamics of parenting*. Thousand Oaks, CA: Sage.

Shannon, S. M. (1990). English in the barrio: The quality of contact among immigrant children. *Hispanic Journal of Behavioral Sciences, 12*, 256–276.

Tse, L. (1995). Language brokering among Latino adolescents: Prevalence, attitudes, and school performance. *Hispanic Journal of Behavioral Sciences, 17*, 180–193.

Tse, L. (1996a). Language brokering in linguistic minority communities: The case of Chinese- and Vietnamese-American students. *The Bilingual Research Journal, 20*, 485–498.

Tse, L. (1996b). Who decides?: The effects of language brokering on home–school communication. *The Journal of Education Issues of Language Minority Students, 16*, 225–234.

United States Census Bureau. (2002). *Coming to America: A profile of the nation's foreign born* (CENBR Publication No. CENBR/01-1). Washington, DC: U.S. Government Printing Office.

Valenzuela, A. (1999). Gender roles and settlement activities among children and their immigrant families. *American Behavioral Scientist, 42*, 720–742.

Vasquez, O. A., Pease-Alvarez, L., & Shannon, S. M. (1994). *Pushing boundaries: Language and culture in a Mexicano community*. New York: Cambridge University Press.

Wells, M., & Jones, R. (2000). Childhood parentification and shame-proneness: A preliminary study. *The American Journal of Family Therapy, 28*, 19–27.

Zelizer, V. A. (1985). *Pricing the priceless child: The changing social value of children*. New York: Basic Books.

14

Similarities and Differences Between First- and Second-Generation Turkish Migrant Mothers in Germany: The Acculturation Gap

Birgit Leyendecker
Axel Schölmerich
Banu Citlak
Ruhr University, Bochum, Germany

INTRODUCTION

The "homo migrans" exists as long as the "homo sapiens"; migration is as much part of the conditio humana as birth, reproduction, disease, and death. . . . Migrations as social processes are answers to more or less complex economical and ecological, social and cultural frameworks of existence.

—Bade (2000, translated by the author)

The economic disequilibrium between nations has led to large migration movements within Europe, specifically into Western Europe. Until the 1950s, most European countries were essentially countries of emigration. It took a long time to realize that these countries turned into targets of immigration as well. In the former West Germany of today, about one third of all children have a migration background. However, not until the year 2000 did Germany pass a law granting citizenship to children born in the country to parents who have been living there for at least 8 years. Many of the labor migrants who originally came with the intention to earn money and to return home as soon as possible were reluctant to realize that they were actually permanently staying in Germany. In particular, many labor migrants from Turkey did not acknowledge the fact that they were likely to stay in Germany and to see their children and grandchildren grow up there.

The failure to recognize Turkish migrants as a sizable, permanent, and growing part of Germany's population has been evident in all areas, especially within the school system. Much research focused on the situation of temporary "guest workers," on specific problem behaviors, especially of adolescents, on the lack of academic success, or on mental health issues see (Leyendecker, 2003). Research on Turkish children, the specific situation of their families, and parenting cognitions as well as practices still remains scarce.

In many aspects, the situation of migrant populations is similar in many countries. However, there are also distinct features unique to particular groups of migrants. Features concerning transnational exchange and reciprocity such as legal situation and immigration policy, religious distinctiveness, ties with the country of origin, family composition, and especially similarities and differences between each parent's length of stay in the host country may lead to difficulties if approached with a unified theory of acculturation. We propose that in order to understand children's acculturation processes, we need to pay closer attention to the generational status of each of their parents. Specifically, within the Turkish community of Germany, two types of acculturation processes can be distinguished. The first type is an "adaptation over generations model," which estimates that the more generations someone's ancestors have lived in a country, the more acculturated the individual is likely to be. For example, a child whose grandparents migrated from Turkey to Germany has parents who were born in Germany and grew up bilingually and biculturally. This child has parents who are likely to share similar experiences of socialization and acculturation due to growing up in Germany. Over the course of three generations, the ties to Turkey are likely to be less close. The second type can be described as an acculturation gap between parents. One parent may be born in Germany and the other parent may just recently have migrated into the country, typically by marriage. German immigration laws support this type of family structure. "Mixed generational status" compared to "joint generational status" may exert considerable influence on the developing child through socialization and acculturation experiences. This acculturation gap is likely to manifest itself in daily life, for instance, in regard to social networks or language proficiency. Furthermore, an increase in the probability of discrepancies between partners' childrearing cognitions and practices can be expected. Moreover, other factors such as living in relatively segregated Turkish neighborhoods may contribute to keeping Turkish culture and language a more palpable experience for a growing child, which leads to a quite different acculturation process.

Most theories of psychological acculturation agree in three considerations. First, acculturation is a process over time that can be described within a segment of the individual life span or throughout several generations. Second, acculturation involves change within both the migrant population and the host country population. Third, acculturation processes differ according to contextual and socioeconomic factors. In this chapter, we focus on the specific situation of Turkish migrants in Germany, as well as the ways in which the acculturation process is shaped by these contextual factors. Generational status of parents is employed as an important moderator.

The goals of this chapter are twofold. First, we want to describe the specific situation of migrant Turkish families in Germany. Second, we want to demonstrate the influence of generational status—"joint" and "mixed" among the parents—on mothers' acculturation. The chapter is divided into four sections. In the first section, we summarize some of the aspects of acculturation that deal with development across migrant generations. In the second section, the characteristics of migration to Germany are described, particularly concerning migration from Turkey to Germany and features unique to the Turkish minority. In the third section, we present data on first- and second-generation immigrant mothers, specifically on their acculturation orientation with regard to their partners' generational status. We close the chapter with some general conclusions and recommendations for future studies on relations among acculturation, parenting cognitions and practices, and child development. In particular, we point out that within some migrant communities, such as the Turkish community in Germany and in other West European countries, the acculturation processes will be increasingly diverse. A closer look at the generational status of each parent might present a key for our understanding of different acculturation venues and thus for understanding parenting and child development in this immigrant community. In particular, we emphasize the need to pay more attention to acculturation gaps between parents and on their possible impact on joint parenting cognitions and practices.

THE DEVELOPMENT OF ACCULTURATION ACROSS MIGRANT GENERATIONS

Much of our information on acculturation is based on migration to the New World, especially to the United States and Canada. Acculturation has been described as a process involving affective, behavioral, and cognitive components (Ward, 2001) as well as change over time (Sam, Kosic, & Oppedal, 2003). Change over time can be studied as development over the individual life span or over subsequent generations.

There is general agreement that the family is a critical arena for the study of processes of acculturation (Booth, Crouter, & Landale, 1997). Studies on migrant families have often focused on the so-called generation gap, including intergenerational conflicts that arise when parents and children are socialized not only into different worlds in a temporal sense but also into different cultures (Buriel & De Ment, 1997; Garcia Coll & Magnuson, 1997). For children of native parents, the difference between home culture and societal culture (Greenfield & Suzuki, 1998) depends exclusively on individual variation and on the speed of social change within a society. For children of foreign-born parents, however, this difference is enhanced by the actual discrepancy between the culture of origin and the culture of the country they live in. The home culture is likely to reflect the culture of origin, whereas the societal culture reflects the majority culture of the country they live in. In case of differences between parents with regard to their own degree of acculturation, the situation becomes more complicated. If parents have similar experiences of growing up in their home country and jointly moving to a host country, or of growing up in a host country as children of immigrant parents, we can assume that these experiences contribute to similar cultural values between partners. However, if parents' exposures to their ancestral culture as well as to their new host country differ, the home culture itself becomes multifaceted, and it is likely that children will experience conflicting messages. Given the likelihood that at least part of the culture of origin has petrified since the time of migration (Greenfield, 1994), chances are that even the perception of the culture of the country of origin differs considerably between first- and second-generation migrant parents. A second-generation mother or father has been raised by parents who take the culture of origin at the time of migration as a reference point. The migrants' perception of their culture of origin is likely to change as a result of the experience of living abroad (Sussman, 2000). The culture of origin is likely to change both as environments for child development as well as in their family attitudes and childrearing practices (Tapia Uribe, LeVine, & LeVine, 1994). Since the first migrants from Turkey came in the 1960s and 1970s, mostly from rural areas, changes in the availability of electricity, schools beyond Grade 5, media exposure, transportation, as well as a decline in the rate of fertility had tremendous influence on the life of children and their families (Akkaya, Özbek, & Sen, 1998). Thus, taking seriously the variability in acculturative status among parents may be an important step in better understanding the situation of children growing up in migrant families.

What Constitutes a Generation?

There appears to be general agreement that adults who migrate to a new host country are described as first-generation immigrants, children already born in the new country (or who migrated as infants or toddlers) are considered to be second-generation immigrants, and their offspring forms the third generation. Children who migrate while they are still attending school are sometimes categorized as the 1.5 generation. Acculturation research on parenting goals and practices is primarily limited to first- and second-generation migrants; on children and adolescents, it is extended to the third generation. For example, in their analyses of a population survey, Jensen and Chitose (1997) combined all native-born individuals with native-born parents under the heading "third generation." Beyond the third generation, people are generally considered as acculturated; according to their ancestral roots, they are associated with a minority or the majority group of the country they live in. There appears to be agreement that major challenges of the acculturation process are limited to the first two or three generations.

In the past two decades, researchers have paid increasing attention to bicultural orientations. Individuals can maintain their original culture as a frame of reference and at the same time can acquire the affective and behavioral components necessary to function competently in the host culture as well. A fully bicultural individual does not live in a world between two cultures but rather in both cultures, with a feeling of belonging to one as well as the other cultural community (Garcia Coll & Magnuson, 1997).

Generally speaking, acculturation is not a simple continuum from low to high (Escobar & Vega, 2000), and there is also evidence that generational status is not necessarily associated with a linear development of acculturation. Despite language deficiencies, foreign born, first-generation immigrant children in the United States may be more motivated and academically more successful or socioemotionally better adjusted when compared to second-generation children already born in the host country or even to their native counterparts (Fuligni, 1998; Phinney, Horenczyk, Liebkind, & Vedder, 2001; Rumbaut, 1995, 1997). Similarly, the religious practices of second-generation Turkish immigrants in Germany are not necessarily a continuation of those of the first generation. Manifold social and political discrimination and sometimes the lack of recognition of their religion by the majority society has turned a considerable part of second-generation Turks to orthodox Islam (Faist, 1999). Notwithstanding these nonlinear processes, we can assume that many of the stressful and uprooting aspects of migration—such as leaving family and friends, experiencing language deficiencies, unknown environment and social customs—are not valid for third-generation children anymore. Individuals who are descendants of people who migrated two generations ago share more similarities with their respective minority or majority group than with recent immigrants.

Marriages Between First- and Second-Generation Migrants

Defining the generational status of children becomes more difficult if their parents consist of mixed generational immigrants. This combination is likely to occur frequently if one or more of the following constraints apply: (1) marriage is the only legal way of entry for new immigrants, (2) migrant families prefer their children to marry someone "untainted" by a host culture perceived as negative, or (3) the home country is easily accessible, migrants stay in close contact with friends and family left behind, and are thus likely to find a partner within this group. We demonstrate in the next section that these three features fostering a combination of first- and second-generation immigrant parents apply for many members of the Turkish community in Germany. The German immigration policy has unintentionally supported this development. Aside from those applying for political asylum and a small group of people who gain entry through their special occupational skills, nowadays family reunion represents the only legal way for Turkish migration to Germany. With the exception of children who were reared in Turkey and joined their parents in Germany within the legal age of 16, most family reunions are marriages. The exact numbers are not available for the entire country, but regional counts in Bavaria and Berlin show that between 50% and 75% of all Turkish men in Germany marry a woman who grew up in Turkey (Bericht der Sachverständigenkommission, 2000; Strassburger, 2000). Regardless of whether these are arranged marriages or love marriages, they are likely to have a difficult start because partners often have very little time to get to know each other before the wedding date (Bericht der Sachverständigenkommission, 2000). In addition, we can assume that partners in these "mixed" marriages have very different socialization experiences as well as an acculturation gap. A closer look at the influence of the generational status of each partner is thus important for understanding diverse pathways of acculturation.

TURKISH MIGRANTS IN GERMANY

Migration to Germany

Immigrants in Germany are from all socioeconomic strata, yet the majority have a low socioeconomic status. On average, they are much younger than the German population. In 2003, only 6% of those with a foreign passport were 65 years of age or older (Bundesamt, 2003). Because the German demographic census does not keep track of ethnic background, there are only estimates about the number of people in Germany with a migration background. It is estimated that between one quarter and one third of all children in the former West Germany have a least one foreign-born parent or do not speak German as their first language. In a representative study on 15-year-old students, 27% of those living in the former West Germany had at least one parent not born in Germany (Baumert, 2001). These numbers are likely to be higher for younger children because disproportionately many people migrate as young adults. In addition, foreign-born women tend to have more children than German women (Bericht der Sachverständigenkommission, 2000). The increasing segregation in many neighborhoods of the bigger cities in Germany has resulted in local switches of the minority and majority population, and many preschools and elementary schools have no or only few children who speak German as their first language. Parallel to other countries, the enormous demographic transformation in Germany is most evident for the younger age groups.

By the end of 2003, 7.3 million people with foreign citizenship lived in Germany (Bundesamt, 2003). Roughly one quarter were EU citizens who could live and work anywhere within the EU, and another quarter (1.9 million) were Turkish migrants in addition to an unknown number of people with Turkish ancestry but with German citizenship. They form the single largest minority group; 26.5% of this group is 18 years of age or younger (Bundesamt, 2003). Specific German immigration laws provide easy access to German citizenship for all East Europeans with German or Jewish ancestry, and between the years 1990 and 2003, 2.3 million East Europeans with German ancestry as well as 180,000 East European Jewish migrants moved to Germany (Bundesamt, 2003). The acquisition of German citizenship, however, remained rather complicated for Turkish citizens until immigration laws were changed in 2000. Now, adults legally living in Germany for 8 years, as well as their descendants, have the right to German citizenship.

The change of citizenship was not only legally difficult but represented an emotional problem for many Turks as well. In contrast to U.S. citizenship, which is highly coveted by migrants in the United States, many Turkish migrants preferred a visa similar to the U.S. green card. Only Kurdish migrants who are not emotionally attached to the Turkish state readily applied for German citizenship. Because dual citizenship for adults is not allowed, to forfeit Turkish citizenship is a difficult step for many migrants and conflicts with loyalty to Turkey and with the plans of returning to Turkey at some point in the future. However, this restriction changed in the year 2005 as the Turkish government, which strives to become a member of the European Union, has encouraged Turks to acquire German citizenship.

Migration From Turkey to Germany

In 1955, Germany—just like some other Northwest European countries—started to recruit temporary laborers, the so-called "guest workers," first from Italy, Spain, Portugal, Greece, and the former Yugoslavia, and in the early 1960s also from Turkey. By 1973, when the recruitment stopped, the first four countries had become members of the European Union. Two reasons worked as an incentive for these groups of people to consider a return migration. The economic situation in their home countries improved considerably, and as citizens of the EU they could move back and forth freely. By contrast, Turkish migrants still faced economic uncertainty on their return, and, in addition, immigration policy did not allow them to reenter the German labor market once they left the country for more than a vacation. Thus, many men and women had their own families move to Germany instead, and they kept postponing the return to Turkey. This second phase of immigration started in the 1970s and resulted in an increase of Turks entering Germany rather than in the anticipated decrease. In 1980, Turkey experienced a military coup that triggered a third wave of immigration to Germany as political refugees, primarily Kurds, sought political asylum in Germany. A representative survey among the Turkish population living in North Rhine-Westphalia, the largest German state, revealed that by the year 2000, the original labor migrants ("guest workers") made up less than 14% of the population, 22% were born in Germany, and the majority came to Germany to unite with family, either to live with their parents or for marriage (Zentrum für Türkeistudien, 2000).

Aside from the so-called marriage migration, two other features characterize a large part of the Turkish community in Germany—their lower schooling when compared to other immigrant samples, and the loyalty and close ties to Turkey and to Turkish culture.

Academic Achievement

Beyond being a key indicator of the socioeconomic status (Hoff, Laursen, & Tardif, 2002), academic achievement presents an important context variable for acculturation inasmuch as it is an indicator of participation in the host society. In the case of Turkish migrants, acquiring a good education presents a high value, and an academically successful child raises the reputation and prestige of the entire family (Citlak, Leyendecker, Schölmerich, Harwood, & Driessen, 2005). The expectations of Turkish parents for their children have even been described as unrealistically high within the Turkish community in Germany (Nauck, 1994; Nauck & Diefenbach, 1997). Many of these parents, however, lack the knowledge or skills that would enable them to actively support their children's academic career. Even though Turks started to migrate to Germany in great numbers in the 1970s, both the German government as well as many migrants from Turkey held on to the idea of a temporary migration. They envisioned their children's future in Turkey, and both the German school administration as well as many parents considered investing into the German language and culture as futile. Aside from language barriers, many Turkish parents had little or no experience with formal schooling in their own childhood and were unfamiliar with the school system. Most Turkish migrants came from remote rural areas, and in contrast to the other migrants, they often had poor schooling. In rural Turkey, schools beyond Grade 5 were often not available at that time. In addition, the German school system is complicated and differs from the Turkish school system. Although exact numbers are not available, the academic career of many immigrant youngsters was also impeded by either moving back and forth between Germany and Turkey or by living with relatives in Turkey and moving to Germany as adolescents while they were still minors who have the right to be reunited with their families. Some Turkish children, especially girls (Karakasoglu-Aydin, 2001) are academically very successful, yet the majority of these children tend to be less successful when compared to German children and other migrant groups (Kristen, 2003). Studies show that Turkish children's lack of academic success can be attributed to their parents' lack of schooling rather than to their culture of origin. The predominantly low schooling success contributes to stereotypes about this particular group of migrants (Baumert, 2001; Kristen, 2003). Today, local school governments have begun to pay closer attention to the specific needs of migrant children, yet at the same time, their situation has deteriorated because they are more likely to live in isolated neighborhoods and to attend highly segregated schools.

Neighborhood Segregation

The tendency to live in ethnically segregated quarters may facilitate the familiarization process on arrival. The downside of such segregated living quarters is that children are likely to attend schools where no or only a few children speak German as their first language and where the learning process is slowed down considerably. Over time, many Germans have either moved out, or they have managed to enroll their children in schools in other neighborhoods. Although part of the population prefers to live in close proximity to friends and especially to relatives (Borck, 1999), the neighborhood segregation is chosen less voluntarily by others. These neighborhoods are often in the less preferred areas of a city where rents are affordable and landlords are willing to rent to foreigners. Within and in proximity to these areas, Turkish businesses are likely to flourish and to provide employment. These businesses often present a niche for people who are more or less excluded from the German job market either because their work and language skills are considered inadequate or because German employees are preferred.

Close Ties to Turkey

The cheap fares for buses and airplanes, as well as the long vacation for workers in Germany, have supported close ties to friends and relatives in Turkey. In addition, the enormous strides made in technology and communication enables people to live in a Turkish enclave in Germany and to choose from a large selection of Turkish TV channels, newspapers, and radio stations. In combination with a predominantly Turkish neighborhood, Turks in Germany are able to hear, speak, read, and write only Turkish, to shop in Turkish stores, to attend meetings of political organizations and voluntary organizations transplanted from Turkey, to have Turkish driving lessons, and to join a Turkish gym. For those who have acquired bilingual and bicultural skills, completed German schools, and who either through work, neighborhood, or friends have contact with the German community, the exclusive Turkish living style might be less attractive. For those, however, who are first-generation migrants, and who are unemployed or employed in businesses catering exclusively to the Turkish community, this version of globalization facilitates a retreat into the migrant variant of Turkish culture and places adolescents at risk of losing their German language skills once they have left school. Because German language skills are paramount for advancing up the social ladder in Germany, a retreat into the virtual and factual Turkish cultural enclave increases the danger of failure. German language skills acquired in Turkey prior to migration are a rare exception. Thus, living in a Turkish environment offers recent migrants little opportunity to learn the German language and to get into contact with the surrounding society. Although families with two second-generation parents often struggle to maintain the Turkish language, the influence of one parent who speaks and understands almost exclusively Turkish and who lives in a Turkish cultural enclave is likely to have an impact on his or her own as well as on the children's social networks and on their access to the surrounding society. Reading books to children, for example, promotes the development of their language skills as well as their later literacy skills (Arnold & Doctoroff, 2003). Bilingual parents can read German books to their children or translate simple picture books, whereas a parent who speaks exclusively Turkish only has limited means of obtaining children's books.

In summary, globalization is not only evident on the economic level but on the cultural level as well. The possibility to virtually live in Turkey and to hear and speak only Turkish and to choose from a wide variety of Turkish TV programs, radio stations, and newspapers is a new development of the 1990s and is likely to keep Turkish culture a primary influence. In combination with segregated neighborhoods and perceived cultural and religious differences to the majority society, Turkish islands are no longer a temporary phenomenon. Instead, they are rather likely to become firmly established ways of living for part of the migrant community, especially for those who prefer marriages with partners who grew up in Turkey. In the next section, we give an example for the differing acculturation orientation of first- and second-generation mothers with regard to their partners' generational status.

JOINT GENERATION AND "MIXED" GENERATION: THE RELATION BETWEEN MOTHERS' CHOICE OF PARTNERS AND MEASURES OF ACCULTURATION

Our study addressed the need for research on normative processes of cultural change following migration by examining the development of acculturation among first- and second-generation Turkish migrant mothers in the Bochum area of Germany. Compared to other migratory populations, there is a higher tendency of men and women of Turkish descent to find a partner from Turkey or at least to marry someone from the Turkish community. Additionally, it is characteristic for the population to have complete families rather than single motherhood, and mothers are typically not employed. The latter is not only supported by a conservative role model within Turkish society (Gümen, Herwartz-Emden, & Westphal, 2000; Kagitcibasi & Sunar, 1997) but by traditional factors of German society as well. The tax system favors one-wage-earner families over two-wage-earner families. Free health insurance for spouses and children is the rule for one-wage-earner families. Moreover, a parent who takes a 3-year leave of absence after the birth of each child is financially supplemented by the government, whereas day care for children below the age of 3 is still scarce. As a result, the number of employed mothers of young children in Germany is very low in comparison to other

European countries and to the United States. For Turkish women, finding a job is difficult, especially for the more recent immigrants who sometimes do not have a working permit. Even if they do, their job training as well as language skills often do not match the demands of the German job market (Herwartz-Emden & Westphal, 1997). However, participation in the job market is not only important as a source of income, but it also offers the chance of getting into contact with the surrounding society. Mothers who have little contact outside their family and neighborhood are less likely to become acculturated.

Sample

Our sample consisted of 61 first-generation and 31 second-generation migrant mothers from Turkey. We report only on the 57 mothers for whom complete data on the acculturation measures are available. A parent was defined as first generation if he or she had migrated to Germany at the age of 15 or older. Second-generation mothers and fathers were either born in Germany or moved to Germany before they entered first grade. They were all children of laborers who were recruited to Germany before 1973. Overall, 28 mothers and 28 fathers were first- and the other 29 mothers and 29 fathers were second-generation immigrants.

First- and Second-Generation Mothers

Mothers' mean age was 27 years (*SD* = 5) for the first generation and 28 years (*SD* = 4) for the second generation. Fathers were several years older, with a mean age of 33 years (*SD* = 9) of those married to a first-generation mothers and 32 years (*SD* = 5) of those married to a second-generation mother. On average, first-generation mothers had 7 years of education (*SD* = 3), and their partners had 9 years of education (*SD* = 2). Second-generation mothers who went to school in Germany had 11 years of education (*SD* = 2), and their partners 10 years (*SD* = 2). Three mothers in the first generation and 5 mothers in the second generation were employed, mostly in part-time jobs. On average, they worked 6.3 hrs. per week (first generation) and 20.6 hrs. per week (second generation). All mothers had at least one child between the ages of 18 and 35 months. All partners were of Turkish descent.

Marriage Migration

Three first-generation women came to Germany with their partners to seek political asylum, and 5 women moved to Germany to be reunited with their parents. As mentioned earlier, to be reared in Turkey and to move to Germany shortly before they reach the age of 16 is not uncommon for children, especially for those whose parents belong to the group of laborers who were recruited before 1973 and who were planning only a temporary stay in Germany. All of these five mothers married a husband who grew up in Turkey as well. The other 20 first-generation women had moved to Germany for marriage. Twelve married a second-generation partner, and the other 8 a partner who grew up in Turkey but migrated to Germany as an adolescent to be reunited with his parents. In sum, aside from the three couples who gained entry through political asylum, 25 couples were composed of one partner who had at least a permanent resident visa and another partner who gained entry through marriage with this person. The majority of the second-generation mothers (n = 17) were married to a second-generation immigrant as well, and the other 12 had married someone from Turkey. One first-generation mother was widowed, one second-generation mother was separated from her husband, and all others were married and living with their partner. In sum, 57% of the first-generation mothers as well as 41% of the second-generation mothers were married to a first-generation father. More than half of the couples (37 out of 57) can be classified as marriage migration inasmuch as one partner lived in Turkey up to the point of marriage with a partner who had at least a permanent resident visa in Germany.

Measuring Acculturation

Acculturation can be defined as "the processes of change in artifacts, customs, and beliefs that result from the contact of societies with different cultural traditions" (The New Encyclopedia Britannica, 1996, p. 57). Involvement in one culture does not require a reduction in involvement in the other culture. Instead, researchers have increasingly emphasized that involvement in the host culture and the culture of origin should be studied as separate phenomena and thus on separate scales (Berry, 1994; Cortes, Rogler, & Malgady, 1994; Garcia Coll & Magnuson, 1997; Phinney, 1990; Rogler, 1994; Szapocznik, Kurtines, & Fernandez, 1980). In this study, we adapted a bicultural measure created by Cortes et al. (1994) originally for Puerto Rican populations. This instrument consists of 21 and 22 items, respectively, that assess separately the individual's orientation toward Turkish and German cultures. The instrument was designed with a 4-point Likert-type scale ranging from *not at all* (1) to *very much* (4). The questions were corresponding: "How much do you enjoy Turkish TV programs" was matched by a question about the enjoyment of German TV programs.

Results

Acculturation Among First- and Second-Generation Mothers

Preliminary exploration of the data revealed a normal unskewed distribution. The Turkish part of the scale and the German part of the scale were uncorrelated, both for the combined sample as well as within each subsample (first- and second-

TABLE 14.1
Involvement in Turkish and German Culture by Parents' Generation Status

Mean Involvement in	*Parents' Generational Status*				
	M1/F1	*M1/F2*	*M2/F1*	*M2/F2*	$F_{(3,53)}$
Turkish culture	3.24	3.26	2.99	2.79	5.0, $p = .004$
German culture	2.31	2.56	2.97	3.05	11.52, $p = .001$

Note. M1 = first-generation mother; F1 = first-generation father; M2 = second-generation mother; F2 = second-generation father.

generation mothers). This confirms the assumption that the two scales are indeed independent of each other and that involvement in one culture does not necessarily affect the involvement in the other culture. A distribution of participants according to the much-used new culture by old culture cross tabulation suggested by Berry (1994) is not appropriate for these data because the mean differences were relatively small. A mean split would have labeled people who do not differ much on the measure as assimilated or integrated. More interesting, however, are the differences between the first- and the second-generation samples. The first-generation mothers were significantly more involved in Turkish culture when compared to the second-generation mothers, $M = 3.25$, $SD = .36$; $M = 2.87$, $SD = .42$, respectively, $F(1, 56) = 13.3, p < .001$. Second-generation mothers were significantly more likely to be involved in German culture when compared to the first-generation mothers, $M = 3.01$, $SD = .40$; $M = 2.42$, $SD = .41$, respectively, $F(1, 56) = 31.0, p < .001$.

Generational Status

In a next step, we looked at the effects of generational status on measures of acculturation. We had a total of four different combinations: Sixteen first-generation mothers had married a first-generation husband, 12 a second-generation husband, 12 mothers of the second-generation were married to a first-generation husband, and another 17 had married someone from the second-generation as well. As shown in Table 14.1, first-generation women married to a first-generation partner were least likely to be involved in German culture, and those married to second-generation partners were most likely to be involved in German culture.

THE ACCULTURATION GAP

In Germany, research on acculturation of the Turkish population is still scarce and to our knowledge, no one has studied the effects of the acculturation gap between parents. Our data show that the choice of partner is likely to influence mothers' acculturation, but the data are incomplete inasmuch as data from fathers were not assessed when we started the data collection in 2001. At that time, we were not aware of the possible implication of a joint or mixed generational status of partners. Today, however, we assume that there are two reasons to take a closer look at the generational status of each parent and the possible acculturation gap between parents. First, we assume that this has implications for our understanding of broad acculturation orientations within the Turkish community. Second, we assume that for the study of child development among migrant communities, we need to pay closer attention to parenting goals and practices with regard to each parent's acculturation experience.

Life Satisfaction: Differences Between First- and Second-Generation Mothers

There appears to be general agreement that the Turkish community is very heterogeneous with regard to acculturation and bicultural competencies (Bericht der Sachverständigenkommission, 2000). Despite adversities such as their parents' low socioeconomic status or the plans for return migration, and a school system that was not prepared to deal with migrants, a small number of second-generation children are academically and/or economically quite successful. They became members of the parliament, teachers, professors, doctors, and lawyers, and numerous small and large businesses have been founded by the offspring of the original labor migrants (Zentrum für Türkeistudien, 2004). The economic and/or academic success of these migrants should contribute to a higher life satisfaction when compared to migrants who are less successful.

We found large differences between first- and second-generation mothers with regard to their life satisfaction in Germany. These differences were also reported by the interviewers who visited the mothers in their homes at three points in time and who gained insight into diverse aspects of their life. Overall, we found the second generation to be well adjusted and content with their life. Even though most women were not working at this point in time, all but one had finished school and almost half ($n = 13$) of these mothers had acquired the Abitur, the German university entrance exam. When asked to rate overall life satisfaction in Germany and the assumed life satisfaction in Turkey, second-generation mothers were more satisfied with their life in Germany. In comparison to the first-generation mothers, they were less likely to assume that their life would be better if they could live in Turkey (Table 14.2).

The differences between first- and second-generation mothers for the question regarding expected life satisfaction in Turkey reflect the longing of first-generation women to be back in Turkey. A sizable number of first-generation mothers were completely isolated (Leyendecker, Schoelmerich, Citlak, & Harwood, 2005) and under close supervision of their husbands' family (Schoelmerich, Leyendecker, Harwood, Citlak, & Miller, 2005). The generational status of partners only mattered in their satisfaction with life in Germany, not at all for the ori-

TABLE 14.2
Life Satisfaction

	Parents' Generational Status				
Question	*M1/F1*	*M1/F2*	*M2/F1*	*M2/F2*	$F_{(3,53)}$
I would be more content living in my country of origin	1.88	1.67	3.58	3.53	23.55, $p = .001$
I am quite content with living in Germany	2.44	1.83	1.67	1.59	3.05, $p = .03$

Note. Mothers were asked to rate these answers 1 = *I fully agree* to 4 = *I fully disagree.* M1 = first-generation mother; F1 = first-generation father; M2 = second-generation mother; F2 = second-generation father.

entation toward their country of origin, which was solely dependent on their own generational status.

Parents' Acculturation Experience

Suarez-Orozco and Suarez-Orozco (2001) found that children of parents who maintained a voice of authority while encouraging them to achieve bicultural competencies had the best chances to take advantage of the opportunities available in the host culture. For the development of bicultural competencies, parents play a key role for their young children as they are the ones who provide pathways to the culture of the majority society.

Parents with a mixed generational status have to deal with more challenges than parents with joint generational status. When they start their new life together, their daily life can be described by the asymmetrical experiences of the two partners. In all probability, the parent who grew up in Germany speaks German, has a larger social network, has his or her family close by, and has at least some access to the majority society. This acculturation gap is even enhanced by a socialization gap. Migrants tend to hold on and to preserve culture from the time of departure, whereas the parent who grew up in Turkey has been socialized in a Turkish culture different from the one in the 1960s. All these factors serve to increase the likelihood that parents have diverse childrearing goals and practices and convey diverse messages to their children. These differences between parents have the potential to compromise their chances to maintain a joint voice of authority.

In combination with segregated neighborhoods and the possibility to virtually live in Turkey, the development of bicultural competencies by the first-generation mothers as well as by their children might be impaired. Several first-generation mothers in our study had made remarkable efforts to learn German, to communicate with their children's teachers, and to encourage their children's involvement with the majority society (e.g., by enrolling them in sport teams). The large majority of the first-generation mothers, however, spoke almost no German and had little contact outside of the Turkish community. For example, when asked about her experiences of discrimination, a first-generation mother who married a second-generation father answered that other people from the Turkish community made fun of her regional dialect. The interviewer repeated the question and asked about experiences of discrimination with Germans. She stated that she could not answer the question because she had no experiences with Germans.

Recent developments suggest that an acculturation gap might also contribute to weaken the strength of Turkish families. Turkish culture has frequently been described as collectivistic and family oriented (Kagitcibasi, 1996; Nauck & Kohlmann, 1999; Pfluger-Schindlbeck, 1989). This strength, however, requires that members of the family share similar norms and values. The sociologist Kelek (2005) points out that about half of the marriages with a partner who grew up in Turkey are arranged marriages, often with a relative and often against the woman's will. In recent years, the break-up of arranged marriages has sometimes led to violent deaths of the women by their male relatives (Gashi, 2005; Kelek, 2005). The anthropologist Schiffauer (2001, 2005) points to the marginalized position of a group of Turkish males who are economically less successful than females in their family. By trying to revitalize ancient traditions from rural villages in Turkey, they believe that they are fortifying the family and the family honor with these killings. From the perspective of an acculturation gap, however, it can be argued that marriages between unequal partners, particularly arranged marriages, have the potential to weaken migrant Turkish families. The increased break-up of these partnerships, as well as the eruptions of the sometimes deadly violence, indicate that these families are potentially at risk.

Among immigrant groups, there have always been parents with a "mixed" generational status. New, however, is the large number of young men and women among the Turkish community who marry someone from their parents' country. Future research on parenting and child development among Turkish migrants in Germany needs to pay more attention to the generational status of both parents. In order to gain more insight into a possible impact of an acculturation gap between parents, research that includes both the mother and father, as well as information on the background of their marriages, is needed.

REFERENCES

Akkaya, C., Özbek, Y., & Sen, F. (1998). *Länderbericht Türkei* [Report on Turkey]. Darmstadt: Primus.

Arnold, D. H., & Doctoroff, G. L. (2003). The early education of socioeconomically disadvantaged children. *Annual Review of Psychology, 54*, 517–545.

Bade, K. J. (2000). *Europa in Bewegung: Migration vom späten 18. Jahrhundert bis zur Gegenwart* [Europe in motion: Migration from the late 18th century until present]. München: Beck.

Baumert, J. (Ed.). (2001). *PISA 2000. Basiskompetenzen von Schülern und Schülerinnen im internationalen Vergleich.* Opladen: Leske und Budrich.

Bericht der Sachverständigenkommission. (2000). *Familien ausländischer Herkunft in Deutschland. Leistungen, Belastungen, Herausforderungen* (6. Familienbericht) [Migrant families in Germany. Achievement, strains, challenges (6th Report on Families)]. *Berlin: Bundesministerium für Familien, Senioren, Frauen und Jugend.*

Berry, J. W. (1994). Acculturative stress. In W. J. Lonner & R. S. Malpass (Eds.), *Psychology and culture* (pp. 211–216). Boston, MA: Allyn & Bacon.

Booth, A., Crouter, A. C., & Landale, N. S. (Eds.). (1997). *Immigration and the family: Research and policy on U.S. immigrants*. Mahwah, NJ: Lawrence Erlbaum Associates.

Borck, C. (1999). Kurdinnen in der Stadt—Stadtaneignung und Wohnortwahl kurdischer Migrantinnen und Migranten in Berlin [Kurdish women in the city—appropriation of the city and choices of Kurdish migrants in Berlin]. In NAVEND (Ed.), *Kurdinnen in der Bundesrepublik Deutschland. Ein Handbuch* (pp. 231–246). Bonn: NAVEND Zentrum für Kurdische Studien.

Bundesamt, S. (2003). *Ausländische Bevölkerung im Bundesgebiet* [Foreign-born population in the federal republic]. Statistisches Bundesamt Deutschland. Retrieved February 2005, from the World Wide Web: www.destatis.de/basis/d/

Buriel, R., & De Ment, T. (1997). Immigration and sociocultural change in Mexican, Chinese, and Vietnamese families. In A. Booth, A. C. Crouter, & N. Landale (Eds.), *Immigration and the family* (pp. 165–200). Mahwah, NJ: Lawrence Erlbaum Associates.

Citlak, B., Leyendecker, B., Schölmerich, A., Harwood, R. L., & Driessen, R. (2005). *Long-term socialization goals of Turkish migrant and German mothers*. Manuscript submitted for publication.

Cortes, D. E., Rogler, L. H., & Malgady, R. G. (1994). Bicultuarity among Puerto Rican adults in the United States. *American Journal of Community Psychology, 22*, 707–721.

Escobar, J. I., & Vega, W. A. (2000). Commentary: Mental health and immigration's AAA: Where are we and where do we go from here? *The Journal of Nervous and Mental Diseases, 188*, 736–740.

Faist, T. (1999). Developing transnational social spaces: The Turkish-German example. In L. Pries (Ed.), *Migration and transnational social spaces* (pp. 37–72). Aldershot: Ashgate.

Fuligni, A. J. (1998). The adjustment of children from immigrant families. *Current Directions in Psychological Science, 7*, 99–103.

Garcia Coll, C., & Magnuson, K. (1997). The psychological experience of immigration: A developmental perspective. In A. Booth, A. C. Crouter, & N. Landale (Eds.), *Immigration and the family: Research and policy on U.S. immigrants* (pp. 91–132). Mahwah, NJ: Lawrence Erlbaum Associates.

Gashi, H. (2005). *Mein Schmerz trägt Deinen Namen. Ein Ehrenmord in Deutschland* [My pain is marked by your name. Murder in the name of honor]. Berlin: Rowohlt.

Greenfield, P. M. (1994). Independence and interdependence as developmental scripts: Implications for theory, research, and practice. In P. M. Greenfield & R. R. Cocking (Eds.), *Cross-cultural roots of minority development* (pp. 1–37). Hillsdale, NJ: Lawrence Erlbaum Associates.

Greenfield, P. M., & Suzuki, L. K. (1998). Culture and human development: Implications for parenting, education, pediatrics, and mental health. In I. E. Sigel & K. A. Renninger (Eds.), *Handbook of child psychology* (5th ed., Vol. 4, pp. 1059–1109). New York: Wiley.

Gümen, S., Herwartz-Emden, L., & Westphal, M. (2000). Vereinbarkeit von Beruf und Familie als weibliches Selbstkonzept [Compatibility of career and family as a female self-concept]. In L. Herwartz-Emden (Ed.), *Einwandererfamilien: Geschlechterverhältnisse, Erziehung und Akkulturation* (pp. 207–232). Osnabrück: Rasch.

Herwartz-Emden, L., & Westphal, M. (1997). *Arbeitsmigrantinnen aus der Türkei in der Bundesrepublik Deutschland. Zwischen Unterdrückung und Emanzipation* [Female Turkish labor migrants in the Federal Republic of Germany. Between oppression and liberation]. Hannover: Niedersächsische Landeszentrale für politische Bildung.

Hoff, E., Laursen, B., & Tardif, T. (2002). Socioeconomic status and parenting. In M. H. Bornstein (Ed.), *Handbook of parenting* (2nd ed., Vol. 2, pp. 231–252). Mahwah, NJ: Lawrence Erlbaum Associates.

Jensen, L., & Chitose, Y. (1997). Immigrant generations. In A. Booth, A. C. Crouter, & N. Landale (Eds.), *Immigration and the family* (pp. 47–61). Mahwah, NJ: Lawrence Erlbaum Associates.

Kagitcibasi, C. (1996). *Family and human development across cultures*. Mahwah, NJ: Lawrence Erlbaum Associates.

Kagitcibasi, C., & Sunar, D. (1997). Familie und Sozialisation in der Türkei [Family and socialization in Turkey]. In B. Nauck & U. Schönpflug (Eds.), *Familien in verschiedenen Kulturen* (pp. 145–161). Stuttgart: Enke.

Karakasoglu-Aydin, Y. (2001). Kinder aus Zuwanderungsfamilien im Bildungssystem [Migrant children and the education system]. In H. Böttcher, K. Klemm, & T. Rauschenbach (Eds.), *Bildung und Soziales in Zahlen. Statistisches Handbuch zu Daten und Trends im Bildungsbereich* (pp. 273–302). Weinheim: Beltz.

Kelek, N. (2005). *Die fremde Braut. Ein Bericht aus dem Inneren des türkischen Lebens in Deutschland* [The foreign bride. A report from the heart of everyday Turkish life in Germany]. Koeln: Kiepenheuer & Witsch.

Kristen, C. (2003). Ethnische Unterschiede im deutschen Schulsystem [Ethnic differences in the German school system]. *Aus Politik und Zeitgeschehen, 21–22*, 26–32.

Leyendecker, B. (2003). Die frühe Kindheit in Migrantenfamilien [Early childhood in migrant families]. In H. Keller (Ed.), *Handbuch der Kleinkindforschung* (3rd ed., pp. 385–435). Bern: Huber.

Leyendecker, B., Schoelmerich, A., Citlak, B., & Harwood, R. L. (2005). *The social network of first and second generation migrant mothers in Germany*. Paper presented at the International Association of Cross-Cultural Psychology, San Sebastian, Spain.

Nauck, B. (1994). Bildungsverhalten in Migrantenfamilien [Educational achievement and migrant families]. In P. Bücher (Ed.), *Kindliche Lebenswelten, Bildung und innerfamiliale Beziehungen. Materialien zum 5. Familienbericht* (Vol. 4, pp. 107–141). München: Deutsches Jugendinstitut.

Nauck, B., & Diefenbach, H. (1997). Bildungsbenachteiligung von Kindern aus Familien ausländischer Herkunft: Eine methodenkritische Diskussion des Forschungsstands und eine empirische Bestandsaufnahme [Academic discrimination of children from migrant families: A critical discussion of the methods and the empirical approaches]. In F. Schmidt (Ed.), *Methodische Probleme der empirischen Erziehungswissenschaft* (pp. 289–307). Hohengehren: Schneider.

Nauck, B., & Kohlmann, A. (1999). Kinship as social capital: Network relationships in Turkish migrant families. In R. Richter & S. Supper (Eds.), *New qualities in the life course* (pp. 199–217). Würzburg: Ergon.

Pfluger-Schindlbeck, I. (1989). *"Achte die Älteren, liebe die Jüngeren". Sozialisation türkischer Kinder* ["Respect the ones older than you, love the ones younger than you." Socialization of Turkish children]. Frankfurt: Athenäum.

Phinney, J. S. (1990). Ethnic identity in adolescents and adults: Review of research. *Psychological Bulletin, 108*, 499–514.

Phinney, J. S., Horenczyk, G., Liebkind, K., & Vedder, P. (2001). Ethnic identity, immigration and well-being: An international perspective. *Journal of Social Issues, 57*, 493–510.

Rogler, L. H. (1994). International migrations: A framework for directing research. *American Psychologist, 49*, 710–718.

Rumbaut, R. G. (1995). The New Californians: Comparative research findings on the educational progress of immigrant children. In R. G. Rumbaut & W. A. Cornelius (Eds.), *California's immigrant children* (pp. 17–69). San Diego: University of California Press.

Rumbaut, R. G. (1997). Ties that bind: Immigration and immigrant families in the United States. In A. Booth, A. C. Crouter, & N. Landale (Eds.), *Immigration and the family* (pp. 3–46). Mahwah, NJ: Lawrence Erlbaum Associates.

Sam, D. L., Kosic, A., & Oppedal, B. (2003). Where is "development" in acculturation theories? *International Society for the Study of Behavioural Development Newsletter* (2, Serial No. 44), 4–7.

Schiffauer, W. (2001). Production of fundamentalism: On the dynamics of producing the radically different. In M. Bal & H. de Fries (Eds.), *Religion and media* (pp. 435–455). Stanford: Stanford University Press.

Schiffauer, W. (2005, Feb. 25). Schlachtfeld Frau [Battlefield woman]. *Süddeutsche Zeitung*, p. 15.

Schoelmerich, A., Leyendecker, B., Harwood, R. L., Citlak, B., & Miller, A. (2005). Variability of the role of grandmothers. In E. Voland, A. Chasiotis, & W. Schievenhövel (Eds.), *The psychological, social and reproductive significance of the second half of life* (pp. 277–292). New York: Rutgers University Press.

Strassburger, G. (2000). Das Heiratsverhalten von Personen ausländischer Nationalität oder Herkunft in Deutschland [The marital patterns of persons with a foreign nationality in Germany]. In Bericht der Sachverständigenkommission (Ed.), *Familien ausländischer Herkunft in Deutschland. Empirische Beiträge zur Familienentwicklung und Akkulturation. Materialien zum 6. Familienbericht* (Vol. 1, pp. 9–48).

Suarez-Orozco, C., & Suarez-Orozco, M. M. (2001). *Children of migration*. Cambridge: Harvard University Press.

Sussman, N. M. (2000). The dynamics of self-identity and cultural repatriation: Why home is not so sweet. *Personality and Social Psychology Review, 4*, 355–373.

Szapocznik, J., Kurtines, W. M., & Fernandez, T. (1980). Bicultural involvement and adjustment in Hispanic American youths. *International Journal of Intercultural Relations, 4*, 353–365.

The New Encyclopedia Britannica. (1996). *Acculturation* (p. 57). Chicago: Encyclopedia Britannica.

Tapia Uribe, F. M., LeVine, R. A., & LeVine, S. (1994). Maternal behavior in a Mexican community: The changing environments of children. In P. M. Greenfield & R. R. Cocking (Eds.), *Cross-cultural roots of minority child development* (pp. 41–54). Hillsdale, NJ: Lawrence Erlbaum Associates.

Ward, C. (2001). The ABCs of acculturation. In D. Matsumoto (Ed.), *The handbook of culture and psychology* (pp. 411–445). Oxford: Oxford University Press.

Zentrum für Türkeistudien. (2000). *Die Lebenssituation und Partizipation türkischer Migranten in Nordrhein-Westfalen. Ergebnisse der zweiten Mehrthemenbefragung* [The situation and participation of Turkish migrants in North Rhine-Westphalia. Results of the second survey]. Essen: Ministerium für Arbeit und Soziales, Qualifikation und Technologie des Landes Nordrhein-Westfalen.

Zentrum für Türkeistudien. (Ed.). (2004). *Türkeijahrbuch des Zentrums für Türkeistudien* [Turkish yearbook of the Center for Turkish Studies]. Münster: Lit Verlag.

IV

Overview of Measurement and Development in Acculturation

15

An Overview of Acculturation and Parent–Child Relationships

Cigdem Kagitcibasi
Koc University, Istanbul, Turkey

INTRODUCTION

This volume is unique in integrating different perspectives and research traditions and presenting a coherent psychological picture of a most complex phenomenon. First, the papers integrate the different topical areas of *acculturation* and *parent–child relationships*. This is a valuable combination, as for some time acculturation was typically studied by social psychologists, and a developmental perspective was lacking. The accumulated knowledge and insights from developmental science provide much needed understanding into the processes of continuity and change at the micro level psychological processes in the context of international migration and ethnic relations. Focusing on parenting, parent–child interaction, adolescent development, and related aspects of family dynamics through culture contact, the studies present rich psychological data and much food for thought. Second, the papers deal with both conceptualization and methodology, bringing a greater sophistication into a field that has been rather descriptive to a large extent. Any serious student of immigration and acculturation who wants to understand the processes underlying these phenomena at the individual and the family levels can derive valuable insights from these chapters. Finally, the volume contains studies conducted and perspectives developed from both American and European acculturation research. Thus integrating the two rather separate research traditions with different immigration histories makes this volume special.

To start, it may be helpful to remind ourselves briefly of the different histories which paved the way to the current variation in the acculturation contexts of the two sides of the Atlantic. Indeed, there are differences in the American and European experiences of immigration and acculturation as well as similarities that derive from the basic nature of culture contact. It is important to see the differences deriving from their disparate historical backgrounds. However, it may be theoretically more important to reveal the similarities which may point to possible universals in the process of human acculturation to culture contact.

HISTORICAL BACKGROUND OF INTERNATIONAL MIGRATION

Immigration is a worldwide phenomenon of growing proportions. Throughout history, human groups have always moved. However, immigration as a socioeconomic phenomenon has become a topic of study for social scientists mainly in the second half of the 20th century. Psychological research on it is of more recent origin even though as a human event, immigration obviously involves psychological aspects. For a number of years, international migration was studied from a macro perspective focusing on its economic, social, and policy aspects, regarding both the sending and the receiving countries, mostly the latter (Kagitcibasi, 1987). Its psychological features emerged as important only recently. Despite being in its "infancy stage" (Hong, Roisman, & Chen, chapter 8, this volume), however, a voluminous body of psychological research on immigration, particularly focusing on acculturation, has already developed.

A cursory look at the field reveals that the bulk of research has been conducted in two main immigration-receiving areas of the world, North America and Western Europe, followed by studies in other receiving regions or countries such as Australia and Israel. Research in North America and Western Europe has been conducted rather independently, without much interface. Various reasons for this come to mind. First, the history of immigration in North America, especially the United States, goes back a much longer period of time, indeed to the beginning of this nation of immigrants. In this multicultural society, the study of intergroup relations, especially racial prejudice against African Americans and anti-Semitism formed the background of the field in social psychology from the 1950s on. Only more recently has acculturation of the various ethnic immigrant groups surfaced as the main psychological topic of study, in response to the immigration of large numbers of Latin and Asian Americans.

Historically, unicultural societies in Europe, on the other hand, experienced the coming of foreigners mainly as "guest workers" who were recruited by governments to rebuild European economies following the devastation of the Second World War, although there had also been continuous immigration from former colonies in some European countries, particularly the United Kingdom. After the first few decades of labor migration, the sharp increases in foreign populations due mostly to family reunification and the coming of refugees challenged and changed unicultural European societies. It took a while for European public opinion to realize that what was assumed to be a temporary state was really a permanent one—that the guest workers were in fact minorities, there to stay (Leyendecker, Scholmerich, & Citlak, chapter 14, this volume). (It also took a while for the guest workers themselves to realize that they were in fact minorities who would probably not return to their country of origin.) This situation brought with it the issue of adjustment of the permanent migrants to the host society and of the host populations to the transformation of their societies from unicultural to multicultural. Psychological work with immigrants took off rather late, in response to and triggered by these issues.

COMMONALITY WITHIN DIVERSITY

Given disparate American and European experiences with immigration, what are some common themes as reflected in the chapters of this volume? What constitute shared experiences within diversity? A great deal of commonality is apparent in the studies presented in this volume, and a basic reason for this is the shared focus on the *micro psychological picture*—that of parent–child relationships. Furthermore, there is also a common *developmental* approach to unravel these dynamics as they are influenced by culture contact and acculturation. Such a developmental perspective is valuable for better understanding some of the intriguing phenomena in family dynamics in the context of culture contact, such as developmental paths and intergenerational gaps in acculturation. As noted by Phinney (chapter 5, this volume), longitudinal research would further enhance the value of the developmental orientation.

The shared orientations have to do with both conceptualization and research methodology. To start, all the authors in this volume recognize the complexity of the phenomena under study, which challenges the researcher to go beyond any simplistic construal of the processes involved. One basic manifestation of the appreciation of this complexity is the rejection of a unidimensional model by the authors and the general endorsement of a bidimensional model of acculturation (Berry, 1997, chapter 2, this volume). This shared perspective on acculturation points to the fact that the interface is with more than one culture, the host culture and the culture of origin, and being close to or identifying with one of these may or may not mean lack of identification with the other. The distinctness of acculturation to each of the relevant cultures allows these acculturation processes to be independent of one another. Thus, acculturation to either, both, or neither one of the relevant cultures, as well as different degrees of each, is possible. Going beyond these "two worlds," multiple and changing worlds may also emerge with shifting challenges and resources (Cooper, 2003). For example, Arends-Tóth and van de Vijver (chapter 3, this volume) refer to views that bring in a third dimension to the acculturation process, the *fusion model*, which can be a synthesis or mixture of the two cultures, resulting in a new entity. It remains to be seen if this third model can be empirically demonstrated to be different from biculturalism. Or there can be other possible outcomes such as immigrant youth identifying with the global "hip hop" youth culture (Kaya, 2001).

Several of the authors in this volume address the issues involved in conceptualization and research methodology. Although there is a shared acceptance of the bidimensional model, it is also criticized for focusing on the end states rather than on the process of acculturation (Hong et al., chapter 8, this volume). Similarly, Birman (chapter 7, this volume) claims that the measures used in the four-fold two-dimensional model become unwieldy in the computation of acculturation gaps between parents and children; therefore, she proposes the orthogonal interaction model to better handle parent–child acculturation gaps. Furthermore, not only generational but also spousal/partner acculturation gaps are considered important to address (Leyendecker et al., chapter 14, this volume). Both types of gaps show variation across different domains of acculturation. Most authors endorse Berry's view that *integration* is the most optimal acculturation strategy. There are nevertheless also some questions raised based on conflicting findings regarding which type of acculturation is more adaptive. For example, some studies show acculturation to the host society to be positively associated with mental health whereas others show a negative relation. The definition or operationalization of acculturation appears to be an issue here, to be taken up later.

The complexity of the issues under study is also due to the fact that acculturation is often situation or domain specific, as pointed out by a number of the authors. Thus, it would be better to construe it not in terms of stable traits but rather as a dynamic process involving changing patterns of behaviors, cognitions and attitudes. In particular, a distinction is made between the public and the private domains where significantly different behavioral patterns emerge ranging from language and identity to choice of friends and food habits (e.g., Arends-Tóth & van de Vijver, chapter 3, and Bornstein & Cote, chapter 9, this volume). The general finding, reflected also in this collection, is greater assimilation in the public domain and more cultural maintenance in the private domain.

Beyond situation and domain specificity, *what* type of psychological phenomenon we study regarding acculturation also makes a difference. For example, Bornstein and Cote (chapter 9, this volume) show that publicly observable parental behaviors get assimilated more than parental cognitions, and cultural practices are more open to change than attitudes. Also it is noted that group level differences tend to be greater than individual level differences, and the former are more influenced by acculturation. These empirical findings need to be substantiated in other spheres of psychological adjustment by research conducted in different acculturation contexts to ascertain if they can be generalized. Within the different domains, a myriad of situations involving families, peers, schools, and communities create links or gaps across the different worlds of children and youth (Cooper, 2003). Mapping how these domain specific situational channels can function as opportunities or constraints would provide us with insights into the vicissitudes in human development in the context of immigration. We also need more comprehensive theoretical perspectives to explain the diverse findings.

Further complexity is seen in the methodology of acculturation research, as discussed at length in this volume. The field is beset with conflicting hypotheses and findings. Given that there is not much theory informing human development in the context of acculturation (Arends-Tóth & van de Vijver, chapter 3, and Bornstein & Cote, chapter 9, this volume), hypotheses are formulated borrowing from existing developmental models, which may have a poor fit for culture contact contexts. For example, psychoanalytically informed individuation models claiming separation from parents to be a requisite of healthy adolescent development are not supported by findings such as the positive contribution of parent–child bonding to psychological health in immigration contexts (e.g., Buriel, Love, & De Ment, chapter 12, this volume). Or parent–adolescent intergenerational value discrepancy tends to be attributed to immigration even though it may reflect an aspect of general developmental processes and is thus seen in the host populations also, as noted by Sam (chapter 6, this volume).

A more problematic approach may take the form of "pathologizing" immigrants, paving the way to stereotypes such as the immigrants being "of poor quality stock." Stereotypes tend to mask in-group diversity and individual differences and therefore reinforce social distance between the host/ dominant society and the ethnic minorities. Negative stereotypes are common despite much evidence regarding countless cases of positive sociocultural adaptation, for example immigrant children being successful in Canadian and American schools despite hardships (Fuligni, 1997, 1998; Kwak, 2003) or Turkish immigrants being successful entrepreneurs, artists, and so forth in Germany. Several factors may play a role in these achievements, among them, supportive and close family relationships, responsibilities toward the family providing the children with a clear direction, and the importance put on education.

Nevertheless, there are conflicting findings regarding the relation of acculturation and family relations, again reflecting complexity in the picture. For example, some research points to weaker family relations being associated with greater acculturation, but other research shows an opposite pattern, and still other research does not find significant relations. The discrepancies may be due to different variables being used in different studies to reflect both acculturation to the host society and also family relations. The latter variables may not be uniformly impacted by acculturation. Or attitude–behavior discrepancy, a long-standing issue in social psychology and parenting, may be a factor here (Arends-Tóth & van de Vijver, chapter 3, and Bornstein & Cote, chapter 9, this volume). The underlying factors responsible for these incompatible findings need to be better understood, calling for theoretical frameworks that can reconcile them. We have more questions than answers. Some of the questions that need to be addressed are: Who is being studied? Which ethnic group? The parent or the child? Which generation of immigrants? Are we studying behavior or attitude or values or cognitions regarding acculturation? Is there a shift to the host culture values? Reassertion of the culture of origin? A fusion or some other combination of values? How much of which? Which behaviors? Where manifested? Some of these issues, as well as the definition of integration are discussed further in the following section.

ISSUES CURRENTLY OUTSTANDING

The studies in this book and the above discussion attest to the richness of this field of inquiry. Although they were late entrants to the field, psychologists' work has greatly enhanced both the scope and the depth of research questions regarding immigration, culture contact, and acculturation. Nevertheless, some potentially significant topics and issues have not yet been dealt with adequately. The coming years may witness growth in these areas of research if there is a recognition that advancement in theory and knowledge can improve our understanding of the phenomena of acculturation and can contribute to the solution of some human problems involved. Interdisciplinary ventures would be especially promising here.

Content of Acculturation

The focus on revealing the *processes* of acculturation has shadowed the study of the *content* of acculturation. In particular, *what* exactly changes in the process of acculturation, and *what* is maintained? This basic question is often answered broadly, in terms of elements or traits of the host culture and those of the culture of origin, such as language, friendship choices, food habits, and the like. What significance do these specific elements or their meanings have for the acculturating people, as well as for the host society, is seldom analyzed. For example, different behavioral patterns emerge in public and private domains, and this is an important issue. However, what makes a specific trait or behavior change in the public sphere, but not in the private sphere of the family, or more generally, which specific traits undergo modification in the acculturation context while others do not and why are questions that need more comprehensive answers.

In some cases those aspects that are more relevant in socio-cultural adaptation (Ward & Kennedy, 1992), that is, the ability to fit in and function effectively in the new society, may undergo change whereas those that are closer home may be maintained. Or, those traits that are considered important or acceptable by the host society may undergo more change. For example, different food habits of ethnic minorities may be tolerated by the host society, even embraced as multicultural enrichment, but some of their different religious practices may be unacceptable. A current example is the practice of animal sacrifice among some Moslem minorities in Europe. There may also be variations in the significance of different traits for the acculturating person and the family such that less significant ones may undergo change more readily than more significant ones. This circumstance may lead to *integration* or even *assimilation* in the public domain but *separation* in the private domain. These are empirical questions that need more research attention as well as clarifying theory.

What is meant by integration may be the crux of the matter. As also noted by Arends-Tóth and van de Vijver (chapter 3, this volume), a great deal of variation occurs within integration. This makes for different meanings attributed to integration in different countries with different immigration histories and policies. For example, in the United States integration mostly means assimilation, but in Canada it implies multiculturalism and therefore maintenance of the culture of origin. As mentioned above, what is desired by the immigrant or tolerated by the dominant society to be maintained appears to be of key importance. The relative *adaptive* function of change or maintenance of specific behaviors, values, and relationships also appears to play a role in the outcome of acculturation. Therefore, going beyond the process, a *functional* perspective is useful in the analysis of the content of acculturation.

An example of what is maintained, that can serve as a case in point, is "relatedness" and parent–child bonding in the family, as for example noted by Buriel and colleagues (chapter 12, this volume). Research points to the adaptive role of relatedness in the context of immigration while at the same time autonomy is attained or aspired for by the adolescent (Grotevant & Cooper, 1998; Kagitcibasi, 2003; Kwak, 2003; see also Buriel et al., chapter 12, this volume; Chao, chapter 13, this volume). To develop an understanding of this apparent dilemma, a conceptual distinction between autonomy and relatedness is useful. Such a distinction questions the psychoanalytically informed views that assume separation to be a requisite of autonomy (Kroger, 1998; Steinberg & Silverberg, 1986). If autonomy–heteronomy (agency dimension) and relatedness–separateness (interpersonal distance dimension) are distinct, then it is possible to have different degrees of each coexisting in a person, thus the feasibility of an "autonomous-related self" (Kagitcibasi, 1996a, 2005). In the context of immigration to an individualistic technological society from a more communal society, new environmental demands are placed on children and youth for autonomous action, for example, in school. Effective socio-cultural adaptation as well as "social comparison processes" would therefore call for aspiring for and developing autonomy. Research shows that such adaptation to the changing environment may reflect on adolescents' demands for more autonomy at home (Phinney, chapter 5, this volume), which may engender parent–child conflict (Kwak, 2003). However, a corresponding intergenerational conflict is often not found regarding relatedness in the family (Grotevant & Cooper, 1998; Kwak, 2003), pointing to the possible emergence of the autonomous-related self in adolescents in the context of acculturation. Thus, studying the development of the self and integrating it into acculturation promises to provide further insight into the dynamic processes we want to understand.

Why is it that there is a shift toward autonomy, especially in the public domain but not a corresponding shift toward separation? The answer lies in the concept of adaptation. Autonomy is adaptive in technological society with high levels of education and specialization that require individual decision making. Lack of autonomy, for example total obedience/submission to authority, would be incompatible to advancing in education and specialized occupations. Thus, autonomy enhancement is an important aspect of sociocultural acculturation (Ward & Kennedy, 1992). However, relatedness is *not* incompatible with the demands of new life styles in the host society, and therefore, it can continue (Kagitcibasi, 1996a, 1996b, in press). Furthermore, relatedness provides psychological support and is especially adaptive in potentially stressful immigration contexts. Going beyond the immigration context, research such as that on "Self Determination Theory" (e.g., Chirkov, Kim, Ryan, & Kaplan, 2003; Ryan & Deci, 2000; Ryan & Lynch, 1989) points to the compatibility of autonomy and close relatedness with parents during adolescence (see Kagitcibasi, 2005, for a review).

Similar analyses of *content* of changes and continuity in different domains would provide us with further insights into acculturation. In this context, understanding what is accepted from which group may be informed by theoretical perspectives on individual-group relations and power differentials such as optimal distinctiveness theory (Brewer, 1990) and social identity theory (Tajfel & Turner, 1979), as well as by an adaptation of attachment theory to culture, as proposed by Hong and colleagues (chapter 8, this volume). As already mentioned, the content of acculturation is also impacted by the context of acculturation, which I address next.

Context of Acculturation

Researchers recognize the importance of context. Nevertheless, many aspects of the contexts of acculturation are not yet adequately attended to. In particular, the more macro characteristics of context, such as the politics of migration and general attitudes about the migrants in the host society, are not always taken into consideration when the focus falls on the acculturating migrant. The host society orientations toward different ethnic minorities show much variation, as noted for example by Hong and colleagues (chapter 8, this volume). The latter authors refer to the "ethnic hierarchy" (Schalk-Soekar, van de Vijver, & Hoogsteder, in press) reflecting the variation in social distance and prejudice the host society maintains regarding different ethnic minority groups. Often the basis for this hierarchy is the extent of perceived difference of the ethnic minority group from host society; the greater the perceived difference of an ethnic minority on some key attributes, the greater is the prejudice against that group (Arends-Tóth & van de Vijver, chapter 3, this volume; Kagitcibasi, 1997). For example, an early study in France (Malewska-Peyre, 1980) showed that the French were more rejecting of North African immigrants compared with Portuguese immigrants even though the former spoke French but the latter did not. Subsequent research corroborated the finding that perceived difference is a factor in discrimination (Mirdal & Ryynanen-Karjalainen, 2004). It is difficult to understand the reasons underlying variations in the acculturation strategies of migrants without taking into account host society sentiments.

The socioeconomic status (SES) of immigrants should also be kept in mind. This is shown to be important in much research. For example, an early study conducted in Australia with ethnic minorities (Cashmore & Goodnow, 1986) found that the observed "ethnic" differences in parental beliefs and attitudes disappeared when SES was controlled. A study conducted with Dutch and Turkish minority adolescents in the Netherlands again found SES explained most of the "ethnic" differences in problem behavior (Darwish Mura, Joung, van Lenthe, Bengi-Arslan, & Crijnen, 2003; see also Leyendecker et al., chapter 14, this volume). Thus, what is readily assumed to be an ethnic characteristic may be the result of low levels of education, low employment status, and the like. It is often the case that ethnic minority status and low SES overlap, which is a challenge because the important point is not just noting the prevalence of a characteristic, but rather understanding its cause. This is particularly important in problem areas such as children's school performance, delinquent behavior, crime, and the like.

Particularly in the context of perceived discrimination, the less than optimal strategies of separation and even marginalization (Berry, chapter 2, this volume) may arise among immigrant groups, often as a reaction to loss of status (Kagitcibasi, 1987, 1997). The issues that emerge in such contexts transcend psychological spheres and may assume political proportions. To understand them adequately, multidisciplinary research orientations would be highly useful. For example, it would be valuable for psychologists and developmental scientists to collaborate with social scientists such as economists, sociologists and political scientists who also study immigration. In particular, when group mobilization, rather than individual action, characterizes the situation, more comprehensive macro approaches may be called for.

The issue of Islam in Europe can serve as a case in point. In one of a series of European Science Foundation "Forward Looks" Workshop on Migration and Transcultural Identities, Nielsen (2001) remarked, "When people talk about multiculturalism in Europe, they generally think of Islam" (Mirdal & Ryynanen-Karjalainen, 2004, p. 16). Indeed, an increasing emphasis is being put on the "otherness" of Islam, which historically used to be external to Europe, but has now become internal, with Moslem immigrants, and therefore even more problematic. In the last years the globally politicized Islam and Islamic terror, a significant base of which is located in Europe, have aggravated the problem. In the eyes of the host society, culture (of the Moslem minorities) *is* their religion, regarding which there are negative sentiments.

There is a dilemma here, because several Western European governments provide financial support to religious activities of ethnic minorities given constitutional provisions that uphold religious tolerance. However, such tolerant multicultural policies actually may *not* foster tolerance in the host society for a number of reasons. First, the increased Moslem identification and mobilization makes these minorities even more *different*, and their "otherness" is accentuated, further fueling rejection by the dominant society (Kaya, 2001; Toelken, 1985). Thus we see an irony of tolerance in government policies leading to intolerance in the host society against Moslem minorities (Kagitcibasi, 1997). Second, in the context of perceived rejection, loss of status and power, Moslem immigrants cling to their religion as an affirmation of group identity and self-worth. This is found to be the case even for those who were not particularly religious in their culture of origin. Indeed, research shows that strengthening group identity is a *consequence* of perceived prejudice and xenophobia (Baumgartl, 1994). This type of a situation may even make migrants vulnerable to radical fundamentalist influences, which in turn pave the way toward further separation from the host society and turning inward, in a vicious cycle. Thus, even though multicultural policies may attempt to foster integration of the different immigrant groups into the host society, they may end up having the opposite effect (Kagitcibasi, 1997). To prevent negative outcomes, serious measures need to be taken with direct implications for policy and applications.

Policy and Applications

Another aspect of immigration and acculturation that needs to be addressed more is policy and applications. A few authors in this volume touch on applied issues that may have some policy relevance. For example, Birman points to possible interventions aimed at easing family tensions that could help students learn or retain their native language. Farver, Eppe, and Ballon point to the value of adapting early childhood programs and parent values to support children's school readiness. Harwood and Feng (chapter 10, this volume) underscore the importance of sound knowledge regarding the growing Latin population in the United States for primary prevention efforts such as social competence promotion or parenting programs and warn against a predominantly problem-focused approach in the study of ethnic groups, which tends to perpetuate stereotypes. However, the applied orientation remains marginal, which is understandable, given the theoretical and methodological emphasis of the volume toward understanding and assessing acculturation and parent–child relationships. Nevertheless, immigration, acculturation, ethnic relations, and their reflections in parent–child interactions constitute global phenomena beset with problems that beg solutions. The solutions are never easy, and applications are carried out not by the researchers but by others. Still, for policies and programs to be of value, they should be informed by sound research. Therefore, these applied issues should also enter the agenda of the researchers studying these phenomena. The reticence of some authors to discuss the policy implications of their research could be due to the fact that the research is in its infancy and that the research findings are sometimes contradictory, as pointed out. Nevertheless, research can provide precious information that we otherwise lack. Thus, its policy relevance should be kept in mind.

Interventions or support programs tend to focus on the migrant, usually the child or adolescent, who is functioning and interacting within the peer group, school, or community. Or the adaptability of the migrant's acculturation strategy, sociocultural adaptation and psychological adjustment are attended to. This focus on the migrant may divert attention from the context of acculturation, discussed earlier. Indeed, as some authors of this volume also note, the overall context of acculturation has not been studied adequately. In particular, preventive measures focusing on the host society are lacking. Some possibilities come to mind that may be especially relevant for the European context. For example multicultural policies can be supported by general "sensitization" efforts to the general population reinforcing an appreciation of the "different" not as deficient but as culturally enriching. Or, more specifically, warning school teachers against low levels of expectations from minority students or inappropriately channeling minority students to less academic tracks. Similarly, social workers could be warned against the attribution of family pathology when they observe strict parental discipline in ethnic minority families (Fisek & Kagitcibasi, 1999; Kagitcibasi, in press).

This point brings us back to a reconsideration of parent–child relationships among ethnic minorities. A great deal of research now shows that, if accompanied by warmth, strict parental discipline which may involve physical discipline (*not* abuse) does not mean parental rejection or hostility. In fact, recent work with ethnic minority families both in Europe and in the United States shows strong parental discipline and expectation of respect from children and adolescents to be the norm (Chao, 1994; Dekovic, Pels, & Model, in press; Kagitcibasi, in press; Kwak, 2003; Lansford, Deater-Deckard, Dodge, Bates, & Pettit, 2003; see also Harwood & Feng; Chao; and Leyendecker et al., chapters 10, 13, and 14, this volume). Actually, for some decades parental discipline and warmth have been shown to be independent orientations. In an early comparison of Turkish and American adolescents' retrospective experiences, Kagitcibasi (1970) found that the two groups did not differ in perceived parental affection, although the Turkish group perceived more parental control. Subsequently, Rohner and Pettengill (1985) and Trommsdorff (1985) showed that parental discipline was perceived as rejection by American and German adolescents but not by Korean and Japanese adolescents. Similarly, Deater-Deckard and Dodge (1997) showed that parent–child behavior links, such as the association between parental physical discipline and child aggression, vary across cultures, depending on the prevalence and acceptability of physical discipline in a culture. Nevertheless, psychoanalytically informed individualistic orientations to family and parenting have labeled strong parental discipline as unhealthy. Host country health professionals such as social workers and clinical psychologists who lack culture-sensitive training may therefore make mistaken interpretations, which can have serious consequences.

CONCLUSIONS

All in all, this volume demonstrates the advanced state of research and conceptualization in the psychological study of acculturation and parent–child relationships in the context of global immigration. Nevertheless, the complexity of the phenomena involved will continue to challenge researchers. Needed at this stage are theoretical frameworks that address the issues with a developmental orientation. Most of the current work on the psychology of acculturation is still of a social psychological nature, and the research designs are typically cross-sectional (e.g., Chun, Organista, & Marin, 2003; Ward, 2001; see Sam, chapter 6, this volume). Developmental perspectives, supported by research utilizing developmental research designs and sound measurement of the variables involved, would greatly enhance our analytical understanding of what is really going on in acculturation. Another promising route to follow would be to look beyond our psychological lenses and to locate the phenomena under study within their socio-political and economic contexts. In this type of endeavor, multidisciplinary research informed by other social scientific viewpoints would go a long way to enrich our outlook. The complex human phenomena we are addressing in acculturation research require multifaceted orientations, at one end delving into the micro developmental dynamics within the family and at the other reaching out to the macro characteristics of the context of immigration and ethnic relations.

REFERENCES

Baumgartl, B. (1994). Xenophobia and racism in Europe. Paper presented at the conference on *Today's Youth and Xenophobia: Breaking the Cycle, Netherlands Institute for Advanced Study*, Wassenaar, The Netherlands.

Berry, J. W. (1997). Immigration, acculturation and adaptation. *Applied Psychology, 46*, 5–68.

Brewer, M. B. (1990). The social self: On being the same and different at the same time. *Personality and Social Psychology Bulletin, 17*, 475–482.

Cashmore, J. A., & Goodnow, J. J. (1986). Influences on Australian parents' values: Ethnicity versus socioeconomic status. *Journal of Cross-Cultural Psychology, 17*, 441–454.

Chao, R. K. (1994). Beyond parental control and authoritarian parenting style: Understanding Chinese parenting through the cultural notion of training. *Child Development, 65*, 1111–1120.

Chirkov, V., Kim, Y., Ryan, R., & Kaplan, U. (2003). Differentiating autonomy from individualism and independence: A self-determination theory perspective on internalization of cultural orientations and well being. *Journal of Personality and Social Psychology, 84*(1), 97–110.

Chun, K. M., Organista, P. B., & Marin, G. (2003). *Acculturation: Advances in theory, measurement and applied research.* Washington: American Psychological Association.

Cooper, C. R. (2003). Bridging multiple worlds: Immigrant youth identity and pathways to college. *International Society for the Study of Behavioural Development Newsletter, 2*(44), 1–4.

Darwish Mura, S., Joung, I. M. A., van Lenthe, F. J., Bengi-Arslan, L., & Crijnen, A. A. M. (2003). Predictors of self-reported problem behaviors in Turkish immigrant and Dutch adolescents in the Netherlands. *Journal of Child Psychology and Psychiatry, 44*, 412–423.

Deater-Deckard, K., & Dodge, K. A. (1997). Externalizing behavior problems and discipline revisited: Nonlinear effects and variation by culture, context and gender. *Psychological Inquiry, 8*, 161–175.

Dekovic, M., Pels, T., & Model, S. (in press). *Unity and diversity in child rearing: Family life in a multicultural society*. Edwin Mellen Press.

Fisek, G., & Kagitcibasi, C. (1999). Multiculturalism and psychotherapy: The Turkish case. In P. Pedersen (Ed.), *Multiculturalism as a Fourth Force* (pp. 75–92). Castleton, NY: Hamilton.

Fuligni, A. J. (1997). The academic achievement of adolescents from immigrant families: The roles of family background, attitudes, and behavior. *Child Development, 68*, 261–273.

Fuligni, A. J. (1998). The adjustment of children from immigrant families. *Current Directions in Psychological Science, 7*, 99–103.

Grotevant, H. D., & Cooper, C. R. (1998). Individuality and connectedness in adolescent development: Review and prospects for research on identity, relationships, and context. In E. Skoe & A. von der Lippe (Eds.), *Personality development in adolescence: A cross-national and life span perspective* (pp. 3–37). London: Routledge.

Kagitcibasi, C. (1970). Social norms and authoritarianism: A Turkish-American comparison. *Journal of Personality and Social Psychology, 16*, 444–451.

Kagitcibasi, C. (1987). Alienation of the outsider: The plight of migrants. *International Migration, 25*, 195–210.

Kagitcibasi, C. (1996a). The autonomous-related self: A new synthesis. *European Psychologist, 1*(3), 180–186.

Kagitcibasi, C. (1996b). *Family and human development across cultures: A view from the other side*. Hillsdale, NJ: Lawrence Erlbaum Associates.

Kagitcibasi, C. (1997). Whither multiculturalism? *Applied Psychology: An International Review, 46*(1), 44–49.

Kagitcibasi, C. (2003). Autonomy, embeddedness and adaptability in immigration contexts. *Human Development, 46*, 145–150.

Kagitcibasi, C. (2005). Autonomy and relatedness in cultural context: Implications for self and family. *Journal of Cross-Cultural Psychology, 36*(4), 403–422.

Kagitcibasi, C. (in press). Preface. In M. Dekovic, T. Pels, & S. Model (Eds.), *Unity and diversity in child rearing: Family life in a multicultural society*. Edwin Mellen Press.

Kaya, A. (2001). *"Zicher in Kreuzberg" Constructing diasporas: Turkish hip-hop youth in Berlin*. London: Transaction.

Kroger, J. (1998). Adolescence as a second separation–individuation process: Critical review of an object relations approach. In E. E. A. Skoe & A. L. von der Lippe (Eds.), *Personality development in adolescence: A cross-national and life span perspective. Adolescence and society* (pp. 172–192). New York: Routledge.

Kwak, K. (2003). Adolescents and their parents: A review of intergenerational family relations for immigrant and non-immigrant families. *Human Development, 46*, 115–136.

Lansford, J. E., Deater-Deckard, K., Dodge, K. A., Bates, J. E., & Pettit, G. S. (2003). Ethnic differences in the link between physical discipline and later adolescent externalizing behaviors. *Journal of Child Psychology and Psychiatry, 44*, 1–13.

Malewska-Peyre, H. (1980). *Conflictual cultural identity of second generation immigrants*. Paper presented at the Workshop on Cultural Identity and Structural Marginalization of Migrant Workers, European Science Foundation.

Mirdal, G. M., & Ryynanen-Karjalainen, L. (2004). Migration and transcultural identities. *European Science Foundation, EFS Forward Look Report 2, October 2004*.

Nielsen, J. S. (2001). Muslims, the state and the public domain in Britain. In R. Bonney, F. Bosbach, & T. Brockmann (Eds.), *Religion and politics in Britain and Germany* (pp. 145–154). Munich: K. G. Saur.

Rohner, R. P., & Pettengill, S. M. (1985). Perceived parental acceptance–rejection and parental control among Korean adolescents. *Child Development, 56*, 524–528.

Ryan, R. M., & Deci, E. L. (2000). Self-determination theory and the facilitation of intrinsic motivation, social development and well being. *American Psychologist, 55*(1), 68–78.

Ryan, R. M., & Lynch, J. H. (1989). Emotional autonomy versus detachment: Revisiting the vicissitudes of adolescence and young adulthood. *Child Development, 60*, 340–356.

Schalk-Soekar, R. G. S., van de Vijver, F. J. R., & Hoogsteder, M. (in press). Migrants' and majority members' orientations toward multiculturalism in the Netherlands. *International Journal of Intercultural Relations*.

Steinberg, L., & Silverberg, S. B. (1986). The vicissitudes of autonomy in early adolescence. *Child Development, 57*, 841–851.

Tajfel, H., & Turner, J. C. (1979). An integrative theory of intergroup conflict. In W. G. Austin & S. Worchel (Eds.), *The social psychology of intergroup relations* (pp. 33–48). Monterey, CA: Brooks-Cole.

Toelken, B. (1985). "Turkenrein" and "Turken, Raus!"—Images of fear and aggression in German gastarbeitterwitze. In I. Basgoz & N. Furniss (Eds.), *Turkish workers in Europe: An interdisciplinary study* (pp. 151–164). Bloomington: Indiana University Turkish Studies.

Trommsdorff, G. (1985). Some comparative aspects of socialization in Japan and Germany. In I. R. Lagnues & Y. H. Poortinga (Eds.), *From a different perspective: Studies of behaviors across cultures* (pp. 231–240). Lisse: Swets & Zeitlinger.

Ward, C. (2001). The ABCs of acculturation. In D. Matsumoto (Ed.), *The handbook of culture and psychology* (pp. 411–446). Oxford: Oxford University Press.

Ward, C., & Kennedy, A. (1992). Locus of control, mood disturbance and social difficulty during cross-cultural transitions. *International Journal of Intercultural Relations, 16*, 175–194.

About the Authors

JUDIT ARENDS-TÓTH is a Postdoctoral Research Fellow in the Faculty of Social and Behavioural Sciences at Tilburg University, the Netherlands. She received her PhD at Tilburg University. Currently, she works on a project concerned with family relationships and acculturation sponsored by the Netherlands Organization for Scientific Research. Her research interests include psychological assessment of acculturation, cultural differences in behavior, and childrearing practices in multicultural contexts.

DANIEL BALLON is completing his BA degree at the University of Southern California. He participates in the Psychology Undergraduate Honors Program and is a McNair Scholar. He plans to attend graduate school in clinical psychology.

JOHN WIDDUP BERRY is Professor Emeritus of Psychology at Queen's University, Canada. He obtained his PhD at the University of Edinburgh. He was previously a Lecturer at the University of Sydney and has been a Visiting Professor at a number of universities, including Nice, Geneva, Bergen, Helsinki, Oxford, Buenos Aires, Tartu, Baroda, Paris, Kwansei Gakuin, and Victoria. He is a Fellow of the Netherlands Institute for Advanced Study in the Humanities and Social Sciences, an Onassis Fellow, and a member of the Canadian Psychological Association, the International Association for Cross-Cultural Psychology, and the International Academy of Intercultural Research. He has served as Secretary General and President of the International Association for Cross-Cultural Psychology and is a member of the Board of Directors of the International Association of Applied Psychology. He received honorary doctorates from the University of Athens and

Universite de Geneve. Berry coauthored *Cross-Cultural Psychology: Research and Applications* and *Human Behaviour in Global Perspective: An Introduction to Cross-Cultural Psychology*. He was the senior editor of the *Handbook of Cross-Cultural Psychology* and is coeditor of the *Cambridge Handbook of Acculturation Psychology*. Berry's main research interests are in the ecology of human behavior and in acculturation and intercultural relations with an emphasis on applications to immigration, educational, and health policy.

DINA BIRMAN is an Assistant Professor of Psychology in the Community and Prevention Research Division at the University of Illinois at Chicago. She received her PhD from the University of Maryland, College Park. She has worked in the Refugee Mental Health Program at the National Institute of Mental Health and Substance Abuse and Mental Health Services Administration, where she provided consultation and technical assistance on mental health issues to the Office for Refugee Resettlement. Her research has focused on understanding the long-term acculturation and adaptation of adolescent, adult, and elderly refugees from the former Soviet Union, Somalia, and Vietnam, school adjustment of refugee children, and the effectiveness of mental health services for refugee youth and families.

MARC H. BORNSTEIN is Senior Investigator and Head of Child and Family Research at the National Institute of Child Health and Human Development. He holds a PhD from Yale University. Bornstein was a Guggenheim Foundation Fellow, and received a RCDA from the NICHD, the Ford Cross-Cultural Research Award from the HRAF, the McCandless Young Scientist Award from the APA, the US PHS Superior Service Award from the NIH, two Japan Society for the Promotion of Science Fellowships, two Awards for Excellence from the American Mensa Education & Research Foundation, and the Arnold Gesell Prize from the Theodor Hellbrügge Foundation. Bornstein has held faculty positions at Princeton University and New York University as well as visiting academic appointments in Munich, London, Paris, New York, Tokyo, and Bamenda. Bornstein is editor emeritus of *Child Development* and editor of *Parenting: Science and Practice*. Bornstein is coauthor of *Development in Infancy* and general editor of *The Crosscurrents in Contemporary Psychology Series* (10 volumes) and the *Monographs in Parenting* (8 volumes). He also edited the *Handbook of Parenting* (Vols. I–V) and coedited *Developmental Science: An Advanced Textbook* as well as a dozen other volumes. He is author of several children's books and puzzles in *The Child's World* series. He has contributed scientific papers in the areas of human experimental, methodological, comparative, developmental, cross-cultural, neuroscientific, pediatric, and aesthetic psychology.

RAYMOND BURIEL is Professor of Psychology and Chicano/a Studies at Pomona College. He received his PhD at the University of California at Riverside.

His research has focused on the acculturation and adjustment of Mexican and other Latino immigrant families, with an emphasis on the characteristics of immigrants that are conducive to success in the United States.

RUTH CHAO is Associate Professor in the Department of Psychology at the University of California, Riverside. She received her PhD from the University of California, Los Angeles. She was formerly at Syracuse University. Her research interests include sociocultural perspectives of parenting and the family, focusing on Asian immigrants. She is currently conducting a longitudinal study examining the effects of parental control, warmth, and parental involvement in school on adolescents' school performance and behavioral adjustment.

JING CHEN is a PhD candidate in the Social–Personality–Organizational Psychology program in the University of Illinois at Urbana–Champaign. Her research interests include behavioral confirmation phenomena in cross-cultural settings and using narrative methods to explore the cultural, emotional, and cognitive ambiguities in the acculturation process. She is examining how the subjectivity of past experience in native and host cultures for bicultural individuals can influence their emotional, cognitive, and behavioral adaptations in the acculturation process and subsequent psychological well-being.

KEVIN M. CHUN is Associate Professor of Psychology and Director of Asian American Studies at the University of San Francisco. He completed his PhD at the University of California at Los Angeles and a Psychology Internship at the Palo Alto Health Care System of the Department of Veterans Affairs. His publications include *Acculturation: Advances in Theory, Measurement, and Applied Research*; *Readings in Ethnic Psychology: African Americans, American Indians, Asian Americans, and Hispanics/Latinos*; and *Psychology of Ethnic Groups in the U.S.* His research focuses on acculturation and its relation to health and psychosocial adjustment for Asian American immigrants and refugees.

BANU CITLAK is a Research Fellow at the Ruhr University of Bochum. She received her PhD at Ruhr University. Her research examines the variability of socialization goals of Turkish migrant mothers in Germany and their involvement with the host culture as well as with the Turkish community. She is coinvestigator in a longitudinal study of relations among parenting cognitions and practices of Turkish parents and their children's socioemotional adjustment and cognitive development.

LINDA R. COTE is a Research Scientist in the Child and Family Research Section at the National Institute of Child Health and Human Development. She received her PhD from Clark University. Thereafter, she was awarded an Intramural Research Training Award from the National Institutes of Health to support a postdoctoral fellowship. Cote was an Assistant Professor in the Psychology Departments at Marymount University and Chapman University. She is a member of the Society for Research in Child Development, National Council on Family Relations, American Psychological Association, International Society for Infant Studies, and International Society for the Study of Behavioral Development. She is also a Certified Family Life Educator by the National Council on Family Relations. Her research interests include the study of parenting and its effects on young immigrant children's cognitive and social development.

TERRI L. DE MENT received her PhD from the Claremont Graduate University. She has been a lecturer at California State University–San Bernardino. She is a member of the American Psychological Association, the American Psychological Society, and the Society for Research in Child Development. De Ment's research interests include socialization of children in immigrant families, the socioemotional impact of language brokering on immigrant children and their families, immigrant adolescents and their parents, and women's conceptions of moral justice.

STEFANIE EPPE is a PhD candidate at the University of Southern California. A native of Costa Rica, Eppe has been involved in a project examining emergent literacy skills of middle- and low-income Costa Rican preschoolers. She has also worked in community violence, victimization and bullying, and children's literacy.

JOANN M. FARVER is an Associate Professor in the Department of Psychology at the University of Southern California. She received her PhD at the University of California–Los Angeles. Farver studies the developmental patterns of multiethnic children in Los Angeles, with a focus on how environmental contexts (home, school, neighborhood, and culture) influence cognitive, socioemotional, and educational outcomes for children. Farver's research reflects her interdisciplinary training in cultural anthropology, education, and child development. Currently, she conducts a large-scale intervention on the emergent literacy skills of inner city preschoolers funded by the National Science Foundation.

XIN FENG is a doctoral candidate at the University of Connecticut. She has focused her research on children's social and emotional development, parent–child interactions, and parental beliefs, particularly in the area of temperament and its influence on the development of competence in different cultural contexts.

ROBIN L. HARWOOD is currently a Visiting Professor at Ruhr University, Bochum, Germany. Previously, she was at the University of Connecticut and the University of New Orleans. She received her PhD from Yale University and was a postdoctoral fellow at the National Institute of Child Health and Human Development. She received a FIRST Award from National Institutes of Health to study culture, mother–infant interactions, and attachment outcomes among middle-class Puerto Rican and Anglo families. She has studied cultural change in childrearing beliefs and practices following migration among Puerto Rican mothers in Connecticut and Turkish mothers in Germany. She is on the editorial board for *Developmental Psychology* and is a member of the Society for Research in Child Development, the American Psychological Association, and the American Anthropological Association. She is the author of *Culture and Attachment: Perceptions of the Child in Context.*

YING-YI HONG is Associate Professor at the University of Illinois at Urbana–Champaign. She received her PhD from Columbia University. She taught at the Hong Kong University of Science and Technology, where she conducted studies to examine cultural priming effects and social identifications of Hong Kong people in responding to the 1997 political transition. Her research on the dynamic influence of culture won the Otto Klineberg Intercultural, International Relations Award conferred by the Society for the Psychological Study of Social Issues and the Young Investigator Award conferred by the International Society for Self and Identity. She is coauthor of *The Social Psychology of Culture.* Hong investigates acculturation and social identification of minority groups in the United States.

CIGDEM KAGITCIBASI is a Professor of Psychology and former Dean at the School of Arts & Sciences at Koç University, İstanbul, Turkey. She received her PhD at the University of California–Berkeley. She was a Visiting Professor at Duke, Columbia, Harvard, and the University of California–Berkeley. She has twice been a fellow of the Netherlands Institute for Advanced Study. She is a founding member of the Turkish Academy of Sciences. She was President of the International Association for Cross-Cultural Psychology and Turkish Psychological Association and Vice-President of the International Union of Psychological Science. She is a fellow of the International Association of Cross-Cultural Psychology. She holds honors and awards, including the American Psychological Association Distinguished Contributions to the International Advancement of Psychology Award and the International Association of Applied Psychology Award for Distinguished Scientific Contributions. Her books include *Handbook of Cross-Cultural Psychology*, *Family and Human Development Across Cultures: A View From the Other Side*, *Individualism and Collectivism*, *Social Behavior Across Cultures*, and *Families Across Cultures: A 30 Nation Psychological Study.* She is involved in both theoretical and applied work with family, parenting, self, early childhood, and human development in cultural contexts. She has directed several applied research projects related to children, women, and families and is involved in large scale educational programs serving their well-being in Turkey and abroad.

BIRGIT LEYENDECKER is a Research Fellow at the Ruhr University in Bochum, Germany. She was educated at the Universities of Marburg and Osnabrück. Her research interests include cultural perspectives on child development and parenting, cultural and psychological adaptation of immigrant children and their families, and linking qualitative and quantitative research. During her time as a Fogarty Fellow at the National Institute of Child Health and Human Development, she was involved in studies of migrant families from Central America and the ecology of mother–infant interaction. Currently, she is Principal Investigator of a longitudinal study on the relation between parenting cognitions and practices in Turkish parents and their children's socioemotional adjustment and cognitive development.

JULIA A. LOVE is a research assistant for the Los Angeles Unified School District and the Quality of Life Research Center and is a doctoral student in the School of Behavioral and Organizational Sciences at Claremont Graduate University. Her research interests include child development within the context of immigrant family socialization, academic achievement, theory of mind, and the link between language brokering and social cognition.

JEAN S. PHINNEY is Professor at California State University, Los Angeles. She received her PhD from the University of California, Los Angeles. She a Fellow of the American Psychological Association and a member of the Society for Research in Child Development, the Society for Research on Adolescence, and the International Association for Cross-Cultural Psychology. She is president-elect of the Society for Research on Identity Formation. She has been an assistant editor for the *Journal of Adolescence*. She has studied ethnic identity and adaptation among adolescents from diverse ethnic and immigrant groups and developed a questionnaire measure of ethnic identity, the Multigroup Ethnic Identity Measure. She is a coeditor of *Immigrant Youth in Cultural Transition: Acculturation, Identity, and Adaptation Across National Contexts*.

GLENN I. ROISMAN is an Assistant Professor at the University of Illinois at Urbana-Champaign. He received his PhD from the University of Minnesota. His interests concern the legacy of childhood experiences as organizing forces in adolescent and adult development. His program of research focuses on the childhood antecedents of adaptation within the developmentally salient contexts of adulthood (work and romantic relationships). The goal of Roisman's program of research is to provide insight into the childhood experiences and resources that scaffold healthy adjustment in the years of maturity, particularly in the context of earlier adversities.

DAVID L. SAM is a Professor at the University of Bergen in Norway where he obtained a PhD. He is a fellow of the International Academy of Intercultural Relations, and he was the recipient of its Early Career Award. Sam was an Associate Scholar at Queen's University, Kingston, Ontario, Canada, Fulbright visiting scholar at the California State University in Los Angeles, and a Visiting Scholar at the University of Hawaii at Manoa. Sam's research interests include the psychology of acculturation and the role of culture in health and human development, and he has published extensively on young immigrants' psychological adaptation.

AXEL SCHÖLMERICH is a Professor of Psychology and Head of the Section on Human Development at the Ruhr University, Bochum, Germany. He received a PhD from the University of Osnabrück, Germany, and a *venia legendi* for Human Development from the University of Mainz. He was a Fogarty Fellow at the National Institute of Child Health and Human Development in Bethesda, MD, and taught at the Universities of Darmstadt and Osnabrück, the Catholic University in Washington, the Martin Luther University in Halle(Saale), and at the Ruhr University, Bochum. His research interests include emotional, cultural, and family processes in human development with a particular focus on early childhood.

FONS J. R. VAN DE VIJVER is Professor of Cross-Cultural Psychology at Tilburg University (the Netherlands) and North-West University (South Africa). He is the current editor-in-chief of the *Journal of Cross-Cultural Psychology*. He is coauthor of *Methods in Cross-Cultural Research*. His research interests include methodological aspects of cross-cultural comparisons (bias and equivalence), cross-cultural differences and similarities in cognitive processes, acculturation, multiculturalism, test translations/adaptations, and psychological assessment in a multicultural context.

Author Index

A

Abidin, R. R., 232, *243*
Abueg, F. R., 76, *77*
Achenbach, T. M., 153, *165*, 279, *295*
Adams, M. J., 226, 227, *243*
Ahearn, F. L., 251, *267*
Ahmadzadeh, V., 23, 26, *29,* 46, 47, *61*
Ahuna, C., 45, *62,* 120, *134*
Ait-Ouarasse, O., 37, *59*
Ajzen, I., 54, *59*
Akkaya, C., 300, *312*
Akutsu, P. D., 56, *59,* 65, 66, *77*, 187, *194*
Alarcón, O., 200, 201, *220*
Alden, L. E., 23, *30,* 45, 47, *61*, 156, *169*
Aldenderfer, M., 91, *94*
Alers, J. O., 203, *222*
Alva, S. A., 249, 251, 265, *270*
Angell, A. L., 233, *246*
Anthony, J. A., 224, 226, 227, 228, 242, *245*
Apostoleris, N. H., 114, *133*
Aranalde, M. D., 114, 120, 129, *134*, 181, *196*
Arends-Tóth, J., 40, 48, 52, *59*
Arey, S. A., 256, *270*
Arndt, J., 141, *168*
Arnold, B., 85, *95,* 119, 122, *133*, 193, *195*, 232, *244*
Arnold, D. H., 224, 242, *245*, 306, *312*
Aronowitz, M., 97, 101, *109*
Arredondo, J., 136, *168*
Asencio, M., 219, *221*
Asner-Self, K. K., 130, *134*
Athey, J. L., 251, *267*
Azuma, H., 179, 184, *194*

B

Bade, K. J., 297, *312*
Bagley, C., 101, *109*
Bahr, S. J., 277, *295*
Balls-Organista, *see* Organista
Banaji, M. R., 148, *166*
Bankston, C. L., 249, *270*
Banting, K., 28, *28*
Baptiste, D. A., 251, 252, 265, *267*
Barankin, T., 225, *244*
Barker, T. A., 226, 227, 228, *245, 247*
Baron, R. M., 138, *166*
Barrett, M. E., 65, *77*
Bartholomew, K., 138, 139, *165, 167*
Bashir, M. R., 98, 100, *109*
Bates, J. E., 329, *331*
Baumgartl, B., 328, *330*
Beauvais, F., 121, 129, *134*
Bebbington, P., 45, *60*

Becker, E., 141, *165*
Bell, R., 115, *134*
Belsky, J., 43, *60*
Benedict, R. 176, *193*
Benet-Martinez, V., 135, 136, 142, 150, *165*, *167*
Bengi-Arslan, L., 327, *330*
Benjet, C., 114, *133*
Benson, J. B., 179, *196*
Bergman, L., 91, *94*
Bernstein, I. H., 46, *61*
Berry, J. W., 13, 16, 18, 19, 20, 22, 23, 24, 25, 26, 27, 28, *28*, *29*, 34, 37, 38, 39, 40, 41, 42, 45, 46, 50, 53, *59*, *60*, 81, 86, 91, 92, *94*, *95*, 98, 99, 100, 101, *109*, 121, 129, *132*, *133*, 138, 139, 156, 157, *165*, 174, 178, 181, 192, *193*, *194*, 202, 213, 219, *221*, 224, 225, 240, *244*, *246*, 308, 309, *313*, 321, *330*
Betancourt, H., 199, 220, *221*
Bhadha, B. R., 119, 121, 123, 125, 131, *133*
Bhatia, D., 144, *165*
Bhavnagri, N., 225, *246*
Birman, D., 45, *59*, 113, 116, 117, 121, 122, 126, 129, 130, 131, *132*, *134*
Blacher, J., 266, *268*
Blashfield, R., 91, *94*
Bochner, S., 24, *30*, 37, 41, *62*, 139, *169*
Boehnlein, J., 65, *77*
Bond, G. L., 227, *244*
Bond, M., 224, *244*
Bonstead-Bruns, M., 114, *133*
Booth, A.,
Borck, C., 305, *313*
Bornholt, L., 115, *134*
Bornstein, M. H., 173, 174, 176, 179, 180, 181, 182, 184, 185, 186, 187, 189, *194*, *195*, *196*
Borthwick-Duffy, S., 266, *268*
Boski, P., 192, 193, *194*
Bourhis, R. Y., 22, *29*, 36, 38, *59*
Bowerman, C. E., 277, *295*
Bowlby, J., 136, 137, 139, *165*
Bowman, B. T., 224, *244*
Bray, J. H., 43, *60*
Brennan, K. A., 140, *165*
Brewer, M. B., 143, *166*, *168*, 326, *330*
Brillon, L., 201, 202, *221*
Brislin, R. W., 178, *194*
Britto, P. R., 229, *244*
Bromberger, J. T., 154, *167*
Bronfenbrenner, U., 69, 70, *77*, 88, *95*, 101, *109*
Brooks, A. J., 56, *59*, 65, *77*
Brossart, D. F., 56, *59*
Brown, J., 173, *195*
Buchanan, R., 117, *132*
Bujaki, M., 19, 22, *29*, 92, *94*, 224, 225, *244*
Buki, L. P., 117, 118, 120, 121, 122, 125, 130, 131, *133*, *134*
Bullock, D., 179, *196*
Bumpas, M. F., 271, *295*
Burgess, S. R., 224, 226, 227, 228, 242, *244*, *245*, *247*
Buriel, R., 100, *109*, 144, *166*, 175, 176, *196*, 224, 229, *244*, *246*, 249, 250, 251, 252, 253, 255, 257, 263, 264, 265, *267*, *268*, *269*. 272, 274, 293, *295*, 299, *313*
Burns, M. S., 224, *244*
Bus, A. G., 228, *244*

C

Calzada, S., 257, *267*
Caporael, L. R., 138, *166*
Cardoza, D., 257, *267*
Carey, J. C., 41, *61*
Carlson, K. S., 139, *166*
Carlson, V. J., 219, *221*
Carter, J., 224, 226, *247*
Cashmore, J. A., 327, *330*
Cassidy, J., 152, *168*
Castaneda, A., 263, *269*
Castillo, L. G., 56, *59*
Cauce, A. M., 198, 200, *221*, 263, *268*
Caudill, W., 176, 185, *194*
Celano, M. P., 45, *59*
Cervantes, R. C., 225, *246*
Chaiken, S., 54, *60*
Chan, S., 252, *268*
Chan-Yip, A., 119, 121, 123, 131, *134*
Chao, R. K., 252, 253, 256, *267*, *268*, 273, *295*, 329, *330*
Chavez, D. V., 249, 250, 251, 253, 255, 263, *267*, 272, 274, 293, *295*
Chen, J., 146, 154, *166*
Chen, M. T., 249, *269*
Chesla, C., 67, *77*
Chiang, K.-H. S., 137, 154, *168*
Chirkov, V., 326, *330*
Chitose, Y., 300, *313*
Chiu, C., 135, 136, 142, 146, *166*, *167*
Choe, J., 118, 121, 131, *133*

Chun, K. M., 14, *29*, 56, *59*, 65, 66, 67, 68, 69, 70, 72, 75, 76, *77*, 187, *194*, 330, *330*
Chung, R. H. G., 116, 124, *133*
Citlak, B., 304, 310, *313*, *314*
Clark, C. L., 140, *165*
Clark, M. M., 228, *244*
Clarke-Stewart, A., 263, *268*
Clement, R., 41, *59*
Coats, S., 140, *169*
Cohen, J., 125, *133*
Cohen, L., 273, *296*
Cohen, P., 125, *133*
Cohen, R. E., 213, *221*
Coleman, H. L., 39, *59*, 145, *167*, 225, *245*
Collins, N. L., 138, *166*
Collins, W. A., 143, 151, 152, *168*
Coltrane, S., 266, *268*
Comer, B., 132, *133*
Conger, K. J., 266, *268*
Conger, R. D., 126, *134*, 265, 266, *268*
Connor, J. W., 184, *194*
Conoley, C. W., 56, *59*
Coon, H., 178, *196*
Cooper, C. R., 322, 325, *330*, *331*
Cortés, D. E., 55, 56, *59*, *61*, 130, *133*, 157, *168*, 201, 209, *221*, *222*, 229, *246*, 252, *269*, 308, *313*
Costigan, C. L., 99, *109*
Cote, L. R., 174, 179, 181, 182, 189, *194*, *195*
Covi, L., 108, *109*
Crawford, J., 241, *244*
Cree, W. K., 200, *222*
Crijnen, A. A. M., 327, *330*
Crnic, K., 201, *221*
Cronbach, L., 72, *77*, 125, *133*
Crouter, A. C., 225, *244*, 271, *295*
Crowne, D. P., 180, *194*
Cuéllar, I., 56, *60*, 85, *95*, 119, 120, 122, *133*, 156, *166*, 178, 193, *195*, 232, *244*
Cummings, E. M., 137, *169*
Curran, M. J., 26, *29*
Cyphers, L., 176, *196*

D

Dagevos, J., 48, *60*
Daley, K. E., 224, *246*
Darwish Mura, S., 327, *330*
Dasen, P. R., 16, *29*, 53, *59*, 100, *109*, 139, *165*
Davidson, D. H., 204, *222*
Davis, H., 229, *245*
De Bot, K., 53, *60*
de Jong, P. F., 224, 229, 242, *244*, *245*
De Ment, T. L., 100, *109*, 229, *244*, 249, 250, 251, 252, 253, 255, 256, 263, *267*, *268*, 272, 274, 293, *295*, 299, *313*
Deater-Deckard, K., 329, *331*
Deaux, K., 158, *166*
deBosset, F., 225, *244*
Deci, E. L., 326, *332*
Dekovic, M., 329, *331*
Delaney, S., 271, *296*
Delgado-Gaitan, C., 114, *133*, 224, 229, 230, *244*
Demetriou, A., 115, *134*
Dennis, J., 266, *268*, 271, *296*
Der, G., 45, *60*
Derogatis, L. R., 108, *109*
Devich-Navarro, M., 86, *95*
Devos, T., 148, *166*
Diaz-Lazaro, C. M., 255, *268*
Diefenbach, H., 304, *314*
Diener, E., 153, *166*, *167*
Dimas, J. M., 252, *268*
Dinh, K. T., 115, *133*
Dobrich, W., 227–228, *246*
Doctoroff, G. L., 306, *312*
Dodge, K. A., 329, *331*
Donà, G., 45, 46, *60*
Donovan, M. S., 224, *244*
Dorner, L., 273, 274, *296*
Dozier, M., 154, *166*
Driessen, R., 304, *313*
Dunn, J., 173, *195*
Durkin, D., 228, *244*
Dykstra, R., 227, *244*

E

Eagly, A. H., 54, *60*
Efklides, A., 115, *134*
Egeland, B., 151, *168*
Elder, G. H., Jr., 265, 266, *268*
El-Khouri, B., 91, *94*
Ellaway, A., 98, *110*
Elliot, J. A., 228, *244*
Entzinger, H., 41, *61*

Eppe, S., 227, 234, *244, 245*
Erikson, E. H., 67, *77*
Erkut, S., 200, 201, *220*
Escobar, J. L., 132, *133*, 301, *313*
Ethier, K. A., 158, *166*
Evans, J., 98, *109*
Evatt Pond, R., 233, *247*

F

Faist, T., 301, *313*
Farver, J. A., 119, 121, 123, 125, 131, *133*
Farver, J. M., 226, 227, 233, 234, *244, 245*
Feldman, S., 65, *78*
Fernandez, D. M., 39, 45, *61*
Fernandez, T., 122, *134*, 308, *315*
Field, T. M., 176, *195*
Fisek, G., 329, *331*
Fishbein, M., 54, *59*
Fisher, C. B., 199, *221*
Fishman, H. C., 64, 68, 69, *78*
Flores, J., 82, 83, 84, 86, 88, *95*
Flyr, M., 271, *296*
Folkman, S., 24, *29*
Forman, B. D., 201, *222*
Forward, J., 100, *111,* 117, 118, 121, 122, *134*
Fowles, D. C., 154, *166*
Fraley, R. C., 138, 157, *166*
Frensch, P. A., 228, *246*
Friedman, S., 263, *268*
Frost, L., 185, *194*
Fuligni, A. J., 57, *60,* 85, 86, 88, *95*, 98, 101, *109, 110,* 240, *245*, 252, 253, 256, *268*, 273, *295*, 301, *313*, 323, *331*
Furby, L., 125, *133*
Furnham, A., 24, *30,* 37, 41, *62*, 139, 158, *166*

G

Gaines, S. O., Jr., 139, *166*
Gallimore, R., 224, 230, *246*
Galperin, C., 176, 179, 180, 184, 185, 186, 187, *194*
Gantous, P., 119, 121, 123, 131, *134*
García Coll, C., 98, *110,* 176, *195,* 200, 201, 202, *220, 221,* 299, 301, 308, *313*
Garcia, J. G., 44, *60,* 198, 199, *221*
Garcia, R. E., 225, *246*
Garrick, R. J., 186, *195*
Gashi, H., 312, *313*
Ge, X., 265, *268*
Georgas, J., 27, *29*
George, C., 152, *166*
Gerton, J., 145, *167*, 225, *245*
Getz, J. G., 43, *60*
Gijsberts, M., 48, *60*
Gil, A. G., 116, *133*, 252, *268*
Ginorio, A., 263, *268*
Gjerde, P. F., 139, *166*, 184, *195*
Goldenberg, C., 229, 241, *245*
Goldwyn, R., 152, *167*
Gonzales, N. A., 220, *221*
Goodnow, J. J., 253, *268*, 271, 272, 273, *295, 296*, 327, *330*
Gordon, E. W., 228, *246*
Gordon, M. M., 38, *60*, 224, *245*
Goto, S. G., 143, *169*
Graves, T., 16, *29,* 34, *60*
Greenberg, J., 136, 141, *166*, *168*, *169*
Greenfield, P. M., 176, *195*, 230, *245*, 299, 300, *313*
Greenwood, C., 224, 226, *247*
Grice, H. P., 152, *167*
Grieve, P. G., 142, *167*
Griffin, D. W., 138, *167*
Griffith, J., 256, *268*
Grizenko, N., 119, 121, 123, 131, *134*
Grolnick, W. S., 114, *133*
Grosjean, F., 273, 273, *296*
Grotevant, H. D., 325, *331*
Grusec, J. E., 273, *296*
Gümen, S., 306, *313*
Gutierrez, J., 225, *245*
Gutierrez, L., 263, *268*
Guyll, M., 154, *167*

H

Hahn, C., 174, *194*
Hall, N., 243, *247*
Hall, S., 154, *167*
Hammer, C. S., 240, *245*
Handwerker, W. P., 219, *221*
Hansen, H. S., 228, *245*
Hao, L., 114, 116, *133, 134*
Hara, H., 186, *195*
Hardy-Fanta, C., 251, *268*
Harkness, S., 105–106, *111*, 185, *195*
Harrell, J. P., 154, *167*

Harris, K. M., 98, *110*
Harris, L. C., 120, *133*, 178, *195*
Harris, R. J., 41, *61*
Harrison, A. O., 252, *268*
Hart, B., 224, 226, *247*
Harwood, R. L., 203, 207, 208, 219, *221*, 304, *313*, 310, *314*
Haynes, O. M., 174, 176, 179, 180, 184, 185, 186, 187, *194*
Hazan, C., 138, *167*
Head, M. R., 271, *295*
Heath, S. B., 228, *245*, 253, *268*
Hecht, S. A., 224, 226–227, 228, *244*, *247*
Hennighausen, K. H., 143, 151, 152, *168*
Henry, S., 140, *169*
Heras, P., 65, *77*, 225, *245*
Hermans, H. J. M., 136, 144, 145, *167*
Hernandez, D. J., 97, *110*, 198, *221*
Herskovits, M. H., 15, *29*, 34, *61*, 224, *246*
Hervis, O., 114, *134*
Herwartz-Emden, L., 306, *313*
Hesse, E., 152, *167*
Hewison, J., 228, *244*
Hinde, R. A., 137, *168*
Hirano-Nakanishi, M., 257, *267*
Hirschman, C., 148, *167*
Ho, C., 68, *77*
Hoff, E., 304, *313*
Hoffman, L., 68, *77*
Hofstede, G., 169, 176, 178, *195*
Hogg, M. A., 136, 142, *167*, *169*
Hollingshead, A. B., 204, *221*
Holloway, S. D., 182, *195*
Holzer, C. E., 256, 258, *269*
Hong, Y., 135, 136, 142, 143, 150, 154, *166*, *167*, *168*, *170*
Hoogsteder, M., 326, *332*
Horenczyk, G., 301, *314*
Horowitz, L. M., 139, *165*
Hovey, J. D., 252, 253, 264, *268*
Huang, L. N., 65, *78*
Hudson, E., 228, 242, *246*
Hui, M. K., 45, *60*
Hunt, L. M., 132, *133*
Hutnik, N., 39, 45, *60*

J

Jackson, J. F., 199, *221*
Jain, A., 43, *60*
Jasso, R., 120, *133*, 178, *195*
Jenkins, R., 201, *221*
Jensen, L., 300, *313*
Joe, G. W., 65, *77*
Jones, C. J., 114, *133*
Jones, R., 294, *296*
Joung, I. M. A., 327, *330*

K

Kagitcibasi, C., 27, *29*, 57, *60*, 306, 312, *313*, 320, 325, 326, 327, 328, 329, *331*
Kalin, R., 18, 19, 22, 28, *29*
Kanno, Y., 136, *167*
Kao, G., 253, *269*
Kaplan, M. S., 56, *60*
Kaplan, N., 152, *166*, *168*
Kaplan, U., 326, *330*
Karakasoglu-Aydin, Y., 304, *314*
Kashima, Y., 45, *62*, 224, *247*
Kaya, A., 322, 328, *331*
Keefe, S. E., 56, *60*, 225, *245*, 252, *269*
Keefer, C. H., 185, *195*
Kelek, N., 312, *314*
Kemmelmeier, M., 178, *196*
Kempen, H. J. G., 136, *167*
Kennedy, A., 34, 37, 45, *62*, 324, 326, *332*
Khoo, G., 45, *62*, 120, *134*
Kibria, N., 249, 253, 263, *269*
Killian, C., 271, *296*
Kim, C., 45, *60*
Kim, G., 118, 121, 131, *133*
Kim, S., 256, 257, *269*
Kim, U., 19, 22, 24, 25, *29*, 41, *59*, 92, *94*, 192, 193, *194*, 224, 225, *244*
Kim, Y., 326, *330*
Kim-Jo, T., 88, 89, 90, *95*
King, C. A., 253, 264, *268*
Kitayama, S., 75, *78*, 175, 176, *196*
Knight, G. P., 220, *221*
Kobak, R. R., 154, *166*
Koch, J., 263, *268*
Kohlmann, A., 312, *314*
Koplow, L., 225, *245*
Kosic, A., 142, *167*, 299, *314*
Kostantareas, M., 225, *244*
Kristen, C., 304, *314*
Kroger, J., 325, *331*
Kruglanski, A. W., 142, *167*, *170*
Kunda, Z., 35, *60*
Kung, M., 135, 142, *167*

Kuo, W. H., 75, *77*
Kurasaki, K., 158, *168*
Kurowski, C. O., 114, *133*
Kurtines, W. M., 56, *62*, 101, *111*, 114, 122, 129, *134*, 181, *196*, 308, *315*
Kwak, K., 99, 100, *110*, 113, 121, *133*, 323, 325, 329, *331*
Kymlicka, W., 28, *28*

L

La Fromboise, T., 145, *167*, 225, *245*
Lachman, M. E., 179, *196*
Lam, M., 252, 253, 256, *268*
Lambert, W. E., 41, *62*
Lamberty, G., 201, *221*
Lansford, J. E., 329, *331*
Lanham, B. B., 186, *195*
Laosa, L. M., 98, *110*
Laroche, M., 45, *60*
Lasry, J., 41, 45, 46, *60, 61*
Laursen, B., 304, *313*
Lawrence, J. A., 102, *111*, 272, *296*
Lawson, E. P., 228, 242, *246*
Lazarus, R. S., 24, *29*
Lebedeva, N., 19, *29*
LeCompte, M. D., 74, *77*
Lecroy, C. W., 56, *59*, 65, *77*
Lee, E., 73, *77*
Lee, P. A., 131, *134*, 145, *169*
Lee, R. M., 118, 121, 131, *133*
Lee-Shin, Y., 226, *244*
LeFevre, J., 224, 228, 242, *246*
Lerner, R. M., 99, *110*
Leseman, P. M., 224, 229, 242, *244, 245*
Leu, J., 136, 150, *165*
Lee, F., 136, 150, *165*
Leung, K., 178, *196*
Leung, P., 65, *77*
LeVine, R. A., 174, *195*, 300, *315*
LeVine, S., 300, *315*
Lew, A., 65, *78*
Lew, S., 72, *78*, 176, *196*
Leyendecker, B., 219, *221*, 298, 304, 310, *313, 314*
Li, Y. H., 158, *166*
Lieber, E., 229, *245*
Liebkind, K., 86, 91, *95*, 99, *110*, 301, *314*
Lightfoot, C., 192, *195*
Linskey, A. O., 258, *269*
Linton, R., 15, *29*, 34, *61*, 224, *246*
Lipman, R. S., 108, *109*
Liu, J. H., 139, *166*
Lonigan, C. J., 224, 226, 227, 228, 233, 234, 242, *244, 245, 247*
Lorenz, F. O., 265, 266, *268*
Lotringen, C., 41, *61*
Love, J., 251, *269*
Lucas, R. E., 153, *167*
Lucca Irizarry, N., 200, 201, 203, 208, 219, *221*
Luo, S.-H., 116, *133*
Lynch, J. H., 326, *332*

M

Ma, T. C., 117, 118, 120, 121, 122, 125, 130, 131, *133*
Machida, S., 182, *195*
Macias, R. F., 250, *269*
Macintyre, S., 98, *110*
MacPhee, D., 179, 180, *195*
Madden, T., 88, *95*, 100, *110*
Madsen, S. D., 143, 151, 152, *168*
Magnuson, K., 98, *110*, 299, 301, 308, *313*
Magnusson, D., 91, *94*
Maguire, L., 207, *221*
Mahler, S. J., 70, *78*
Main, M., 152, *166, 167, 168*
Maital, S., 179, 184, *194*
Mak, W., 75, *78*, 81, 82, *95*, 155, 159, *170*
Maldonado, M., 225, *246*
Maldonado, R. E., 56, *60*, 85, *95*, 119, 122, *133*, 156, *166*, 193, *195*, 232, *244*
Malewska-Peyre, H., 326, *331*
Malgady, R. G., 55, *61*, 130, *133*, 157, *168*, 201, 209, *221*, *222*, 229, *246*, 252, *269*, 308, *313*
Malz, T. A., 174, *196*
Mannetti, L., 142, *167*
Marcia, J., 92, *95*
Marín, B. V., 56, *61*, 160, *169*, 174, 175, 176, *196*
Marín, G., 14, *29*, 44, 56, 57, *60, 61*, 65, 75, *77, 78*, 160, *169*, 174, 175, 176, *196*, 229, *245*, 330, *330*
Marks, G., 56, *60*
Markus, H. R., 75, *78*, 175, 176, *196*
Marlowe, D., 180, *194*
Marotta, S. A., 198, 199, *221*
Masgoret, A.-M., 102, *110*

Mathew, J., 119, 121, 123, 131, *134*
Matthews, K. A., 154, *167*
Mau, W.-C., 114, *134*
Mautino, K. S., 97, *110*
Mavreas, V., 45, *60*
McAdams, D. P., 155, *168*
McAdoo, H. P., 201, *221*
McDowell, D., 271, *296*
McHale, S. M., 271, *295*
McKay, L., 98, *110*
McQueen, A., 43, *60*
McQuillan, J., 249, *269*, 272, 273, 274, 275, 293, *296*
Meehl, P., 72, *77*
Mendoza, R. H., 43, 56, *61*
Menjivar, C., 271, *296*
Merali, N., 113, 118, 120, 121, 122, 123, 131, *134*
Messe, L. A., 41, 45, *61*, 117, 122, 129, 130, *134*, 157, *168*
Messinger, E., 225, *245*
Meyer, E. C., 201, 202, *221*
Meza, M., 274, *296*
Miccio, A. W., 240, *245*
Miller, A. M., 207, 219, *221*, 310, *314*
Miller, J. G., 203, 208, 219, *221*
Minagawa, M., 186, *195*
Minde, K., 101, *110*, 225, *245*
Minde, R., 101, *110*, 225, *245*
Minde, T., 24, *29*, 225, *244*
Minuchin, S., 64, 68, 69, *78*
Mirdal, G. M., 327, *331*
Model, S., 329, *331*
Moïse, L. C., 22, *29*, 36, 38, *59*
Mok, D., 24, *29*, 225, *244*
Monker, J. A., 228, *246*
Montana, P., 251, *268*
Moon, C., 227, 242, *246*
Moran, V. R., 249, 250, 251, 253, 255, 263, *267*, 272, 274, 293, *295*
Morgan-Lopez, A. A., 200, 220, *221*, *222*
Morris, M. W., 135, 136, 142, 150, *165*, *167*
Moyerman, D. R., 201, *222*
Murphy, H. B. M., 18, *29*, 98, *110*
Murphy, J., 140, *169*

N

Nagata, D. K., 41, 56, *61*, 193, *196*
Narang, S. K., 119, 121, 123, 125, 131, *133*
Nauck, B., 56, *61*, 304, 312, *314*
Negy, C., 37, 41, 44, 55, *61*
Neighbors, H., 154, *170*
Newman, R. S., 227, *247*
Ngo, P. Y. L., 174, *196*
Ngo, V., 118, 121, 131, *133*
Nguyen, D., 119, 121, 123, 131, *134*
Nguyen, H. H., 41, 45, *61*, 117, 122, 129, 130, *134*, 157, *168*
Nguyen, N., 115, 134
Nielsen, J. S., 327, *331*
Niemann, Y. F., 136, *168*
No, S., 136, 150, *167*, *168*
Noels, K. A., 41, *59*
Nunnally, J. C., 46, *61*
Nyberg, B., 56, *60*, 156, *166*

O

Oakes, P., 136, *169*
Oetting, G. R., 121, 129, *134*
Ogino, M., 176, 179, 184, *194*, *196*
Okagaki, L., 228, *246*
Olmedo, E. L., 34, 41, *61*, 121, 129, *132*, 181, *194*
Olsen, L., 249, *269*, 271, 275, *296*
Ong, A., 88, *95*, 100, *110*
Onishi, M., 139, *166*
Oppedal, B., 101, 107, *110*, *111*, 299, *314*
Orellana, M. F., 272, 273, 274, 294, *296*
Organista, K. C., 158, *168*
Organista, P. B., 14, *29*, 75, *77*, 158, *168*, 330, *330*
Osorio, S., 88, 89, *95*
Otero-Sabogal, R., 56, 57, *61*, 65, *78*, 160, *169*
Oyserman, D., 178, *196*
Özbek, Y., 300, *312*

P

Pacheco, A. M., 200, 201, *221*
Pachter, L. M., 176, *195*
Padilla, A. M., 41, *61*, 225, *245*, *246*, 252, *269*
Padrón, E., 151, *168*
Painter, K. M., 176, 180, 185, 186, 187, *194*
Park, R. E., 136, *168*
Parke, R. D., 175, 176, *196*, 266, *268*, 271, *296*

Pascual, L., 176, 180, 185, 186, 187, *194*
Patel, N., 225, *246*
Paulhus, D. L., 23, *30*, 45, 47, *61*, 156, *169*
Pawliuk, N., 119, 121, 123, 131, *134*
Payne, A. C., 233, *246*
Pease-Alvarez, L., 249, *269*
Pelligrini, A., 228, *244*
Pels, T., 329, *331*
Perez, W., 249, 250, 251, 253, 255, 263, *267*, 272, 274, 293, *295*
Perez-Stable, E. J., 56, 57, *61*, 65, *78*, 160, *169*
Perez-Vidal, A., 114, 129, *134*
Perreault, S., 22, *29*, 36, 38, *59*
Persky, I., 126, *134*
Pettengill, S. M., 329, *331*
Pettigrew, T. F., 47, *61*
Pettit, G. S., 329, *331*
Pfluger-Schindlbeck, I., 312, *314*
Phalet, K., 41, 55, 58, *61*, *62*
Pham, T. B., 41, *61*
Phinney, J. S., 23, 27, *29*, 82, 83, 84, 85, 86, 88, 91, *94*, *95*, 98, 99, 101, *109*, 100, *110*, 145, 160, *168*, 201, *222*, 224, 225, 240, *246*, 301, 308, *314*
Piaget, J., 188, *196*
Pickett, C. L., 143, *166*, *168*
Pierro, A., 142, *167*
Pine, C. J., 252, *268*
Poortinga, Y. H., 16, 27, *29*, 53, *59*, 100, *109*, 139, *165*
Portes, A. R., 105, *110*, 114, 116, *134*
Pouliasi, K., 143, *169*
Power, S., 19, 22, *29*, 92, *94*, 224, 225, *244*
Power, T., 225, *246*
Prins, K. S., 47, 53, *62*
Pulido, L., 273, 274, *296*
Pumariega, A. J., 258, *269*
Pyszczynski, T., 136, 141, *166*, *168*, *169*

Q

Quintero-Salinas, R., 258, *269*
Quiroz, B., 230, *245*

R

Raeff, C., 230, *245*
Ram, A., 144, *165*
Ramirez, M., 263, *269*
Ramirez, R. R., 299, *222*
Rashotte, C. A., 226, 227, 234, *247*
Read, S. J., 138, *166*
Redfield, R., 15, *29*, 34, *61*, 224, *246*
Reese, L., 224, 230, *246*
Regeser López, S., 199, 220, *221*
Reicher, S., 136, *169*
Reigadas, E., 257, 264, *267*
Revilla, L. A., 65, *77*, 225, *245*
Reynolds, J., 274, *296*
Richels, K., 108, *109*
Richmond, A., 18, *29*
Rick, K., 100, *111*, 117, 118, 121, 122, *134*
Rickard-Figueroa, K., 72, *78*
Riley, C., 65, *77*
Rio, A., 114, 129, *134*
Roberts, R. E., 56, *60*, 156, *166*
Rodriguez, C. E., 203, *222*
Rodríguez, M. D., 198, 200, *221*
Rodriguez, R., 101, *111*
Rodriguez, V., 136, *168*
Rogler, L. H., 55, *61*, 130, *133*, 157, *168*, 201, 202, 209, *221*, *222*, 229, *246*, 252, *269*, 308, *313*, *314*
Rohner, R. P., 329, *331*
Roisman, G. I., 137, 143, 151, 152, 154, *166*, *168*
Romero, A. J., 136, *168*
Roosa, M. W., 200, *222*
Rosenberg, M., 108, *111*
Rosenblatt, R., 223, *246*
Rosenthal, D., 65, *78*,115, *134*
Ross, M., 143, *168*
Rowell, T. E., 137, *168*
Røysamb, E., 107, *110*
Rudmin, F. W., 23, 26, *29*, 46, 47, *61*, 151, 157, *169*, 192, *196*
Rueschenberg, E., 224, *246*
Rueter, M., 126, *134*
Rumbaut, R. G., 105, *110*, 114, *134*, 146, *169*, 197, 207, *222*, 240, *246*, 252, 253, *269*, 301, *314*
Ryan, R. M., 326, *330*, *332*
Ryder, A. G., 23, *30*, 45, 47, *61*, 156, *169*
Ryynanen-Karjalainen, L., 327, *331*

S

Sabogal, F., 56, 57, *61*, 65, *78*, 160, *169*
Saenz, D., 220, *221*

Sam, D. L., 23, 26, 27, *29,* 53, *59,* 86, *94*, 98, 99, 100, 101, 107, *109, 110, 111*, 174, 181, 192, *194*, 225, 240, *246*, *244*, 299, *314*
Sameroff, A., 225, *245*
Sanchez Korrol, V., 203, *222*
Sanchez, J. I., 39, 45, *61*
Santisteban, D. A., 114, 129, *134*
Saracho, O. N., 229, *246*
Sarason, B. R., 115, *133*
Sarason, I. G., 115, *133*
Sayegh, L., 41, 45, 46, *60, 61*
Scarborough, H. S., 227–228, *246*
Schachter, S., 137, *169*
Schalk-Soekar, R. G. S., 57–58, *61*, 326, *332*
Schaller, J., 101, *111*
Schensul, J. J., 74, *77*
Schiffauer, W., 312, *314*
Schimel, J., 141, *168*
Schneider, S., 132, *133*
Schoelmerich, A., 208, 219, *221*, 304, 310, *313, 314*
Schooler, C., 176, *194*
Schulze, P. A., 208, *221*
Schwab, J., 256, *270*
Scopetta, M. A., 114, 120, 129, *134*, 181, *196*
Segall, M. H., 16, *29,* 53, *59*, 100, *109*, 139, *165*
Sen, F., 300, *312*
Senécal, S., 22, *29,* 36, 38, *59*
Sénéchal, M., 224, 228, 242, *246*
Shannon, S. M., 249, 250, 251, *269*, 274, *296*
Shaver, P. R., 67, *78,* 138, 140, *165*, *166*, *167*
Shimada, E., 45, *62*, 224, *247*
Siantz, M. L. d. L.. 98, *111*
Silva-Palacios, V., 252, *270*
Silver, M. D., 143, *168*
Silverberg, S. B., 325, *332*
Simons, R. L., 265, 266, *268*
Simpkins, S., 271, *296*
Simpson, D. D., 65, *77*
Sirignano, S. W., 179, *196*
Sirolli, A., 220, *221*
Smith, E. R., 140, *169*
Smith, J. A., 155, *169*
Sodowsky, G. R., 41, *61*
Solomon, S., 136, 141, *166*, *168*, *169*
Soto, E., 67, *78*
Sparrow, L. M., 135, *169*
Specter, M. M., 200, *222*
Sroufe, L. A., 143, 151, 152, *168*
Stanovich, K. E., 226, *246*
Steinberg, L., 325, *332*
Steiner, V., 233, *247*
Stevenson, H. W., 227, *247*
Stollak, G. E., 41, 45, *61* 117, 122, 129, 130, *134*, 157, *168*
Stonequist, E., 92, *95*
Strassburger, G., 302, *315*
Strickland, B. R., 219, 220, *222*
Strom, R. D., 117, 118, 120, 121, 122, 125, 130, 131, *133*
Strom, S. K., 117, 118, 120, 121, 122, 125, 130, 131, *133*
Stuewig, J., 56, *59,* 65, *77*
Su, T. F., 99, *109*
Suarez-Orozco, C. E., 253, *269*, 311, *315*
Suarez-Orozco, M. M., 253, *269*, 311, *315*
Suh, E., 153, *167*
Suinn, R. M., 45, *62,* 72, *78*, 120, *134*, 176, *196*
Suizzo, M., 174, *194*
Sullivan, J., 229, *245*
Sunar, D., 306, *314*
Super, C. M., 105–106, *111*, 185, *195*
Sussman, N. M., 300, *315*
Sutton, C. R., 203, *222*
Suzuki, L. K., 176, *195*, 299, *313*
Swanson, J. W., 258, *269*
Swyngedouw, M., 58, *61*
Szapocznik, J., 56, *62*, 101, *111*, 114, 120, 122, 129, *134*, 181, *196*, 308, *315*

T

Tajfel, H., 144, *169*, 326, *332*
Takenaka, A., 136, *169*
Taliaferro, J., 154, *167*
Tamis-LeMonda, C. S., 176, 180, 185, 186, *194, 196*
Tan, S., 65, *77*
Tapia Uribe, F. M., 300, *315*
Tardif, T., 304, *313*
Tatarko, A., 19, *29*
Taylor, D., 22, *29,* 41, *62*
Teale, W. H., 226, *247*
Therrien, M., 199, *222*
Thijs, J., 45, *62*
Thomas, E. M., 224, 228, *246*
Thomas, T., 225, *247*
Tienda, M., 253, *269*

Tilly, C., 202, *222*
Tobin, J. J., 204, *222*
Toda, S., 176, *196*
Toelken, B., 328, *332*
Torgesen, J. K., 226, 227, 234, *247*
Trafimow, D., 143, *169*
Tran, H., 65, *77*
Triandis, H. C., 45, *62*, 75, *78*, 143, *169*, 176, *196*, 224, *247*
Trickett, E. J., 45, *59*, 113, 114, 117, 122, 126, 130, 131, *132*, *133*, *134*
Trimble, J. E., 121, 129, *132*, 181, *194*
Trommsdorff, G., 329, *332*
Tsai, J. L., 131, *134*, 137, 145, 154, *168*, *169*
Tsai, Y. M., 75, *77*
Tse, L., 249, 250, 255, 259, 263, *269*, 272, 273, 274, 275, 293, *296*
Tseng, V., 88, *95*, 252, 253, 256, *268*, 273, *295*
Tsuda, T., 136, *169*
Turner, J. C., 136, 144, *169*, 326, *332*
Tyler, F. B., 45, *59*

U

Uba, L., 176, 187, *196*
Uhlenhuth, E. H., 108, *109*

V

Valdés, G., 229, 230, *247*, 252, 253, 264, *269*
Valenzuela, A., 253, *269*, 271, 272, 273, 274, *296*
Valsiner, J., 102, *111*, 192, *195*
van de Vijver, F. J. R., 27, *29*, 37, 40, 41, 48, 52, 55, 57–58, *59*, *61*, *62*, 178, *196*, 326, *332*
van IJzendoorn, M. H., 139, 151, *169*, 228, *244*
van Lenthe, F. J., 327, *330*
van Oudenhoven, J. P., 47, 53, *62*
Van Praag, C., 48, *60*
Vasquez Calzada, J. L., 200, *222*
Vasquez, A., 155, *169*
Vasquez, O. A., 249, *269*, 274, 275, *296*
Vasquez, R., 257, *267*
Vázquez García, H., 200, 201, *220*
Vedder, P., 23, 27, *29*, 81, 86, 91, *94*, *95*, 98, 99, 101, *109*, 301, *314*
Vega, W. A., 116, 132, *133*, 202, *222*, 252, *268*, 301, *313*
Ventura-Cook, E., 208, *221*
Verkuyten, M., 45, *62*, 143, *169*
Vigil, P., 72, *78*
Vilhjalmsdottir, P., 88, 89, *95*
Villanueva, C. M., 250, 251, 255, 263, *268*
Villareal, M., 45, *62*, 224, *247*
Villarruel, F. A. 199, *221*
Vinokurov, A., 117, *132*
Virta, E., 98, 100, *111*
Vu, K. C., 65, *77*
Vygotsky, L., 188, *196*

W

Wagner, R. K., 226, 227, 234, *247*
Wagstaff, D. A., 240, *245*
Walker, D., 224, 226, *247*
Waller, N. G., 157, *166*
Ward, C., 25, 26, *30*, 34, 37, 41, 45, *62*, 99, 102, *110*, *111*, 136, 139, *167*, *169*, 192, *196*, 299, *315*, 330, *332*
Warheit, G. J., 256, *270*
Warton, P. M., 271, *296*
Wasik, B. H., 201, *221*
Waters, E., 137, *169*
Waters, M., 146, *169*
Webster, D. M., 142, *167*, *170*
Weinstock, S. A., 44, *62*
Weisner, T., 229, *245*
Weisskirch, R. S., 249, 251, 265, *270*
Wells, G., 227, 242, *246*
Wells, M., 294, *296*
Werner, E. E., 202, *222*
Westin, C., 98, *111*
Westphal, M., 306, *313*
Wetherell, M., 136, *169*
Whitbeck, L. B., 266, *268*
Whitehurst, G. J., 224, 226, 228, 233, 242, *245*, *246*, *247*
Widmayer, S. M., 176, *195*
Willemsma, G., 47, 53, *62*
Williams, D. R., 154, *170*
Williams, H. L., 115, *134*
Wilson, A. E., 143, *168*
Wilson, M., 252, *268*
Wilson, S. P., 208, *221*
Wiseman, R. L., 116, *133*
Wolf, E. R., 200, 201, *222*
Wong, R. Y-M., 143, *170*
Wong-Fillmore, L., 252, *270*
Wong-Rieger, D., 34, *62*

Woods, D. J., 37, 41, 44, 55, *61*
Wu, D. Y. H., 204, *222*

X

Xu, Y., 227, *244*
Xun, W. Q. E., 143, *168*

Y

Yang, K., 224, *244*
Yee, B. W. K., 65, *78*
Ying, Y. W., 67, *78*, 131, *134*, 145, 157, 159, *169, 170*
Yip, T., 86, *95*, 273, *295*
Young, M., 19, 22, *29,* 92, *94*, 224, 225, *244*

Z

Zaharna, R. S., 136, *170*
Zambrana, R. E., 252, *270*
Zane, N. W. S., 75, *78,* 81, 82, *95*, 155, 159, *170*
Zea, M. C., 130, *134*
Zelizer, V A., 272, 293, *296*
Zhou, M., 99, 101, *111*, 249, *270*
Zigler, E., 243, *247*
Zimmerman, I., 233, *247*

Subject Index

A

Accultural adjustment, 24
Acculturation
  attitudes, 50, 54
  concept of, 14
  content of, 324
  context of, 326
  continuity and discontinuity of change, 99
  cultural contexts of, 16
  cultural factors, 100
  definitions, 13, 35, 79, 94, 102, 201, 224, 308
  development model, 102–103, 107
  development pathways, 104–105
  family role, 55, 116, 311
  over generations, 298
  measures, 192, 308
  multidimensional process, 224
  mutual nature of, 14
  person-oriented approach, 91
  policy, 328
  psychological, 16, 19, 34, 298
  redefined by National Institute of Child Health and Human Development, 5
  research methodology, 323
  uniformity, lack of, 11
  universal and group-specific aspects, 53
Acculturation gaps, *see also* Assessment of acculturation
  actual gaps, 119, 131
  assimilation discrepancy, 122
  case study, 126–129
  comparative studies, 115
  computation, 120
  between generations, 311
  independent measures, 130
  interaction approach, 123–125
  Language, Identity, and Behavior Scale, 126, 130
  matched/mismatched groups, 123
  models, 120
  between parents, 298
  perceived gaps, 117, 131
  suggestions for measurements, 129–130
Acculturation strategies, 14, 19, 23, 25, 140, 202
  assimilation, 18, 20, 225, 233, 325
  exclusion, 22
  integration, 20, 53, 225, 233, 322, 325
  marginalization, 18, 225, 233
  melting pot, 22
  multiculturalism, 22
  segregation, 18
  separation, 20, 225, 233, 325
Acculturative stress, 22, 24, 25, 116, 225

Adaptation, 25
  of immigrant children, 97
Assessment of acculturation, 41, 55
  demographics, 43
  guidelines, 42–44
  mainstream and heritage cultures, 43
  multivariate analyses of covariance (MANCOVAs), 237
  multivariate analyses of variance (MANOVAs), 181, 189, 214, 237
  in the Netherlands, 47
  orientations, 44–47, 48
  rating scale, 2332
  single-index measures, 44
  Tukey HSD tests, 181, 189
  two-dimensional measures, 129
  univariate analyses of variance (ANOVAs), 181, 189, 237

B

Behavioral shifts, *see also* Accultural adjustment
  cultural conflict, 24
  cultural learning, 24
  cultural shedding, 24
Bicultural individuals, 135, 142–143, 150

C

Cluster analysis
  diffuse, 23
  ethnic, 23
  integrated, 23
  national, 23
Cultural attachment
  Adult Attachment Interview, 151–152
  assessment, 151
  consensual validation, 142
  Cultural Attachment Interview, 152, 161–165
  definition, 137
  development of, 144
    first-generation immigrants, 146
    later generation ethnic minorities, 148
  security of, 138
  to social groups, 137–138, 140
  terror management, 141
Culture brokering, *see* Latinos
Culture shock, *see* Acculturative stress

D

Dimensionality, *see also* Variables
  bidimensional model, 39, 322
  fusion model, 39, 321
  unidimensional model, 38

F

Family, *see also* Acculturation, Acculturation gap, Language brokering
  adjustment, 116
  changes in relationships, 56
  contributions of children, 272, 294
  developmental issues, 69
  dynamics, 68
  ecologies, 69–70
  generation gap, 299
  generations, definitions, 300–302
  models of changes, 56, 57
  research strategies, 71
    constructs, 75
    domain-specific assessment, 75
    ethnographic observation, 74
    family narratives, 74
    geograms, 73
    transnational social fields, 74
  structure and subsystems, 64–68

I

Immigrants, *see also* Parenting cognitions
  acculturation experiences, 34, 114
  acculturation context, 37
  challenges in acculturizing, 4
  Chinese American, 72, 116
  commonality, 321
  Dutch, in Canada, 53
  International Organization of Migration, 4
  Native Americans, 3
  neighborhood segregation, 305, 311
  socioeconomic status, 327
  Turkish, in the Netherlands, 47–48
  Turkish, in Germany, 298, 302, 310
Immigration, 197, 223, 297, 303, 320

L

Language brokering, *see also* Latinos
  advantages, social and cognitive, 251

disadvantages for children, 251, 275
gender roles, 253, 258, 261
measures
academic success, 253
bilingualism, 279
Child Behavioral Checklist (CBCL), 279
demographic information, 258
Depression Scale, 256, 259
educational aspirations and expectations, 257, 264
English and Spanish proficiency, 257
family characteristics, 280
frequency of translation, 277, 280
Language Brokering Scale (LBS), 255
Parent–Child Bonding Scale (PCBS), 256
parental education, 257
Parental Identification, 277
parent–child relationships, 251–252, 258, 261, 263, 264, 271, 288, 292
Latinos, *see also* Immigration
children's school performance, 224, 241
culture brokering, 249
definition, 198
English language learners, 240, 254
family values, 229
language brokering, 249, 250
maintenance of culture, 210, 215
migration, 201
Migratory Experiences Interview, 208
Puerto Ricans, 200
research methods, 203
social networks, 207, 216
socioeconomic status, 199
in the United States, 198, 199, 200, 203
Literacy, *see also* Assessment of acculturation
bilingual education, 241
child interest, 228
home environment, 228, 230, 241
oral language, 226, 233, 237
phonological processing abilities, 227, 234
print knowledge, 227, 234, 237

P

Parenting cognitions, 173, 191
of attributions, 179, 182
among immigrants, 174
of knowledge, 179, 184
of parenting style, 180, 185
self-perceptions, 179, 184
Parenting practices, 188, 227

R

Research and acculturation models
social-cognition approach, 34
social-learning approach, 34
stress-and-coping approach, 34

S

Social Science Research Council, 15
Suinn Lew Asian Self-Identity Acculturation Scale (SL-ASIA), 72, 176

T

Terror management, *see* Cultural attachment
Turks, *see also* Immigrants
acculturation processes, 298
acculturation gap, 312
acculturation of mothers, 306–308

V

Variables
academic achievement, 304
acculturation conditions, 35
acculturation orientations, 37
acculturation outcomes, 37
change over time, 80, 81, 85
cross-sectional studies, 85, 100
domain specificity, 37, 40, 52
generations, 81
longitudinal studies, 85
markers of time, 80, 85–86
separate consideration of, 81
underlying factors of change, 87